SOCIO-ECONOMIC SCENARIO OF THE NORTH EAST INDIA

About the Author

R.K. Das Choudhury did his graduation in Science from Gauhati University in 1969 and M.Sc in Statistics in 1971 from Dibrugarh University. Initially, he started his service career in 1972 with the Directorate of Economic and Statistics, Government of Assam and then in 1978, he joined the Directorate of Economics and Statistics, Government of Arunachal Pradesh and finally retired from there as Joint Director on 31st December, 2007. While in service, he obtained his Ph.D. degree from the North Eastern Hill University (NEHU), Sillong. Apart from administrative and financial knowledge, Dr. Das Choudhury has vast experience in National Sample Survey (NSS), both in Field Operations and in Tabulation and Publication of NSS Reports. He had special contribution in the field of improvement of Sample Design for selection of sample households/ sample enterprises for detailed survey in the Hilly Areas of North Eastern Region. Dr. Das Choudhury also worked in the North Eastern Council Secretariat, Sillong for about 10 (ten) years (on deputation) in various capacities and gathered enough experience in Planning, processing of projects for financial sanctions, preparation of financial reports, Evaluation and Monitoring of completed projects, preparation of Data Bank etc. There are three published books in his credit. Presently he is working on a Bengali Novel entitled "Chadmabeshi".

SOCIO-ECONOMIC SCENARIO OF THE NORTH EAST INDIA

R.K. DAS CHOUDHURY

CONCEPT PUBLISHING COMPANY PVT. LTD.,
NEW DELHI-110059

ISBN-13: 978-81-8069-909-2

First Published 2013

Published and Printed by

Concept Since 1974

Concept Publishing Company Pvt. Ltd.
A/15-16, Commercial Block, Mohan Garden
New Delhi-110059 (India)
T: 25351460, 25351794, *F*: 091-11-25357109
E: publishing@conceptpub.com, W: www.conceptpub.com
Editorial Office: H-13, Bali Nagar, New Delhi-110 015, India.

Cataloging in Publication Data--*Courtesy:* D.K. Agencies (P) Ltd. <docinfo@dkagencies.com>

Das Choudhury, R. K., 1949-
Socio-economic scenario of the North East India / R.K. Das Choudhury.
p. cm.
Includes bibliographical references (p.) and index.
ISBN 9788180699092

1. India, Northeastern—Social conditions. 2. India, Northeastern—Economic conditions. 3. India, Northeastern—Social conditions—Statistics. 4. India, Northeastern—Economic conditions—Statistics. I. Title.

DDC 306.09541 23

Foreword

Today, the North Eastern Region of India is included among the laggard regions of the country. Moreover, continued volatile politico-social climate in the region right from the time of independence has repeatedly sent warning signal to the power centres at different levels in the country many a times in the past. It is an irony that most often these warnings were not only misinterpreted, but also received condemnations within the prevailing binary logic in a self-proclaimed unitary system i.e. one nation state, one geo-body, one language (culture), one standard time, one currency, one constitution, one legal system, one rationality and one planning strategy, etc. It was constructed as a case of difficult choices between rational versus irrational or national versus anti-national or regional versus national at the power centres. The North East, particularly its political economy, ethics and ethos were considered both irrational as well as impediments in the progress and dynamism of the country as a whole. It was argued that, but for the lack of involvement and enthusiasm among the people of the region in accepting the newly found unitary national identity, its development and modernization magic mantras centering around 'development' the region could have been among the other developed regions/states of the country. To placate the resenting and anguished people from the region, the unitary nation states at different point of times dolled out the concepts like: multiparty democracy, decentralized planning and federal system of governance etc. But, in reality these were all strategies to reinforce the one and the same unitary system. Say for example, the so-called decentralized planning was nothing but replication of the same bureaucratic structures of planning at the national, state, district, block and village levels. Similarly, the so-called multiparty democracy too is a strategy adopted by the existing potentates to occupy all the spaces that should theoretically belong to the parties that form the government and that are in the opposition and even those that want to overthrow the system and replace it with a new one i.e. the left parties.

In the backdrop of such a war of positions, little scopes are made available for moderation on either side (the unitary system and the aspirants of regional identity). In case of the North Eastern Region of India, it was the unilateral decision of the power centres that has so far constructed the North Eastern Region as an 'irrational' within the overarching 'rational national interests'. So, in the ongoing war between the irrational 'North East' and the rational national interests, it is the former, that has to yield before the latter. Such type of unilateralism on the part of the 'rational' which is largely responsible for creating an impasse between the aspirations of the people of the region and the response they receive from the power elites at the centre. Persistent unilateralism contributed in perpetuating the process of generalized alienation and deterritorialisation of the otherwise traditional communities in the region.

Consequently, it has become so alarming that it now threatens the unity and integrity of the country. Now, it has become a major concern to many nationalists and development theoreticians alike. Scholars have expressed their anxieties about the prevailing state of affairs in the region and the discourses that have persisted between the politics of plural regional identities and unitary national identity and they have also tried to suggest models and strategies for ameliorating the ills of the region. Like the pluralities of the identities in the region the emphasis of the scholars have also been quite diverse as far the North Eastern Region is concerned.

For many, the term 'India's North East Region' conveys an idea of territoriality or geographical location of a region. But, in reality the geographical identity of any region is not all that important if not the least significant. A true North East is more of a cultural, ideological and economic identity. And above all, it symbolizes a typical mindset and power relation, which is ambiguous as much as is full of apparent and real contradictions. Viewed from the nationalist perspectives, it is both the pathology as well as the negation of the same. It continues to pose some of the formidable challenges before the otherwise so-called success stories of Nation State formation in India. This region is not only diverse in terms of its rich and vivid cultural heritage, but it is also a dwelling place of numerous dormant and subaltern nationalities which have so far refused to bite the bullets offered to them by the protagonists of the pan Indian nation in the name of development, modernization and national integrity etc. Consequently, the region continues to suffer from innumerable development handicaps, which are contingent upon the success story of nation formation. For want of proper enthusiasm and support among the people of the region for the nationalist projects, the dissents are interpreted as anti-national activities.

Taking a deconstructionist approach to the term the 'North East' in the context of development would reveal that the 'North' is considered synonymous to developed regions[1]. It is the 'other' to the backward 'South', which is not only a 'Post Colony' but also accounts for being a classic case of secular marginalization. Its identity lies in being subservient to the vibrant North. This particular identity the 'North' shares with the 'East' (Orient), which is also the archetype of the subordinate, and hegemonised one[2]. In post-colonial discourses the 'East' is an epitome of Occident's greatest, richest and oldest colonies[3]. Moreover, it is once again a relationship of power, domination and varying degree of a complex hegemony[4]. This particular identity is most appropriate to the North Eastern Region of India. It is a region that symbolizes the negation of Hirschman's 'North' but justifies being an extreme case of Said's 'Orient'. Consequently, this region does not only form the geographical periphery of India, but it is also the economic, political and cultural periphery of the same and above all torn between two diametrically opposite mindsets and loyalties. The magnitudes of peripheralisation is so intense and well pronounced that some scholars preferred to identify this region with a classic case of marginalization leading to internal colonization.

It all indicates that the sufferings and neglects of the North Eastern Region have encompassed not only in terms of its economic, social, cultural, political and psychological dimensions but it has also suffered in terms of distorted discourses and epistemological constructs. Most often these distortions and misrepresentations have been done due to improper knowledge and understanding of the region. In this book,

Dr. R.K. Das Choudhury has made a sincere attempt to remove some of the misrepresentations and epistemological distortions. Dr. Das Choudhury is a well-known Statistician. After completing his Master in Statistics, he joined the Directorate of Economics and Statistics, Government of Assam and after working there for a few years, he got a better opportunity in the Directorate of Economics and Statistics, Government of Arunachal Pradesh and joined there. His service career in the Directorate was primarily associated with the National Sample Survey Organisation (NSSO), both Field Operations as well as Tabulation of the State level data. At the later stage, being the Technical Head of the Directorate and overall in charge of NSSO, he acquired in-depth knowledge of socio-economic studies, method of data collection, data management and publication of reports. Moreover, he presented a paper on 'Ways and means of controlling non-sampling errors in large scale sample surveys' in the Seminar arranged in Guwahati on 25th May, 2001 by the National Sample Survey Organization (NSSO) on the occasion of NSSO Golden Jubilee Celebration, which was very much appreciated and the same paper was published in the Report on Seminar on Survey Practices. He also presented another paper on 'The method of selection of sample households/enterprises for detailed survey, in the heterogeneous field conditions prevailing in the North Eastern States', in the Seminar organized in Shillong by the Indian Statistical Institute (ISI), Kolkata. Further, he worked in the North Eastern Council Secretariat, Shillong for about 10 (ten) years and acquired the knowledge of formulation of Annual and Five Year Plans, Examining projects/schemes for implementation, Evaluation and Monitoring of completed projects/schemes, etc. During his service, he also completed his Doctorate on 'Manpower Planning and Economic Development in Arunachal Pradesh' from the North Eastern Hill University (NEHU), Shillong and later on, his Thesis was published as a book with some additions. These are all indicative of his persistent engagement with the issues and themes related to the North Eastern Region and his competence to say something meaningful and different on the basis of his vast infield experience. His first book has already created a benchmark for many scholars. The present book, which covered the entire North Eastern Region including Sikkim, has all the acumen to create yet another benchmark for future research and discourses on the region as a whole. This book is so intense and wide in terms of its content that, it will be difficult for the scholars interested in the study on the region, to ignore.

Professor B.S. Butola,
Centre for the Study of Regional Development,
School of Social Sciences,
Jawaharlal Nehru University,
New Delhi-110 067.

NOTES

1. Albert, O. Hirschman (1981): *Essay in Trespassing Economics to Politics and Beyond*; Cambridge University Press, Cambridge, England.
2. Edward, W. Said (1995): *Orientalism Western Conceptions of the Orient*, Penguin Books, India.
3. Said: *ibid.*, p. 3.
4. Said: *ibid.*, p. 5.

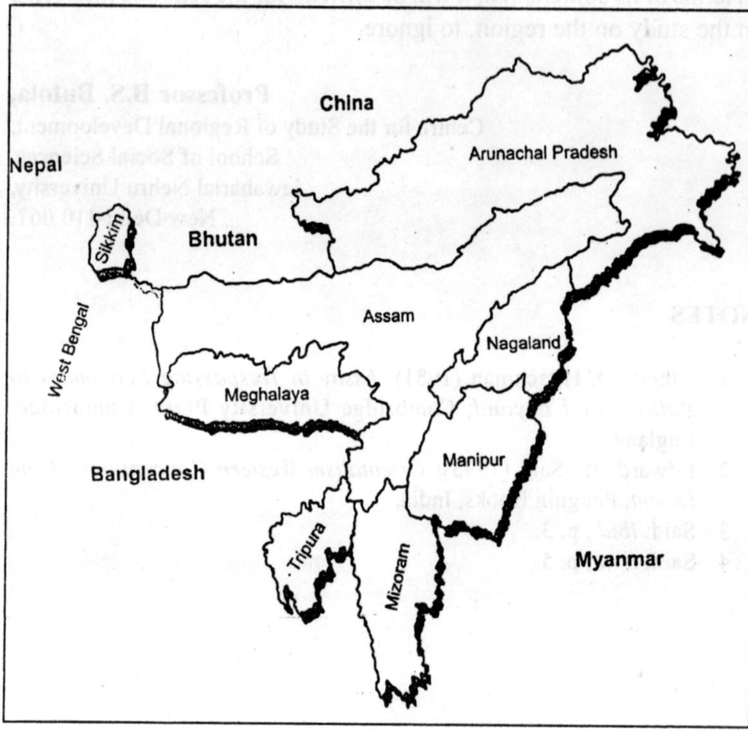

Map of The North East India

Preface

I spent my entire service life in the North Eastern Region and my work was more or less connected to socio-economic studies, collecting and analyzing statistical data, preparing reports for publication, making financial statements, formulation of Annual Plans and Five Year Plans, Evaluation and Monitoring of Projects, creation of Data Bank etc. The very nature of my job always inspired me for creative work and gradually I developed interest for that. And the first achievement in that line was my book entitled "Human Capital and Manpower Planning in North East". But while doing that work, I had to face a lot of problems for collecting information as many of the required information were either not available or were partly available or were very old. However, my inquisitiveness compelled me to continue this kind of work and to do something more for this region.

Non-availability of information is a common problem in the North Eastern Region for any kind of socio-economic studies. This kind of study requires huge amount of data for a longer period on various subjects and in an uniform manner. Continuity, consistency and reliability of data are the other pre-requisites for any kind of analytical study for finding trends and drawing conclusions. But that is very much missing in this region. The Directorate of Economics and Statistics is the nodal Department in the State for collection, compilation and dissemination of data on socio-economic aspects and development activities. All the Directorate of Economics and Statistics of this region are publishing various reports with the same name or similar name every year, but in their own ways. That means, they are not following any standard format and as such, there is no uniformity in the items of information as well as in the way of presentation of data. The Central Statistical Organisation (CSO), New Delhi, on many occasions, suggested for identifying the items of information and for standardizing the formats for presenting the data in different reports of the States for maintaining uniformity and continuity. Unfortunately that was not materialized. Therefore, it is really very difficult to make any comparative study of different States of this region using State level reports. Most of the reports also suffer from inconsistency of data, non-response and lack of updation. The North Eastern Development Finance Corporation Ltd. (NEDFi), Guwahati was established with a view to create Data Bank for the North Eastern States and for publishing developmental reports, besides other works. But the reports of NEDFi as well as the data put up in their website also suffer from similar drawbacks. I wish, one day, these problems will go away and the future writers and scholars will not find such difficulties in their works.

However, I was very much fortunate that, at the end of my service life, I was in NEC and got the opportunity to go through many of the reports of different Central Ministries, Planning Commission, Central Statistical Organisation, reports of NEC and also could utilize fully the benefit of the NEC Library. On getting all these facilities, I conceived the idea of writing this book at the end of 2007 and tried to give a comparative picture of the socio-economic scenario of each of the North Eastern States including Sikkim. I also tried to compare the position of the North Eastern Region with the country as a whole, wherever possible. The data used in some of the chapters of this book are quite old because, some are decadal in nature and in some cases the latest position was not available. However, every effort was taken to use latest data from the available reports and also from the website of different Ministries, Organisations, Departments, etc.

I am very much thankful to all the Ministries, Planning Commission, Central Statistical Organisation (CSO), North Eastern Council Secretariat (NEC), Shillong and other Departments and Institutions, whose reports I have used and mentioned their names in my book. I am also very much thankful to the Librarian and other staff of the NEC Library, who always helped me in providing books, journals, reports, etc. My special thanks are due to Prof. B.S. Butola of Jawaharlal Nehru University, New Delhi who has been the source of inspiration for me from a long time. Under his constant guidance and support, I could write two books on the North East. According to me, the present book is a better one, and I hope, the comparative picture of all the North Eastern States including Sikkim, given in this book, will be useful for identifying the deficiencies and shortcomings of different States and will help in formulating and implementing future plans for all round development of the States. This will also be useful for the research scholars. The general readers may find it beneficial for knowing the socio-economic scenario of all the N.E. States from one place.

I will be extremely happy, if I find that, this book is useful in any way. And that will be the satisfaction and fulfilment of my endeavour. I hope, the readers will excuse me, if there is any omission or commission and will suggest for improvement.

Kolkata, **R.K. Das Choudhury**
Dec., 2010

Contents

Introduction

Human beings are social beings and they have some basic needs like food, shelter, clothing, education, health, employment, recreation, sex, parenthood and freedom. Freedom is a term, which can be used in many senses. In its most abstract sense, it means 'the absence of external obstacles to the realisation of needs or acquiring of desires'. Taking in its abstract sense, freedom may be increased either by maximizing power or by minimizing wants. That means, the external conditions can modify human nature, and that harmony between the two is to be sought by a mutual interaction. If a man is taken from one environment and suddenly put to another, he may be by no means free, but the new environment may not give him freedom, as it can give freedom only to those who are accustomed to it. Therefore, we cannot deal with freedom without taking into account the possibility of variable desires owing to changing environment[1]. However, whatever may be involved in freedom, but certainly no person is free who is deprived of the basic needs which constitute the bare minimum of freedom.

This brings us to the definition of 'society'. It is obvious that the above-mentioned minimum of freedom can be better secured in a society than by an individual, moreover, sex and parenthood are essentially social. The society can be defined as a group of persons who co-operate for certain purposes. As far as human beings are concerned, the most primitive social group is the family. Economic social groups came quite early; though the groups which co-operate in war are not so primitive[2]. In the modern world, economics and war are the main motives for social cohesion. It is also a fact that a well organized society can protect its people as well as can meet their basic requirements in a better way. The civilized people have a far more elaborate social organization. They want to develop further and to catch up with the other developed groups and to be liked by them. Here comes the role of the Government to regulate the social and economic life of the people of a State, Region or a Country and to provide them the basic requirements in a planned and efficient way.

Culture is another important aspect of human development. It can be said that, culture is a continuous process of acquiring knowledge, enrichment of mind, being magnanimous and containing anger. Knowledge may not necessarily be academic. It can be agricultural, trade and commerce, industrial, religious, political, and the like, through which one can earn his bread. The immediate requirement of a person is food, and for that, he or she has to interact with the nature and with the surroundings. However, the mode of interaction varies over time. In early stages, with low level of technology and primitive institutional set-up, the interaction might have been aggressive amongst different groups. It is believed that, such interaction was common and acquiring supremacy by one group over the other was very often regarded as showing of might and considered as status symbol. But with the passes of time, this brute supremacy gave way to supremacy in terms of acquiring knowledge. Thinking of people started changing and eventually pen took the place of sword.

This brought in a radical change and people could realize that war is not the answer for all round development. It has been found that, due to anger or some dispute or for personal gain or for some other reasons, people or groups of people fight amongst each other, but in the process, many of the innocent people give their lives and their families face irreparable damages and losses. Anger is not a good thing, and if due to anger or whimsically, anybody takes any action or decision, the result of this may not always be good and in many occasions, the people is to repent. To contain anger, realization of people is a must and that realization can come, only when people are civilized and educated. Winston Churchill once said, "civilization means a society based upon the opinion of civilians. It means that violence, the rule of warriors and despotic chiefs, the conditions of camps and warfare, of riot and tyranny, give place to Parliaments where laws are made, and independent courts of justice in which over long periods those laws are maintained".

To achieve such cherished ideals, education has a significant role to play. Education can enlarge the mental horizon of people, through which one can see and understand others and can built-up the capacity of judging, what is good and what is bad and can develop a good culture. The moment one can attain such a capacity, he or she can educate himself or herself further and can develop his or her sense of intelligence and responsibilities for becoming a good citizen who can take part in public affairs and in the act of nation building. This also reduces the problems of running the Government, as it is a known fact that, the civilized and educated people can be governed very easily than the uncivilized and uneducated people. According to John Ruskin "education is the leading of human souls to what is best, and making what is best out of them; and these two objectives are always attainable together, and by the same means. The training which makes men happiest in themselves also makes them most serviceable to others".

The uncivilized, uncultured and uneducated people do not understand the intricacies of running a Government and also its limitations. They sometimes pose for getting something which is not just and ultimately that turns out to be a matter of discontent and displeasure. They finally think that, they are not a part of the society and being deprived of their freedom. In this connection, Mahatma Gandhi said "I value individual freedom but you must not forget that man is essentially a social being....unrestricted individualism is the law of the beast of the jungle. Willing submission to social restraint for the sake of the well-being of society enriches both the individual and the society".

Culture is not a frozen set of values and practices. It is constantly recreated as people question, adopt and redefine their values and practices to changing realities and exchanges of ideas[3].

To inculcate this, people need certain freedom. Cultural liberty is the capability of people to live and be what they choose, with adequate opportunity to consider other options[4]. These options and adequate opportunities are the main things. These are to be created by human beings and also to be enjoyed by them. Here comes the question of education and knowledge. Only the educated and knowledgeable persons can do that for their own benefit as well as for the benefit of the people. Common people are also required to be educated, so that they can understand and can choose what they want. Food, shelter, clothing, education, health, and employment are the basic minimum requirements of all people. These are essential for leading a normal life. Apart from these, there are desirable requirements e.g. good house, best education, highly paid employment, motor car, telephone, radio, television, freeze and all other amenities that are required for leading a luxurious life. The desirable requirements, now-a-days, have become a status symbol and everybody aspires to acquire at least a few of these items. And it is a known fact that, the society, in which, more number of persons, having desirable requirements, is more developed.

Here comes the question of means and opportunities of acquiring the essential and desirable requirements, that means, the economic condition of an individual as well as the infrastructure available to him. The economic condition of a person depends upon his income which in turn depends upon his work or employment. From this analogy, again one can say that, a society, in which, more people are employed and their economic condition is good, i.e. the purchasing power is more, is more developed. From this, it can be concluded that, the root of development is human beings and their work. But human wants are unlimited, whereas the work is limited and the purchasing power of a person may not grow with the same proportion of his wants. However, the economic condition of a person can be improved, if he can get proper education and employment at the right time. The talent and working capacity of a person is not fixed and also not same as any other. Only avenues and opportunities are required at the right time and at the right place to inculcate and improve the position.

The cultural dimensions of human development require careful attention for three reasons. First, cultural liberty is an important aspect of human freedom, central to the capability of people to live as they would like and to have the opportunity to choose from the options they have—or can have. Second, even though there has been much discussion in recent years about culture and civilization, the focus has been less on cultural liberty and more on recognizing—

even celebrating—cultural conservatism. Third, cultural liberty is important not only in the cultural sphere, but also in the successes and failures in social, political and economic spheres. Moreover, different dimensions of human life have strong interrelations with each other. Even poverty, a central economic idea, cannot be adequately understood without bringing in cultural considerations. Indeed, the close link between cultural deprivation and economic poverty was noted by no less an economist than Adam Smith, whose works have, as it happens, illuminated the relevance of human development[5].

Cultural diversity is another important aspect of human development. Cultural diversity in a society can give all the people in that society, irrespective of their background, the opportunity to enjoy a wider range of cultural choice. If diversity is not allowed, many choices become meaningless. Cultural diversity may be both a consequence of the exercise of human freedom and a source of societal enrichment. A culturally diverse society can bring benefits to others through the variety of experiences that they are, as a consequence, in a position to enjoy. However, the availability of opportunity for education, employment and other cultural choices depend upon the socio-economic condition of the society or in other words, on the socio-economic scenario of the State, Region or the Country.

The North Eastern Region consists of seven States viz. Arunachal Pradesh, Assam, Manipur, Meghalaya, Mizoram, Nagaland and Tripura. This Region is also called the land of seven sisters. However, for the purpose of Development Activities, the State of Sikkim came under the purview of the North Eastern Council, which is a Regional Planning Body, by an Act of Parliament, in December, 2002. All the States of this Region, except Assam are mostly hilly. Assam is also having hilly regions, but it is comparatively less than the plain areas of the State. The States of this region are very much unique in their own Geographic, Demographic and in other Socio-economic aspects, which have been analyzed by different scholars differently at various points of time. Here is an attempt to place the problems and opportunities present in this region in a wider and comprehensive canvas.

NOTES

1. *Sceptical Essays*, Bertrand Russell, Unwin Hyman Limited, 15-17 Broadwick Street, London, p. 130.
2. *ibid.*, p. 130-31.
3. *Human Development Report 2004*, Cultural Liberty in Today's Diverse World, Oxford University Press, p. 4.
4. *ibid.*, p. 4.
5. *ibid.*, p. 13.

2

Geophysical Scenario

The North Eastern Region is situated in the North East extremity of our country. It is bounded by China in the North, Myanmar and Bangladesh in the South, Myanmar in the East and Nepal and West Bengal in the West. The total Geographical Area (notional area) of the North Eastern Region including Sikkim is 2,62,191 sq. kms. Historically, successive legal and administrative decisions taken between 1874 and 1935 gave distinct identity to the areas of this Region. The British administration initially treated the hill areas of the North East as a "Non-Regulated Areas", and then declared them as "Backward Tracts" and finally "Excluded Areas" and "Partially Excluded Areas". A brief history of each of the North Eastern States is given below:

Arunachal Pradesh

Arunachal Pradesh is a thinly populated mountainous State lies roughly between 26° 28′ N and 29° 30′ N latitudes and 91° 30′ E and 97° 30′ E longitudes on the North East extremity of India. The State is having a total area of 83,743 sq.kms. forming India's international boundaries with Bhutan in the West, Tibet in the North-West, China in the North and Myanmar in the South-East. From the south it is bordered by the State of Assam. The overall hilly feature of the State shows that it gradually rises from about 350 metres height in the foot-hills in north bank of river Brahmaputra to mighty convolutions of mountain ranges and spurs over 6,000 metres in the Greater and Trans Himalayas. It is a tangle of deep gorge like valleys, densely wooded mountain slopes, dissected by numerous torrents and rivers, deep river valleys and a belt of tropical rain forest[1].

Arunachal Pradesh is one of the very few States of India which has a very large area under forest. According to the published land-use statistics provided by the State as well as the Central Government, the total forest cover is legally notified as 52,000 sq. kms. (i.e. about 62.1 per cent of the total Geographical area of the State) while the satellite imagery data generated by NRSA, Hyderabad recorded it as 71,405 sq. kms. (i.e. about 85.3 per cent)[2]. The rich forest cover of the state is also vivid in terms of variety of plant species and vegetation. It ranges from swampy rain forest at the foothills and low-lying areas in the eastern part of the state to the tropical and subtropical vegetation cover up to the height of approximately 2,134 metres. This vegetation zone is distinguished by valuable trees of great size, plentiful climbers and abundant undergrowth. Among the climbers, cane is most noticeable. Orchids of numerous varieties are also in abundance. Beyond 2,134 and up to 2,734 metres, there are deciduous and mixed deciduous forests comprising mainly of walnut, oak, chestnut, pine, spruce and rhododendron. Beyond it and up to an altitude of 3,658 metres, the wide stretch of area is generally claimed by conifers. Going still further up, the flora yields to plentiful rhododendrons of dwarfish stature and wild strawberry bushes. Above 4,877 metres and right up to the snow line, is the region of alpine meadow.

Like the flora, the deeply wooded terrains of Arunachal Pradesh are also rich in fauna. Among the great variety of wildlife in the State, the most commonly noticed are tiger, black panther, black deer, leopard, wild elephant, barking deer, musk deer, monkey and langur, wild buffalo, wild goat, flying fox and many other kinds of birds[3]. Apart from these, the state is very rich in natural resources like water and hydroelectric potentials. Moreover, the unexplored and adventurous terrain of this strategically sensitive state has vast potentials for the development of tourism industry.

The State of Arunachal Pradesh is the homeland of about 20 major tribes and more than 100 sub-tribes. The major tribes are Sherdukpen, Monpa, Aka, Miji, Khoa, Bagni, Nishi, Hill Miri, Apatani, Tagin, Memba and Khamba, Adi, Mishmi, Khamti, Singpoh, Nocte, Wancho, Tangsa, Lisu, etc. According to historians and other scholars, the tribal people of the State with Mongoloid characters had a South East Asian origin and their migration to Arunachal Pradesh took place in prehistoric times[4]. The racial affiliation of the people of this State has been described by scholars as Mongoloid, Palio-mongoloid and so on. But Anthropologists also noticed deviation in racial type among different sections of the same group, particularly among the ethnic groups spreading along the central parts of the state and these are considered to be the earliest migrants to this area.

The tribal people of Arunachal Pradesh are predominantly agriculturists. The rural people mostly depend on agriculture, free collection from surrounding forests, hunting, fishing, etc. for their livelihood. Since, the area is not much exposed to agricultural development as compared to other areas of the country, the age-old traditional method of shifting (*jhum*) cultivation is still prevalent in the agricultural pursuits. Limited availability of flat land, lack of protective measures for land development, paucity of irrigation facilities has offered limited choice before the rural people, which made them compelled to pursue the traditional method of jhum cultivation. However, the Apatanis of lower Subansiri district, gifted with some amount of flat land, have been pursuing settled rice cultivation in an improved manner for a long time. Though, improvements have also been noticed among the Adis of Pasighat, Mebo, Roing, Dambuk, Khamtis of Chaukham and Namsai, Monpas of Tawang and Dirang in this regard, but the situation is far from satisfaction.

The historical accounts of Arunachal Pradesh and its people dates back to the late Ahom period in the eighteenth century. It appears from the historical evidences that "*Sukapa*" the founder of the Ahom Kingdom came across the Patkoi hills in early thirteenth century. After the conquest of Assam by the Ahoms, it was found that the Akas, Daflas, Miris, Mishmis, Nagas, etc. living in the mountains of the North and East of Brahmaputra valley were in the habit of coming down in the plains contiguous to their respective hills and taking by force whatever they found before them. To prevent the tribes men from such rapacious attacks, the Ahom rulers initially applied force but failed. Ultimately, they introduced the policy of payment of *Posa* (allowance) to the tribes men in order to maintain a good relation and to keep them in good humour.

The decline of Ahom monarchy dates back to the middle of the eighteenth century. The British annexed the whole of Assam in 1838 and constituted it into a Non-Regulated Province of the British Empire in India[5]. Moreover, to regulate relations with the tribal people of North East India, the British laid down a restrictive line what came to be known as '*Inner Line*' in 1874. Later on, the then Government of India, extended the Assam Frontier Tracts Regulation of 1880 to the hills inhabited by Abors, Miris, Mishmis, Singphos, Nagas, Khamtis, Bhutias, Akas, Daflas and other tribes in the year 1914 through a notification issued by its Foreign and Political Department. As a result the hills inhabited by the tribes mentioned above were separated from Darrang and Lakhimpur Districts of Assam and constituted into the *North Eastern Frontier Tract*[6].

With rapid expansion of administration in the interior of the Frontier Tracts, spatial interaction at the intra and inter-regional levels increased manifolds. Moreover, it was realized that an efficient administrative machinery is a must for executing various developmental programmes. Accordingly, momentous reorganization took place in the year 1954. The promulgation of the North East Frontier (Administration) Regulation, 1954, inaugurated a full-scale and integrated administrative structure for the entire area under the name of North East Frontier Agency (NEFA) for the first time[7].

However, the political and constitutional development of late sixties, lead towards a separate direction and on 21st January, 1972, NEFA attained the status of Union Territory (UT) with the new name of Arunachal Pradesh. On 15th August, 1975, the Union Territory was endowed with the Legislative Assembly and the first general election was held in 1978. The Union Territory of Arunachal Pradesh, finally attained the status of a full-fledged state on 20th February, 1987. The State is now having 16 Districts, 44 Sub-Divisions, 85 CD/IRD Blocks, 169 Circles and 17 Urban Towns[8]. But, as per 2001 census, there were 3863 villages and a total of 1097968 population.

Assam

The erstwhile State of Assam which was called North-East India, situated between 89° 46′ E and 97° 4′ E longitude and 28° 15′ N and 24° N latitude[9]. The history of the pre-historic and proto-historic periods of Assam is shrouded in mystery and very little is known about this period. The *Mahabharata*, *Vishnupurana*, *Kalika Purana* and *Yoginitantra* indicate that in the early period, it was known as *Pragjyotisha* and later as Kamarupa and was ruled by Kings who had appellation of Danaba-Asura which suggest their non-Aryan origin[10].

The earliest historic record is found in the account of the Chinese pilgrim Hiuen-Tsang, who visited Kamarupa in 640 A.D. It was a strong and prosperous kingdom ruled by a Hindu King named Bhaskar Varman. Hiuen-Tsang placed the circumference of the kingdom at 10,000 lee from which Winningham infers that it must have included, at that time, the whole of Brahmaputra valley, Cooch-Behar and Bhutan[11].

After the visit of Hiuen-Tsang, the history of Kamarupa again became obscure and the veil was lifted by a dynasty founded by Pralambha about the year 800 A.D. The new dynasty ruled for about 200 years when it gave way to the Palas at about 1000 A.D. After a century and a half, Pala Dynasty was brought under the Pala Dynasty of Bengal by Ram Pala[12].

In the 13th century, a new kingdom known as Kamatapura comprising a small portion of the kingdom of Kamarupa came into existence. The establishment of Muslim power in Bengal affected the course of the history of Assam considerably. While Assam became a constant prey of the Muhammadan invasions from Bengal, the Ahoms made their way into Assam early in the 13th century across the Patkai range. At the end of the 15th century, a new dynasty of Kochas was established by one Biswa Singh. The Koches then launched a systematic warfare against the Ahoms for territorial expansion. During the latter part of the reign of King Nara-Narayana, the most powerful and glorious king of the dynasty, a division was made in the kingdom with the river Sankosh as the boundary between them. The new branch of the Koch dynasty with their headquarters at Baruagarh ruled over the kingdom which came to be known as Kamarupa. The territory of this kingdom was gradually absorbed by the Ahoms when the last powerful king of the dynasty, Parikshit, was carried off to Delhi by the Muhammadans[13].

The Ahoms, a Shan tribe, came to the Brahmaputra valley from Burma about the year 1226. After establishing firmly in the upper Brahmaputra valley, they followed a policy of expansion and by

1700 A.D., conquered the territories once included in the kingdom of Kamarupa. In 1695 Rudra Singh, the greatest of Ahom princes, ascended the throne and completed the conquest of the whole Brahmaputra valley. In 1780, Gourinath succeeded to the throne and his reign was marked chiefly by the rising of the Moamarias which shook the foundations of the Ahom kingdom. Gourinath in utter distress applied for help to the British, who succeeded in suppressing the Moamaria rebellion and defeated Kisen Narayan, the king of old Darrang, and in 1809, Chandra Kanta Singh succeeded to the throne[14].

It was found that Badan Bar Phukan who became jealous of the power of the Bor Gohain, the Ahom Prime Minister, sought the help of the British to oust the Bor Gohain from his position. But, having failed to persuade the British, he went to the Court of the King of Ava in Burma and succeeded eventually in getting his support. As a result, a huge Burmese army came to Assam towards the end of 1816. At this critical juncture, the Ahom Prime Minister died and all responsibility fell on his eldest son who was quite inexperienced in conducting the affairs of the state. The Burmese then continued with their triumphant march, and the new Bor Gohain fled away to Guwahati. The Bor Gohain who suspected the Ahom King Chandra Kanta, having conspired to through him over to the enemy, invited an Ahom Prince Purandar Singh and put him up as a pretender to the Ahom throne. In the meantime, the Bor Phukan who enjoyed momentary glory, was assassinated in another court intrigue. But, at one stage, both Chandra Kanta and the pretender Purandar Singh sought British help for driving the Burmese occupation army. But in the meanwhile, Burmese army created great havoc and finally succeeded in enticing Chandra Kanta to leave British protection. He was then immediately seized and confined. The Burmese also continued to give offense to the British across the border and demanded surrender of fugitives who had sought shelter in the British territory. The British finally declared war against Burmese on the 5th March, 1824. The war lasted for about two years and ultimately the Burmese army retreated before the superior might of the British which put an end to the Burmese occupation of Assam. The British finally annexed the whole of Assam in 1838 and constituted it into a Non-Regulated Province of the British empire in India and the region was brought under direct British rule[15].

The British rule in Assam ended with the independence of India on 15th August, 1947. The present State of Assam is having a geographical area of 78,438 sq. kms. and is surrounded by seven North Eastern States viz. Arunachal Pradesh, Nagaland, Manipur, Mizoram, Tripura, Meghalaya, West Bengal and two other countries viz. Bhutan and Bangladesh. The total population of Assam was 26655528 as per 2001 census. The population of the State can be divided in to two broad groups viz. non-tribal and tribal. The non-tribal people generally lives in the two major river systems in the twenty two districts of the Brahmaputra valley and the three districts of Barak velley. Whereas, the tribal people generally lives in the hill districts. There are about 23 different tribes, like Bodo Kacharis, Karbis, Lalings, Khasis, Jaintias, Garos, Dimasas, Hmars, Rengma Nagas, etc. The overall density of population of the State was 340 persons per sq. kms. However, the density of population was less in the two hill districts of Karbi-Anglong and the North Cachar Hills. For administrative and revenue purposes, the State has 27 (twenty-seven) districts including the newly created Kamrup (Metro) district and 4 (four) districts under the newly created Bodoland Territorial Council (BTC) areas viz. Kokrajhar, Baska, Chirang and Udalguri[16].

Agriculture is the main source of livelihood of majority of the people of this State. The State is also very rich in timber products, tea and oil besides many other industrial and economic activities.

Manipur

Manipur is one of the seven sisters of the North Eastern Region, situated between 93.03° E and 94.78° E longitudes and 23.80° N and 25.68° N latitudes. The State is a charming place encircled by nine hill ranges on all sides with a small and beautiful oval valley at the centre. The State has 352 kms. long international border with Myanmar to the South-East and 502 kms. long border with the adjacent state of Nagaland on the North, while Cachar District of Assam on the West and Mizoram on the South and South-West. The total Geographical area (notional) of the State is 22327 sq. kms. The altitude of the State, above the mean sea level, varies from 790 metres to 2020 metres. It has sub-tropical temperate climate.

The early history of the State of Manipur can be seen from the

State Royal Chronicle, called the Cheitharol Kumbaba which covers the period from 33 AD to 1890 AD. During this period, altogether 74 (seventy-four) kings ruled the State, of which Nongda Lairen Pakhangba (33 AD to 121 AD) was the first and Kulachandra was the last. At that time, Manipur was a small independent kingdom.

Manipur lost her independence to the British India in the year, 1891. From 1892 onwards, it became a princely native state under the political control of Government of British India. Accordingly, the administration of the State came to be handed over to a political agent by vesting all executive powers in him. This British Paramountcy continued till 1947 when India got independence.

According to a merger agreement between Maharaja Budhachandra, the then king of Manipur and the Government of India, signed on 21st September, 1949, the State was merged into India as a part C-category on the 15th October, 1949. As a result, Manipur came under the administrative control of a Chief Commissioner assisted by an Advisory Council of 14 (fourteen) members. But from the year1957, a Territorial Council with 70 (seventy) members headed by a Chairman replaced the Advisory Council and this was continued till 1963 when Manipur became a single district Union Territory. Later on, the Territorial Council was replaced by a Legislative Assembly of 30 (thirty) members and a Council of Ministers. In the year, 1972, Manipur became a full-fledged state within the Indian Union with a Governor as the Head of the state and the members of the Legislative Assembly was also doubled to 60 (sixty)[17].

The State of Manipur is divided naturally into two tracts viz. the hills and the dales. The hill comprises of five districts viz. Senapati, Tamenglong, Churachandpur, Chandel and Ukhrul. While, the valley comprises of four districts viz. Imphal East, Imphal West, Bishnupur and Thoubal. The valley area of Manipur consists of two main parts, one is the Imphal valley, right at the heart of the state and the other is Jiri valley, in the west beyond the hill ranges bordering the Cachar district of Assam[18]. The total population of the State as per 2001 census was 2166788 (excluding the population figures of Mao Maran, Paomata and Purul sub-divisions of Senapati district where the census results were cancelled due to technical and administrative reasons). The people include Meiteis, Nagas, Meite Pangals and other communities. The overall population density of the state was though

97 persons per sq. km. but the population is mainly concentrated in the valleys where the density was 628 persons per sq. km[19].

Agriculture is the main source of livelihood of majority of the people of Manipur. In the hills, the people follow the traditional method of shifting cultivation. Permanent cultivation is generally practiced in the valley districts. Terrace cultivation is also practiced in some of the pockets of the hills where jhuming or shifting cultivation is widely adopted[20].

Meghalaya

The State of Meghalaya is situated between 98° 47′ E and 97° 47′ E longitudes and 25° 5′ N and 26° 10′ N latitudes bounded by the Goalpara, Kamrup and Nowgong districts of Assam on the North, Karbi Anglong and North Cachar Hills on the East and Bangladesh on the South West. The State is broadly divided into three natural sectors viz. (i) The Central Plateau, (ii) The Southern Border Area, and (iii) The Northern Border Area.

The Central Plateau forms the highest region of the State. It comprises mainly with the high land of the Khasi and Jaintia Hills and situated more or less in the centre of the state having an altitude approximately between 1230 metres and 1850 metres above mean sea level. From the Shillong Peak, it stretches out to a distance of about 50 kms. directly towards the south, 65 kms. towards the south-west and 28 kms. towards the south-east and merges with the Southern Border Areas. Similarly, it stretches out to a distance of about 20 kms. towards the north and merges with Norhern Border Areas. The Central Plateau is the source of most of the streams viz. Umngot, Kopili, Umiam Mawphlang, Umiam Khwan, Myntdu, Umkhen, Myntang and others[21].

The Southern Border Area is highly irregular. It is more or less a continuation of the Central Plateau and up to a few kms. with interruptions here and there caused by sudden drops and depressions. As it recedes further and moves closer to the border of Bangladesh, the sudden drops and depressions become more prominent till they abruptly end in sheer precipices. This is specially true in the case of Khasi and Jaintia Hills. From the foot of the precipices, the area continues for some more distance in the form of a vast stretch of flat land till it merges with the border of Bangladesh at an elevation of mostly 200 to 300 metres. However, along the border of the Garo Hills, there are no sudden drops, depression or precipices. This region receives the heaviest and most copious rainfall in the state[22].

The Northern Border Area lies in the north of the State and merges with the districts of Goalpara, Kamrup and Nowgong of Assam. The feature of the Northern Border Area is more or less similar to the Central Plateau with the gradual downward move till it merges with the border of Assam. This region gets less rainfall and has a sub-tropical climate[23].

The present State of Meghalaya with its headquarters at Shillong was originally a part of Assam. At its initial stage, it was consisted of two districts viz. the Garo Hills district and the united Khasi-Jaintia district. It became an Autonomous State on 1st April, 1970, but it did not retain that status for long. Under the North Eastern Areas (Regulation) Act, 1971, Meghalaya became a full-fledged State and it was formally inaugurated on 21st January, 1972. On 22nd February, 1972, the Jaintia Hills district was created. In October, 1976, two new districts viz. East Garo Hills district with its headquarters at Williamnagar, and West Khasi Hills district with its headquarters at Nongstoin were created[24]. Later on, in the month of June, 1992, two more districts viz. Ri-Bhoi and South Garo Hills were created and thus, the total number of districts in Meghalaya reached to 7 (seven).

The total Geographical area of the State is 22429 sq. kms. and the total population as per 2001 census was 2318822, having a density of 103 persons per sq. km. The inhabitants of this State are mainly Khasis, Jaintias, Garos, Bhois, Wars, etc. The Khasis, Jaintias, Bhois and Wars are collectively known as the Hynniewtrep people predominantly inhabit the districts of East Meghalaya. They are also known to be one of the earliest ethnic group of settlers in the Indian sub-continent, belonging to the Proto Austroloid Monkhmer race. The Garo Hills are predominantly inhabited by the Garos, belonging to the Bodo family of the Tibeto-Burman race, said to have migrated from Tibet. The Garos prefer to call themselves as Achiks and the land they inhabit as the Achik-land. The Khasi-Pnars inhabit the eastern part of Meghalaya, in the Khasi and Jaintia Hills. Khasis residing in Jaintia Hills are now better known as Jaintias. They are also called Pnars. The Khasis, occupying the northern lowlands and foothills, are generally called Bhois and those who live in the southern tracts are called Wars[25].

The people of Meghalaya, mainly the rural masses, depend on agriculture. Agriculture is the main source of their livelihood and they primarily follow the age old method of Jhum cultivation. Terrace cultivation is done in the gentle slopes of the Khasi Hills. Besides this, wet cultivation is also practiced in the inter-mountain plains in the Khasi and Jaintia Hills and in the low-lying border areas of the Garo Hills[26]. The State of Meghalaya is very rich in the production of potato, cabbage, cauliflower, ginger, turmeric, orange, banana, pineapple, etc.

Mizoram

The State of Mizoram is situated between 22° 19′N and 24° 19′ N latitude and 92° 16′ E and 93° 26′ E longitude covering an area of 21087 sq. kms. The State is bounded by Assam and Manipur on the North and North-East, Myanmar on the East and South, Tripura on the North-West and Bangladesh on the South-West.

Mizoram is a mountainous State. It consists of seven long north-south traversing parallel ranges with intervening valleys which form a panoramic physiographic feature of 'Tongueshaped' area or hogsback, the middle portion is high and tappers downwards in north-south direction[27]. Further, the whole area is divided into three natural regions viz. (i) Mountainous region, (ii) Ridges and high land regions, and (iii) Plain land or Flat land (low land areas).

The Mountainous terrain region can be further sub-divided into (a) Mountainous region of north-east, (b) Mountainous region of central Mizoram, and (c) Mountainous region of south-east region.

The Mountainous terrain of north-east is above 1500 metres, having very less population and agricultural facilities. The central region falls under Chalfilh range in which Zopuitlang (1992 metres) and Bualpuitlang are prominent. The highest peak of Blue Mountain (2165 metres, Phawngpui) falls in the southern region and the river Kolodyne passes through it.

Low-lying areas in Mizoram are very rare except a few small patches between mountain ranges. In the north-west Mizoram, between the rivers Longkhaih and Tlawng, there is a small area below

600 metres near Lokichera and Bhairabi. Near Demagiri, the river Karnphuli and its tributaries form another small low-lying area. Down south, the low land lies west of Tuichawng and its tributaries. In the east, near Champhai covering an area of 11 sq. kms, is a flat land and in the Mat river basin near Thenzol and north-Vanlaiphai, there is another small low-lying area, which are suitable for wet rice cultivation[28].

The early history of the Mizos is virtually based on legends, traditions, customs and beliefs. There is common belief among the Mizos that, their ancestors emigrated from a place called 'Chhingluing'. Historians and Anthropologists are of the opinion that this place is in the southern China. In some recent studies too, it was found that the Mizos came from the east and their original home was in Mekong Valley. K. Zawla, a historian asserts that the Mizo people came to the Chindwin belt about 996 A.D. and lived there for about 200 years. Later on, they left that place and during their movement around 1466 A.D., the first place of halt was at Lengtlang and each family grouped together and each sub-tribe settled in separate villages. The sub-tribes were the Lusei, Ralte, Chawangthu, Khiangte, Hauhnar, Chuange, Chuanthang, Ngente, Punte and Parte. Westward movement of the Mizos from Lentlang to the present Mizo State took place between 1700 and 1730 A.D.[29].

The present State of Mizoram was a part of Assam and was known as Lushai Hills District. In 1954, the nomenclature of the Lushai Hills District was changed to Mizo Hills District by an Act of Parliament. Later on, the District was elevated to the status of Union Territory with the name 'Mizoram' in 1972 and subsequently it became a full-fledged state on 20th February, 1987[30]. At present the state is having 8 (eight) districts viz. Mamit, Kolasib, Aizawl, Champhai, Serchhip, Lunglei, Lawngtlai and Saiha.

The total population of Mizoram as per 2001 census was 888573 and most of them are depending on agriculture and allied activities for their livelihood. They are generally practicing the age old method of *Jhum* cultivation on hilly slopes. The scope of settled cultivation in Mizoram is very much limited as the availability of flat land is very less. However, wet rice cultivation is being practiced in the low-lying areas available in between the mountain ranges and river basins. The main food crops in Mizoram are paddy, maize, pulse, vegetables, ginger, chilly, sugarcane, etc. The State of Mizoram, on the other hand, is very much suitable for pisciculture and sufficient quantity of fish of different kinds is being produced every year.

Nagaland

The State of Nagaland is situated between 25° 60′ N and 27° 40′ N latitude and 93° 20′ E and 95° 15′ E longitude spreading over an area of 16579 sq. kms. The State is bounded by Assam and Arunachal Pradesh on the North, Manipur on the South, Myanmar on the East and Assam on the West. Nagaland is predominantly a tribal state. The entire tribal population is divided into twenty major tribal groups. The dominant tribes which have their well-defined territorial jurisdiction are—Aos, Angamis, Changs, Chakhesang, Kabuis, Kacharis, Khein Mangas, Konyaks, Kukis, Lothas, Maos, Mikirs, Phoms, Rengmas, Sangtams, Semas, Thankuls, Yimchungars and Zelliang[31].

The early history of Nagas is not much known as there is hardly any record available on this. However, it is seen that, at about 2000 years B.C., Mongolians came to India through Barma and Tibet. Some of these people settled in Garo Hills, while Kukis and Bodos settled in Cachar Hills. The Cacharis started ruling over northern Assam and Dimapur was said to be the capital of Cacharis. More details about Nagas could be found from the references of emissaries and evidence of cultural relations that grown up with the Cacharis in the later part of 14th century.

It is believed that, Sukhpa, the founder of Ahom Kingdom came to Assam from Burma through Tirap region of Arunachal Pradesh around 1228 A.D. and had their first contacts with the tribal communities of Nocte, Konyak and Wanchas. Later on, with the gradual expansion of the Ahom Kingdom, the Aos and Lothas also came in contact with the Ahoms. However, though there were frequent clashes among these tribes and Lothas, Ahoms could somehow manage to keep their control over this region and also could maintain more or less a good relation with the Nagas. It was found that Nagas used to present gifts and tributes to Ahoms and they in turn allowed Nagas to carry out revenue-free cultivation of paddy in the fields and fishing in the bills. Moreover, so long Nagas were refrained from raids on the plain people, Ahoms did not interfere in the daily activities of the Nagas.

But in the year 1536, Ahom made an expedition against the Nagas to subside the Konyak uprising, but failed. Subsequently, a large Ahom force was sent who brutally murdered hundreds of people at Dimapur and finally defeated the Konyak. But that was not the end, the Konyak and the Lothats carried out their raids on the plain people on different occasions but the Ahom rulers could succeed in defeating the tribal people and finally could establish their authority on the Naga Hills and as such, there was no major untoward incident occurred in these hills in the eighteenth century[32].

The British came in contact with the Nagas in the early period of the nineteenth century and found that it is very difficult to control the Nagas. Initially, the British made a series of raids and adopted changing policies to contain the Naga hostilities but could not succeed. Later on, they thought of developing friendly relations with the Nagas and accordingly, Lieutenant Bigge made two friendly missions to Naga Hills in 1840-42 and succeeded in that. On demand of the Naga Chief, he opened a salt depot at Dimapur and because of that good gesture, he became very popular among the tribals. Further, with the help of Captain Gordon, Bigge also succeeded in demarcating a boundary, separating the Naga country from Manipur[33].

The British established its authority and control over the Naga territory in 1866 in pursuance of the decision taken by the Government of India on the recommendations of the Lieutenant Governor of Assam. In 1881 a separate Naga Hills District was formed and the British followed the policy of consolidating their authority in the region and also pursued steady penetration into the interior. In 1890, Mokokchung Sub-division was formed and in 1922, Primi (Akhegwo) and Meloni (Meluri) were annexed to the Naga Hills District. Later on, the Naga Hills District Council was formed in order to bring all the Nagas under one banner. In April, 1946, the Council became Naga National Council (NNC) and had its first Conference at Wokha[34].

The Naga territory remained split between Assam and North East Frontier Agency even after India's independence in 1947, despite a vocal movement advocating the political union of all Nagas. In 1957, the Indian Government established a single Naga administrative unit under Indian rule. Later on, in 1960, the Indian Government agreed to make Nagaland a self-governing State within India. Finally, the State was officially inaugurated on 1st December, 1963[35]. The State is now having 8 (eight) districts viz. Kohima, Dimapur, Phek, Mokokchung, Wokha, Zunheboto, Tuensang and Mon.

Nagaland is a hilly tribal State. The general elevation ranges from 914 metres to 3840 metres above the sea level. The Barail Range locally known as Radliura, enters the state from north Cachar and after passing through Kohima goes in the direction of Wokha. Owing to a sudden rise of the Barail Range on its northern face, about 12 kms. wide miniature type of Dun (valley) is formed in between the Barail Range and Samaguling Hills. The Patkai Range forms a watershed which constitutes the International boundary between India and Myanmar. Saraniati situated in Tuensang district is the highest peak of the State which is 3877 metres above sea level[36].

The State was having a total population of 1990036 as per 2001 census, spreading over a Geographical area of 16579 sq. kms. with a density of 120 persons per sq. km. Agriculture is the main stay of the people of Nagaland. In the hill slopes, the people generally practice Jhum cultivation. However, in recent times, people have started terrace cultivation and the Government is also encouraging them by givin loans and subsidies for this purpose. The main crops of the State are Paddy, Wheat, Maize, Bajra, Jowar, Millets, Cereals, Pulse, Oilseeds, etc. The State is also rich in flora and fauna.

Tripura

The State of Tripura is situated between 22° 56′ N and 24° 32′ N latitude and 91° 09′ E and 92° 20′ E longitude spreading over an area of 10492 sq. kms[37]. The state is almost surrounded by Bangladesh on three sides with an international border of 856 kms. leaving a small strip of about 30 kms. on the North, by which, it is having the link with the rest of the country through the Karimganj District of Assam. The State is also having a boundary of about 160 kms. with Mizoram on the North Eastern side[38].

Topographically, the State can broadly be divided into hill ranges, plain lands including valleys, and river basins. The hill ranges gradually gain height from west to east and generally run from north to south losing altitude till they merge with the plains of Bangladesh. The six main hill ranges in Tripura are the Jampui, Sakhan, the Longtharai-Atharamura, the Sardang, the Baramura-Devtamura and Atharamura Ranges. The Jampui Range is situated in Dharmanagar sub-division and is 74 kms. in length. One of its peaks, the Betling Sib (1000 metres) is the highest altitude found in Tripura and is mainly inhabited by the Lushais and the Reangs. The Sakhan range forms the boundary of Dharmanagar and Kailashahar sub-division and its northern part, is known as the Unakuti. The length of this range is 58 kms. and that of Unokuti is 20 kms. Its highest peak is the Sakhan (840 metres) and this range is mainly inhabited by the Lushais and the Darlongs. The Longtharai range forms the boundary of Kailashahar and Kamalpur sub-division and is about 48 kms. long. Its highest peak is Longtharai (515 metres). The Atharamura Range starts from the Amarpur sub-division and then runs into the southern part of Khowai sub-division and thereafter along the boundary of Khowai and Kamalpur sub-divisions, it merges into the plains of Bangladesh. It rises at Niungmarueta to a height of 514 metres and derives its name from the fact that, it has eighteen peaks. Two offshoots of this range run towards south-east and west meeting Longtharai and Baramura ranges respectively. The Baramura range is about 47 kms. and that of its lower portion known as the Devata range is about 85 kms[39].

The early history of Tripura is clouded in mystery and romance. This can be seen from the Bengali poem Rajmala or Chronicles of Tripura, the early part of which was composed in 1458 A.D. by Tripuri priest Durlabhendra and two of his Brahmin associates, Sukheshwar and Baneshwar. The early King of Tripura, King Chengthum-fa was very weak, but his wife, Queen Tripura Sundari was very brave and strong and once fought a war with her troops against the army of the Emperor of Gaur and won the war. The victorious Queen belonged to a Raj which traces its descent to Drujho, the son of Yajati, the supreme ruler. Drujho ultimately became a sanyasi and abdicated his throne in favour of his son Tripur. But Tripur unleashed a reign of terror and oppression. Under his rule, his subjects reached to a stage of great poverty and starvation and ultimately emigrated to Hiramba (Cachar), but had to return soon as they did not get any help from the Raja there. They then worshipped Shiva, who promised to help them if they worship Chaturdash Deveta. Their prayers were answered when

Tripur's widow gave birth to Trilochan, who was immediately made the King by his grateful people. The tales of his wisdom then spread far and wide and ultimately Hiramba King offered him his daughter in marriage which was solemnized with great joy[40].

After a reign of conquest and glory, Trilochan was succeeded by the youngest of his twelve sons, Dakshin, who was the choice of both his father and their subjects. Rajeshwar, the sixty-first king of Tripura had no son; so he in his anger fired an arrow at a Shivalingam. Shiva cursed him that he would have no son, but to propitiate the great God, Rajeshwar offered a human sacrifice which pleased Shiva and Rajeshwar was blessed with a son by the name of Micholee. At the time of Pratit, the seventy-first Raja, Tripura and Cachar were bound in a strong alliance. This treaty survived the storm and stress of subsequent history.

The fame of Tripura nationalism was however, tarnished by Ratan-pha, an exile in Gaur, who invited the Turkish Sultan, Togral to conquer the Kingdom. He successfully invaded the State with the help of the Mohammedan troops and ascended the throne after beheading his brother. The Gaur Sultan conferred upon him the title of *Manik*, probably in 1279 A.D., which the Tripura Rajas retained to these days. Dharma Manikya ascended the throne in 1407 A.D. and ruled till 1458 A.D. Up to his time, human sacrifice was very much in vogue, but he ruled that such sacrifice should only be offered three times a year. Dharma Manikya was a great King and was a patron of learning. Under his patronage, the work on the first part of Rajmala was started. He died after a long and peaceful reign. But an inter-regnum followed after his death till Dhanya Manikya became the Raja in 1490 A.D.[41]

Dhanya Manikya was the greatest of the Tripura Kings. With the help of his Queen, Kamala Devi, he tried to remove a number of baneful caste restrictions among his troops. He was a great patron of literature and wanted to popularize Bengali. Dhanya Manikya was also a worshiper of the lingam and built many temples and got artists to carve beautiful images. He died in 1520 A.D. and was succeeded by his son Dev Manikya. Dev Manikya was a tantrik and a great devotee of Shakti. He was assassinated by a priest, but the priest was in turn killed by the army chief who put first Indra and then Vijoy, the late Raja's two sons, on the throne. Vijoy Manikya (1535-1583 A.D.)

was a very powerful ruler, but unfortunately died of small-pox after ruling for 47 years. His son, Anantha Manikya (1583-1585 A.D.) succeeded him. However, Gopi Prasad strangled his son-in-law and sat on the throne as Udai Manikya. Udai Manikya (1585-1596 A.D.) decorated his capital Rangamati with beautiful tanks, buildings, temples and renamed it as Udaipur. He was later on poisoned and his son Jai Manikya (1596-1597 A.D.) succeeded him, but for a very short period. His son, Amar Manikya (1597-1611 A.D.) beheaded his father as well as his uncle Runag Narayan who was trying to kill him, and ascended the throne.

Up to this time, the Tripura Kings had successfully repelled all external invasions and had carried the glory of their state beyond the bank of the Brahmaputra and the Padma. But when Mughals defeated the Tripura troops and marched on Udaipur, Amar Manikya fled away to the forests and subsequently committed suicide. He was succeeded by his son Rajdhar Manikya (1611-1613 A.D.) who made a temple of Vishnu and distributed land to the Brahmins. He was accidentally drowned in the river Gomati as he bent to drink water in which the image of Vishnu had been washed. After his death, his son Jasadhar Manikya (1613-1623 A.D.) became the King. During his time, he was repeatedly at war with Mughals. In 1620, Nawab Fateh Jung invaded Tripura and after a fierce fighting managed to subdue Jasadhar Manikya and took him to Delhi as prisoner along with a large number of elephants and horses. However, having refused restoration of his throne on condition of paying a tribute, Jasadhar Manikya was exiled to Benaras where he died at the age of 72[42].

In the meantime, Tripura was systematically plundered by the Mughal Governors of Udaipur, but ultimately a dreadful plague forced them to leave Udaipur. However, in 1625 A.D., Kalyan Manikya, a kinsman was sworn into the throne of Jasadhar by the people of Tripura. Kalyan Manikya (1625-1659 A.D.) was a kind and religious man, but was a strong ruler. He defied the Mughals and refused to pay any tribute. Kalyan Manikya had to fight several times with the powerful Mughal troops, but finally the valiant Tripura troops were overcome by Shah Shuja in 1658 and for the first time in the history, Tripura came to be included in the rent roll of a foreign power. However, it appears from the available history that, the rent assessed by Shah Shuja was never paid and there was a feeling amongst the people that, Tripura had been independent and ultimately their defeat of 1658 was almost forgotten.

Kalyan Manikya was succeeded by Govind Manikya, whose reign was interrupted by his half-brother, Nakshatra Rai, who ruled between 1660-1666 A.D. as Chattra Manikya. After his death due to small pox, Govind Manikya regained his throne and ruled till 1669. Within this short period, he became very popular and resisted successfully all attempts by the Mughals to oust him from the throne. He was succeeded by his son Ram Manikya (1669-1682 A.D.) whose reign was quite uneventful. But after his death, his younger brother Narendra Manikya usurped the throne, but later on, he was deposed and Ratna Manikya (1684-1712 A.D.) regained the throne. The throne was then seized by Ghanshyam Thakur, the second son of Ram Manikya and assumed the title of Mahendra Manikya (1712-1714 A.D.) and then, he was succeeded by his younger brother, Dharma Manikya (1714-1744 A.D.)[43].

Tripura then faced many ups and downs and it was also marked by sordid court intrigues, when all the contenders were trying to ingratiate themselves with the Mughal Nawab. But finally Krishna Manikya ascended the throne, when the Muslim glory was on the wane in India. However, at that time, the Mughals occupied the lowlands of Tripura leaving the hill areas under the control of Raja. The East India Company in the meantime, attacked the plains of Tripura and Krishna Manikya (1760-1783 A.D.) was made the Raja of Hill Tripura. He was succeeded by his nephew, Jajdhar Manikya (1785-1804 A.D.). After his death, a five year inter-regnum followed, during which anarchy prevailed in the State. Ultimately, in 1808 A.D. the English recognized Durga Manikya (1809-1813 A.D.) and invested him as Raja. Since then, every Raja received investiture from the English and was called upon to pay nazar. The rulers of Tripura continued to describe the state as Swadhina Tripura, but the state soon fell in line with the other feudatory states of India.

The relations of the subsequent Rajas of Tripura with the English were based solely on the concern to regain as much of their territory as possible. During the time of Isan Chandra Manikya (1850-1862 A.D.), he tried to receive the sympathetic consideration from the British authorities in the matter of fixation of the boundaries, but could not do that. He was succeeded by Bir Chandra Manikya

(1862-1896 A.D.), Radha Kishore Manikya (1896-1909 A.D.), Birendra Kishore Manikya (1909-1923 A.D.) and Bir Bikram Manikya (1923-1946 A.D.). All of them tried to impress the British for fixing their boundaries in accordance with the correct historical position, but could not succeed. The last of these Rajas, Kirit Manikya, retained the title, some privileges, and a sizeable privy purse when his state acceded to the Indian Union in 1949 till these were withdrawn by the President of India in 1970 and he became a commoner, thus ending a dynasty over two millennium old[44].

Tripura became a Union Territory on 1st July, 1963 and finally attained the status of a full-fledged State on 21st January, 1972. Presently, the State is having 4 (four) Districts viz. West Tripura, South Tripura, North Tripura and Dhalai District. The total geographical area of the State is 10492 sq. kms. having a total population of 31,99,203 as per 2001 census with a population density of 305 persons per sq. km. The State is mostly hilly and about 60 per cent of the area has been classified as forest and about 27 per cent is available for cultivation. The State has many rain-fed, non-perennial rivers and streams flowing to the neighbouring Bangladesh. The major rivers are Gomati, Howrah, Dhalai, Muhuri, Feni, Juri which swell in monsoons, but they become shallow during the rest of the year. The hill areas of the State is mainly inhabited by the tribal people. There are 19 (nineteen) sub-tribes amongst the Scheduled Tribes (STs) people with their own cultural identity. They are Tripuri, Reang, Jamatia, Chakma, Lusai, Mog, Garo, Kuki, Chaimal, Uchai, Halam, Khasia, Bhutia, Kunda, Orang, Lepcha, Santal, Bhil and Noatia.

The hill people mainly pursue the age old method of Jhum cultivation. However, the high rainfall and good quality soil made the plain areas suitable for settled cultivation. A significant area of the state is under fruits and plantation crops. The major crops grown in plantations are tea, rubber, cashew, orange and pineapple. Jackfruit, banana, lemon, coconut and arecanut are also grown mainly on the homestead. The state is also rich in power potentials[45].

Sikkim

Sikkim is basically a mountain State belonging to the Eastern Himalayas. It is situated between 27° 4′ and 28° 7′ north latitude and

88° 11′ and 88° 56′ east longitude. The State is completely a mountain-locked one, bordering on the north by Tibet (China), on the east by Tibet (China) and Bhutan, on the west by Nepal and on the south, the hill division of Darjeeling District of West Bengal. The State covers an area of 7096 sq. kms. stretching for about 113 kms. from south to north and only 64 km. from west to east. The mountain ranges vary from about 3040 metres to over 8500 metres on all the three sides of north, west and east[46].

The early history of Sikkim is not much known. However, the Lepchas are believed to be the original inhabitants of 'Sikkim Proper' and the name 'Sikkim' is said to be derived from two Limbu words 'Su Him', means 'new house' (meant for the Limbu girl, from east Nepal, married to Lepcha boy at that time). The words later changed to 'Sukhim' which ultimately came to be 'Sikkim' in anglicized form. The original Lepchas, however, called their homeland as Nyema-el which means 'the holly land'.

Sikkim has been invaded many times by the Bhutias from the north bringing with them the Tibetan culture, the Tibetan language, the Lamaistic Buddhism along with a mixture of Pastoral and semi-settled agricultural life, while the Nepalese coming from the west, brought in Indo-Aryan languages, Hinduism and a settled agricultural practice. It is seen that, the infiltration of the Tibetans started long before 15th century when traders, farmers and the Lamas came here in search of new opportunities. The Tibetans, at that time, were at a higher cultural level than the Lepchas and as such could provide facilities for various branches of learning including medicine, mathematics and astronomy[47].

However, it is seen that, the credit of organizing the Lepchas into a society for the first time went to a person known as Tur Ve Pa No who was eventually elected as the leader or king called 'Punu' in around 1400 A.D. By this time, the Limbus from Nepal took occupation of the south-western part of Sikkim and they used to come in conflict with the Lepchas and in one such conflict, Punu was killed. And, the kingship ended after three more Punus following the death of the first one. Thereafter, the Lepchas resorted to electing leaders to advise on religious and social matters of the community which gradually shifted itself to the region around Kanchenjunga under continuous pressure of the Limbus.

In the second quarter of the 17th century A.D., three highly placed Lamas came from Tibet to convert the Sikkimese people into Buddhism and in their search for the descendent of Guru Tashe, a Tibetan noble, they came in contact of a person known as Phuntsog (Panchoo) Namgyal at Gangtok who happened to be his great-grandson and proclaimed him as the Gyalpo or king of Sikkim in 1641 at Yoksam, giving him the title of Chogyal or the Dharmaraj. The kingdom was divided into 12 (twelve) Dzongs or Districts and each of them was placed under a Lepcha Governor. And at that time, the kingdom was spread up to Chumbi valley in the north in Tibet and the present Darjeeling District of West Bengal.

The reign of Chogyal continued for about hundred and fifty years. However, in 1706 the Bhutanese army invaded Sikkim but was finally defeated by Tibet which came to its rescue and in gratitude of that, the great monastery of Pemayangtse was built by the king of Sikkim. But the peace was for a temporary period, and with the emergence of Gurkha power in Nepal, a number of invasions were conducted into Sikkim in the middle of 18th century causing great hardship besides bringing significant changes to the social structure of Sikkim with a lasting effect. The Gurkhas gradually came to represent an important section of the Nepalese population in Sikkim and ultimately, the Nepalese in general, started encroaching upon the forests of Sikkim and cutting down valuable timber. There was neither much resistance to immigration from Tibet, nor any restrictions to the entry of Nepalese in Sikkim, rather some people welcomed them for various type of construction works and for the development of resources of a less populated area like Sikkim[48].

The relation between Sikkim and the British represented by the East India Company began sometimes in 1814-15 and in terms of a treaty signed by Sikkim in 1817, the East India Company agreed to hand over the territory captured by Nepal to Sikkim and the political boundary between Nepal and Sikkim was fixed along the rivers Mahananda and Mechi and the Singalia range. But Sikkim forfeited her independence for good by this treaty, since according to article 3 of the treaty (Treaty of Titalia), Sikkim lost the right to take any independent decision in any of its disputes with Nepal or other neighbouring states. This was followed by the loss of Darjeeling which Sikkim was forced to cede to the East India Company as a gift in

1835. The East India Company further acquired an additional territory of Sikkim covering 640 sq. miles as a sequel to its military expedition to Sikkim in 1849 on a flimsy pretext. Though the whole of Sikkim was not physically annexed to British India in view of political consideration, affecting its relationship with other Himalayan states like Nepal, Tibet and Bhutan, the Government of India sent a military expedition in 1860 and reduced the power of the king almost to subservience by the Treaty of 1861 which brought Sikkim under the control of British India, making it a *de facto* protectorate of the Government of India[49].

In 1889, a political officer was appointed with his headquarters at Gangtok, the capital of Sikkim for the first time. During his time, he encouraged Nepalese immigrants who eventually subsided the interests of the original people of Lepcha and the Tibetan origin in Sikkim. But on the other hand, he took up many developmental measures like laying tracks into densely forested hills, introduction of apple cultivation, cloth weaving, carpet making, copper mining, opening schools and hospitals, etc. All these, along with the measures taken on improving the land tenure system, land rent etc. contributed very much towards the all-round development of Sikkim.

But the cultural differences between groups of people together with superiority of the Nepalese made the situation acrimonious in terms of political authority, which was vested with the king and his advisers, favouring Bhutia-Lepcha interests. However, at the time of attaining India's independence in 1947, the growing discontent found an opportunity to replace monarchy with an elected Government reflecting majority interest. And the formation of the Sikkim State Congress in December, 1947 was the first step in this direction, demanding among other things a popular interim Government to function till merger with India. This prompted the then Maharaja to organize Sikkim National Party which stood for an independent Sikkim. But later on, the two parties came to an agreement on Sikkim continuing to be an Indian Protectorate in respect of external affairs, defence, communication and enjoy internal autonomy. A treaty to this effect was signed with the India Government in December, 1950. The first general election for local self-Government was held in 1953 for which both the Nepalese and the Lepcha-Bhutia groups were allotted six seats each, keeping out another six to be nominated by the king. But in course of time, the relation between the king and the members of the Sikkim Congress gradually became very bitter and finally in 1974 election, the Sikkim Congress won a thumping victory with a tally of 31 out of 32 seats in the Assembly, which advocated Sikkim's participation in the political and economic institutions of India. Accordingly, a special opinion poll was held on 14th April, 1974 and the result went overwhelmingly in favour of merger, which ultimately took place on 26th April, 1975 making Sikkim a full-fledged State of India[50].

Sikkim is a mountainous State spreading over an area of 7096 sq. kms. having a total population of 540851 with a density of 76 persons per sq. km. as per 2001 census. The State is divided into four Districts viz. North Sikkim, East Sikkim, South Sikkim and West Sikkim. The inhabitants of this State are mainly Lepchas, Bhutias and Nepalese. The majority of population of North Sikkim comprises of Lepchas and Bhutias. The Lepchas are predominantly concentrated in the Dzongu Areas and the Bhutias are seen from Kabi-Tingda to Lachen-Lachung. Nepalese are found mixed up around Phodong, Mangshila and Mangan. Lepchas and Bhutias are usually Buddhists and Nepalese are Hindus[51].

Another important aspect of the State is that, most of its area comes under forest and under the category of barren land and other non-agricultural area, leaving a small part of it for agriculture. The forest of the State is very rich in stunning varieties of orchids, rhododendron, bamboo groves, medicinal plants, large cardamom, tea, etc. However, in the land available for cultivation, the people of Sikkim practices both terrace and jhum cultivation in association with animal husbandry. The agricultural practice in Sikkim is much more advanced and the most remarkable feature of agriculture is that, the practice of mono-cropping has largely been replaced by double or triple cropping system irrespective of altitudinal or agroclimatic handicaps. This has changed the character and nature of production and made it possible to get higher returns with the introduction of short duration, photo-intensive high yielding varieties of paddy, maize and dwarf wheat. Simultaneously, the animal husbandry sector also went up to a significant change with the introduction of improved technology[52].

NOTES

1. J.N. Chowdhury, *Arunachal Through the Ages*, published by Smti Jaya Chowdhury, Shillong, 1982, p. 1.
2. Surendra Singh, North Eastern Hill University, Shillong, *A Resource Atlas of Arunachal Pradesh, 1999*, p. 59.
3. J.N. Chowdhury, *Arunachal Panorama*, published by Smti Jaya Chowdhury, Shillong, 1973, p. 15.
4. J.N. Chowdhury, *Arunachal Through the Ages*, op cit., p. 63.
5. *ibid.*, pp. 83-86.
6. *ibid.*, pp. 218-223.
7. *ibid.*, pp. 242-43.
8. Directorate of Economics and Statistics, Government of Arunachal Pradesh, Itanagar, *Arunachal Pradesh at a Glance*, 2004, p. 4.
9. M.L. Bose, *Social History of Assam*, Concept Publishing Company, New Delhi, p. 15.
10. *ibid.*, p. 37.
11. *ibid.*, p. 37.
12. *ibid.*, p. 37.
13. *ibid.*, p. 38.
14. *ibid.*, pp. 38-39.
15. J.N. Chowdhury, *Arunachal Through the Ages*, op cit., pp. 83-86.
16. Directorate of Economics and Statistics, Assam, *Economic Survey*, Assam 2005-06, p. 5.
17. Directorate of Economics and Statistics, Government of Manipur, *Economic Survey*, Manipur, 2002-03, p. i.
18. *ibid.*, p. ii.
19. *ibid.*, p. ii.
20. *ibid.*, pp. 67, 72.
21. D.D. Mali, *An Introduction to the Economy of Meghalaya*, Ratna's Mascot, G.S. Road, Shillong p. 2.
22. *ibid.*, p. 2.
23. *ibid.*, p. 2-3.
24. *ibid.*, p. 1.
25. P.L. Sanjeev Reddy and P.C. Shekar Reddy, *Peace and Development in Northeast*, Mittal Publications, New Delhi, p. 22.
26. D.D. Mali, *An Introduction to the Economy of Meghalaya, op cit.*, p. 39.
27. S.N. Singh, *Mizoram: Historical, Geographical, Social, Economic, Political and Administrative*, Mittal Publications, p. 13.
28. *ibid.*, p. 17.
29. *ibid.*, pp. 28, 29.

30. *ibid.*, pp. 4, 5.
31. S.A. Rahman (Chief Editor), *The Beautiful India—Nagaland*, Published by Reference Press, New Delhi, pp. 39, 40.
32. *ibid.*, pp. 12, 13.
33. *ibid.*, p. 14, 15.
34. *ibid.*, pp. 21, 22.
35. P.L. Sanjeev Reddy and P.C. Shekar Reddy, *Peace and Development in Northeast, op. cit.* p. 23.
36. S.A. Rahman (Chief Editor), *The Beautiful India—Nagaland, op. cit*, p. 41.
37. Directorate of Economics and Statistics, Planning (Statistics) Department, Government of Tripura, *Economic Review of Tripura*, 2003-04, p. 1.
38. Omesh Saigal, *Tripura: Its History and Culture*, Published by Concept Publishing Company, New Delhi, 1978, p. 17.
39. *ibid.*, pp. 18, 19.
40. *ibid.*, pp. 29-31.
41. *ibid.*, pp. 32-33.
42. *ibid.*, pp. 33-36.
43. *ibid.*, pp. 37-38.
44. *ibid.*, pp. 38-40.
45. *Economic Review of Tripura, 2003-04, op. cit.* pp. 1-5.
46. B. Bhattacharya, *Sikkim—Land and People*, Omsons Publications, New Delhi-110 027, pp. 5, 6.
47. *ibid.*, pp. 1, 2.
48. *ibid.*, pp. 2, 3.
49. *ibid.*, p. 3.
50. *ibid.*, pp. 4, 5.
51. P.L. Sanjeev Reddy and P.C. Shekar Reddy, *Peace and Development in Northeast, op. cit.* p. 17.
52. B. Bhattacharya, *Sikkim—Land and People*, *op. cit.* pp. 27-29, 56, 57.

3

Demographic Scenario

The total Geographical Area (notional area) of the North Eastern Region including Sikkim is 2,62,191 sq. kms. which is about 7.98 per cent of the total Geographical Area of our country, while the total population of this region was 3,88,57,769 which was only about 3.78 per cent of the total population of our country as per 2001 census. The State of Assam, though, is the second largest State in terms of Geographical area, yet it is the homeland of the highest number of persons i.e. 68.60 per cent of the population of this region with an equally highest density of 340 persons per sq. km. The State of Arunachal Pradesh is though the largest, but it accounted for only 2.82 per cent of population of this region with a density of 13 persons per sq. km, which was the lowest of this region. On the other hand, though, Tripura is the second smallest State, but it was accommodating the second highest number of persons i.e. 8.23 per cent of the population of this region and also with the second highest density of 305 persons per sq. km. as per 2001 census. The States of Manipur and Meghalaya are almost equal in terms of Geographical areas, but slight difference was there in terms of population contents. Manipur was having 5.58 per cent and Meghalaya was having 5.97 per cent of population of this region with the density of 97 and 103 respectively. Mizoram is though slightly smaller in size than Manipur and Meghalaya, but according to 2001 census, it was having only 2.29 per cent of the population of this region with a density of 42 persons per sq. km. Sikkim is the smallest state and though it was having only 1.39 per cent of population, but the density of population was 76 persons per sq. km, which was the third lowest in this region. The density of population of the North Eastern Region excluding Sikkim was 150 and including Sikkim, it was 148 persons per sq. km. as against the all India figure of 313 persons per sq. km as per 2001 census.

The States viz. Arunachal Pradesh, Meghalaya, Mizoram and Nagaland are tribal dominated States. Among these four States, as per 2001 census, the proportion of tribal people in Mizoram was the highest, which was 94.46 per cent of its total population. In Nagaland, it was the second highest of 89.15 per cent, then comes the position of Meghalaya, which was 85.94 per cent followed by Arunachal Pradesh with 64.22 per cent. The total number of tribal people in Assam was 3308570, which was though only 12.41 per cent of its total population, but that number was greater than the total number of population of any other state of this region. However, the total tribal people of the North Eastern Region as a whole was though 26.93 per cent of the total population of this Region, but it was only 12.41 per cent of the total tribal population of the Country and only 1.02 per cent of the total population of India as per 2001 census. Among all the North Eastern States, the density of tribal population was the highest of 107 persons per sq. km. in Nagaland, followed by 95 in Tripura, 89 in Meghalaya, 42 in Assam, 40 in Mizoram and 33 in Manipur. The lowest density of tribal population was in Arunachal Pradesh, which was 8 and the second lowest was 16 in Sikkim. The density of tribal population of the North Eastern Region as a whole was 40 as against the all India tribal density figure of 26 persons per sq. km as per 2001 census. Further details can be seen from Appendix-3.1.

It is a fact that, even now most of the people of our country are living in the rural areas. This is more so in case of tribal people. It appears from Appendix-3.2, which has been prepared on the basis of the information of 2001 census that, 72.18 per cent of population of our Country was living in rural areas and only 27.82 per cent was in urban areas. In case of North Eastern Region, the percentage of rural people was much higher to the extent of 84.34 per cent and only 15.66 per cent of population was in urban areas. However, in case of tribal people of this region, the situation was different. It is seen that, 91.71 per cent of the tribal people of our country was living in rural areas and only 8.29 per cent was in urban areas. Whereas, in the

North Eastern Region, 87.85 per cent of the tribal people was living in rural areas and 12.15 per cent was in the urban areas as per 2001 census. This is because of the fact that, many of the states of this region are hilly and tribal dominated, and a large number of tribal people are living in the hill towns of this region.

The household size is an important demographic indicator. A household is ordinarily defined as a group of persons normally staying together and taking food from a common kitchen, and the size of the household is taken as the number of persons in that group. Temporary guests are not considered as household members and similarly temporary stay away of household members are also ignored while counting the household size. It can be seen from Appendix-3.2 that, the overall household size in almost all the states of North Eastern Region was above 5 (five) and was more or less same as the national average with the exception of Nagaland, Tripura and Sikkim. The overall household size in Nagaland was the highest and it was more than 6 (six), whereas, it was more than 4 (four) but less than 5 (five) in both the states of Tripura and Sikkim. Further, the household size in the rural areas was more than the overall household size and again, the overall household size was more than the household size in the urban areas of all the North Eastern States as well as in the country. That means, on an average, every household in the rural areas was having more number of people than every household in the urban areas.

The sex ratio is another important Demographic Indicator. This is defined as the number of females per thousand males. As per 2001 census, the sex ratio shows an interesting feature in different states of the North Eastern Region. It is seen that, the overall sex ratio in Sikkim was the lowest, which was 875 and the second lowest was in Arunachal Pradesh, which was 893. The overall sex ratio in all other states as well as of this region as a whole was ranging from 900 of Nagaland to 978 of Manipur. The other interesting feature was that, the overall sex ratio in Arunachal Pradesh, Assam, Nagaland and Sikkim was more than urban but less than rural. That means, more females per thousand males were there in the rural areas of these States. The rural sex ratio was the lowest of 880 in Sikkim and the highest of 944 in Assam. On the other hand, in Manipur, Meghalaya, Mizoram and Tripura, the urban sex ratio was more than the overall sex ratio, and the overall sex ratio was more than the sex ratio of the rural areas of these States. That means, the number of females per thousand males were more in urban areas than in the rural areas of these States. The lowest urban sex ratio was 948 of Mizoram and the highest of 1009 of Manipur. That indicates a very significant Demographic feature, i.e., in urban areas of Manipur, the females had out numbered the males and it was also an indicator of higher birth rate in the urban areas of Manipur. In case of North Eastern Region and the country as a whole, the rural sex ratio was more than the overall sex ratio as well as the sex ratio of the urban areas. The rural sex ratio in NER and in the country was almost same, which was 943 and 946 respectively, but the urban sex ratio was exactly the same and it was 900 for both. Further, details can be seen from Appendix-3.2.

From the Sample Registration System (SRS) Bulletin, published in October, 2006 by the Registrar General of India (RGI), New Delhi, it has been found that, among all the North Eastern States, the overall birth rate in Meghalaya was the highest, which was 25.1 followed by Assam, which was 25. The overall birth rate in Arunachal Pradesh was the third highest, which was 23.3 and was very much close to the National figure of 23.8. The overall birth rate in all other North Eastern States was ranging from the lowest of 14.7 of Manipur to the highest of 19.9 of Sikkim. Further, it has been found that, the birth rate was more in the rural areas of all the North Eastern States as well as the country as a whole with the exception of Manipur, where the birth rate was more in the urban areas. This was perhaps because of the fact that, the sex ratio in urban areas of Manipur was very high. In case of rural birth rate, Meghalaya was again on the top with 27.3 and Assam was very much close with 26.6. The rural birth rate was the lowest of 14.5 of Manipur whereas, Nagaland and Tripura were having the same rate of 16.5, which was the second lowest. The urban birth rate was the lowest of 14.4 of Mizoram and the highest of 18.7 of Arunachal Pradesh, but that was less than the National figure of 19.1. That means, the birth rate in urban areas of all the North Eastern States was less than the all India urban figure.

The death rate was also showing some unique features in all the North Eastern States. The overall death rate in Nagaland was the lowest, which was 3.8 and it was 8.7 in case of Assam which was the highest and was also more than the overall figure of 7.6 of the country as a whole. Further, it has been found that, in the rural areas, the death rate was more than the urban areas as well as the overall death rate in all the North Eastern States except Manipur. In Manipur, the death rate in urban areas was more than the death rate in rural areas as well as the overall death rate of Manipur. However, the overall infant mortality rate was the lowest of the order of 13 in Manipur, but it was the highest of the order of 68 in Assam which was also more than the overall figure of 58 of the country as a whole. Moreover, it has been found that, the infant mortality rate in rural areas of all the North Eastern States and also of the country as a whole, was more than the urban areas as well as of the overall infant mortality rate with the exception of Manipur and Nagaland. In Manipur and Nagaland, the infant mortality rate in rural areas was less than the urban areas as well as the overall mortality rate in these two states.

However, the overall natural growth rate was the lowest in Tripura which was 10.3 and it was 18.3 in Arunachal Pradesh, which was the highest amongst all the North Eastern States as well as the overall figure of 16.3 of the country as a whole. Moreover, it has been found that, the natural growth rate was more in rural areas than the urban areas as well as the overall natural growth rate in all the North Eastern States and also in the country as a whole except the same two states of Manipur and Nagaland, where it was just in the reverse way. Further, details can be seen from Appendix-3.3.

The children occupy a significant portion of the population of our country, and it is more so in the North Eastern Region. From the results of 2001 population census, it appears that, the overall percentage of children in the age group of 0-6 years of the North Eastern Region, which was 16.54, was more than the national figure of 15.93. Moreover, the most interesting feature of the children of the age group of 0-6 years was that, in all the North Eastern States except Manipur, the percentage of female children was more than the percentage of male children. That means in all these States, female children were more than the male children, in the age group of 0-6 years. In Manipur, the percentage of male children was more than the female children and there was a significant difference in the number of male and female children of the age group of 0-6 years, as their percentages were 14.39 and 14.09 respectively. In the national context, it also appears that, though there was no much difference in the percentages of male and female children of age group of 0-6 years, which were 15.97 and 15.88 respectively, but in reality, the number of male children was quite bigger than the number of female children.

The other important feature of the children of the age group of 0-6 years was that, amongst all the North Eastern States, the percentage of female children in Meghalaya was the highest of the order of 20.19 and in Tripura, it was the lowest of the order of 13.77. Further, it appears that, amongst the rural areas of all the North Eastern States, the percentage of female children of the age group of 0-6 years in Meghalaya was also the highest to the extent of 21.53, and that was also much higher than the all India rural figure of 16.92 per cent. That means, in rural areas of Meghalaya, there were more female children of the age group of 0-6 years. However, in case of urban areas of the North Eastern States, the scenario was different. In this case, the percentage of female children of the age group of 0-6 years in Arunachal Pradesh was the highest of the order of 17.77, while in Tripura, it was the lowest of the order of 9.7 which was also much less than the all India urban figure of 13.1 per cent. Further, details can be seen from Appendix-3.4.

The educational scenario (excluding the children of the age group of 0-6 years) of the North Eastern States is not uniform and it largely vary from state to state. It has been seen that, the people of Mizoram are more educated and their average percentage of literacy was 88.80 as per 2001 census. Further, the percentage of literacy of the rural people of Mizoram, was though a bit less to the level of 81.27 per cent, but it was quite high to the extent of 96.13 per cent for the urban people. The other significant aspect was that, both the Male and Female people of urban areas are equally educated and having a very high percentage of literacy of 96.43 and 95.80 respectively. In terms of percentage of literacy, Tripura came in the 2nd position with 73.19 per cent. The urban Males and Females are also highly educated and their percentage of literacy was 93.21 and 85.03 respectively as per 2001 census. The percentage of literacy of the other States of North Eastern Region, except Arunachal Pradesh, was ranging between 62.56 of Meghalaya to 70.53 of Manipur. The average percentage of literacy of Arunachal Pradesh was the lowest in this region and it was to the level of 54.34 per cent. The average percentage for the rural people was though at the level of 47.83 per cent, but for the urban people, it was quite high to the extent of 78.26 per cent. Further, according to 2001 census, the average percentage of literacy of the North Eastern Region as a whole was 65.07, for rural it was 61.01 and for urban it was 85.66 per cent, which were more than the National figures of 64.84, 58.74 and 79.92 per cent respectively. More details can be seen from Appendix-3.4.

The growth of population in the North Eastern States shows a very peculiar trend. In Appendix-3.5, the population trend in the North Eastern States as well as in the country has been shown from the population census year, 1901 to 2001 i.e. for a period of 100 years. However, in case of Arunachal Pradesh, the 1st population census was conducted in 1961 and the population at that time was 3.37 lakh, but within next 20 years, the population became little less than double and within another 20 years, it increased to more than three times. The population in Assam in the year, 1901 was 32.90 lakh and it became more than double within a period of 40 years and finally went up to more than eight times within a period of 100 years. The growth of population in Manipur at the initial stages was almost similar to Assam. In 1901, the population of Manipur was 2.84 lakh and it became little less than double within a period of 40 years, then went up to little more than five times within 80 years and finally reached to more than eight times within a period of 100 years. The population growth in Meghalaya was a bit slow. In 1901, the population of Meghalaya was 3.41 lakh and it became little less than double within a period of 50 years and within next fifty years, it reached to little less than seven times.

The growth of population in the States of Mizoram, Nagaland and Tripura was very fast. In Mizoram, though the population growth at the initial stages was a bit slow, but it increased very rapidly in the later years. In 1901, the population of Mizoram was though 0.82 lakh, but it became little less than double within a period of 40 years and within next 40 years, it went up to more than six times and finally reached to almost eleven times within a period of 100 years. In Nagaland also, though the growth of population at the initial stages was slow, but at the later years, population increased very rapidly. It is seen that, the population of Nagaland in 1901 was 1.02 lakh, but it increased to little less than double within a period of 40 years and after that it picked up the momentum and reached to more than five times within next 30 years and then in every 10 years, the population went up to more than seven times, then to more than ten times and finally reached to much more than nineteen times within a period of 100 years. The growth of population of Tripura was also more or less similar to Nagaland. The population of Tripura in the year 1901 was though 1.73 lakh, but within a period of 40 years, it went up to little less than three times and then to nine times within next 30 years and then in every 10 years, it went up to little less than twelve times and then to almost sixteen times and finally reached to little less than nineteen times within a period of 100 years. The growth of population in Sikkim was not that fast. The population of Sikkim in 1901 was 0.59 lakh and after a period of 40 years, it became little more than double and then within next 30 years, it reached to little less than four times and then in the next 20 years, it went up to little less than seven times and finally reached to little less than ten times within a period of 100 years.

The phenomenal growth of population in the three North Eastern States viz. Mizoram, Nagaland and Tripura, particularly Nagaland and Tripura, perhaps cannot be attributed to the natural growth process. This high rate of growth of population in these states might be due to the time to time influx of people from other areas in search of employment and other economic activities. The population growth in the North Eastern Region as a while, including Sikkim was not that fast. It is seen that the population of North Eastern Region in 1901 was 43.31 lakh and it became little more than double within a period of 40 years and then it became little less than six times within a period of next 40 years and finally reached to more than nine times within a period of 100 years. However, the growth of population of our country as a whole was much slow as compared to the North Eastern States. In 1901, the population of the country was 23.84 crore and within a period of next 50 years, it increased to 36.11 crore i.e. much less than double and finally reached to 102.87 crore i.e. much less than five times within a period of 100 years. The details can be seen from Appendix-3.5.

In Appendix-3.6, the decadal variation in population, change in decadal variation and average exponential growth rate of population in the North Eastern States and in the country have been shown for the last three decades i.e. from 1971-1981,1981-1991 and 1991-2001. In case of decadal growth rate, it is seen that, the rate of growth in the states of Arunachal Pradesh, Assam, Meghalaya and Tripura, was more during 1981-1991 than 1971-1981 and then again it decreased during 1991-2001 in these states. In the States of Manipur, Mizoram and the country as a whole, the decadal growth rate showed a declining trend in the consecutive periods of 1981-1991 and 1991-2001. The State of Sikkim showed a different trend. First, the decadal growth rate decreased during 1981-1991 and then again it increased during 1991-2001. However, the State of Nagaland registered a unique trend of increasing decadal growth rate in the two successive periods of 1981-1991 and 1991-2001.

In case of average annual exponential growth rate, all the North Eastern States and the country as a whole, showed the trend exactly in the same fashion as they had shown in the case of decadal growth rate during the periods, 1971-1981, 1981-1991 and 1991-2001. Further, details including the extent of changes in the growth rates in different periods can be seen from Appendix-3.6.

Further, from Appendix-3.6, it is seen that, for all the States, except Nagaland and Sikkim, both the decadal growth rate as well as the average annual exponential growth rate was the lowest during the period 1991-2001. This declining trend was perhaps due to the various measures, that the individuals, the State Governments as well as the Central Government have taken up for controlling the growth of population. However, in case of Sikkim, though the decadal growth rate and average annual exponential growth rate showed some ups and downs, but in case of Nagaland, both of these rates showed a steadily increasing trend. This is definitely not a good sign as the rapid increase of population may create many socio-economic problems in the long run. From above, it has already been seen that the population of North Eastern States was increasing quite faster, and it is perhaps high time to look into the matter in a broader perspective and to find out the ways and means to check the growth of population for the overall development of this region.

However, in order to show the future population scenario of the North Eastern States, an attempt has been made to calculate the projected population of each of the States and also for the country for a period of twenty-five years i.e. from 2001 to 2025. For calculating the projected population, the average annual exponential growth rate during the period 1991-2001 from Appendix-3.6 has been taken for all the states and also for India, which was the lowest, except Nagaland. For Nagaland, the average of the average annual exponential growth rates for the three periods i.e. for 1971-1981, 1981-1991 and 1991-2001 has been taken with the idea that this will perhaps give a better picture for the State. The details of projected population for all the North Eastern States and for the country up to 2025 can be seen from Appendix-3.7.

From Appendix-3.7, it can be seen that, how the population of 2001 of each of the North Eastern States and of the country is growing during a period of 25 years. It appears that, the growth rate of population is less in Tripura and Assam, but it is very high in Nagaland. In case of Tripura, the population will increase by 15.94 per cent during the first decade i.e. during 2001-2011, then it will increase by 34.42 per cent during the second decade i.e. during 2011-2021 and finally it will increase by 42.61 per cent during the period from 2021 to 2025. In case of Assam, the population will increase by 18.71 per cent during 2001-2011, by 40.92 per cent during 2011-2021 and finally it will increase by 50.93 per cent during the period from 2021 to 2025. The State of Manipur comes in the third position. The population of the State will increase by 24.55 per cent during 2001-2011, by 55.14 per cent during 2011-2021 and finally it will increase by 69.38 per cent during the period from 2021 to 2025. Next is the position of Arunachal Pradesh. The population of the State will increase by 26.64 per cent during 2001-2011, by 60.38 per cent during 2011-2021 and finally it will increase by 76.27 per cent during the period from 2021 to 2025.

The State of Mizoram occupies the fifth position. The population of Mizoram will though increase by a lesser percentage of 20.38 during the first decade i.e. during 2001-2011, but it will go up to 64.82 per cent during 2011-2021 and finally it will reach to 82.15 per cent during the period from 2021 to 2025. The State of Meghalaya is in the sixth position. It is seen that the population of the State will increase by 30.15 per cent during 2001-2011, by 69.38 per cent during 2011-2021 and finally it will increase by 88.21 per cent during the period from 2021 to 2025. The State of Sikkim occupies the seventh position. The population of Sikkim will increase by 32.58 per cent during 2001-2011, by 75.76 per cent during 2011-2021 and finally it will increase by 96.75 per cent during the period from 2021 to 2025. The State of Nagaland is in the top position in respect of population growth. It is seen that, during the first decade i.e. during 2001-2011, though the population will increase at a rate of 55.24 per cent, but the growth of population will reach to 140.99 per cent during the next decade i.e. during 2011-2021 and finally it will reach to 187.34 per cent during the period from 2021 to 2025. This is very much alarming and perhaps there is an urgent need to look into the matter properly.

The high rate of growth of population in Nagaland also contributed significantly towards the growth of population of the North Eastern Region. It is seen that, the population of the North Eastern Region including Sikkim will though increase by 22.01 per cent during the first decade i.e. during 2001-2011, but it will go up to 49.60 per cent during the second decade i.e. during 2011-2021 and finally the population will increase by 62.57 per cent during the period from 2021 to 2025. However, it appears that the population of the country as a whole will grow at a slower rate than the rate of the North Eastern Region. It is seen that, the population of the country will increase by 21.30 per cent during 2001-2011 and then by 47.14 per cent during 2011-2021 and ultimately the population of the country will increase by 58.96 per cent during the period from 2021 to 2025. Further, details can be seen from Appendix-3.7.

The projected population shown in Appendix-3.7 will simply give an idea about the probable population in each of the North Eastern States, all the States of the region taking together and the country as a whole, in each year during a period of twenty-five years i.e. from 2001 to 2025. This projection has been done on the basis of the average annual exponential growth rate of different North Eastern States and the country during the decade 1991-2001 and it is expected that, the growth rate will definitely decrease in the subsequent decades. The people of our country are becoming more and more educated and are able to understand the necessity of controlling population growth. Moreover, the Central Government as well as the State Governments are taking every effort for providing various facilities and incentives towards family planning and social welfare. Keeping this in mind, it is hoped that, the population of the North Eastern States as well as of our country will grow with a lower rate and the actual population will be much less than the projected population shown in Appendix-3.7, in the years to come.

4

Land Use Scenario

As mentioned earlier, the total Geographical Area of the North East India, including Sikkim is 262191 sq. kms., which is only 7.98 per cent of the total Geographical Area of our country. The North Eastern States, except Assam, are generally hilly and most of the areas are under forest cover. Amongst all the North Eastern States, Arunachal Pradesh is the largest having a total area of 83743 sq. kms., which is 31.94 per cent of the total area of this region. The State of Arunachal Pradesh is though the largest in area, but 61.55 per cent of this i.e. 51540 sq. kms. is recorded forest area and 81.22 per cent i.e. 68019 sq. kms. is under forest cover, leaving a small portion of only 15724 sq. kms. i.e. only 18.78 per cent for other purposes. The State of Assam is the second largest having a total area of 78438 sq. kms. and it accounts for 29.92 per cent of the total area of this region. The recorded forest area of Assam is only 27018 sq. kms., which is 34.45 per cent and the area under forest cover is 27826 sq. kms. i.e. 35.48 per cent of its Geographical Area. The remaining portion of 50612 sq. kms. i.e. 64.52 per cent is other area.

The States of Manipur, Meghalaya and Mizoram are almost equal in terms of Geographical Area, but are varying in case of area under forest and forest cover. Manipur is having an area of 22327 sq. kms., which is only 8.52 per cent of the total area of this region. The total recorded forest area of Manipur is 17418 sq. kms., which is 78.01 per cent of its Geographical Area, but the area under forest cover is 17219 sq. kms. i.e. 77.12 per cent, leaving a portion of only 5108 sq. kms. i.e. only 22.88 per cent of its area for other purposes. The total Geographical area of Meghalaya is 22429 sq. kms., which accounts for 8.55 per cent of the total area of this region. The recorded forest area of Meghalaya is comparatively less to the extent of 9496 sq. kms., which is 42.34 per cent, but the area under forest cover is quite high to the tune of 16839 sq. kms. i.e. 75.08 per cent of its Geographical area, leaving a portion of only 5590 sq. kms. i.e. only 24.92 per cent for other purposes. Amongst these three states, Mizoram is the smallest having a total Geographical area of 21087 sq. kms., which is 8.04 per cent of the total area of this region. The recorded forest area of Mizoram is 16717 sq. kms. i.e. 79.30 per cent and the area under forest cover is even more to the extent of 18430 sq. kms., which is 87.42 per cent of its total area, leaving only 2651 sq. kms. i.e. only 12.58 per cent for other purposes.

The States of Nagaland, Tripura and Sikkim are the smaller States in terms of Geographical area. The total Geographical area of Nagaland is 16579 sq. kms. and it accounts for 6.32 per cent of the area of this region. The recorded forest area of Nagaland is though little more than half of its Geographical area, but the area under forest cover is quite high to the extent of 13609 sq. kms. i.e. 82.09 per cent and 2970 sq. kms. i.e. 17.91 per cent is other area. The State of Tripura is the second smallest state of this region. It is having a total Geographical area of 10492 sq. kms., which is only 4 per cent of the total area of this region. The recorded forest area of Tripura is 6293 sq. kms. i.e. 60.01 per cent and the area under forest cover is 8093 sq. kms. i.e. 77.18 per cent of its total area leaving a small portion of 2393 sq. kms. i.e. 22.82 per cent for other purposes. Sikkim is the smallest State of this region. It has a Geographical area of 7096 sq. kms., which is only 2.71 per cent of the total area of this region. The recorded forest area of Sikkim is though 5841 sq. kms. i.e. 82.31 per cent, but the actual area under forest cover is much less to the tune of 3262 sq. kms. i.e. only 45.97 per cent of its total area. The total Geographical area of the country as a whole is 3287263 sq. kms. and out of this, only 774740 sq. kms. i.e. 23.57 per cent is the recorded forest area and the area under forest cover is even less to the extent of 678333 sq. kms. i.e. 20.64 per cent of its total Geographical area. Further details, can be seen from Appendix-4.1 and Appendix-4.2.

Forest is generally described as a tract of land having plant community largely consisting of trees and other woody vegetation. In our country a tract of land is recognized as forest if it is largely proclaimed to be a forest under the forest law (Indian Forest Act of 1927 or the relevant State Forest Act) and it is recorded/notified as forest in Government records. However, it may so happen that, a part or the whole of such forest area, at any point of time, may not have trees on it, but still all the provisions of the forest law under which it is notified will be applicable to it. The recorded forest area is further categorized into (i) Reserved Forest, (ii) Protected Forest, and (iii) Un-classed Forest. Reserved Forest is an area notified under the provisions of the Indian Forest Act or the State Forest Acts having a greater degree of protection. Protected Forests are also notified under the provisions of the Indian Forest Act or the State Forest Act, but the restrictions are less severe. Un-classed Forest is an area recorded as forest but not included in reserved or protected forest category. Ownership status of such forests varies from forest to forest and from state to state[1].

Forest cover is defined as an area more than 1 (one) hectare in extent and having tree canopy density of 10 per cent and above[2]. In the North Eastern States, forest is comprising mainly of valuable trees like shal, teak, pine, oak, walnut, chestnut, large cardamom, rhododendron, etc. and of the climbers like cane, bamboo, etc. The forest is generally of two kinds e.g. (i) Dense Forest, and (ii) Open Forest. The Dense Forest is defined as 'all lands with a forest cover having a canopy density of 40 per cent and above' and the Open Forest is defined as 'all lands with a forest cover having a canopy density of 10 to 40 per cent'[3]. The forest cover again is not a static one, it can be changed to non-forest also. If an area that was earlier classified as forest but now owing to harvesting of trees or degradation, has been classified as non-forest in the current assessment, it signifies loss in forest cover. On the other hand, if an area that was non-forest in the earlier assessment is found to have tree vegetation cover in the current assessment, there is said to be a gain in forest cover. The difference between the sum-total of all such gains and losses is described as 'net change' in forest cover[4].

The Appendix-4.3 will give an idea about the change in forest cover between 2001 Assessment and 2003 Assessment in all the North Eastern States and the country as a whole. From this, it appears that, in Assam, though the loss of Dense Forest was the highest to the extent of 2788 sq. kms., but there was a gain in the Open Forest to the tune of 2900 sq. kms. and thereby there was a net gain of 112 sq. kms. of forest cover. The second highest loss of Dense Forest was in the state of Mizoram, amounting to 1448 sq. kms., but here also there was a gain in the Open Forest to the extent of 2384 sq. kms. and therefore, there was a net gain of 936 sq. kms. of forest cover. The State of Arunachal Pradesh also lost its Dense Forest to the tune of 421 sq. kms. and though there was a gain of 395 sq. kms. in the Open Forest, still there was a net loss of 26 sq. kms. of forest cover. Further, it can be mentioned that, Arunachal Pradesh was the only State in this region, which lost 26 sq. kms. of its Dense Forest over a period of two years, which was not a good sign at all. The State of Sikkim was also in that category. But, though it lost 29 sq. kms. of its Dense Forest, but on the other hand, it gained 98 sq. kms. of Open Forest and as such there was a net gain of 69 sq. kms. of forest cover in Sikkim.

In Manipur, there was a gain of 828 sq. kms. of Dense Forest, but again it lost 535 sq. kms. of its Open Forest and thereby, there was a net gain of 293 sq. kms. of forest cover. Meghalaya was another unique state in this region, which gained both of its Dense Forest as well as Open Forest to the extent of 810 sq. kms. and 445 sq. kms. respectively registering a net gain of 1255 sq. kms. within a period of two years, which was definitely a very good sign. The State of Nagaland could not achieve much. It could gain only 314 sq. kms. of Dense Forest, but at the same time it lost 50 sq. kms. of its Open Forest leaving an overall gain of 264 sq. kms. of forest cover. The position of Tripura was also not that bad. The State could gain 1583 sq. kms. in the Dense Forest and even though it lost 555 sq. kms. of its Open Forest, still there was a net gain of 1028 sq. kms. of forest cover within a period of two years. On the whole, it can be seen that, the position of North East India was better than the position of the country as a whole in case of forest cover. This region as a whole, though lost 1151 sq. kms. of its Dense Forest, but on the other hand, it could gain 5082 sq. kms. of Open Forest registering a net gain of 3931 sq. kms. of forest cover. As against this, there was a loss of 26245 sq. kms. of Dense Forest in the country as a whole and though it could gain 29040 sq. kms. of Open Forest, still the net gain was only 2795 sq. kms. Further, details can be seen from Appendix-4.3.

To find the land utilization pattern, it is seen that, there are two kinds of land, one is Geographical area and the other is Reporting area. The Geographical area of a State means the area provided by the Office of the Surveyor General of India. Whereas, the Reporting area stands for the area for which data on land use classification of area are available or estimates of classification of area are derived[5]. The Reporting area is broadly divided into nine classes viz. (i) Forests, (ii) Area put to non-agricultural use, (iii) Barren and unculturable land, (iv) Permanent pastures and other grazing lands, (v) Land under misc. tree crops and groves, (vi) Culturable wasteland, (vii) Fallow land, (viii) Net area sown, and (ix) Area sown more than once.

The area under non-agricultural use includes all land occupied by buildings, roads and railways or under water, e.g. rivers and canals, and other land put to uses other than agriculture. Barren and unculturable land means, all land covered by mountains, deserts, etc. and the land which cannot be brought under cultivation except at an exorbitant cost is classified as unculturable. Permanent pasture and other grazing land include all grazing land whether it is permanent pasture and meadows or not. Village common grazing land is also included under this category. The culturable wasteland means, the land which is available for cultivation, but not cultivated during the last five years or more in succession including the current year for some reasons or the other. Fallow land implies all land, which were taken up for cultivation, but are temporarily out of cultivation for a period of not less than one year and not more than five years. Fallow land has been divided into two parts e.g. (i) Current fallow, which means, land lying fallow for a period of one year, and (ii) Other fallow, means land which are lying fallow for more than one year but less than five years. However, the Net area sown represents the total area sown with crops and orchards. And the Area sown more than once indicates the areas on which crops are grown more than once during the agricultural year and this is obtained by deducting the Net area sown from the total cropped area[6].

The Land utilization pattern during the year 2003-04 in different states of the North East India and in the country as a whole can be seen from Appendix-4.4. From this, it appears that, the Reporting area of Arunachal Pradesh was 5498 thousand hectares, which was much less than the Geographical area, and out of the Reporting area, 5154 thousand hectares i.e. 93.74 per cent was under forest and 180 thousand hectares i.e. 3.27 per cent was under non-agricultural use including fallow land and therefore, the area available for crop was very less. The net area sown was only 164 thousand hectares i.e. only 2.98 per cent of the Reporting area. However, the positive side of this was that, 60.37 per cent of the net cropped area was sown more than once, that means, though the availability of cropped area was less, but the utilization of the cropped area was more in Arunachal Pradesh. The Reporting area of Assam was 7850 thousand hectares, which was slightly more than the Geographical area. The forest area of Assam was comparatively much less than the other North Eastern States. Assam was having 1933 thousand hectares of forest area, which was only 24.62 per cent of the Reporting area, but the area put to non-agricultural use including barren and unculturable land was quite high to the extent of 2533 thousand hectares, i.e. 32.27 per cent of the Reporting area. The other uncultivated and fallow land was also not less, which was 609 thousand hectares i.e. 7.76 per cent. In spite of all these, the net area sown was quite high to the extent of 2774 thousand hectares i.e. 35.34 per cent of the Reporting area. The area sown more than once was also not very less, which was 1188 thousand hectares i.e. 42.83 per cent of the net area sown and it indicated that both Kharif and Rabi crops were very much prevalent there.

The Reporting area of Manipur was much less than the Geographical area. The Reporting area was only 1945 thousand hectares and 87.04 per cent of it i.e. 1693 thousand hectares was under forest. The area not available for cultivation including other uncultivated area was only 35 thousand hectares i.e. only 1.80 per cent of the Reporting area. The net area sown was also not much, it was only 217 thousand hectares i.e. 11.16 per cent of the Reporting area. Moreover, the area sown more than once was quite less, it was even less than 500 hectares. The Reporting area of Meghalaya was also little less than the Geographical area. The Reporting area was 2227 thousand hectares, but the area under forest was comparatively less. It was only 951 thousand hectares i.e. 42.70 per cent, but the area not available for cultivation was 215 thousand hectares i.e. 9.65 per cent and the other uncultivated land including fallow land was quite high to the extent of 834 thousand hectares i.e. 37.45 per cent of the Reporting area. Therefore, the net area sown was quite less to the tune of 227 thousand hectares i.e. only 10.19 per cent of the

Reporting area. The area sown more than once was also less to the extent of only 46 thousand hectares, which was 20.26 per cent of the net area sown. The State of Mizoram was showing somewhat different characteristics. The Reporting area of this State was though not much less than the Geographical area, but the area under forest was quite high and the fallow land was also not less. It appears that, the Reporting area of the State was 2085 thousand hectares and out of that, 1594 thousand hectares i.e. 76.45 per cent was under forest. The area not available for cultivation together with other uncultivated land was though 161 thousand hectares i.e. 7.72 per cent, but the fallow land was quite more to the tune of 233 thousand hectares, which was 11.18 per cent of the Reporting area. The net area sown on the other hand, was very less to the extent of 98 thousand hectares i.e. only 4.70 per cent of the Reporting area and due to non-availability of information on the area sown more than once, it was also not possible to understand the extent of utilization of the cropped area.

The Reporting area of Nagaland was also less than the Geographical area. The Reporting area of the State was 1583 thousand hectares and little more than half of it i.e. 54.52 per cent was under forest. The area not available for cultivation was though not much, but other uncultivated land was 179 thousand hectares i.e. 11.31 per cent and the fallow land was 160 thousand hectares i.e. 10.11 per cent of the Reporting area. The net area sown was however 305 thousand hectares, which was 19.27 per cent of the Reporting area and the area sown more than once was 65 thousand hectares i.e. 21.31 per cent of the net area sown. The State of Tripura was showing a unique position. Its Reporting area was the same as the Geographical area of 1049 thousand hectares. The area under forest was more than half to the extent of 606 thousand hectares i.e. 57.77 per cent. The area put to non-agricultural use including barren and unculturable land was though 134 thousand hectares i.e. 12.77 per cent of the Reporting area, but the fallow and other uncultivated land was comparatively less. The net area sown was proportionately a bit more to the tune of 280 thousand hectares, which was 26.69 per cent of the Reporting area and the area sown more than once was 53 thousand hectares i.e. 18.93 per cent of the net area sown. The Reporting area of Sikkim was however, less than its Geographical area. The Reporting area of the State was 672 thousand hectares and the area under forest was though 265 thousand hectares i.e. 39.43 per cent, but almost an equal amount of area measuring 250 thousand hectares i.e. 37.20 per cent of the Reporting area was put to non-agricultural use, including Barren and unculturable land. The net area sown in Sikkim was only 110 thousand hectares, which was 16.37 per cent of the Reporting area and the area sown more than once was 11 thousand hectares, i.e. only 10 per cent of the net area sown.

The Land utilization pattern of the country as a whole was quite different from the position of the North Eastern Region. The Reporting area of the country was though less than the Geographical area and even though a good amount of area was not available for cultivation, still the proportion of net area sown was much more than the proportion of net area sown of this region, as the area under forest of the country as a whole was proportionately much less. The Reporting area of the country was 305843 thousand hectares and the area under forest was 69700 thousand hectares, which was only 22.79 per cent and was much less as compared to the figure of 57 per cent of the North Eastern Region. And because of that, though 31.15 per cent of the Reporting area of the country, as against the figure of 24.77 per cent, was not available for cultivation together with the land under miscellaneous tree crops and groves and fallow land, still the net area sown of the country was 140883 thousand hectares, which was 46.06 per cent of the Reporting area, as against the figure of only 18.22 per cent of the N.E. Region. However, the proportion of area sown more than once in the country as well as in this region were almost equal i.e. 35.32 per cent and 35.02 per cent respectively. That indicates that the extent of utilization of the cropped area of N.E. Region was more or less same as the country as a whole. Further details can be seen from Appendix-4.4.

The Appendix-4.5 gives an idea about the irrigated area and area under foodgrains with cropping intensity during the year, 2003-04 in North East India as well as in the country. It has been found that, amongst all the North Eastern States, extent of utilization of the cropped area was more in Arunachal Pradesh, that means, the cropping intensity was more there. As per definition, the cropping intensity is the ratio of net area sown to the total cropped area[7]. Therefore, it is seen that the cropping intensity was the highest of the order of 160.4 per cent in Arunachal Pradesh. The irrigated area was also not less, but the irrigation was not done by Government canals or tanks or wells, it was generally through other sources and the extent of net irrigated area was 42 thousand hectares i.e. 25.6 per cent of the net cultivated area. The area under foodgrains was 191 thousand hectares, which was 72.6 per cent of the total cropped area. The cropping intensity was the second highest of the order of 142.8 per cent in Assam. The source of irrigation in Assam was mainly Government canals and to some extent through other sources also. The net irrigated area was 172 thousand hectares i.e. 6.2 per cent of the net cultivated area, but the area under foodgrains was quite high to the extent of 2742 thousand hectares, which was 69.2 per cent of the total cropped area.

The cropping intensity in Manipur was only 100 per cent, as the area sown more than once was very less in this State. Further, it appears that, the sources of irrigation like Government or private canals or tanks and tubewells, etc. were not much there and the irrigation was done mainly through other sources. The net irrigated area was 40 thousand hectares, which was only 18.4 per cent of the net cultivated area. The area under foodgrains was however 166 thousand hectares, which was 76.5 per cent of the total cropped area. The cropping intensity in Meghalaya was 119.8 per cent. The source of irrigation in this State was mainly Government and private canals and the net area irrigated was 60 thousand hectares i.e. 26.4 per cent of the net cultivated area. But the area under foodgrains was 135 thousand hectares, which was 49.6 per cent of the total cropped area of the State. The cropping intensity in Mizoram was also appears to be only 100 per cent, as the information on the area sown more than once was not available. Like Meghalaya, the source of irrigation in Mizoram was also mainly Government and private canals and the net irrigated area in this State was 16 thousand hectares, which was only 16.3 per cent of the net cultivated area whereas, the area under foodgrains was 75 thousand hectares i.e. 76.5 per cent of the total cropped area.

The cropping intensity in Nagaland was the third highest to the extent of 121.3 per cent. The net irrigated area was also more to the tune of 67 thousand hectares, which was 22 per cent of the net cultivated area, but the irrigation was done mainly through other sources. The area under foodgrains was also more to the extent of 263 thousand hectares i.e. 71.1 per cent of the total cropped area. In

Tripura, the cropping intensity was 118.9 per cent. Unlike other States, irrigation was done in Tripura mainly through Government canals, tanks and wells. The net irrigated area was 40 thousand hectares, which was 14.3 per cent of the net cultivated area, but the area under foodgrains was more to the tune of 250 thousand hectares i.e. 75.1 per cent of the total cropped area of the State. The cropping intensity in Sikkim was not much, as the area sown more than once was less in this State. The cropping intensity was only 110 per cent. The net irrigated area was also less, which was only 9 thousand hectares i.e. only 8.2 per cent of the net cultivated area and irrigation was mainly done through other sources. However, the area under foodgrains was 72 thousand hectares i.e. 59.5 per cent of the total cropped area of the State.

The cropping intensity of the country as a whole was 135.3 per cent, which was more or less same to the figure of 135 per cent of the North Eastern Region. But the proportion of net irrigated area was much more to the extent of 39.1 per cent of the net cultivated area, as against the figure of only 10.7 per cent of the N.E. Region. But all the sources of irrigation like Government and private canals, tanks, tubewells, other wells and also the other sources were used for irrigating the land in other parts of our country. However, it appears that, the proportion of area under foodgrains to total cropped area in the country as a whole was less to the extent of 64.8 per cent, whereas in the North Eastern Region, it was 69.1 per cent. This indicates that, the extent of utilization of land for foodgrains was proportionately more in the North Eastern Region than in the country as a whole. Further, details can be seen from Appendix-4.5 and Appendix-4.6.

The foodgrains production in the North Eastern States is primarily confined to rice, wheat, maize, small millets, gram and tar. Amongst the oilseeds, mainly mustard, groundnut and soyabean can be mentioned, while other crops like sugarcane, cotton and jute are also grow in most of the States of this region. The details of area, production and yield rate of these crops in different States of North Eastern Region as well as in the country as a whole can be seen from Appendix-4.7. From this it appears that, though the cropping intensity in Manipur was not much, but the yield rates of rice, maize and also of total foodgrains were the highest amongst all the North Eastern States. The yield rate of rice was 2472 kg/hectare, maize was 2781 kg/hectare and of total foodgrains was 2390 kg/hectare respectively. The production of oilseeds was also there, but the yield rate was not that good, it was only 444 kg/hectare. However, the production of sugarcane was quite good and the yield rate was 36333 kg/hectare, which was the fourth highest in this region. The yield rate of total foodgrains in Tripura was also very good. It was 2179 kg/hectare, which was though the second highest, but the yield rate of wheat was the highest of the order of 2545 kg/hectare and of rice was the second highest of 2247 kg/hectare. The other crops like sugarcane and jute were also grown there and the yield rate of both of these two crops were the highest of the order of 47636 kg/hectare and 1482 kg/hectare respectively.

The yield rate of total foodgrains was the third highest of 1888 kg/hectare in Mizoram. The yield rate of rice alone was also the third highest of 1900 kg/hectare, but of maize, it was the second highest of 2093 kg/hectare. Other crops like oilseeds, sugarcane and cotton are also grown there. The yield rate of cotton was the highest of the order of 442 kg/hectare in this State. The main foodgrains in Meghalaya are rice, maize, small millets and pulses. The yield rate of total pulses was though the highest of 1385 kg/hectare and of rice was 1737 kg/hectare, but the yield rate of total foodgrains was 1674 kg/hectare, which was the fourth highest in this region. Amongst other crops, oilseeds, cotton and jute were also grown there and the yield rate of jute was 909 kg/hectare, which was the third highest. The yield rate of total foodgrains was though the fifth highest of 1577 kg/hectare in Nagaland, but the yield rate of small millet was the highest of 1000 kg/hectare and of maize was the third highest of 1800 kg/hectare. The yield rate of total oilseeds was also the highest of the order of 1165 kg/hectare and of sugarcane was the second highest of 47367 kg/hectare. In respect of yield rate of total foodgrains, Sikkim comes in the sixth position. The yield rate of total foodgrains in this State was 1406 kg/hectare. However, the yield rate of maize was slightly better to the extent of 1586 kg/hectare, which was the fourth highest and of wheat was 1456 kg/hectare and of rice was 1469 kg/hectare, which were fifth and sixth highest respectively. Amongst other crops, only oilseeds were grown there and the yield rate of total oilseeds was 768 kg/hectare, which was the third highest.

In case of Assam, it appears that, though the net area under crop was much more to the extent of 35.34 per cent of the Reporting area of the State, but the yield rates of the crops were not that good. The yield rate of total foodgrains was only 1405 kg/hectare, which was the second lowest in this region. The yield rate of rice alone was also the second lowest of the order of 1460 kg/hectare, wheat was the third lowest of 1066 kg/hectare and of maize was 724 kg/hectare, which was the lowest among all the States of this region. However, the position was a bit better in case of sugarcane and jute. The yield rate of sugarcane was 36983 kg/hectare, which was the third highest and of jute was 1272 kg/hectare, which was the second highest. The yield rate in Arunachal Pradesh was also not good. It appears that, though the cropping intensity in this State was the highest, still the yield rate of total foodgrains was only 1178 kg/hectare and it was the lowest in this region. And perhaps, because of this reason, the proportion of area sown more than once was more in Arunachal Pradesh. However, the only hope was that the yield rate of both wheat and small millet was the second highest of the order of 2023 kg/hectare and 955 kg/hectare and the yield rate of total pulses was the third highest of 1046 kg/hectare. Oilseeds were also grown in this State and the yield rate of this was also good to the extent of 1042 kg/hectare, which was the second highest in this region.

However, it appears that, for almost all the crops, the yield rate in the North Eastern Region was less than the yield rate in the country as a whole. The yield rate of the major crops like rice, wheat and maize in N.E. Region was 1589 kg/hectare, 1219 kg/hectare and 1538 kg/hectare as against the all India figures of 1984 kg/hectare, 2602 kg/hectare and 1907 kg/hectare respectively, while the yield rate of total foodgrains was also less to the extent of 1525 kg/hectare as against the all India figure of 1652 kg/hectare. In case of other crops like sugarcane, cotton and jute, the yield rate was also less in this region. The yield rate of these crops in N.E. Region was 36608 kg/hectare, 178 kg/hectare and 1235 kg/hectare as against the all India figures of 64752 kg/hectare, 318 kg/hectare and 2186 kg/hectare respectively. But it appears that, the exception was only with the oilseeds. The yield rate of total oilseeds in this region was much more to the extent of 2162 kg/hectare as against the all India figure of 885 kg/hectare. Further, details can be seen from Appendix-4.7.

The North Eastern States are also producing fruits. The main fruits are banana, pineapple, mango, orange, jackfruit, papaya, litchi, guava, etc. These fruits are grown almost in all the States of this region. Other fruits like apple, pears, plum, coconut, arecanut, walnut, cashewnut, etc. are also grown in some of the States. However, the area under horticulture is not much. The details of area, production and yield rate of fruits during the three years from 2000-01 to 2002-03 in different States of N.E. Region and the country as a whole can be seen from Appendix-4.8. From this it appears that, the proportion of area under fruits was more in Tripura and the yield rate was also high there. It can be seen that, on an average, the area under fruit crops was 28.53 thousand hectares, which was 2.72 per cent of the Reporting area, and the State was producing 15913 kgs. of fruits per hectare. The yield rate of fruit crops in Assam was also good. The average area under fruit crops was 103.20 thousand hectares, which was 1.31 per cent of the Reporting area of the State and it was producing, on an average, 12138 kgs. of fruits per hectare and it was the second highest rate in this region. The average area under fruits in Nagaland was though 19.40 thousand hectares i.e. 1.23 per cent of the Reporting area, but the average yield rate of fruit crops was 10530 kg/hectare, which was the third highest in this region. The area under fruits in Meghalaya was though less, but the yield rate was not that bad. The State was having, on an average, 21.13 thousand hectares i.e. only 0.95 per cent of the Reporting area under fruits, but it was producing 8521 kgs. of fruits per hectare, which was the fourth highest rate amongst the States of N.E. Region.

The yield rate of fruits in the States of Manipur, Mizoram, Arunachal Pradesh and Sikkim was generally less. In Manipur, it can be seen that, though the average area under fruit crops was comparatively more to the extent of 25.83 thousand hectares i.e. 1.33 per cent of the Reporting area, but the yield rate was only 5034 kg/hectare, which was the fifth highest in this region. The yield rate of fruits in Mizoram was further less to the extent of 3414 kg/hectare. The average area under fruits was also less to the tune of 18.07 thousand hectares i.e. only 0.87 per cent of the Reporting area of the State. The State of Arunachal Pradesh however, showed some different picture. It is seen that, the State was having, on an average, the second largest area of 44.50 thousand hectare i.e. 0.81 per cent of the Reporting area, but it was producing only 2474 kgs. of fruits per hectare, which was the second lowest rate in this region. However, the State is very much famous in production of apple and it got many prizes in all India competition. The State of Sikkim was in the last position in respect of yield rate of fruits. The average area under fruits was though comparatively high to the extent of 10.57 thousand hectares i.e. 1.57 per cent of the Reporting area, but the production was only 904 kg/hectare. The position of fruit production in the country as a whole was better than the position of North East India. Though the proportion of average area under fruits in North Eastern Region and in the country as a whole was more or less same, which were 1.18 per cent and 1.27 per cent of the respective Reporting areas, but the average yield rate of North Eastern Region as a whole was only 8886 kg/hectare as against the all India figure of 11269 kg/hectare, which was quite more. Further, details can be seen from Appendix-4.8.

Along with fruit crops, the North Eastern States are also growing vegetables. The main vegetables are potato, tomato, brinjal, cabbage, cauliflower, onion, peas, lady's-finger, beans, etc. and other crops like sweet potato, ginger, turmeric, chillies, etc. are also grown in almost all the States of this region. However, the area under vegetables is comparatively less. The details of area, production and yield rate of vegetables during a period of three years from 2000-01 to 2002-03 in different States of North East India and of the country as a whole can be seen from Appendix-4.9. From this, it appears that, the proportion of area under vegetables and also the yield rate were more in the State of Assam. On an average, Assam was having 235.90 thousand hectares of land under vegetables, which was 3.01 per cent of its Reporting area and was producing 11429 kgs. of vegetables per hectare. In case of yield rate of vegetables, Tripura though came next to Assam, but it was having exactly the same proportion of land under vegetables. The average area under vegetables in Tripura was 31.57 thousand hectares, which was also 3.01 per cent of the Reporting area of the State and, on an average, producing 11001 kgs. of vegetables per hectare, which was little less than the production rate of Assam. The proportion of land under vegetables and the yield rate in Nagaland were also not bad. It is seen that, the average area under vegetables was 19.97 thousand hectares i.e. 1.26 per cent of the Reporting area and it was producing 10673 kgs. of vegetables per hectare, which was the third highest rate in this region. The proportion of land under vegetables in Meghalaya was quite high, but it came after Nagaland in respect of yield rate. The average area under vegetables in Meghalaya was 37.17 thousand hectares i.e. 1.67 per cent of the Reporting area, but the yield rate was 8132 kg/hectare, which was the fourth highest amongst the N.E. States. However, some of the vegetables like potato, cabbage, cauliflower and turmeric are very famous and are grown in abundance.

The area under vegetables as well as the yield rate in the States of Mizoram, Manipur, Sikkim and Arunachal Pradesh were comparatively less. In Mizoram, the average area under vegetables was 6.33 thousand hectares i.e. only 0.30 per cent of the Reporting area and the yield rate was 6630 kg/hectare, which was the fourth lowest amongst the N.E. States. The average area under vegetables in Manipur was 10.63 thousand hectares, which was 0.55 per cent of the Reporting area of the State, but the yield rate was 6461 kg/hectare, which was the third lowest. The proportion of land under vegetables in Sikkim was though a bit more amongst all the four States of this group, but the yield rate was the second lowest. In Sikkim, the average area under vegetables was 13.93 thousand hectares, which was 2.07 per cent of the Reporting area, but the State was producing only 4279 kgs. of vegetables per hectare. The State of Arunachal Pradesh was in the last position in respect of production of vegetables. The average area under vegetables was 20.77 thousand hectares, which was 0.38 per cent of the Reporting area of the State and it was producing only 3999 kgs. of vegetables per hectare, which was the lowest rate of this Region. From Appendix-4.9, it can be seen that the proportion of area under vegetables as well as the production rate in North East India were low as compared to the position of the country as a whole. In N.E. Region the average area under vegetables was 376.27 thousand hectares, which was 1.64 per cent of the Reporting area and the Region was producing on an average 10106 kgs. of vegetables per hectare, whereas the average area under vegetables in the country as a whole was 6165.87 thousand hectares, i.e. 2.02 per cent of the Reporting area and it was producing 14445 kgs. of vegetables per hectare, which was much more than the production rate of this Region. Further, details can be seen from Appendix-4.9.

The use of chemical fertilizer for production of different type of crops in the North Eastern States except Assam, is very less. This is perhaps due to the geographical condition, nature of cultivation and to some extent, due to social taboo in some of the States. The hill people are primarily doing jhum cultivation and prefer to use compost manure. However, the consumption pattern of chemical fertilizers viz. Nitrogen (N), Phosphate (P_2O_5) and Potash (K_2O) for Kharif crops and Rabi crops during 2004-05 and 2005-06 in the North Eastern States and in the country as a whole can be seen from Appendix-4.10. From this it can be seen that, the consumption of Nitrogen was generally more than the other two types of fertilizers in all the States of this Region as well as in the country as a whole. Further, it also appears that, in the hilly region, the consumption of Nitrogen was more for Kharif crops, but in the plain areas like Assam, Tripura and in the country as a whole, it was more for Rabi crops.

In Assam, on an average, 182.01 thousand tonnes of fertilizers were used every year for production of crops and out of this, Nitrogen accounted for almost half i.e. 47.10 per cent. The average consumption of fertilizer in Manipur was 17.30 thousand tonnes per year, but the proportion of Nitrogen was quite high to the extent of 84.22 per cent. In Tripura, the average consumption of fertilizer was 14.01 thousand tonnes per year and the proportion of Nitrogen was also high to the tune of 68.74 per cent. Fertilizer was also used in Meghalaya, though not in large quantity. On an average, 4.92 thousand tonnes of fertilizers were used every year and out of this, the share of Nitrogen was 59.35 per cent. However, in all other States of this Region, though people are using fertilizer, but the amount is very less. The average consumption of fertilizer in the country as a whole was quite high to the extent of 19369.34 thousand tonnes per year and out of that, the share of Nitrogen was 63.08 per cent. But in comparison to all India position, the consumption of fertilizer was very less in the North Eastern Region. It was only 1.27 per cent of the total consumption of the country and in case of Nitrogen, it was even less to the extent of 0.94 per cent of the total Nitrogen consumption of the country as a whole. Further, details can be seen from Appendix-4.10.

On the whole, it can be seen that, the land use scenario of the North East India is completely different from the other parts of the country. The States of this region except Assam are mostly hilly and more than two-third area of each State is forest area or covered under forest. The extent of area not available for cultivation including fallow land in each State is also not less and therefore, the area available for cultivation is very less. The area available for cultivation was only 3 to 5 per cent of the Reporting area in Arunachal Pradesh and Mizoram. It was 10 to 12 per cent in Meghalaya and Manipur, 16 to 20 per cent in Sikkim and Nagaland. But, in Tripura and Assam, it was slightly more than 26 and 35 per cent of the respective Reporting areas, as against the all India figure of 46 per cent. In case of crop production, though the yield rate in some of the States like Tripura and Assam was more than the National rate, but the yield rate of the North Eastern Region as a whole was much less than the National figure of 11269 kg/hectare. In case of production of vegetables, the position of N.E. Region was also not good. The production rate of vegetables in all the States of this region was much less, in some States, it was almost one-fourth of the National yield rate of 14445 kg/hectare.

The reason of such low yield rate of crops and vegetables in North East India can perhaps be attributed to so many factors. The most prominent one is the geographical condition and the method of cultivation. The hill people are mostly pursuing the age old method of jhum cultivation in the hill slopes, as the availability of flat land for permanent cultivation is very less. For jhum cultivation, people are mostly using compost manure, but the problem is, the rain wash away the fertility of the top soil every time exposing the roots of the crop trees which makes the tree weak resulting in low productivity. Moreover, though the hill people are trying to do terrace cultivation in the moderate slope or in the valley type land wherever available, but due to absence of proper irrigation facilities, they are not getting the desired result. The other important factor is non-availability of proper road, infrastructure and marketing facilities. The people in the interior places sometimes loose their interest of growing more, as they do not get the marketing facilities for their surplus production and have to through away particularly the perishable goods like fruits and vegetables.

However, it is an accepted fact that, the jhum cultivation is bad, it is an inferior method of cultivation, low productivity, uneconomical, the cause of deforestation and soil erosion and so on and so fourth. Many discussions, debates, studies, researches, etc. also have been taken place to find out an alternative of jhuming, but so far nothing concrete could be found out. The problem is, jhum cultivation is the way of life of the hill people and it is not very easy to solve this complex problem and to provide an alternate way of life to the hill people. However, to control or to reduce jhum cultivation, some of the Scholars suggested for terrace cultivation and water resource development. Some of them even went a step further and suggested for diversified farming together with a system comprising of agricultural and horticultural crops combined with animal husbandry, fishery and poultry farming, as an alternative way to replace jhuming to permanent cultivation. But only time can say, whether this can actually be an alternative way of life of the hill people and can replace the age old method of jhuming to the modern method of settled cultivation or not.

NOTES

1. *State of Forest Report, 2003*, Forest Survey of India, Ministry of Environment and Forest, Dehradun, p. 5.
2. *ibid.*, p. 8.
3. *ibid.*, pp. 123-24.
4. *ibid.*, p. 18.
5. *Fertilizer Statistics, 2005-06*, the Fertilizer Association of India, New Delhi, p II-7.
6. *ibid.*, pp II-7, II-8.
7. *ibid.*, p II-8.

5

Communication Scenario

The North East India is connected to the State of West Bengal *vis-à-vis* with the rest of the country through a narrow strip of land, which is known as chicken neck, at a point called Srirampur, Assam. The means of communication in this region are road, rail, air and waterways. Of all these, road plays the most important role in the life of the people and for their all-round development. It is needless to say that, without the very basic amenity like road communication, no other infrastructure can develop and the socio-economic activities cannot take place. Rail is the other important communication system for the common people, but it has many limitations as almost all the States of North Eastern Region except Assam and Tripura are hilly and practically no rail communication could be established so far. Air communication also could not be developed in a bigger way in the North Eastern Region due to so many factors. The topography of this region is the greatest hurdle for development of road communication as well as Airports. In the hills, there is hardly any flat land convenient for construction of runways and other infrastructure for landing and taking off the Aircrafts. The economic viability is the other important factor. The construction cost and the maintenance charges of Airports in this hilly region is quite high, but the availability of goods and passengers are less as this is a costly way of transportation system. Waterways are the cheapest form of communication, but again, because of the geographic condition, the turbulent hilly rivers are not navigable and therefore, the water transport in the hilly States of this region is almost non-existent.

It is seen that the road communication system in the North East India was initially very poor and its development practically started only after the independence of our country and with the beginning of First Five Year Plan in the Year, 1951-52. It can be seen that, even in India, very little attention had been given to road development till 1920s. It is only after the First World War, when motor transport increased considerably, the inadequacy of Indian roads were felt all over the country. Therefore, in 1927, the Council of State adopted a resolution for the improvement of the road system and a Road Development Committee under Dr. M.R. Jayakar was set-up. The Committee reported that, road development was beyond the capacity of the Provincial Governments and that, considering the national importance of roads, the Central Government ought to bear a substantial portion of the cost. And in pursuance of this, the Central Road Fund was formed in 1929, and that was the turning point in the history of road development in India. The Central Road Fund derived its revenue from the proceeds of customs and excise duties levied on motor spirit at the rate of 3.5 paise per litre, and 20 per cent of this income used to be credited to the Central Road Fund for the administration, research and investigation and the remaining 80 per ce. used to be distributed among the States and Union Territories on the basis of the volume of motor spirit consumed by them[1].

The first major attempt for development of road, which was taken in India is known as Nagpur Plan 1943. The objective of that Plan was to see that no village would be more than 5 miles (i.e. 8.05 kms.) from a main road in agricultural area and 20 miles (i.e. 32.19 kms.) in non-agricultural area, and the target fixed was to obtain a density of 16 kms. of road length per 100 sq. kms. of area by 1961. For the next 20 years (i.e. 1961-81) another plan, known as Bombay Plan was drawn with the aim that, no village would be more than 4 miles (i.e. 6.44 kms.) from a metalled road and 1.4 miles (i.e. 2.25 kms.) from any road in developed and agricultural area, 8 miles (i.e. 12.87 kms.) from a metalled road and 3 miles (i.e. 4.83 kms.) from any road in semi-developed area, 12 miles (i.e. 19.31 kms.) from a metalled road and 5 miles (i.e. 8.05 kms.) from any road in undeveloped area. Further, the target was fixed to achieve an overall road density of 32.50 kms. per 100 sq. kms. of area. In the meantime, the Border Roads Organisation (BRO) was also set-up in 1960 with a view to provide road communication in the North and North Eastern Region of the country in order to speed up the socio-economic development of these regions. The Organisation gradually expanded further and is functioning in underdeveloped and remote regions of our border States and constructing roads in the high altitudes of the Himalayas[2].

The progress of road construction in the North Eastern Region is comparatively much slow mainly due to its geographic and climatic conditions, remoteness and insufficient resources. Most of the areas of this region are hilly and it is not very easy to construct roads in the hilly terrains. It can be seen that, the target of Nagpur Plan though could be achieved by all the States of this region at a much later stage, but the target of Bombay Plan could not be achieved by the States of Arunachal Pradesh, Mizoram and Sikkim even in 2002. The details of roads up to 31st March, 2002 in respect of all the States of North Eastern Region as well as of the country as a whole can be seen from Appendix-5.1 to Appendix-5.6. From these, it can be seen that, Arunachal Pradesh was having a total road length of 18365 kms. and a road density of only 21.93 kms. per 100 sq. kms. of area, which was the lowest in this region, but on the other hand, it was providing 1669.55 kms. of road for every lakh of its population, which was the highest amongst all the North Eastern States. However, out of the total road length, Highways accounts for 93.75 per cent i.e. 17218 kms. and National Highways was only 2.13 per cent i.e. 392 kms. The condition of the Highways was again not very good. It can be seen that, only 32.59 per cent of the Highways was surfaced and 67.41 per cent was un-surfaced, of which 73.88 per cent was again not motorable. The length of PWD roads was 12169 kms., which was 66.26 per cent of the total road length of the State. Moreover, a major portion i.e. 57.01 per cent of the PWD road was un-surfaced, and out of this, 56.46 per cent was not motorable. The road under Forest Department in Arunachal Pradesh was not much. It was only 1111 kms. i.e. 6.05 per cent of the total road length of the State. On the other hand, the positive side of this was that, though most of the road under forest i.e. 96.31 per cent was un-surfaced, but 85.51 per cent of this was motorable. The urban road in Arunachal Pradesh was also not much. It was only 36 kms. and the entire road length was surfaced and motorable.

The road length in Mizoram was not much. It was only 5075

kms. with a road density of only 24.07 kms. per 100 sq. kms. of area and was providing 563.89 kms. of road to every lakh population of the State. But the plus point was that, 95.09 per cent of the total road was Highways and the National Highways occupied a total length of 927 kms., which was 18.27 per cent of the total road length of Mizoram. The Highways were also mostly surfaced and though, 40.59 per cent of this was un-surfaced, but the entire length of 1959 kms. was motorable. The length of PWD road in Mizoram was 3730 kms., which was 73.50 per cent of the total road length of the State. It is seen that, almost half i.e. 50.97 per cent of the PWD road was though un-surfaced, but the whole length of 1901 kms. was motorable. The road under Forest Department in Mizoram was much less to the extent of only 239 kms. i.e. only 4.71 per cent of the total road length of the State and the entire length was un-surfaced, moreover, most of the un-surfaced road i.e. 51.88 per cent was not motorable. The urban road in Mizoram was also very less. It was only 10 kms., but the whole length was surfaced and motorable.

Sikkim is the third State in N.E. India, which could not fulfil the target of Bombay Plan even in 2002. The State was having only 2019 kms. of road with a road density of 28.45 kms. per 100 sq. kms. of area and was providing 336.50 kms. of road for every lakh population of the State. However, out of the total road, 1918 kms. i.e. 95 per cent was Highways and the National Highways was 62 kms., which was only 3.07 per cent of the total road length of the State. The Highways were mostly surfaced and only 409 kms. i.e. 21.32 per cent was un-surfaced, but the entire length was motorable. The PWD road occupied more than two-third of the total road length of Sikkim. It was 1670 kms. i.e. 82.71 per cent and out of this, only 409 kms. i.e. 24.49 per cent though un-surfaced, but the entire length was motorable. The road under Forest Department was also very less, it was only 65 kms. and out of this, 64 kms. was un-surface, moreover, 46.87 per cent of the un-surfaced road was again not motorable. The urban road in Sikkim was comparatively not that less. It was 36 kms. and the entire length was surfaced and motorable.

Amongst all the North Eastern States, road density was the highest in Tripura. The State was having a total road length of 16296 kms. with a road density of 155.41 kms per 100 sq. kms. of area and was providing 509.25 kms. of road for every lakh population of the State.

The length of Highways in the State was 14740 kms. i.e. 90.45 per cent, and the National Highways was 400 kms., which accounted for 2.45 per cent of the total length of road of the State. However, though the road density was the highest in Tripura, but the condition of the Highways was not that good. It is seen that, out of the total Highways, only 28.46 per cent was surfaced and 71.54 per cent was un-surfaced. Moreover, out of the total un-surfaced road of 10545 kms., 51.63 per cent i.e. 5444 kms. was not motorable. The PWD road in Tripura was also not much. It was only 5569 kms. i.e. 34.17 per cent of the total road length of the State and out of this, 34.30 per cent i.e. 1910 kms. was though un-surfaced, but the entire length was of course motorable. The road under Forest Department in Tripura was 1328 kms. i.e. 8.15 per cent, but almost the entire length i.e. 99.17 per cent of this was un-surfaced and not motorable. The urban road in Tripura was 228 kms. and out of this, 41 kms. i.e. 17.98 per cent was un-surfaced and 13 kms. of that was again not motorable.

The road density was the second highest in Nagaland. The State was having a total road length of 21021 kms. with a density of 126.79 kms. per 100 sq. kms. of area and was providing 1051.05 kms. of road for every lakh population of the State. However, out of the total road length, 20180 kms. i.e. 96 per cent was Highways and 369 kms. i.e. 1.76 per cent was National Highways. The road density of the State was though the second highest, but the condition of the Highways was not that good. It appears that, only 31.45 per cent of this was surfaced and 68.55 per cent was un-surfaced and again 1430 kms. i.e. 10.33 per cent of the un-surfaced road was not motorable. The length of PWD road in Nagaland was 6273 kms. and out of this, 5328 kms. i.e. 84.94 per cent was un-surfaced and also 406 kms. i.e. 7.62 per cent of the un-surfaced road was not motorable. The road under forest department in the State was 725 kms. and out of this, 720 kms. i.e. 99.31 per cent was though un-surfaced, but the positive side of this was that, the entire length was motorable. The length of urban road in the State was 96 kms. and only 2 kms. was un-surfaced, of which 1 km. was not motorable.

The State of Assam comes in the third highest position in respect of road density. The State was having a total road length of 89486 kms. with a density of 114.09 kms. per 100 sq. kms. of area and was providing 328.99 kms. of road for every lakh population of the State.

The Highways was 78471 kms. i.e. 87.69 per cent and the National Highways was 2836 kms., which accounted for only 3.71 per cent of the total length of road of the State. However, the condition of the Highways in Assam was not that good. It appears that, only 13.23 per cent of the Highways was surfaced and 86.77 per cent was un-surfaced, and again a big portion of the un-surfaced road measuring 19355 kms. i.e. 28.43 per cent was not motorable. The length of PWD road in Assam was 26416 kms., which was 29.52 per cent of the total length of road of the State. Further, it appears that, more than two-third i.e. 21683 kms. of the PWD road was un-surfaced and out of that, 4688 kms. i.e. 21.62 per cent was not motorable. The length of road under Forest Department was 6076 kms., which was 6.79 per cent of the total road, and most of this, i.e. 95.56 per cent was un-surfaced. Moreover, a total of 2368 kms. i.e. 40.79 per cent of the un-surfaced road, was not motorable. The length of urban road in Assam was quite high to the extent of 3904 kms., which was 4.36 per cent of the total road of the State, but the un-surfaced portion of this was not less. Almost half, i.e. 1882 kms. was un-surfaced and out of this, 644 kms. i.e. 34.22 per cent was not motorable.

The State of Manipur was in the fourth position in respect of road density. The State was having a total road length of 11434 kms. with a road density of 51.21 kms. per 100 sq. kms. of area and was providing 476.42 kms. of road for every lakh population of the State. Out of the total road length, 10882 kms. i.e. 95.17 per cent was Highways and the National Highways was 954 kms. i.e. 8.43 per cent of the total road length of the State. Further, it appears that, 34.75 per cent of the Highways was surfaced and 65.25 per cent was un-surfaced. The total length of un-surfaced road was 7100 kms. and 20.25 per cent of this was not motorable. The length of PWD road in Manipur was 6638 kms. and a big portion of this, measuring 4824 kms. i.e. 72.67 per cent was un-surfaced. Moreover, out of the un-surfaced road, 1438 kms. i.e. 29.81 per cent was again not motorable. The road under Forest Department was not much in Manipur. It was only 417 kms. i.e. 3.65 per cent of the total road of the State and the entire road length under forest was though un-surfaced, but it was motorable. The length of urban road in the State was 135 kms. and out of this, 54 kms. i.e. 40 per cent was un-surfaced, but motorable.

The State of Meghalaya was though in the fifth position in respect of road density, but the road condition of the State, in general, was a bit better. The State was having a total road length of 9565 kms. with a road density of 42.65 kms. per 100 sq. kms. of area and was also providing 398.54 kms. of road for every lakh population of the State. The length of Highways of the State was 8165 kms. i.e. 85.36 per cent and the National Highways was 717 kms. i.e. 7.50 per cent of the total road length of the State. The condition of the Highways was comparatively better. It is seen that, 78.18 per cent of the Highways was surfaced and only 21.82 per cent was un-surfaced. The length of PWD road was also quite high to the extent of 6013 kms. i.e. 52.59 per cent of the total road of the State. Further, out of the total PWD road, 81.72 per cent was surfaced and the remaining 18.28 per cent, measuring 1099 kms. was though un-surfaced, but the entire length was motorable. However, the condition of the road under Forest Department in Meghalaya was not that good. The length of road under forest in the State was 1081 kms. and almost the entire length i.e. 99.63 per cent of this was un-surfaced. Moreover, more than two-third of the un-surfaced road, measuring 874 kms. was also not motorable. The length of urban road in Meghalaya was 106 kms. and a very small portion of this measuring only 4 kms. was un-surfaced, of which, 3 kms. was not motorable.

However, compare to the position of the country, the position of the North Eastern Region as a whole, was not good in many respects. It can be seen that, the road density of this region was 66.09 kms. per 100 sq. kms. of area as against the all India figure of 74.73 kms. Further, in case of Highways, it appears that, in N.E. Region, only 26.26 per cent of the Highways was surfaced and 73.74 per cent was un-surfaced. Whereas, 59.32 per cent of the Highways of the country was surfaced and only 40.68 per cent was un-surfaced. The position was further bad in case of PWD road. It can be seen that, only 35.61 per cent of the PWD road of this region was surfaced and 64.39 per cent was un-surfaced, but 83.17 per cent of the PWD road of the country was surfaced and only 16.83 per cent was un-surfaced. The position of the road under Forest Department was also no better. In N.E. Region, only 3.01 per cent of the forest road was surfaced and 96.99 per cent was un-surfaced, as against the position of the country of 10.68 per cent and 89.32 per cent respectively. The percentage of urban road in N.E. Region was also much less. It was only 2.64 per cent of the total road of this region, whereas, in case of the country as a whole, it was 10.18 per cent. Moreover, out of the total urban road of this region, 56.43 per cent was surfaced and 43.57 per cent was un-surfaced, but in case of the country as a whole, it was 76 per cent and 24 per cent respectively. Further, details can be seen from Appendix-5.1 to Appendix-5.6.

For construction of roads in the North Eastern Region, besides (BRO), the North Eastern Council (NEC) is also playing an important role. The Council is not only providing fund to the BRO for construction of roads and bridges in this region, but also funding the State Governments mainly for the construction of inter-state roads and the roads of economic importance. In addition to that, the Council is also providing fund for construction of major bridges and for the maintenance of the roads constructed under NEC Plan. However, in addition to NEC Plan, the States of this Region are having their own separate plans for construction of roads and bridges. The position of state sector outlay and expenditure for Ninth Plan and the outlay for the Tenth Plan and also for the years, 2002-03 and 2003-04 for different States of the North Eastern Region and the country as a whole can be seen from Appendix-5.7.

It can be seen from the nature of expenditure that, the progress of work for construction of roads and bridges in the North Eastern Region was slow, as none of the States could spend the allocated money during Ninth Plan. Only the States of Meghalaya and Sikkim could spend little more than 90 per cent of their respective allocations. The State of Assam also could spend 81.02 per cent and Mizoram 77.04 per cent. But the expenditure for all other States was much less. The States of Arunachal Pradesh and Manipur could spend 67.57 per cent and 61.79 per cent of their respective allocations. The expenditure of Nagaland and Tripura was further less. Nagaland though could spend only 58.11 per cent, but Tripura could not spend even half of its allocated money. However, the overall expenditure of the North Eastern Region as a whole was 72.44 per cent of its allocation, whereas, the expenditure figure of the country as a whole was much more, it was even more than its allocation and was of the order of 103.19 per cent of its outlay.

The outlay of different States for Tenth Plan was not uniform.

The allocation figures had been reduced by 9 to 47 per cent for most of the States who could not spend 75 per cent of their allotted money during Ninth Plan. But, on the other hand, the allocation figures for some of the States like Sikkim and Mizoram had been increased by 78 to 128 per cent of their respective allocations of Ninth Plan. The allocation for the country as a whole had also been increased by 65 per cent during Tenth Plan. However, the outlay for different States for Tenth Plan may not necessarily been decreased or increased on the basis of expenditure during Ninth Plan, but it may be, as per the requirement of the respective States. Further, details can be seen from Appendix-5.7.

Whenever we talk about the necessity or the utility of the road, the first thing comes to our mind is that, it is one of the basic amenities and the means of movement of human beings and goods. In the earlier days, people could walk miles together and sometimes taking loads on their heads, but now-a-days, people are so busy and generally they do not want to walk even a small distance. In the present days walking is not necessary also because, various kinds of vehicles have been developed for carrying human beings and goods and gradually that has become a necessity of life of the people. The people are not only using vehicles for their own purposes, but for business and other economic activities also. Therefore, in recent times, the growth in the number of vehicles is so fast that, the capacity of the roads for carrying such increasing number of vehicles is gradually decreasing and that is becoming a cause of concern for the Governments as well as for the public.

The Appendix-5.8 will give the details of the type and the number of Motor Vehicles registered as on 31st March of 2001-02 and 2003-04 in different States of North East India and in the country as a whole. However, the data for Arunachal Pradesh is available for only one year and that too, is of 1996-97 and, therefore, no comparative study for showing the recent trend could be made. In case of Assam, it appears that, the highest increase was in the number of Auto-Rickshaws. Within a period of two years, it increased by 30.48 per cent. Next was Two-wheelers, which increased by 26.73 per cent and then comes cars with an increase of 24.65 per cent. The average number of vehicles per km. of road was 6.66, but it went up to 8.12 within two years with a growth rate of 21.92 per cent.

The State of Manipur showed a high growth of 64.89 per cent in cars, 40.30 per cent in Two-wheelers and 45.17 per cent in buses within a period of six years. The average number of vehicles per km. of road was the highest of 9.30 in Manipur during 2003-04. The State of Meghalaya though showed a declining trend in case of goods vehicles, but it showed an increase of 14.55 per cent in Buses, 13.55 per cent in cars and 11.43 per cent in Taxis within a period of one year and the average number of vehicles per km. of road was 7.67 during 2002-03.

The State of Mizoram though showed a declining trend in case of miscellaneous vehicles, but it showed a very high growth of 108.99 per cent in Jeeps, followed by 83.79 per cent in Auto-Rickshaws and 29.68 per cent in cars within a period of two years. The average number of vehicles per km. of road was though 6.66, but it went up to 8.30 with a growth rate of 24.62 per cent within that period. Nagaland showed a very different picture. The declining trend was in most categories of vehicles, but there was a record increase of 362.83 per cent in taxis, 161.71 per cent in miscellaneous vehicles and 24.19 per cent in goods vehicles within a period of two years and on an average, there were more than 8 vehicles per km. of road during that period. The State of Tripura also showed some declining trend in case of Taxis and Buses, but the growth rate was quite high to the extent of 75.05 per cent in case of cars, 53.93 per cent in Auto-Rickshaws and 35.57 per cent in Two-wheelers. The average number of vehicles per km. of road in Tripura was comparatively less. It was 3.52 during 2001-02, but it increased to 4.64 during 2002-03 with a growth rate of 31.82 per cent. In Sikkim, the maximum increase was in the case of cars. It increased with a rate of 79.46 per cent, followed by taxis with 44.78 per cent and then by buses and goods vehicles, both with about 40 per cent. The average number of vehicles per km. of road was 6.42 in 2001-02, but it went up to 8.54 in 2003-04 with a growth rate of 33.02 per cent, which was the second highest in this region. However, in the North Eastern Region as a whole, the growth rate of almost all types of vehicles, except taxis, Auto-Rickshaws and miscellaneous vehicles, was less than the growth rate of the country as a whole. The average number of vehicles per km. of road in this region was 7.12 in 2003-04, which was much less than the figure of 29.60 of the country as a whole at that time. The growth rate was also less to the extent of 18.47 per cent, as against the all India rate of 23.54 per cent. Further, details can be seen from Appendix-5.8.

Railway is the other most convenient communication system for short as well as for long journey and due to availability of variety in the accommodation procedure, all sections of people can avail that without much problem. But again, mainly due to geographic condition, the railway network could not be established so far in most of the States of this region. The position of the railway network as on 31st March, 2004 in different States of N.E. Region and in the country as a whole can be seen from Appendix-5.9. From this, it can be seen that, there was no railway network at all in the States of Meghalaya and Sikkim. However, recently a proposal has been taken up for connecting Byrnihat of Meghalaya with Assam by a railway line. The States of Arunachal Pradesh, Manipur and Mizoram were though included in the Railway Map of the North Eastern Region, but these were actually for name sake, as all these three States were having Metre Gauge line of 1.26 km., 1.35 km. and 1.50 km. respectively. The State of Nagaland was having a bit more to the extent of 11.13 kms. of Broad Gauge and 1.72 km. of Metre Gauge line. The position of Tripura was slightly better. It was having 64.42 kms. of Metre Gauge line and moreover, the capital city of Agartala has also been connected by Rail recently. Amongst all the States of this region, Assam is the only State, which was having a total railway line of 2517.23 kms. of which, 1227.70 kms. was Broad Gauge and 1289.53 kms. was Metre Gauge. The length of railway line was 2.81 per cent of the total road length of Assam and with a density of 3.21 kms. of railway line per 100 sq. kms. of area of the State. The length of railway line in the country as a whole was 63122 kms., out of which, 45622 kms. was Broad Gauge, 14364 kms. was Metre Gauge and 3136 kms. was Narrow Gauge. The total length of the railway line was 2.57 per cent of the total road length of the country and was having a density of 1.92 km. of railway line per 100 sq. kms. of area as on March, 2003.

Waterway is another convenient and cheaper mode of transport of goods and people, though it takes comparatively more time than the other forms of transportation. However, in this case also, there are some problems. The rivers in the hilly regions are basically turbulent and are mostly not navigable, except for some water sports. Only the rivers, which are flowing in the plains, like Brahmaputra, Barak, Longai, Katakhal, Kushihara, etc. are navigable and are convenient for transportation. In earlier days, these waterways of North Eastern Region were very much in use for transportation of Goods and for maintenance of trade relation with East Bengal and West Bengal. But after the formation of Bangladesh, these trade routes were closed and gradually it lost its importance. However, the Government of India is now trying to revive the trade relation with Bangladesh and Myanmar and to develop the waterways of this region with all modern transportation facilities. The Ministry of External Affairs has already commissioned a study through RITES on feasibility of the multi-modal Kaladan River route from Mizoram to Sittwe port in Myanmar and then by sea to Kolkata port. The Brahmaputra River from Dhubri to Sadiya, a distance of 891 kms. already declared as National Waterway-II in 1988 and the proposal for declaring the River Barak from Lakhipur to Bhanga, a distance of 121 kms. as National Waterway-VI is also under process. The North Eastern Council, Shillong is also actively associated with the improvement of Water Transport in this region[3].

Air is the most quickest form of communication system, though it is a bit costly and not always within the reach of the common people. However, since most of the interior places of this region are inaccessible and the road as well as the rail communication system is also very much inadequate, therefore, the air connectivity is the only other viable means of transportation for intra-state and inter-state movement and also for the linkage of this region with the other part of the country. For this purpose, 14 numbers of big and small Airports viz. Agartala, Aizawl, Bagdogra, Dibrugarh, Dimapur, Guwahati, Imphal, Jorhat, Kamalpur, Lilabari, Silchar, Shillong, Tejpur, and Teju are already there in operation. However, due to infrastructure constraints, the Shillong Airport is not effectively functional. Moreover, a number of non-operational Airports viz. Along, Daporijo, Pasighat, Ziro, Tezu, Kailashahar, Khowai, Rupsi, Tura, Turial and Shella are also there in different states of this region and works are going on for making these Airports operational.

The main airlines operating in this region include Indian Airlines, Alliance Air, Jet Airways, Kingfisher, Spicejet, Air Sahara and Indigo.

Moreover, the Government of India has granted an initial NOC, 2006 to M/s. Sky King Aviation to operate scheduled air services within the North Eastern Region. Besides aircraft operations, helicopter services are also there in the N.E. Region. Pawan Hans Helicopters Ltd. have deployed various categories of helicopters in four States of this region which include one helicopter each in Meghalaya, Tripura, Sikkim and Arunachal Pradesh. In addition to that, Jagson Airlines has deployed one helicopter in Arunachal Pradesh and there is one more Dauphin Helicopter of Pawan Hans, which is in lease to Ministry of Home Affairs (MHA) for operational requirements[4].

The North Eastern Council, Shillong is playing a major role in the development of Airports of this region and also funding for procurement of ATR-42 by Alliance Air for operating these Aircrafts in this region. Moreover, the Airport Authority of India (AAI) with the financial support from NEC, could invest a capital of Rs. 180.69 crore during Tenth Plan for development of Airports in N.E. Region. The AAI has also planned for investment of Rs. 651 crore in this region during Eleventh Plan, which includes an outlay of Rs. 379 crore for the three proposed Greenfield Airports. The major Airports of N.E. Region are primarily Agartala and Guwahati where night landing operations are possible. Moreover, the Guwahati and Bagdogra Airports in the meanwhile attained the status of International Airports also. The Instrument Landing Systems (ILS) are however, in place at Agartala, Guwahati, Dibrugarh, Dimapur and Imphal. Various other projects involving installation of navigational equipments e.g. Communication, Navigation and Surveillance (CNS), Doppler Very High Frequency Range (DVR), Digital Satellite Communication Network (DSCN), Digital Automatic Terminal Information Service (DATIS), Digital Video Tape Recorder (DVTR) etc. are going on in various Airports of this region[5].

Though all the Airports of North Eastern Region are not equally busy, but some of them are very much busy and handling a big number of flights, passengers and cargo per day. The Appendix-5.10 will give the details of Domestic Traffic of various Airports of this region per day during 2004-05. From this, it can be seen that, Guwahati was the busiest Airport and on an average, it was handling 38 flights, 1637 passengers and 14 tonnes of cargo per day. The next busiest Airport was Agartala, which was handling 12 flights, 631 passengers and

9 tonnes of cargo per day. Dibrugarh and Bagdogra were also quite busy and on an average each of them was though handling 9 flights per day, but Bagdogra was handling much more passengers than Dibrugarh. The average number of passengers for Bagdogra was 473 and for Dibrugarh was 263 per day. The Imphal Airport was also quite busy and it was handling on an average 6 flights, 354 passengers and 5 tonnes of cargo per day. Aizawl and Dimapur Airports were handling 4 flights every day. However, though both of them were handling the same amount of 1 tonne of cargo, but Aizawl was handling more passengers i.e. 139 numbers and Dimapur was only 80 numbers per day. The Jorhat Airport was also having on an average 2 flights and 99 passengers per day. Further, details can be seen from Appendix-5.10.

The details of Domestic and International Passenger Traffic handled at various Airports of North Eastern Region during the year, 2004-05 can be seen from Appendix-5.11. From this, it can be seen that, Guwahati and Bagdogra Airports were having International Operations and were very busy throughout the year. The Guwahati Airport was having 13871 flights and was handling the highest number of 597676 passengers, 4308 tonnes of freight and 675 tonnes of mail during the year, 2004-05. Bagdogra Airport, on the other hand, was having 3148 number of flights, 172620 number of passengers, 418 tonnes of freight and 226 tonnes of mails during the same year. The Agartala Airport though not having the International operations, but was having the second highest number of 4503 flights, 230333 number of passengers, 2869 tonnes of freight and 495 tonnes of mails. Imphal was the other busy Airport, which was having 2236 flights, the fourth highest number of 129103 passengers, 1515 tonnes of freights and 351 tonnes of mails during 2004-05. The Dibrugarh Airport was though having 3121 flights, which was more than the figure of Imphal, but it handled 95837 number of passengers, which was much less than the figure of Imphal. But the most noticeable feature was that, Dibrugarh handled the second highest of 520 tonnes of mails in 2004-05. Aizawl and Dimapur Airports were also busy and each of them was having more than 1300 flights and handled 50773 and 29280 numbers of passengers respectively during that period. Further details about the embarkation and disembarkation of passengers, loading and unloading of freights and mails in each Airport of this region can be seen from Appendix-5.11.

The North Eastern Council, Shillong is not only providing money for the construction of roads and bridges and for development of Waterways and Airports, but it is also providing fund to the State Governments of this region for implementation of various schemes/ projects, primarily of regional nature, for all round development of the North East Region. Besides State Governments, the North Eastern Council also implemented many other schemes/projects, through some Autonomous Institutions and other Organisations like NEEPCO and PGCIL, CWC, CIWTC, Brahmaputra Board (BB), N.F. Railways, etc. and invested a total amount of Rs. 7483 crore since its inception up to the month of February, 2006 for the development of this region. The details of investment can be seen from Appendix-5.12.

The other forms of communication systems are Post and Telegraph and Telecommunication. Post and Telegraph is the oldest form of communication system and though it is a slow process, even then, it is meeting the needs of the people from time immemorial. However, the development of Postal Service in the North Eastern Region is comparatively slow mainly due to the geographic condition, sparse population and remoteness of the population habitats. In the North Eastern Region, more than 80 per cent population are living in the rural areas and even now, there are localities, where foot march is the only option and it takes a number of days to reach there. In spite of all these, the Postal Network of this region is gradually growing. The position of the Postal Service in different States of N.E. Region as well as in the country as a whole as on 31st March, 2008 can be seen from Appendix-5.13.

From this, it can be seen that, except Mizoram, more than 92 per cent of the Post Offices are situated in the rural areas. Amongst all the North Eastern States, postal service is comparatively better in Mizoram. The State was having 85.89 per cent of the Post Offices in rural areas and 14.11 per cent in urban areas. Further, there was one Post Office for every 2620 persons and it was covering an area of 52.19 sq. kms. Next was the position of Sikkim, where there was one Post Office for every 2751 persons and it was covering a lesser area of 34.12 sq. kms. The Postal Service in Tripura was though in the third position in terms of population, but its position was the best in terms of coverage of area. For every 3551 persons, the State was having one Post Office and it was covering the lowest area of only

10.82 sq. kms., that indicates, concentration of population is more in Tripura. The position of Manipur was also not that bad, but 98.42 per cent of its Post Offices were in the rural areas. However, the State was having one Post Office for every 3844 persons and it was serving an area of 32.08 sq. kms.

The State of Arunachal Pradesh was though having one Post Office for every 4332 persons, but each Post Office was covering the largest area of 280.08 sq. kms. This is mainly because, Arunachal Pradesh is very big and mostly hilly and more than 80 per cent of its area is under forest cover. Moreover, compare to the area, the population of the State is much less and the rural people are very much scattered. In Meghalaya, 94.24 per cent of the Post Offices were in rural areas. The State was having one Post Office for every 5738 persons and it was serving an area of 46.15 sq. kms. The Postal Service in the State of Assam was also good. Though the State was having 92.51 per cent of its Post Offices in rural areas, but for every 7250 persons, there was one Post Office and it was covering the second smallest area of 19.58 sq. km., which indicates that, population concentration is more in Assam. The Postal Service in Nagaland was not that good. The State was having one Post Office for every 8280 persons, which was the highest number in this region, and each Post Office was also covering the third largest area of 50.70 sq. kms.

However, it appears that, the overall position of the Postal Service in the North Eastern Region was not that bad as compared to the position of the country as a whole. It can be seen that, in the North Eastern Region, 92.89 per cent of the Post Offices were in the rural areas as against the all India figure of 89.37 per cent. That means, in N.E. Region, rural coverage was better. But the negative side of this was that, though there was one Post Office for every 5893 persons as against the all India figure of 6871 persons, the area served by each Post Office was much more to the extent of 35.45 sq. kms. as against the all India figure of 21.12 sq. kms. That means, the Postal density in terms of area, was more in the country as a whole than the Postal density of the North Eastern Region.

The Telecommunication is another form of communication system, which is very fast and convenient. This system is gradually reducing the workload of Postal Services, particularly the work of collection and delivery of letters, to a great extent. With the advent of

Telephone and recent development of Mobile and Internet technology, people are changing the age-old habit of writing letters in Postcards, Inlands or in Envelopes. The mobile services have brought a sea change in the communication system, which people could not even think, in a few years back. The most important aspect of Cellular Service is that, even the poor people can also afford it and the mobile set can be carried along wherever one is going and can contact or can send SMS to any one whenever he wants.

However, the growth of Telecommunication is comparatively slow in the North Eastern Region due to its geographical location and hilly terrains, which made the physical connectivity difficult. But with the development of Internet technology and cellular services, the physical barriers are gradually loosing its significance. The Cellular Mobile Services introduced in the North Eastern Region only in the year 2003. Moreover, due to security reasons, there are some restrictions in expansion of the services, particularly in the border areas, even now. Bharat Sanchar Nigam Ltd. (BSNL) is the main service provider in this region. Besides BSNL, Reliance, Airtel, Vodafone, Idea, etc. are also there and doing a good job in the field of Mobile Services. The Central Government and its implementing agency, BSNL are very much aware about the communication needs of this region. Keeping this in mind, the year 2007 was declared as the "Year of Development of Telecom Network in N.E. Region" and an ambitious expansion Plan was taken up and special importance was given for rural connectivity. To cover the rural areas, BSNL introduced the Plan of providing Village Public Telephone (VPT) for the benefit of the rural people[6]. The details of Telecommunication and Cellular Services can be seen from Appendix-5.14 (a) and 5.14 (b).

From Appendix-5.14 (a), it appears that, amongst all the North Eastern States, the position of Telephone connection (fixed) in relation to estimated households of the respective States during 2004 to 2006 was better in Mizoram and Arunachal Pradesh. In Mizoram, on an average, for every 3.62 households, there was 1 (one) telephone and 2.77 per cent of the total telephones were provided with Internet connection. In Arunachal Pradesh, 1 (one) telephone was there for every 4.02 households and 2.66 per cent of the total telephones were provided with Internet connection. The position of Meghalaya was also better, as the State was having 1 (one) telephone for every 6.52 households and Internet connection was provided for 2.20 per cent of the total telephones. The position of Nagaland was not that bad. There was 1 (one) telephone for every 8.15 households and 3.10 per cent of the total telephones were provided with Internet connection. Next was the position of Tripura, which was though having 1 (one) telephone for every 8.33 households, but 4.88 per cent of the total telephones were provided with Internet connection, which was the highest amongst all the N.E. States. The position of Manipur and Assam was though at the bottom in terms of telephone connections, but their position was much better in respect of Internet connections. In Manipur, though for every 9.37 households, there was 1 (one) telephone, but 3.38 per cent of the total telephones were provided with Internet connection, which was the second highest in this region. In Assam, for every 9.55 households, there was 1 (one) telephone and Internet connection was provided for 3.29 per cent of the total telephones, and that was the third highest. The overall position of the North Eastern Region as a whole was similar to Tripura. The region was having 1 (one) telephone for every 8.42 households and 3.28 per cent of the total telephones of this region were provided with Internet connection. The growth of Internet service in the North Eastern Region is comparatively slow because, the Internet service is a recent development and it will take some more time to understand the utility and applicability of this service and to become popular in this region.

As regards Village Public Telephone (VPT), in relation to 2001 census villages, the State of Tripura was on the top, as 94.48 per cent of its villages were provided with VPT. Assam was in the second position with 84.17 per cent. The position of Nagaland, Mizoram and Manipur were also not that bad. In Nagaland, 77.30 per cent of the Villages were provided with VPT, whereas in Mizoram, it was 74.79 per cent and in Manipur, 66.29 per cent of the villages were provided with VPT. The position of Meghalaya and Arunachal Pradesh were rather poor. In the State of Meghalaya, though 46.17 per cent of its villages were provided with VPT, but in Arunachal Pradesh, only 19.78 per cent of its villages were having VPT facilities.

This was perhaps due to the topographic condition of the State. However, the overall position of the N.E. Region was not that bad, as 71.22 per cent of its villages were provided with Village Public Telephone facility.

The Cellular Mobile service at that period was in its initial stage and only two service providers viz. Reliance and BSNL were there. At the initial stage, the progress of Mobile Service in the North Eastern Region was also slow due to its geographic condition as well as its security considerations. The initial position of the BSNL Mobile Service in relation to the projected population of the respective years and States of this region can be seen from Appendix-5.14 (a). From this, it appears that, the Mobile Service in the States of Mizoram, Tripura and Assam was slightly better. In Mizoram, it can be seen that, on an average, for every 30 persons, there was a Mobile. In Tripura, one Mobile was there for every 90 persons and in Assam, for every 125 persons, there was a Mobile. The position of Nagaland and Manipur was not that good. In Nagaland, every 538 persons were having one Mobile and in Manipur, for every 890 persons, there was 1 (one) mobile. But the BSNL Mobile Service in the States of Arunachal Pradesh and Meghalaya was very much in its initial stage. Moreover, at the beginning, Reliance Mobile Service was there in Meghalaya and people were taking Reliance connections.

However, the situation gradually started changing and one more service provider viz. Bharti Airtel came to North Eastern Region. Recently, Vodafone has started its activities and Tata Indicom as well as Idea, are also planning to come to this region. This has created a competitive market and people can now expect a better service, as competition always improves the quality. The Mobile Phone has now become very much popular in this region and the growth of this sector is quite fast and that has created a negative growth in the Wireline subscribers. Now-a-days, people are surrendering the Land Line Phones and going for the mobiles. A clear picture of the number of Mobile and Wireline subscribers in different Circles of the North Eastern Region, as on March and April, 2008 can be seen from Appendix-5.14 (b).

From this, it can be seen that, there were four types of Mobile Services viz. Bharti Airtel, Reliance, Aircel and BSNL were available in North East Circle-I, comprising of Meghalaya, Mizoram and Tripura, and also in Assam Circle, but in North East Circle-II, comprising of Arunachal Pradesh, Manipur and Nagaland, only BSNL Service was available. Further, it appears that, in N.E. Circle-I, there was a growth of 5.01 per cent in the total number of mobile subscribers within March to April, 2008 and that raised the Mobile density to 24.48, on the basis of projected population of 2008. That means, for every 100 persons, there were 24.48 mobiles. In other words, it can be said that, 1 (one) Mobile was there for every 4.08 persons. In this Circle, Aircel subscribers were more and it accounted for 34.19 per cent of the total subscribers followed by Bharti Airtel with 29.80 per cent, Reliance with 19.04 per cent and BSNL with 16.97 per cent as on April, 2008. However, the number of Wireline subscribers in this Circle went down by 0.31 per cent within a month.

In Assam Circle, the growth of mobile subscribers was 4.83 per cent within March to April, 2008 and that raised the mobile density to 13.68 or in other words, 1 (one) mobile was there for every 7.33 persons. In Assam Circle also, Aircel subscribers were more and it accounted for 29.29 per cent of the total subscribers followed by BSNL with 24.78 per cent, Reliance with 23.47 per cent and Bharti Airtel with 22.46 per cent as on April, 2008. In this Circle, the Wireline subscribers also showed a negative growth of 0.86 per cent during March to April, 2008.

In North East Circle-II, BSNL was the only Cellular Service provider and perhaps due to that, the Mobile density was also the lowest there. The mobile density was only 5.70 or in other words, it can be said that, there was 1 (one) mobile for every 17.54 persons. In case of Wireline subscribers, it appears that, the number of Wireline subscribers decreased with a rate of 2.27 per cent and that was the highest negative growth during March to April, 2008 in this region.

The overall position of Cellular Service in the North Eastern Region was not satisfactory. It was much behind the overall position of the country. The mobile density of the N.E. Region as a whole was only 14.26 as compared to the overall density of 22.86 of the country, on the basis of projected population of 2008. In other words, it can be said that, there was 1 (one) mobile for every 7.01 persons in the North Eastern Region as against the all India figure of 4.37 persons. However, it is seen that the growth of Cellular Service caused a recession in the Wireline Service (fixed) and as a result, the number of Wireline subscribers were gradually decreasing all over the country. This decrease was a bit faster in the North Eastern Region as it could be seen that, the rate of decrease was 0.94 per cent in this region as against the all India rate of 0.52 per cent during March to April, 2008.

Further details can be seen from Appendix-5.14 (a) and Appendix-5.14 (b).

The other mode of communication system is Radio and Doordarshan. This is not only informative but educative and entertaining also. Now-a-days, so many important things are happening everywhere, in every aspect of our life, and all over the world. Through Radio and Television, we can keep ourselves updated about these happenings immediately after its occurrence or some of the things we can even listen through Radio or can watch live through Television. In the present world, Radio and Television have become a part of life and people cannot think with it. In some of the rural areas, though people cannot watch Television due to power problem, but they are keeping Radio sets for their information and entertainment. The Government is also taking interest on this aspect and proving Community Listening Sets in the rural areas for the benefit of the rural people. The details of Radio and Television Network in different States of the North Eastern Region as on January, 2006 can be seen from Appendix-5.15.

In the North Eastern Region, Arunachal Pradesh is the biggest State in terms of area. It was having a total of 5 Radio Stations and was broadcasting 17 languages and dialects. On the other hand, though the State was having only 1 (one) Doordarshan Kendra, but it was having the highest number of 49 Relay Kendras, mainly due to its geographic condition and scattered population habitats. The State of Assam was having the maximum of 11 numbers of Radio Stations and was broadcasting the highest of 28 languages and dialects. The State was also having the highest of 3 numbers of Doordarshan Kendras, but the second highest of 29 numbers of Relay Kendras. The position of Manipur and Sikkim was exactly the same. Each of these two States was having only one Radio Station and one Doordarshan Kendra. The position of Meghalaya was better than others. This State was having 6 Radio Stations and was broadcasting 8 languages and dialects and also having 2 Doordarshan Kendras with 10 Relay Kendras. The position of Mizoram and Tripura was the same. Each of the States was having 3 (three) Radio Stations and 1 (one) Doordarshan Kendra. The State of Nagaland was though having only 4 Radio Stations, but it was broadcasting the second highest of 18 numbers of languages and dialects. The State was also having 1 (one) Doordarshan Kendra with third highest of 14 numbers of Relay Kendras. However, the N.E. Region as a whole was having 34 Radio Stations and was broadcasting 6 main languages and 60 dialects. The region was also having 11 Doordarshan Kendras with 136 Relay Kendras. Further details can be seen from Appendix-5.15.

The Newspapers and Periodicals are the other form of communication system, which record all kinds of news and events that are happening in the world over day by day and by reading these, one can keep himself or herself informed about all these happenings sitting at home. The Newspapers and Periodicals not only generate interest, but also extend the mental horizon of people and make them fit to participate usefully in an educated and cultured society. Moreover, the number of Newspapers and Periodicals and the extent of their circulation also determine the level of any educated society. In this respect, some of the States of the North Eastern Region are lagging a bit behind. There are so many reasons for this, but the most significant ones are the geographic condition, lack of infrastructure and the educational standard. However, Appendix-5.16 (a) and Appendix-5.16 (b) will give a clear picture of the type and number of registered Newspapers and Periodicals and their languages, that were available in different States of this region as on 2004-05.

From this, it appears that, Assam was having the highest number of 476 Newspapers and Periodicals and out of these, 239 were in Assamese, 94 were in Bengali, 63 were in English, 14 were in Hindi and the number of Dailies were 50, Weeklies were 191 and Monthlies were 108. The State of Manipur was having the second highest number of 153 Newspapers and Periodicals and out of these, 18 were in English, 43 were Bi-lingual and 79 others. The State was having the highest of 55 numbers of Dailies and 42 Monthlies. Mizoram came in the third position having 134 numbers of Newspapers and Periodicals and out of these, 4 were in English, 10 were Bi-lingual and the remaining were others. There were 43 Dailies, 14 Tri/Bi-weeklies, 36 Weeklies and 24 Monthlies in the State. Tripura was in the fourth position having 111 Newspapers and Periodicals, of which 24 were Dailies, 59 Weeklies and 13 Monthlies. These were mostly in Bengali i.e. 84 were in Bengali, 13 were in English and 9 were Bi-lingual.

Meghalaya was having comparatively less to the extent of only 76 numbers of Newspapers and Periodicals. Out of these, 21 were in

English, 13 were Bi-lingual and 39 others. There were 5 Dailies, 33 Weeklies and 17 Monthlies in the State. The availability of Newspapers and Periodicals in the States of Sikkim, Nagaland and Arunachal Pradesh was very less. Sikkim was though having 37 numbers of Newspapers and Periodicals, but there was only 1 Daily, 2 Tri/Bi-weeklies and 27 Weeklies. Only 10 of these were in English, 2 were Bi-lingual, 1 was in Hindi and the remaining in other languages. Nagaland was having only 17 Newspapers and Periodicals and these were mostly in English. There were 5 Dailies, 9 Weeklies and only 1 Monthly in the State. The State of Arunachal Pradesh was having the lowest number of only 13 Newspapers and Periodicals and out of these, 10 were in English. There were 4 Dailies and an equal number of Weeklies were available in the State. Further, details can be seen from Appendix-5.16 (a) and Appendix-5.16 (b).

NOTES

1. *Manorama Year Book, 1984*, Manorama Publishing House, Kottayam, India, p. 516.
2. *Report of Working Group* on Transport Sector for preparation of perspective plan in North Eastern Region up to 2000 AD, NEC Secretariat, August, 1987 p. 7.
3. *3rd Sectoral Summit* of the North Eastern Council, Shillong, held in Guwahati from 9th to 11th March, 2007.
4. *5th Sectoral Summit* of the North Eastern Council, Shillong, held at Aizawl on 18th April and 11th May, 2007.
5. *ibid.*
6. *7th special Sectoral Summit* of the North Eastern Council, Shillong, held at Kohima on 31st July and 1st August, 2007.

6

Educational Scenario

The word education has a very wide meaning and implication and therefore, it is really very difficult to define it by a single definition or two. From time immemorial, philosophers, educationists, scholars, and many others tried to define education in their own ways. Aristotle defined education as a "creation of a sound mind in a sound body". John Stuart Mill opined that "whatever helps to shape the human being to make what he is, or hinder him from being what he is not—is part of his education". According to Adams, education is "a conscious and deliberate process in which one personality acts upon another in order to modify the development of the other by the communication and manipulation of knowledge". Dewey said, education is "the development of all those capacities in the individual which will enable him to control his environment and fulfil his possibilities". To Derry education means "the full and harmonious development and artistically effective expression of all the seven faculties or powers of man (senses, imagination, mechanical and intellectual memory, intellect, emotions and will), to be achieved, by the pupils' own personal practice or conscious exercise of each specific power, under the guidance of teachers, and the help of divine grace, in preparation for the highest and happiest life, here and hereafter". According to Gandhiji education means "all-round drawing out of the best in child and man-body, mind and spirit". Charles E. Skinner said "education is a phase of social process which is fostered by society for the purpose of fitting its members for life in the group". According to Nunn education is "the complete development of individuality so that he can make an original contribution to human life according to his best capacity".

From the above, it appears that whatever may be the definition of education or whatever may be the individual perception on education, but it is a fact that education is the means of development of human body and mind and enrichment of knowledge for leading a healthy life and building up of a prosperous society or nation. In a fast changing world, education is undoubtedly a dynamic force, which requires continuous updation, reorganization and reconstruction of experience and integration of activities, both formal and non-formal. Apart from formal education, which is required for career building, there are many other aspects that are integrally related to self-development. With the new challenges of time, along with formal education, one has to be always alert about other aspects of self-improvement, which include body language, personality development, time management, creativity, communication skills and convincing capacity etc. besides development of the very vital aspect of positive attitude.

Education is primarily a State subject, though it is included in the Concurrent List of the Constitution of our country. The Central Government has little to do with it, particularly at the primary level. The Central Government comes into the picture in secondary education and in the higher education and research, the Central Government has the higher role. However, due to sharing of power between Central and State Governments and also because of the States themselves differing in their needs, resources, policies and in administrative mechanisms, the educational scenario of our country shows wide regional disparities. It is in this context, a National Policy on Education (NPE) was formulated on the basis of the recommendations of the Education Commission under Dr. D.C. Kothari and it was adopted by the Parliament in 1968. This policy stressed the following objectives: (i) free and compulsory education up to the age of 14, (ii) improved status, emoluments and education of teachers, (iii) three-language formula and development of regional languages, (iv) equalization of education of science and research, (v) development of education for agriculture and industry, (vi) improvement in quality and production of inexpensive text-books, and (vii) investment of 6 per cent of national income in education[1].

Further, as laid down in the National Policy on Education (NPE), the Central Advisory Board of Education adopted a unanimous resolution recommending that, the new pattern of 10 +2 +3 should be introduced all over the country during the Fifth Plan period i.e. during 1974-79. Moreover, the Vice Chancellors' Conference held on 30th September, 1975 decided that, 10+2 should be the pre-university level and the new enriched 3-year first degree course should be launched from the academic year, 1979-80[2]. Thus, the new pattern of education envisaged an integrated course of fifteen years' duration leading to first degree. The first ten years in school covering Primary, Middle and High School or Secondary, the next two years in Higher Secondary Schools, Intermediate or Pre-university Colleges, as the case may be and the remaining three years in Colleges leading to the Bachelor degree in general courses like Arts, Science and Commerce. But in case of Bachelor degree in Engineering, Medical and other technical subjects, the pattern and the duration are different than that of the general courses. However, the new pattern of School education could be adopted by different States and Union Territories of our country at different points of time and in the meanwhile, many researches have been done and various ways and measures have been taken to enrich the educational system of our country.

The significant step towards this direction was universalisation of education. In this connection, the Government of India set-up a Working Group and in August, 1980, the Group submitted its report indicating the policies to be adopted in the eighties for equalizing educational opportunities among all sections of the people. The Working Group further pointed out that, "education is a crucial input in the development of human resources ...... and that it should find its rightful place as a basic input in national planning. Investments in education should reflect its pivotal role"[3]. The programme of universalisation of elementary education became one of the two topmost priority programmes in the field of education, the other being the Adult Education Programme.

For implementing the programme of universalisation of elementary education, the States adopted a number of measures for increasing enrolment in schools, retaining the children in the schools up to class-VIII. These include providing mid-day meals, un-graded school system at the primary stage, policy of no detention till class-VIII but with comprehensive evaluation, multiple point entry in formal schools, introduction of play-way methods in class I-II with the adoption of dynamic teaching, teacher improvement and above all, reform of primary curriculum including socially useful productive work as recommended by the Ishwarbhai Patel Committee[4]. Moreover, the Constitution of our Country provides for free and compulsory education upto the age of 14 and the States are adopting this in accordance with their convenience. The students belonging to the Scheduled Castes and Scheduled Tribes are getting free education all through in all the States and Union Territories. In addition, they are also provided with funds for books and other accessories and in certain States with free boarding[5].

The National Council of Educational Research and Training (NCERT) established in 1961 assists the Union Ministry of Education in the formulation and implementation of its policies in school education. The Council also works in co-operation with State Education Departments and Universities and with other Institutions for promotion of education and maintains close contacts with International Organizations. Moreover, the Council developed new curricula and syllabi for class I to XII in the new (10 + 2 + 3) pattern of education and suggests modifications/improvements in this respect from time to time. The Central Board of Secondary Education (CBSE), New Delhi introduced the new pattern of education from 1975. The first examination for class-X took place in 1977 and for class-XII in 1979[6]. Now-a-days, many of the Schools of different States are following the CBSE course.

Kendriya Vidyalaya Sangathan (KVS) i.e. the scheme of Central Schools was approved by the Government of India in November, 1962. The main objective of this scheme is to encourage the growth of Secondary Schools having a common syllabus and medium of instruction and for providing uniform educational facilities throughout the country for the children of transferable Central Government employees including Defence personnel. The Sangathan has been making considerable efforts for improving the professional competence of all categories of teaching and supervisory staff of Kendriya Vidyalayas by organizing in-service education courses for them. Moreover, to make the Vidyalayas as Model Institutions, many educational reforms ranging from improving instructional techniques to evaluation procedures have been adopted[7].

The National Adult Education Programme (NAEP) was inaugurated on 2nd October i.e. on Gandhi Jayanti Day in 1978. In an estimate made in the year, 1980, it was found that more than 230 million people of our country above the age of 15 years cannot read or write. Therefore, the National Adult Education Programme started with an objective of covering at least 65 million illiterate people in the age group of 15 to 35 years within a period of 5 years i.e. by 1983-84. The most important aspect of this programme is to impart literacy in one hand, and to keep literacy alive among the impartees on the other. Keeping this in mind, the programme was made to cover a four-fold objectives, which are (i) Literacy with assured follow up, (ii) Conventional functional literacy supportive of a dominant development programme, (iii) Literacy with learning-cum-action groups, and (iv) Literacy for the formation of organizations of the poor[8].

Sarva Shiksha Abhiyan (SSA)

For universalisation of elementary education, the Government of India launched another programme called Sarva Shiksha Abhiyan (SSA). It is actually an effort to universalise elementary education by community-ownership of the school system. This is in response to the demand for quality basic education all over the country. The SSA programme is also an attempt to provide an opportunity for improving human capabilities to all children, through provision of community-owned quality education in a mission mode. The Sarva Shiksha Abhiyan (SSA) has two aspects—(i) It provides a wide convergent framework for implementation of Elementary Education Schemes, and (ii) It is also a programme with budget provision for strengthening vital areas to achieve universalisation of elementary education.

The main objective of Sarva Shiksha Abhiyan is to provide useful and relevant elementary education for all children in the age group of 6 to 14 years by 2010. Besides this, SSA also has another goal to bridge social, regional and gender gaps, with the active participation of the community in the management of schools. The special feature of the Sarva Shiksha Abhiyan is that, it allows States/UTs to have their own management structures, respecting the diversity that exists in these structures across the States. This, however, does not mean that decentralization will not be monitored. In fact, the effort is to empower schools to take their own decisions, within the overall management context of a State/UT. For this purpose, the States will have to set-up the State Level Implementation Society and the State Level Implementation Societies have to have effective monitoring and operational support units. The Sarva Shiksha Abhiyan will also have a community-based monitoring system. The Educational Management Information System (EMIS) will incorporate provision for correlation of school level data with community-based information from micro-planning and surveys. Besides this, every school will have a notice board showing all the grants received by the school and the details thereof.

The Sarva Shiksha Abhiyan also emphasizes quality education and, therefore, it is necessary to periodically monitor and evaluate all aspects of pedagogical inputs like curriculum and textbook development, teacher training packages and classroom processes, amongst others. In this effort, the role of community assumes paramount significance. The community leaders and groups need to be sensitized on the issues related to monitoring of children's progress and other quality related school activities[9].

Girls' Education

The Government of India, since beginning, has given high priority for the education of the girls. In spite of that, the disparity between the education of boys and girls still persists. However, the National Commitment to provide free and compulsory education to all children in the age group of 6 to 14 years has now become a Fundamental Rights of every child in our country after the passing of the Constitution (86th Amendment) Act in December, 2002[10]. The Sarva Shiksha Abhiyan or the 'Education for All' programme also recognizes that, ensuring girls' education requires changes not only in the education system, but also in societal norms and attitudes. Therefore, a two-pronged gender strategy has been adopted to make the education system responsive to the needs of the girls through targeted interventions which serve as a pull factor to enhance access and retention of girls in schools and on the other hand, to generate a community demand for girls' education through training and mobilization[11].

The National Programme for Education of Girls for Elementary Level (NPEGEL), launched in September, 2003 is an integral but distinct component of the Sarva Shiksha Abhiyan. It provides additional provisions for enhancing the education of underprivileged/ disadvantaged girls at elementary level through more intense community mobilization, the development of model schools in clusters, gender sensitization of teachers, development of gender sensitive learning materials, early child care and education facilities and provision of need based incentives like escorts, stationery, work books and uniforms, etc. for girls.

Kasturba Gandhi Balika Vidyalaya (KGBV) is another scheme launched in July, 2004 for setting up residential schools at upper primary level for girls belonging predominantly to the SC, ST, OBC and minority communities. This scheme is being implemented in educationally backward blocks of the country where the female rural literacy is below the national average and gender gap in literacy is above the national average. The special feature of this scheme is that, it provides for a minimum reservation of 75 per cent of the seats for girls belonging to SC, ST, OBC or minority communities and priority for the remaining 25 per cent, is accorded to girls from families below poverty line. This scheme covers 24 States and the Union Territory of Dadra and Nagar Haveli. Six of the North Eastern States viz. Assam, Arunachal Pradesh, Manipur, Meghalaya, Mizoram and Tripura are amongst the 24 States of our country. The Government of India, up to March, 2007, sanctioned 2180 KGBVs and out of that, 1226 KGBVs are reported to have been made operational and 80853 girls enrolled in them[12].

The initial educational scenario of the North East India is not very clear as no systematic chronicle on this is available. However, from the available information, it was found that, in olden days the system of Gurukul and Sanskrit Tools were prevalent in Assam, Manipur and Tripura. Later on, it was further found that, the Foreign Missionaries who came in this region in the middle of the nineteenth century were the pioneers in propagating education. The Welsh Presbyterian Missionaries first established primary schools in 1841 in Khasi Hills. The Baptist Missionaries then started primary schools in Garo Hills in 1873 and the present Christian Girls' High School in Tura, established in 1882, was one of the earliest institutions established by this Missionaries. The Catholic Missionaries who came to these hills later, played an important role in case of higher education and established the first high school viz. Shillong Government Boys' High School in 1880[13]. Manipur was an independent Princely State till 1891. But when the English Missionaries were permitted to enter into Manipur, the King Chandra Kiriti, gave his consent for establishing a school at Imphal and accordingly the school was established in 1885. However, female education in those days was not encouraged in Manipur. But the situation gradually changed and in 1899, a girls' educational institution was first established and 12 girls were enrolled[14]. Since then, the educational scenario of the North East India started changing and during British period, several educational institutions were also established in different places of this region.

However, even after all these, the educational facilities in many parts of this region were very poor till independence of our country. Moreover, the situation could not make much improvement immediately after independence. The growth of education in the North Eastern States, in true sense, and in a systematic way, started only with the beginning of Planning era in 1951-52. The State Governments got the opportunity of identifying their needs, the resources available and the deficiencies, and could formulate their Plans accordingly for the development of education in their respective States. The States so far, have passed through Tenth Five Year Plans and many Annual Plans and now stepped in to the Eleventh Five Year Plan and made considerable progress in the field of education in all these years. The number of educational institutions and enrolments have increased, literacy has gone up and many technical and vocational institutions have come up. In other words, the overall educational scenario has changed manifold, though many more miles are yet to go.

The position of various educational institutions as on 30th September, 2004 in different States of North East India and the country as a whole can be see from Appendix-6.1. From this, it can also be found that a total number of 74962 institutions were there in the eight North Eastern States including Sikkim, which was about 6 per cent of the total number of 1281953 institutions of our country. These numbers further showed that, on an average, there were 1.81 number of educational institutions per thousand population in the North

Eastern Region as against 1.17 number of educational institutions per thousand population of our country, calculated on the basis of projected population for the year 2004 as shown in Appendix-3.7. However, all the North Eastern States were not having all kinds of educational institutions and also not in the same proportion.

In case of Primary/Junior Basic Schools, amongst all the North Eastern States, the position of Meghalaya was on the top. It was having 23.31 number of Primary/Junior Basic Schools per ten thousand population, followed by Mizoram having 15.46 numbers. Then came the position of Arunachal Pradesh and Sikkim having almost the same numbers of 11.63 and 11.62 Primary/Junior Basic Schools per ten thousand population of their respective States. The position of Assam and Manipur was closer having 10.71 and 10.41 numbers of Primary/Junior Basic Schools per ten thousand population of their respective States. The position of Nagaland and Tripura was on the lower side having 6.69 and 5.31 numbers respectively. The overall position of the North Eastern Region was however better having 10.95 numbers of Primary/Junior Basic Schools per ten thousand population, than the all India figure of 7.04.

In case of Middle/Senior Basic Schools, the position of Mizoram was on the top having 9.80 numbers of Middle/Senior Basic Schools per ten thousand population. This followed by Meghalaya having 7.01 and then by Arunachal Pradesh having 4.20 numbers of Middle/Senior Basic Schools per ten thousand population of their respective states. The position of Manipur and Sikkim was closer with 3.39 and 3.14 respectively. The position of Tripura, Assam and Nagaland was on the lower side having 2.99, 2.90 and 2.11 numbers of Middle/Senior Basic Schools per ten thousand population of their respective states. In this case also, the overall position of North Eastern Region was better having 3.34 numbers of Middle/Senior Basic Schools per ten thousand population, than the figure of 2.52 of the country as a whole.

In case of High/Post Basic Schools, Mizoram was again on the top having 4.65 numbers of High/Post Basic Schools per ten thousand population. This followed by Meghalaya with 2.51 and then by Manipur with 2.40 numbers of High/Post Basic Schools per ten thousand population of the respective States. Amongst the other five States, the position of Sikkim was slightly better with 1.86, then came the position of Assam with 1.65, followed by Nagaland with 1.48,

Tripura with 1.22 and Arunachal Pradesh with 1.15 numbers of High/ Post Basic Schools per ten thousand population of the respective States. However, the overall position of North Eastern Region was better with 1.76 than the position of the country as a whole having 0.93 number of High/Post Basic Schools per ten thousand population.

The position of Pre-Degree Junior College/Higher Secondary Schools was slightly different. In this case, it is found that the position of Sikkim was on the top with 8.50 numbers of Pre-Degree Junior College/Higher Secondary Schools per lakh population of the State. This followed by Tripura with 7.27, Mizoram with 6.99 and Arunachal Pradesh with 6.62 numbers of Pre-Degree Junior College/Higher Secondary Schools per lakh population of the respective States. After that, came the position of Manipur having 4.82, followed by Meghalaya with 3.19, Assam with 2.65 and then by Nagaland with 1.89 numbers of Pre-Degree Junior College/Higher Secondary Schools per lakh population of the respective States. This however, does not mean that, the availability of educational facilities up to the level of Pre-Degree/Higher Secondary were less in the States like Assam, Manipur, Meghalaya and Nagaland. Actually, in these States, more number of Colleges were there, which included the Pre-Degree/ Higher Secondary level of education also.

The management of educational institutions is another important aspect. The Appendix-6.2 will give a clear picture of the category of management of different type of educational institutions in the States of North Eastern Region as well as in the country as a whole as on 30th September, 2004. From this, it is seen that, the Primary/Junior Basic Schools in Assam, Arunachal Pradesh, Nagaland, Manipur, Mizoram and Sikkim were mostly managed by the Government. But in Tripura, 69.37 per cent of the Primary/Junior Basic Schools were managed by the Local Bodies and 29.22 per cent by the Government. The position of Meghalaya was again different from others. In Meghalaya, 43.39 per cent of the Primary/Junior Basic Schools were managed by the Government, 42.30 per cent were Private Aided and 14.31 per cent were Private Unaided. The position of the country as a whole was also more or less similar to Meghalaya. It is seen that, 43.33 per cent of the Primary/Junior Basic Schools of our country were managed by the Government, 46.87 per cent by Local Bodies and the remaining were Private Aided and Unaided.

In case of Middle/Senior Basic Schools, it appears that most of the institutions in Arunachal Pradesh, Assam, Tripura and Sikkim were managed by the Government. In Mizoram and Nagaland also, almost 60 per cent of the institutions were managed by the Government. The position of Manipur and Meghalaya was again different. In Manipur, it is seen that, 36.94 per cent of the Middle/ Senior Basic Schools were managed by the Government and 51.74 per cent were Private Unaided. Whereas, in Meghalaya, only 3.18 per cent institutions were managed by the Government and 55.71 per cent were Private Aided and 41.10 per cent were Private Unaided. However, the position of the country as a whole showed that, 42.96 per cent of the Middle/Senior Basic Schools were managed by the Government and 29.24 per cent were by the Local Bodies. Whereas, 6.41 per cent of the institutions were Private Aided and 21.39 per cent were Private Unaided.

The position of High/Post Basic Schools showed that, most of these institutions in Arunachal Pradesh, Tripura and Sikkim, and also more than 60 per cent of them in Assam were managed by the Government. The position of Mizoram, Nagaland, Manipur and Meghalaya was different and it appears that, 42.70 per cent in Mizoram, 34.52 per cent in Nagaland, 31.29 per cent in Manipur and only 3.33 per cent of the High/Post Basic Schools in Meghalaya were managed by the Government. Private Aided High/Post Basic Schools were more in Nagaland and Meghalaya having 65.48 per cent and 61.49 per cent respectively. Whereas, Private Unaided High/Post Basic Schools were more in Mizoram with 53.03 per cent and in Manipur with 51.36 per cent. The position of the country as a whole showed that, 31.66 per cent of High/Post Basic Schools were managed by the Government, 11.30 per cent by the Local Bodies and an equal percentage of 28.52 High/Post Basic Schools were Private Aided and Private Unaided.

In case of Pre-Degree Junior College/Higher Secondary Schools, it appears that more than 85 per cent of these institutions in Arunachal Pradesh, Assam, Tripura and Sikkim were managed by the Government. In Manipur, Government managed institutions were 46.61 per cent and in Mizoram, Meghalaya and Nagaland, these were 29.85 per cent, 27.50 per cent and 20.93 per cent respectively. Private Aided Pre-Degree Junior College/Higher Secondary Schools were more in Nagaland having 79.07 per cent and in Meghalaya it was 50 per cent. Whereas, the Private Unaided institutions were more in Mizoram with 59.70 per cent and in Manipur with 53.39 per cent. The position of Pre-Degree Junior College/Higher Secondary Schools in our country showed that, 36.08 per cent of these institutions were managed by the Government and only 1.09 per cent by the Local Bodies. But in case of Private Schools, it appears that, 31.04 per cent of Pre-Degree Junior College/Higher Secondary Schools were Private Aided and almost an equal percentage of 31.79 were Private Unaided. Further, details can be seen from Appendix-6.2.

The enrolment position as on 30th September, 2004 in different educational institutions of North Eastern States and of our country can be seen from Appendix-6.3. It is seen that, amongst all the North Eastern States, the percentage of students in Meghalaya was the highest, that means, 42.14 per cent of the estimated population of 2004 of the State were enrolled in different educational institutions. The position of Tripura was the second highest with 37.81 per cent followed by Manipur with 33.62 per cent, Sikkim with 32.21 per cent and then by Arunachal Pradesh with 30.51 per cent of the estimated population of 2004 of the respective States. The enrolment percentage was comparatively less in other States. In Nagaland, it was 25.76 per cent, in Assam, it was 25.62 per cent and in Mizoram, it was 22.93 per cent of the estimated population of 2004 of the respective States. However, the enrolment percentage in all the states as well as the overall enrolment figure of 28.26 per cent of the North Eastern Region as a whole was higher than the overall enrolment figure of 21.79 per cent of the estimated population of 2004 of the country as a whole.

The State of Meghalaya showed another distinct characteristic. This is the only State amongst all the North Eastern States, where the enrolment percentage of Girls was more than the Boys. It is seen that, out of the total enrolment, the percentage of Girls was 50.83 and the percentage of Boys was 49.17. The percentage of enrolment of Boys in all other North Eastern States was more. The State of Arunachal Pradesh was having the highest enrolment percentage for Boys and lowest for Girls with 55.50 and 44.50 per cent respectively. This followed by Assam with 52.32 and 47.68 per cent and then by Tripura with 52.21 and 47.79 per cent, Manipur with 52.12 and 47.88

per cent, Nagaland with 51.95 and 48.05 per cent, Mizoram with 51.78 and 48.22 per cent and finally by Sikkim with 50.73 and 49.27 per cent respectively. The enrolment percentage for Boys in the North Eastern Region as a whole was 52.05, which was less than the all India figure of 54.89 per cent for Boys. But the enrolment percentage for Girls of the North Eastern Region showed a better picture with 47.95 than the all India figure for Girls of 45.11 per cent. That means, proportionately, more number of Girls of the North East India were attending schools/colleges than the proportional figure for the Girls of the country as a whole. This is definitely a good sign pertaining to the Girls education in the North Eastern Region.

The position of institution-wise number of Teachers as on 30th September, 2004 in all the States of North East India and the country as a whole can be seen from Appendix-6.4. The Appendix-6.5 will give some of the very vital indicators like Student-Teacher Ratio, number of Female Teachers per 100 Male Teachers and percentage of Trained Teachers in different educational institutions of the North Eastern Region and in the country as a whole as on 30th September, 2004. These indicators are very much helpful for getting a clear picture of the educational scenario of a State or of a country.

From Appendix-6.5, it appears that, amongst all the North Eastern States, Mizoram was having the best Student-Teacher Ratio in all types of educational institutions starting from Primary/Junior Basic Schools to Pre-Degree Junior College/Higher Secondary Schools and even in Higher Educational Institutions also. This Ratio ranges from the lowest of 8 in Middle/Senior Basic Schools to the highest of 17 in Primary/Junior Basic Schools. That means, in the educational institutions of Mizoram, the number of Students per Teacher were less and as such, each Teacher could give more attention to everyone and this definitely helped in improving the quality of education of every Student.

The Student-Teacher Ratio in Sikkim, Nagaland and Manipur was also good. In Sikkim, it was ranging from 11 in High/Post Basic Schools to 22 in Primary/Junior Basic Schools, in Nagaland, it was from 16 in Middle/Senior Basic Schools to 35 in Pre-Degree Junior College/Higher Secondary Schools and in Manipur, it was from 23 in Pre-Degree Junior College/Higher Secondary Schools to 30 in Primary/Junior Basic Schools. The Student-Teacher Ratio in Assam, Meghalaya and in

Tripura showed some wide variation. In Assam, it was ranging from 16 in Middle/Senior Basic Schools to 42 in Primary/Junior Basic Schools. Whereas, in Meghalaya, it varied from 16, both in Middle/Senior Basic Schools and Pre-Degree Junior College/Higher Secondary Schools to 44 in Primary/Junior Basic Schools and in Tripura, it was ranging from 15 in Middle/Senior Basic Schools to 54 in Primary/Junior Basic Schools. This showed that, in Assam, Meghalaya and Tripura, less number of Teachers were there in the lower level Schools. The Student-Teacher Ratio in Arunachal Pradesh, was though not very good, but it showed some uniformity and it was ranging from 28 in High/Post Basic Schools to 34 in Primary/Junior Basic Schools. However, the Student-Teacher Ratio in all the educational institutions of the North Eastern Region was comparatively better than the position of the country as a whole. In North Eastern Region, it was ranging from 16 in Middle/Senior Basic Schools to 39 in Primary/Junior Basic Schools. Whereas, in India, it was varying from 32 in High/Post Basic Schools to 46 in Primary/Junior Basic Schools. The Student-Teacher Ratio showed that, in general, the lower level educational institutions were having comparatively less number of Teachers than other institutions.

The Appendix-6.5 also indicates some other important aspects of Teachers. From this, it can be seen that, in the States like Meghalaya, Manipur, Mizoram, Nagaland and Sikkim, the number of Female Teachers were quite high in almost all types of educational institutions. In case of Primary/Junior Basic Schools, the number of Female Teachers were equal to the number of Male Teachers in Sikkim. And in Mizoram, it was almost equal, that means, there were 98 Female Teachers per 100 Male Teachers in Mizoram. In case of Pre-Degree Junior College/Higher Secondary Schools, the number of Female Teachers were even more than the number of Male Teachers in the States like Meghalaya and Nagaland. This number was 118 per 100 Male Teachers in Meghalaya and 105 per 100 Male Teachers in Nagaland. However, amongst all the North Eastern States, the number of Female Teachers were comparatively less in the States of Arunachal Pradesh, Assam and Tripura. But the position of the country as a whole showed another unique aspect of the Female Teachers. It can be seen that, in all types of educational institutions starting from Primary/Junior Basic Schools to Pre-Degree Junior College/Higher

Secondary Schools, the average number of Female Teachers were ranging from 60 to 64 per 100 Male Teachers of the respective educational institutions. This indicates that, considerable number of Female Teachers, were there in the educational institutions of our country. Further, details can be seen from Appendix-6.5.

The role of Teachers, particularly at the lower levels of education, is immense as they are the makers of the future generation. In other words, it can be said that, Teachers are the architects of building up the educational foundation and the character of the younger generation and also making them aware about their future and at the same time inspiring them to face the challenges of life. Each young mind is like a ball of clay and a Teacher can give the shape of that ball as he likes and as his knowledge permits. In this connection, John Adams describes the teacher as a "maker of man". Teacher is the torch-bearer of race and guardian of the future of mankind. He is essentially a nation builder and the key-man on whom depends the future of the child and the mankind. He also plays an important role in shaping and moulding the personality of a child[15]. It is of course a fact that, all young minds are not equally capable of receiving and retaining the things, whatever they have been taught, but it is true that, quality teaching will definitely improve the quality of every student. However, the quality teaching depends on merit and educational standard of the Teachers and at the same time, their training, time to time. Periodical training and re-training of the Teachers are not only essential for improving their teaching capacity, but also for keeping them abreast with the new methods of teaching and also with the changes, that are being taking place world over day by day.

In this connection Rabindra Nath Tagore said, "A teacher can never truly teach unless he is still learning himself". He further said, "The whole world is a School for me and I am the student of every one, and in various ways, I am learning new things day and night". To emphasize the quality of a teacher, Martin said, "In order to be a good teacher one should be a good student". John Ruskin said, "Education is the leading of human souls to what is best, and making what is best out of them; and these two objects are always attainable together, and by the same means. The training which makes men happiest in themselves also makes them most serviceable to others". It is true that, there is no end of knowledge or learning. One can improve upon his knowledge by coming in contact with persons of more experience and ability, and he should not feel shy to learn from them.

The position of Trained Teachers in the North Eastern States as well as in the country as a whole, as on 30th September, 2004 can be seen from Appendix-6.5. From this, it appears that, there was a shortage of Trained Teachers in almost all the States of this region. Amongst all the North Eastern States, the position of Mizoram, Sikkim, Meghalaya and Manipur was slightly better. In Mizoram, the percentage of Trained Teachers in Primary/Junior Basic and Middle/Senior Basic Schools was though 58 and 60 respectively, but in High/Post Basic Schools and Pre-Degree Junior College/Higher Secondary Schools, it was only 42 and 29 per cent respectively. The State of Sikkim showed slightly better picture than Mizoram in the higher levels of education. In Sikkim, the percentage of Trained Teachers in Primary/Junior Basic and Middle/Senior Basic Schools was though 50 and 42, but in High/Post Basic Schools and Pre-Degree Junior College/Higher Secondary Schools, it was 44 and 51 per cent respectively. In Meghalaya, the percentage of Trained Teacher was though 45 in the Primary/Junior Basic Schools, but it was only 36 per cent in each of the higher levels starting from Middle/Senior Basic Schools to Pre-Degree Junior College/Higher Secondary Schools.

On the other hand, the percentage of Trained Teachers in Manipur was though in the lower side with 32 and 31 per cent in Primary/Junior Basic and Middle/Senior Basic Schools, but it was slightly in the higher side with 41 and 40 per cent in High/Post Basic Schools and Pre-Degree Junior College/Higher Secondary Schools respectively. However, the position of Trained Teachers was much better in the country as a whole in all levels of education. The most noticeable feature of this was that, the percentage of Trained Teachers starting at 86 in Primary/Junior Basic Schools, it gradually increased to 87 per cent in Middle/Senior Basic Schools, 89 per cent in High/Post-Basic Schools and finally reached to 90 per cent in Pre-Degree Junior College/Higher Secondary Schools. From all these, it appears that, the position of Trained Teachers was much better in other States than in the States of North Eastern Region. It can also be said that, the higher level Schools in other States were having more number of Trained Teachers, which was a very good indication of quality education and of making quality Students in higher levels also.

The position of Scheduled Caste Students in the North Eastern States and in India as a whole, as on 30th September, 2004 can be seen from Appendix-6.6. From this, it appears that, amongst all the North Eastern States, Scheduled Caste Students in Arunachal Pradesh, Mizoram and Meghalaya was very less and Nagaland did not have any Scheduled Caste Student. Out of total number of Students of the respective States, the percentage of Scheduled Caste Students was only 0.18 in Arunachal Pradesh, 0.35 in Mizoram and 0.75 in Meghalaya, taking together all the educational institutions starting from Pre-Primary/Pre-Basic Schools to Pre-Degree Junior College/ Higher Secondary Schools. The overall percentage of Scheduled Caste Students in the above-mentioned institutions was the highest to the extent of 12.00 in Tripura, followed by Assam with 9.97 per cent, Sikkim with 4.55 per cent and then by Manipur with 2.54 per cent. The overall position of Scheduled Caste Students in the North Eastern Region as a whole was 7.76 per cent, which was much lower than the all India figure of 16.52 per cent.

The number of Scheduled Caste Students in the North Eastern States, particularly in the tribal dominated States like Nagaland, Arunachal Pradesh, Mizoram and Meghalaya are very less. But whatever may be their numbers, out of this, it appears that, the enrolment of Scheduled Caste Girls, were quite encouraging in all the States and it was even more than the Boys in Sikkim. The percentage of Scheduled Caste Girls Student in Sikkim was 50.24 and that of Boys was 49.76. The enrolment percentage of Scheduled Caste Girls was also quite high to the extent of 49.41 per cent in Mizoram, followed by 47.82 per cent in Manipur, 47.77 per cent in Assam, 46.65 per cent in Tripura, 46.52 per cent in Meghalaya and the lowest of 37.61 per cent in Arunachal Pradesh. However, the percentage of Scheduled Caste Girls student of the North Eastern Region as a whole was 47.59, which was even more than the all India figure of 42.95 per cent. This implies that, proportionately, more number of Scheduled Caste Girls were attending educational institutions in the North Eastern Region than the Scheduled Caste Girls of the country as a whole. Further, details can be seen from Appendix-6.6.

In the North Eastern Region, the States like Mizoram, Nagaland, Meghalaya and Arunachal Pradesh are tribal dominated States and therefore, the enrolment percentage of tribal students in different educational institutions are more in these States. From Appendix-6.7, it can be seen that, out of the total number of students, the percentage of Scheduled Tribe Students was the highest to the extent of 96.31 per cent in Mizoram. The second highest of the order of 69.91 per cent was in Nagaland and then it came to 64.99 per cent in Meghalaya followed by 64 per cent in Arunachal Pradesh. But in other States, the tribal population is comparatively less and therefore, the percentage of Scheduled Tribe Students is also less. However, amongst them, the percentage of Scheduled Tribe Students was more to the extent of 28.01 per cent in Manipur, followed by 24.28 per cent in Sikkim, 19.71 per cent in Tripura and 15.07 per cent in Assam. The overall percentage of Scheduled Tribe Students in the North Eastern Region as a whole was 26.93, which was quite higher than the all India figure of 8.75 per cent.

The Scheduled Tribe Girls of the North Eastern States are not lagging much behind in the field of education, they are rather, ahead of the Scheduled Tribe Boys in some of the States. From Appendix-6.7, it can be seen that, the overall enrolment percentage of Scheduled Tribe Girls was more to the extent of 51.41 per cent in Sikkim and 50.99 per cent in Meghalaya. In other States, though the overall enrolment percentage of Scheduled Tribe Girls was less than the Scheduled Tribe Boys, but their percentage difference was not much. It can be seen that, the enrolment percentage for Scheduled Tribe Girls was 48.33 in Mizoram, 47.61 in Nagaland, 47.36 in Assam, 46.77 in Manipur, 45.54 in Arunachal Pradesh and 45.40 per cent in Tripura. The most noticeable feature regarding the education of the Scheduled Tribe Girls of the North Eastern Region was that, the overall enrolment percentage of Scheduled Tribe Girls in each of the North Eastern States was higher than the overall percentage figure of 44.86 for the Scheduled Tribe Girls of the country as a whole. That indicates that, proportionately, more number of Scheduled Tribe Girls of the North Eastern Region, were attending educational institutions than the Scheduled Tribe Girls of the country as a whole.

Dropout or discontinuation of studies by the students at the successive levels of education is a natural phenomenon. There might be so many reasons, but amongst these, the *five* main reasons for such dropouts are (i) Not interested for further studies, (ii) Financial inability of parents or guardians, (iii) Higher educational facilities are not available at the place of residence or nearby, (iv) Due to bad performance or failure, and (v) Requirement for participation in household duties or household industries or enterprise or for other economic activities. It is a fact that, the educational facilities are less in the rural areas and the economic condition of most of the rural people is also poor, and because of these reasons, the rate of dropouts is more in the rural areas than in the urban areas.

The dropout rates at different levels of education in the North East India as well as in the country as a whole, can be seen from Appendix-6.8. From this, it appears that, amongst all the North Eastern States, Manipur was having the lowest dropout rates at all the three levels of Primary having 31.18 per cent, Middle having 32.80 per cent and Secondary having 43.02 per cent. In Nagaland, it was the second lowest at Primary and Middle levels with 42.69 per cent and 42.49 per cent respectively, while at Secondary level, it was the third lowest with 67.29 per cent. In Tripura, the dropout rate was the third lowest of the order of 43.20 per cent at Primary level, fourth lowest with 64.15 per cent at Middle level and fifth lowest having 73.36 per cent at the Secondary level. In Arunachal Pradesh, it was the fourth lowest at both Primary and Secondary levels having 46.85 per cent and 70.79 per cent respectively, but third lowest with 62.63 per cent at the Middle level.

The dropout rate in Assam was very high. It was the highest at both Primary and Middle levels having 50.07 per cent and 73.38 per cent and third highest of the order of 74.96 per cent at Secondary level. In Meghalaya, it was the second highest at both Primary and Secondary levels having 49.97 per cent and 79.15 per cent respectively, whereas at Middle level, it was the fourth highest to the extent of 64.21 per cent. In Mizoram, like literacy rate, the dropout rate was also quite high at various levels of education. It was the third highest at both the levels of Primary and Middle with 49.84 per cent and 66.84 per cent respectively, whereas, it was the seventh highest to the extent of 66.95 per cent at Secondary level. The dropout rate in Sikkim was also very high. At Primary level, though it was the fourth highest of the order of 49.44 per cent and the second highest having 71.22 per cent at Middle level, but it was the highest amongst all the North Eastern States to the extent of 82.30 per cent at Secondary level. That indicates that maximum number of students are dropping out at the Secondary level and very few students are reaching to the level of Higher Secondary in Sikkim.

The other noticeable feature is that, in all the North Eastern States, except Arunachal Pradesh, Manipur and Nagaland, the dropout rate for Boys was more than the dropout rate for Girls at Primary level. At Middle level, the dropout rate for Boys was also more than the dropout rate for Girls in all the States, except Assam, Nagaland and Tripura. This was also true at the Secondary level except for the States of Arunachal Pradesh and Nagaland. This means that, proportionately, more Boys are discontinuing their studies at the early age in the North Eastern States. However, compare to the North Eastern Region, the dropout rate in the country as a whole was much less in all levels of education. At Primary level, it was only 29 per cent, at Middle level, it was 50.84 per cent and at Secondary level, it was 61.92 per cent. In case of Girls, the dropout rate at Primary level was though less, but it was more than the dropout rate for Boys at both Middle and Secondary levels, in the country as a whole. Further, details can be seen from Appendix-6.8.

The dropout rates of the Scheduled Caste Students of the North East India and of the country can be seen from Appendix-6.9. Amongst the North Eastern States, the information on the dropout rates of Scheduled Caste Students for the States of Nagaland and Mizoram were not available. However, from the available records of the other states, it appears that, the dropout rates of the Scheduled Caste Students for the State of Arunachal Pradesh was the lowest at both Primary and Middle levels with 20 per cent and 38.18 per cent respectively, but it was the second lowest having 17.07 per cent at Secondary level. In Manipur, this rate was the lowest with 1.16 per cent at Secondary level, but it was the second lowest with 31.62 per cent at Primary level. Tripura was at the third lowest position at all the three levels of Primary, Middle and Secondary with 35.26 per cent, 66.20 per cent and 70.02 per cent respectively.

The dropout rate of the Scheduled Caste Students in the States of Sikkim, Assam and Meghalaya was higher. In Sikkim, it was the highest of the order of 85.23 per cent and 75.49 per cent at Secondary and Middle levels, but at the Primary level, it was the third highest having 48.55 per cent. In Assam, the dropout rate of the Scheduled

Caste Students was the highest to the extent of 53.15 per cent at Primary level, second highest with 70.30 per cent at Middle level and third highest having 71.01 per cent at Secondary level. In case of Meghalaya, it was the second highest at both Primary and Secondary levels with 49.41 per cent and 75.48 per cent respectively, whereas at Middle level, it was the fourth highest with 62.37 per cent.

Further, it appears that, the dropout rate of the Scheduled Caste Boys was more than the Scheduled Caste Girls in all the states of Assam, Meghalaya, Sikkim and Manipur with 55.85 per cent, 52.04 per cent, 51.82 per cent and 37.14 per cent respectively at Primary level. In Middle level, it was more in Sikkim and Meghalaya with 79.83 per cent and 63.38 per cent respectively, but at secondary level, except Tripura, the dropout rate of the Scheduled Caste Boys was more than the Girls in all the States of Sikkim, Meghalaya, Assam, Arunachal Pradesh and Manipur having 86.13 per cent, 76.08 per cent, 72.65 per cent, 17.86 per cent and 1.17 per cent respectively. This indicates that, more number of Scheduled Caste Boys were discontinuing their studies at an early age in the North Eastern States. However, the dropout rate of the Scheduled Caste Students for the country as a whole was 34.21 per cent at Primary level, 57.26 per cent at Middle level and 71.25 per cent at Secondary level. But the dropout rate of the Scheduled Caste Girls was more than the Scheduled Caste Boys at all levels of Primary having 36.14 per cent, Middle with 59.95 per cent and Secondary with 74.17 per cent in our country. Further, details can be seen from Appendix-6.9.

The dropout rate of the Scheduled Tribe Students of the North East India and the country as a whole, can be seen from Appendix-6.10. From this, it appears that, in the States of Sikkim, Nagaland, Mizoram and Manipur, the dropout rate of the Scheduled Tribe Students was comparatively less. In Sikkim, it was the lowest having 24.47 per cent at Primary level and second lowest at both Middle and Secondary levels with 44.49 per cent and 67.72 per cent respectively. In Nagaland, this rate was lowest at Middle level having 42.93 per cent, but second lowest with 38.78 per cent at Primary level and third lowest with 68.75 per cent at Secondary level. The position of dropout rate of the Scheduled Tribe Students of Mizoram was better at the higher level, but it was not that good at the lower levels. In Secondary level, though it was the lowest with 66.64 per cent, but it was the fourth lowest at both Primary and Middle levels with 49.79 per cent and 66.28 per cent respectively. The dropout rates of the Scheduled Tribe Students of Manipur showed some ups and downs. These rates were though third and fourth lowest having 57.16 per cent and 72.18 per cent at Middle and Secondary levels respectively, but it was the sixth lowest or in other words, it was the third highest to the extent of 51 per cent at the Primary level.

The dropout rate of the Scheduled Tribe Students was comparatively more in the States of Tripura, Assam, Meghalaya and Arunachal Pradesh. In Tripura, it was the highest at all the levels of Primary, Middle and Secondary with 58.84 per cent, 81.40 per cent and 85.99 per cent respectively. In Assam, it was the second highest at both Primary and Middle levels with 54.98 per cent and 75.53 per cent, but at the Secondary level, it was the third highest having 77.18 per cent. In this group, the position of Arunachal Pradesh was slightly better. The dropout rate of the Scheduled Tribe Students of this State was the third lowest at Primary level with 47.83 per cent, but it was the fourth highest at both Middle and Secondary levels having 67.37 per cent and 74.05 per cent respectively.

From this Appendix-6.10, it also appears that the dropout rate of the Scheduled Tribe Boys was more than the Scheduled Tribe Girls at Primary level in all the States of Assam, Meghalaya, Mizoram, Arunachal Pradesh, Nagaland and Sikkim having 58.65 per cent, 54.17 per cent, 50.77 per cent, 47.91 per cent, 39.71 per cent and 30.51 per cent respectively. At Middle level, it was more in the States of Meghalaya, Mizoram, Arunachal Pradesh, Manipur, Sikkim and Nagaland with 70.68 per cent, 68.39 per cent, 68.03 per cent, 57.69 per cent, 52.14 per cent and 44.78 per cent respectively. However, at the Secondary level, the dropout rate of the Scheduled Tribe Boys was though more in the States of Assam, Sikkim, Manipur and Mizoram having 78.15 per cent, 73.02 per cent, 72.27 per cent and 69.21 per cent respectively, but the dropout rate of the Scheduled Tribe Girls was more in the States of Tripura, Meghalaya, Arunachal Pradesh and Nagaland having 87.06 per cent, 82.87 per cent, 74.89 per cent and 68.86 per cent respectively. On the whole, in case of Scheduled Caste Boys also, it is seen that, more number of them were discontinuing their studies at an early age in the North Eastern States. The dropout rate for the country as a whole was 42.32 per cent at Primary level, 65.87 per cent at Middle level and 78.97 per cent at Secondary level. In case of Scheduled Tribe Girls, though this rate was less with 42.04 per cent at Primary level, but it was more at both Middle and Secondary levels with 67.09 per cent and 80.66 per cent respectively. Further, details can be seen from Appendix-6.10.

The literacy rate is generally taken in to account for finding the status of educational development of a state. Therefore, to know the position of educational development of the North Eastern States as well as of the country, the Appendix-6.11 can be seen. From this, it appears that, amongst all the North Eastern States, the overall literacy rate in Mizoram was the highest to the extent of 88.80 per cent as per 2001 census. In rural areas, it was though a bit less with 81.27 per cent, but in urban areas, it was very high to the extent of 96.13 per cent. The overall literacy rate in Tripura was the second highest of the order of 73.19 per cent. It was also the second highest in both rural and urban areas with 69.72 per cent and 89.21 per cent respectively. Manipur came in the third highest position with overall literacy rate of 70.53 per cent. In rural areas, it also occupied the third highest position with 67.29 per cent, but in urban areas, it was the seventh highest with 79.28 per cent. Sikkim stood in the fourth highest position with overall literacy rate of 68.81 per cent. It was also the fourth in rural areas with 66.82 per cent, but in urban areas, it was in the sixth position with 83.91 per cent.

The literacy rate was comparatively less in the States of Nagaland, Assam, Meghalaya and Arunachal Pradesh. In Nagaland, the overall literacy rate was in the fifth position with 66.59 per cent. The literacy rate of both rural and urban areas was also in the fifth position with 62.79 per cent and 84.74 per cent respectively. The State of Assam was in the sixth position with overall literacy rate of 63.25 per cent. In rural areas, it was in the fourth position with 59.73 per cent, but in urban areas, it was in fourth position having 85.34 per cent. Then came the position, of Meghalaya. The overall literacy rate of the State was in the seventh position with 62.56 per cent. In rural areas, it was also in the seventh position with 56.29 per cent, but in urban areas, it was in the third position having 86.30 per cent. Arunachal Pradesh came in the eighth and the last position in all three categories of overall literacy rate as well as in rural and urban areas having 54.34 per cent, 47.83 per cent and 78.26 per cent respectively. The overall literacy rate of the country as a whole as per 2001 census was 64.84 per cent, which was even more than the literacy rate of Assam, Meghalaya and Arunachal Pradesh. In rural areas, the literacy rate of our country was 58.74 per cent, which was more than the literacy rates of Meghalaya and Arunachal Pradesh and in urban areas, it was 79.92 per cent, which was also more than the urban literacy rates of Manipur and Arunachal Pradesh. Further, details can be seen from Appendix-6.11.

The literacy rate for Scheduled Caste people as per 2001 census can be seen from Appendix-6.12. It appears that, in this case also, the position of Mizoram was on the top with overall literacy rate of 89.20 per cent, having 88.89 per cent in rural areas and 89.30 per cent in urban areas. Tripura was in the second highest position on overall literacy as well as in literacy rate of rural areas having 74.68 per cent and 73.59 per cent respectively, but in urban areas, it was in the third highest position having 79.51 per cent. Manipur stood in the third highest position in respect of overall and of rural literacy with 72.32 per cent and 70.76 per cent respectively, but it was in the fifth highest position in respect of urban literacy having 73.14 per cent. Arunachal Pradesh came in the fourth highest position in respect of overall and of rural literacy with 67.64 per cent and 65.87 per cent respectively, but it was in the sixth highest position in respect of urban literacy having 69.28 per cent.

Assam was in the fifth highest position on overall literacy as well as in literacy rate of rural areas having 66.78 per cent and 64.92 per cent respectively, but in urban areas, it was in the fourth highest position having 76.86 per cent. In case of Scheduled Caste literacy, Sikkim came in the sixth highest position in respect of overall literacy having 63.04 per cent and it was also in the sixth position for rural areas having 60.23 per cent, but it was in the second highest position in case of urban literacy having 81.99 per cent. Meghalaya came in the last position in all the three categories of overall literacy as well as of the literacy rate in rural and urban areas having 56.27 per cent, 51.91 per cent and 63.57 per cent respectively. In respect of Scheduled Caste Literacy, it appears that, the overall literacy for the country as a whole was 54.69 per cent. In rural areas, it was 51.16 per cent and in urban areas, it was 68.12 per cent. Here, the most noticeable feature is that, each of these three rates was less than the rate of each of the North Eastern States in the respective category except for urban-areas of Meghalaya. That means, the Scheduled Caste literacy rate was more in each and every State of North East India than the Scheduled Caste literacy rate of the country as a whole. Further, details can be seen from Appendix-6.12.

The literacy rate of the Scheduled Tribe people of the North Eastern States and the country as a whole as per 2001 census can be seen from Appendix-6.13. From this, it appears that, amongst all the States of this region, Mizoram was in the top in all the three categories of overall literacy and also in rural and urban areas having 89.34 per cent, 82 per cent and 96.77 per cent respectively. The State of Sikkim, though came in the second highest position in respect of overall literacy as well as of rural literacy having 67.14 per cent and 65.37 per cent respectively, but it was in the sixth highest position in case of urban literacy having 84.89 per cent. Nagaland stood in the third highest position in both the cases of overall literacy as well as in the literacy rate of urban areas having 65.95 per cent and 88.70 per cent respectively, but it was in the fourth highest position in case of rural literacy with 62.55 per cent. The State of Manipur was though in the fourth highest position in case of overall literacy having 65.85 per cent, but it was in the third highest position in case of rural literacy with 65.09 per cent and was in the seventh highest position in case of urban literacy having 80.94 per cent.

The Scheduled Tribe literacy rate was comparatively less in the States of Assam, Meghalaya, Tripura and Arunachal Pradesh. In case of Assam, the literacy rate was in the fifth highest position in respect of overall and rural literacy having 62.52 per cent and 61.29 per cent respectively, but it was in the fourth highest position with 86.75 per cent in respect of urban areas. The State of Meghalaya was in the sixth highest position in respect of both overall literacy and in the literacy rate of rural areas with 61.34 per cent and 56.36 per cent respectively, but it was in the fifth highest position in case of urban literacy with 86.67 per cent. The State of Tripura though stood in the seventh position in case of overall and in rural literacy having 56.48 per cent and 55.46 per cent respectively, but it was in the second highest position in case of urban literacy having 91.97 per cent. Arunachal Pradesh was in the eighth and the last position in respect of all the three categories of overall, rural and urban literacy having 49.62 per cent, 45.04 and 77.39 per cent respectively.

The literacy rate of the Scheduled Tribe people of our country as a whole was also very poor. The overall literacy rate was only 47.10 per cent, which was less than the literacy rate of the Scheduled Tribe people of any of the North Eastern States. The literacy rate of the Scheduled Tribe people of our country in rural areas was 45.02 per cent and in urban areas, it was 69.09 per cent. These two rates were also less than the literacy rate of the Scheduled Tribe people of any of the North Eastern States in the respective category. From this, it can be concluded that, proportionately, more number of Scheduled Tribe People are literate in the North East India. Further, details can be seen from Appendix-6.13.

The Government of India as well as the State Governments are always trying for the overall development of education sector and are introducing various schemes and also adopting new methods for improvement of literacy of our country. These have yielded positive results and the literacy rate of the States as well as of the country as a whole are gradually improving. This improvement can be seen from Appendix-6.14, which will indicate the gender-wise literacy rates as per 1991 and 2001 census, literacy gaps and also the decadal changes (1991-2001) in the literacy rates in various States of the North Eastern Region and the country as a whole.

From this, it appears that, amongst all the North Eastern States, the male-female literacy gap in Mizoram was the lowest of the order of 7.01 per cent in 1991 census and this has reduced to 3.97 per cent in 2001 census. This indicates that, in Mizoram, the females are also equally literate and their literacy gap with the males was reducing faster. But on the other hand, the decadal change in the literacy rate was at the second lowest of 5.11 per cent in respect of males and 8.15 per cent in respect of females, which means, the overall growth in the number of educated persons was slow in Mizoram, though the females are becoming educated at a faster pace than the males. This is perhaps due to the fact that, Mizoram already having maximum number of literate persons. The male-female literacy gap in Meghalaya was the second lowest having 8.27 per cent in 1991 census, but this has gone down to 5.82 per cent in 2001 census, which was also the second lowest. That means, in Meghalaya also, the females are equally educated and their literacy gap with the males was reducing faster. However, the decadal change in literacy rate was the second highest for both males and females with 12.31 per cent and 14.76 per cent respectively. This indicates that, in Meghalaya, though the number of literate males and females are increasing faster, but the rate of growth for females was more.

The male-female literacy gap in Nagaland was though the third lowest of the order of 12.87 per cent in 1991 census and 9.70 per cent in 2001 census, but the decadal change in the literacy rate was the lowest for both males and females having only 3.54 per cent and 6.71 per cent respectively. That means, in Nagaland, comparatively, the females are not that much educated and the rate of change in the literacy was also very slow for both males and females, though the rate of change was a bit more for females than males. The male-female literacy gap in Assam was the fourth lowest of the order of 18.84 per cent in 1991 census and there was not much change in it and remained at 16.67 per cent in 2001 census. But, the decadal change in the literacy rate was in the fourth lowest having 9.41 per cent for males and it was in the third lowest with 11.58 per cent for females. That means, in Assam, the number of educated females are comparatively less and the decadal change in the literacy rate was also slow for both males and females, though the number of educated females was growing faster.

The male-female literacy gap was quite high in the States of Manipur, Arunachal Pradesh, Tripura and Sikkim. In Manipur, it was the highest to the extent of 24.03 per cent in 1991 census, but though it came down to 19.80 per cent in 2001 census, still it remained at the second highest position. The decadal change in literacy rate was the third lowest with 8.70 per cent in case of males and it was the fourth lowest having 12.93 per cent in case of females. These indicate that, in Manipur, compare to literate males, literate females were very less and the decadal change in the literacy rate was also slow for both males and females. The male-female literacy gap was the second highest in Arunachal Pradesh to the extent of 21.76 per cent in 1991 census, but there was hardly any change and it remained at 20.30 per cent in 2001 census. However, the decadal change in literacy rate was the highest of the order of 12.38 per cent for males and it was the third highest with 13.84 per cent for females. That means, though the literate females are less in Arunachal Pradesh, but the positive aspect was that, the literacy was increasing at a higher rate for both males and females in that State.

The male-female literacy gap was also quite high in the State of Tripura. It was the third highest to the extent of 20.93 per cent in 1991 census and it came down to only 16.11 per cent in 2001 census. However, the decadal change in the literacy rate was the third highest with 10.44 per cent for males, but it was the highest to the extent of 15.26 per cent for females. That indicates, though the number of literate females was comparatively less in Tripura, but their number was increasing very fast and minimizing the male-female literacy gap with a greater speed. In Sikkim, the male-female literacy gap was also high. It was the fourth highest with 18.94 per cent in 1991 census and it came down to only 15.64 per cent in 2001 census. But the decadal change in the literacy rate was the fourth highest for both males and females with 10.34 per cent and 13.64 per cent respectively. That indicates, in Sikkim, the literacy rate was increasing faster and though the number of literate females were less than literate males, but the number of literate females was increasing with a faster pace. In fact, it appears that, in all the North Eastern States, the female literacy was increasing rapidly which is a very good sign for the overall development of this region.

The male-female literacy gap in our country as a whole was also quite high. In 1991 census, it was of the order of 24.85 per cent, but it came down to only 21.59 per cent in 2001 census. The decadal change in the literacy rate was 11.13 per cent for males and 14.39 per cent for females, which were not that high. From this, it appears that, the figure of male-female literacy gap in our country as a whole in both the census of 1991 and 2001 was more than the figure of male-female literacy gap of any of the North Eastern States in the corresponding census periods. That means, proportionately, the number of literate females were more in North East India than in the Country as a whole. However, though the decadal change in the literacy rate was not that high in our country, but the only hope was that, the female literacy of our country was increasing with a higher pace than that of the males. Therefore, it can be concluded that, the steps taken by the Central and State Governments for the development of education, particularly female education, are fruitful and these not only helping in increasing female literacy, but also paving the way for reducing the male-female literacy gap in our country.

However, the literacy rate is though considered as the indicator of educational development, but this alone cannot specify the quality and level of education of the people. The literacy rate is generally calculated once in ten years, at the time of Population census. And while calculating this rate, only the total number of literate people is taken into account, not their quality and level of education. Moreover, the census way of defining a literate person is that — 'one who can read and write anything with understanding in any language'. That means, the people who are having very little knowledge or in some cases, can simply write their names, are treated as literate, and are being considered in the literate group while calculating literacy rate. Therefore, in true sense, the literacy rate is not enough for determining the level of educational development of a State or of a country and also the qualitative aspects of its people as well as of their skills and levels of education, which are very much required for all round development of that State or that country. Present world is running after industrial and technological development and this is possible only when the education sector is well equipped with proper infrastructure together with qualified and sincere teachers who could produce adequate number of professional and skilled manpower for such development. Any kind of compromise with the quality, skill and level of education of the teachers as well as of the students will be disastrous. Right thinking persons with adequate knowledge should be in the helm of affairs and keeping themselves above their own or group interest, they should always think for the interest of the young minds who are the nation builders. Otherwise, though there might be temporary glory or benefit, but it may so happen that, not to speak of nation building, rather, one day they may have to repent for their own deeds or their next generation may have to suffer for that and at that time, they may curse them for the wrong things that they have done. And at that time, it will be too late and there may not be any way of coming out of that misery.

Finance is also a very important aspect of educational development. The position of expenditure on education in the year, 2004-05 in the States of North East India and also in the country as a whole can be seen from Appendix-6.15. From this, it can be seen that, amongst all the North Eastern States, the percentage of expenditure on education in Tripura was the highest to the extent of 25.63 per cent of its Total Budget. But in spite of that, the per capita expenditure was the third highest of Rs. 1698.53. In case of percentage of expenditure on education, Assam though came in the second position with 19.82 per cent of its Total Budget, but in case of per capita expenditure, it was in the lowest position with Rs. 1108.97. Manipur stood in the third highest position spending 19.48 per cent of its Total Budget on education, but it remained in the fifth highest position in case of per capita expenditure with Rs. 1448.56. The State of Meghalaya was though coming in the fourth position with the percentage of expenditure on education having 18.53 per cent of its Total Budget, but it remained in the seventh position in case of per capita expenditure with Rs. 1243.28.

The State of Mizoram is considered as educationally developed and even though the State spent only 15.99 per cent of its Total Budget on education, but the per capita expenditure was the second highest of Rs. 2568.51, which was a positive sign for development of education of the State. Nagaland was in the sixth position in respect of both percentage of expenditure on education and per capita expenditure, spending 14.55 per cent of its Total Budget and having per capita expenditure of Rs. 1282.30. The State of Arunachal Pradesh was in the seventh position in case of percentage of expenditure on education with 11.43 per cent of its Total Budget, but in case of per capita expenditure, it was in the fourth highest position having Rs. 1539.53. The percentage of expenditure on education in Sikkim was though in the eighth and last position with only 9.18 per cent of its Total Budget, but in case of per capita expenditure, the State was in the highest position having Rs. 2927.81. That indicates, the Government of Sikkim was taking much care for the educational development of the State. However, it can be seen that, the percentage of expenditure on education for the country as a whole was though 12.76 per cent of its Total Budget, but the per capita expenditure, compare to the North Eastern States, was very less to the extent of only Rs. 969. This indicates that, all the North Eastern States, on an average, were spending more money per person on education.

Inspite of all these, it is a fact that, the standard of education in the North Eastern Region is still not up to the mark. Though some students of this region are scoring very high marks and some of them are topping the list of merit in the state level examinations, but they cannot do very well in the entrance examinations of many of the renowned Medical and Engineering Colleges and also in the all India level entrance tests like PMT, AIEEE, IIT, IIM, CAT, NET, IAS, IPS etc. It cannot be denied that, the success rate of the North Eastern Candidates in such examinations is very low. The few candidates those who are becoming successful, are mostly getting coaching in the coaching centres located outside North East India. Though some coaching centres are there within North Eastern Region, particularly in Guwahati, but these are yet to go a long way to catch up with the standard of the coaching centres located in Delhi, Bombay, Kota, Kolkata, Kanpur, Hyderabad, Chennai, Patna, etc.

One can have some idea about the success level of the students of this region from the results of IIT-JEE. It can be seen that, in 2008, 19982 students appeared in the examination and out of them, only 193 i.e. only 0.96 per cent students of Guwahati region could successfully complete the IIT Joint Entrance Examination against the all India pass percentage of 2.77. But again, out of these 193 successful candidates, only 97 belong to general category and the remaining 96 i.e. almost half were from reserved category e.g. — other backward class 63, Scheduled Caste 25 and Scheduled Tribe 8. In 2007, 15675 students appeared for IIT-JEE from Guwahati region and out of them, only 153 i.e. only 0.97 per cent could come out successful. Instances were also there that some of the students even discontinued their studies halfway as they could not cope up with the standard of education. However, in 2008 Shri Uttam Sikaria topped the Guwahati region and ranked 199 in all India level. Shri Sikaria took coaching at Kota for appearing this examination. Regarding coaching facilities in Guwahati, he said, "There is no competitive environment here which is essential for such competitive and tough examination in Guwahati"[16].

In case of IIM, PMT and AIEEE, the position is more or less the same. A very few students of this region are securing good ranks in all India merit list and are getting admission through all India counselling. However, for AIEEE, there is a provision of separate State-wise merit list for Scheduled Caste (SC), Scheduled Tribe (ST) and for General category students and also for each State, category-wise some seats in different disciplines are reserved in various National Institution of Technologies (NITs). The students those who are securing good ranks in the State list are getting admission in the

NITs through State Counselling and opting for the subjects as per their choice, depending on their merit and availability. But it is a fact that, most of the students, particularly of General category, those who are securing good ranks in the State merit list, are taking coaching from the Coaching Centres located outside North East Region. Even for preparation for All India Civil Service or Police Service Examination, the candidates from this region are generally going to Delhi for coaching, though their success rate is very less.

In Shillong, though one or two organizations are trying to start coaching centres from last few years, but they also could not make much success in their endeavour. Mainly two reasons are coming on their way. The first one is, non-availability of adequate number of students for running a coaching centre and the second one is non availability of qualified and efficient teachers. One of the coaching centres, at the beginning, though started the centre with a few students and brought some qualified and efficient teachers, mostly from south India and made some success, but again in the very next year, the number of students remained almost the same and as such, they could not bring those teachers since it was not economically viable. However, they tried to bring the teachers from Kolkata, but that also did not work and ultimately they had to manage somehow with the teachers from the local colleges. Coaching centres need specialized teachers as well as the specific programme of action. The only purpose of this is to prepare the students for appearing in the entrance tests. Therefore, the students should also have that standard and ability to cope up with the curriculum of the coaching centre for becoming successful in the competitive examinations.

Shillong got the light of education much earlier. Once upon a time it was considered as the seat of learning and its glory was spreading far and wide. In this regard, it was mentioned that, "in the past, Shillong had been a favoured destination for thousands of students not only from different parts of the country but outside as well. But, with the decline in quality education, there has been a sharp drop in the numbers of students coming from outside". However, regarding the reason for declining in quality education, it was said that, "Shillong has over the years lost the stature with a downslide in academic standards largely because of the absence of a viable education policy"[17]. In this connection, the Chief Minister of

Meghalaya said, "In the past, Shillong was known as the centre of education, however we lack technical education. It is now high time to have such institutions". He further said, "Unless we have quality education and competent teaching faculty right from the lower levels especially in rural areas, it is difficult to improve education at the higher level". The Chief Secretary of Meghalaya opined that, "mere graduation is no assurance for a job. The youth need skills to procure a settled job"[18].

Now it is a well accepted fact that, the quality of education has really gone down. But is it true that the quality has gone down largely because of the absence of a viable education policy? Or is it something else? If the declining in quality education is attributed to absence of a viable education policy alone, thank God, it can be rectified; a new policy can be formulated. But, if it is because of the process of implementation of the policy, then what to do? Education is such a thing which always needs honesty, hard work, quality and merit. Compromising with the quality and merit of students or teachers at any stage is disastrous. Today who is a student, tomorrow he may be a teacher or today who is a teacher, yesterday he was a student. Student-Teacher relation is complementary. If student is good, then he can be a good teacher or if teacher is good, then he can produce many good students. Therefore, the downfall in the quality of education might be because of compromising with the quality and merit of students and teachers. This can very well be understood, if the guardians, educationists and the policy makers think about themselves, particularly about their student life and the type and quality of teachers they had and if they compare their situation with the present situation, then it would not be very difficult to understand, where lies the defects.

The educational scenario in Assam is no better. The downfall of the education sector started long back. A few years ago one of the leading Newspaper of the State while describing the condition of the schools wrote, "The pathetic state of government-run schools, where a vast majority of the students get enrolled every year, has been another serious concern, as is the mushrooming of private schools that keep flouting all norms governing education. Large-scale corruption in the recruitment process, where monetary considerations override merit, has resulted in a huge number of undeserving candidates getting appointed as teachers in government schools. The consequence is too evident to merit any mention. The rot in education has now reached such a stage that even Gauhati University, the most revered seat of learning, has found itself embroiled in an unprecedented scam involving answer script evaluation". Regarding reform of education, the paper further pointed out that, "the trouble with our governments is that they make far too many promises without backing those by realistic measures. If the Chief Minister is indeed serious about reforming the education system, then let him begin by cleansing the recruitment process of school teachers, which has touched an all-time low"[19].

The reform of a much respected subject like education, perhaps does not lie on simply making a good policy and setting up of a few general and technical institutions, it goes much beyond that. The first and foremost thing is the attitude towards education. Education should be above politics, personal influence, religion, caste, etc. There should be only honesty, sincerity, hard work, quality and merit. Education should not be made a commodity so that, like other things, one can purchase a seat for study or a post for employment. The educational institutions should not simply be the places of employment for everyone, only the deserving candidates should come in such institutions. There should not be any compromise with the quality, merit and the level of education of such persons. The educational institutions should be well equipped with necessary instruments and machineries and also with other required infrastructures for all round physical and mental development of the students. It is also very much essential to see that the schools, particularly the lower level schools in rural areas are functioning properly and the teachers are attending schools regularly. The teachers should get proper respect and they should be paid well so that they need not have to think for leading a responsible and respectable life. There should be adequate provisions for training and re-training of all teachers for increasing their knowledge and the capacity of teaching. Proper Coaching Centres with expert faculties should be established for coaching the students for appearing at the all India level entrance examinations and making them successful in such examinations. There is no dearth of talent in the North East, but what is lacking is the honesty and attitude towards education. Instead of providing so many relaxations, one should think as to how the talents can be harnessed and the capacity of learning can be increased. Relaxations are not the solution of any problem, rather these are the weapons of destruction of the capacity and quality of individuals resulting in permanent damage of the society as a whole. This is perhaps the high time to understand the consequences and keeping that in mind, remedial measures should be taken for improving the quality of education so that the students of this region can compete with others and can go along with them or even further.

NOTES

1. *Manorama Year Book*, 1984, Manorama Publishing House, Kottayam, p. 533.
2. *ibid.*, p. 533.
3. *ibid.*, p. 534.
4. *ibid.*, p. 534.
5. *ibid.*, p. 534.
6. *ibid.*, p. 535.
7. *ibid.*, pp. 535, 36.
8. *ibid.*, p. 536.
9. *Website of the Ministry of Human Resource Development*, Government of India, New Delhi.
10. *ibid.*
11. *ibid.*
12. *ibid.*
13. *Socio-Economic Review*, 2003, Directorate of Economics and Statistics, Government of Meghalaya, Shillong, p. 23.
14. A paper on "Social Context of Education in Manipur" by Ms. Salam Jeebanlata, Centre for Educational Studies, SSS J.N.U., New Delhi, pp. 1, 2.
15. J.C. Aggarwal, *School Organisation and Administration*, Doaba House, Booksellers and Publishers, Delhi, p. 75.
16. *The Times of India*, 31st May, 2008, p. 5.
17. *The Times of India*, 1st June, 2008, p. 4.
18. *The Shillong Times*, 18th June, 2008, pp. 1, 5.
19. *The Assam Tribune*, 7th January, 2006 p. 6.

7

Health and Family Welfare Scenario

Health and Family Welfare is one of the most essential services, which is required not only for the survival of humanity, but also for leading a healthy and happy life by the people. Human being is prone to diseases and the duty of the Doctor is to diagnose diseases and prescribe for their treatment. Therefore, the Doctor is the friend of humanity and his service should be available to all who need it. He is not only curing diseases, but in many occasions, giving a second life to people and therefore, his services will be needed as long as man is subject to disease and death. In the words of World Health Organization (WHO), health is 'a state of complete physical, mental and social well being and not merely the absence of disease or deformity'. Therefore, only a well planned and well organized Health and Family Welfare services can fulfil that requirements and can prove the dream of WHO into a reality.

Public health in our country is primarily the responsibility of the State Government. But, the Ministry of Health and Family Welfare of the Central Government has however a part to play for improving the health of the people by sponsoring and also supporting different schemes. The broad objective of the health programmes have been not only to control and eradicate communicable diseases but also to provide curative and preventive measures through health services. To improve the health services, particularly in the rural areas, the Government of India launched the National Rural Health Mission (NRHM) in 2005 and under this a lot of emphasis had been given on strengthening of rural health infrastructure including physical infrastructure and building, manpower and other facilities. The basic features of NRHM are provision of accessible, affordable, accountable, effective and reliable primary health care facilities especially to the poor and vulnerable sections of the population, bridging the gap in rural health care services through creation of a cadre of Accredited Social Health Activists (ASHA), improved health care, decentralized planning, ensuring population stabilization, intersectoral convergence and maintaining gender balance[1].

The important health programmes are—

(i) *Reproductive and Child Health (RCH).* The second phase of this programme was launched on 1st April, 2005 for a period of 5 years to improve the performance of family welfare in reducing maternal and infant morbidity and mortality and unwanted pregnancies in order to stabilize population.

(ii) *Universal Immunization Programme.* The programme was initially launched in the urban areas in 1985 and was subsequently extended to cover the entire country by 1990. Under this programme, vaccines are given to infants and pregnant women for controlling vaccine-preventable diseases like childhood Tuberculosis (BCG), Diphtheria, Pertussis and Tetanus (DPT), Measles, Poliomyelitis (OPV) and Neonatal Tetanus (NNT).

(iii) *Pulse Polio Programme.* Under this programme, supplementary immunization activities have been intensified to cover all children up to the age of 5 (five) years.

(iv) *National Vector Borne Disease Control Programme.* It is an umbrella programme for control of vector borne diseases and the objectives are in tandem with the goals set out in the NHP 2002 and Millennium Development Goals (MDGs).

(v) *National Tuberculosis Control Programme.* The Revised National TB Control Programme (RNTCP) using Directly Observed Treatment Short-course (DOTS) strategy is being implemented with the objective of covering at least 85 per cent of new sputum positive patients to be put on treatment and detection of at least 70 per cent of such patients.

(vi) *National AIDS (Acquired Immune Deficiency Syndrome) Control Programme.* The first phase of this programme was launched in 1992, and encouraged by the progress of this, a second phase was formulated by the Government in 1999 with two key objectives viz. (a) reducing the spread of HIV infection, and (b) strengthening the capacity to respond to HIV/AIDS on a long term basis.

(vii) *National Leprosy Eradication Programme.* The aim of this programme is to eliminate Leprosy from our country. The programme has been decentralized in all the States and the Leprosy services have also been completely integrated with the general health care system. The achievement of this programme is quite satisfactory and the prevalence rate has come down to 0.85/10,000 population by May, 2006[2].

(viii) *Control of Non-communicable Diseases.* In this connection, research at ICMR focusing on identifying risk factors, their control strategies, is in progress.

(ix) *Integrated Disease Surveillance Project (IDSP).* This project was initiated in November, 2004 with the support of World Bank with a view to establishment and operation of a central level Disease Surveillance Unit, integration and strengthening of disease surveillance at State and District levels, improvement of laboratory support and training for disease surveillance and action. The diseases covered under this project include water-borne diseases and emerging diseases, while the surveillance includes water quality monitoring/surveillance.

(x) *Ayurveda, Yoga and Naturopathy, Unani, Siddha and Homoeopathy (AYUSH).* Mainstreaming of AYUSH in the health care delivery network has been envisaged in the NRHM with the focus on improvement and upgradation of standard of education, standardization of drugs and quality control, sustainable collection and cultivation of medicinal plants.

(xi) *Women and Child Development.* The three dimensional strategy for development of women, namely social empowerment, economic empowerment and gender justice continued to be the main focus of this programme. Moreover, measures to uplift health and nutrition standard of women under ICDS include health check up for pregnant women and lactating mothers, pre-and post-natal care and supplementary nutrition[3].

(xii) *Janani Suraksha Yojana (JSY)*. Janani Suraksha Yojana (JSY) is a safe motherhood intervention under the National Rural Health Mission (NRHM) being implemented with the objective of reducing maternal and neo-natal mortality by promoting institutional delivery among the poor pregnant women. This Yojana, launched on 12th April, 2005, by the Hon'ble Prime Minister, is being implemented in all States and UTs with special focus on low performing states. JSY is a 100 per cent centrally sponsored scheme and it integrates cash assistance with delivery and post-delivery care. The success of the scheme would be determined by the increase in institutional delivery among the poor families[4].

The Health and Family Welfare scenario of the North Eastern Region, particularly of the rural areas, is not very encouraging. This is primary due to inadequacy in Health Institutions and other Health Infrastructure, lack of Doctors and Health Assistants, shortage of medicines and other essential items. The Geographic condition of the hilly States of this region is not very congenial for the development of healthcare infrastructure in the rural areas. The healthcare services of NER is predominantly urban based. Due to the absence of basic amenities like proper road communication, transportation, housing accommodation, electricity, water supply, sanitation, social environment, etc. Doctors and Health Workers are reluctant to go to the rural areas. On the other hand, many of the rural people prefer to go for the traditional method of treatment and as such, even when, health centers exist, people do not make full use of these centers. However, there is an overall shortage of modern medical diagnostic and therapeutic aids, superspeciality services, specialized Doctors etc. even in the existing institutions of the urban areas. Moreover, the few laboratories and ancillary diagnostic facilities that exist in some of the North Eastern States are fairly primitive. Patients with serious ailments or complications or requiring advanced investigations are very often, required to go to Guwahati, Kolkata, Delhi, Bombay, Chennai, Vellore etc. for their treatment.

The position of the Health Institutions and other Health

Infrastructure in different States of N.E. Region as on 31st March, 2007 can be seen from Appendix-7.1. It appears that, amongst all the North Eastern States, Assam was having the maximum of 5842 number of Health Institutions, of which 3 are Medical Colleges with Post-Graduation Courses, 20 District Hospitals, 5109 Sub-Centres, 610 Primary Health Centres (PHCs) and 100 Community Health Centres (CHCs). The State was also having the maximum of 393 number of Ayurvedic Dispensaries, besides 1 Ayurvedic Hospital, 3 Homoeopathic Hospitals, 75 Homoeopathic Dispensaries and 1 Unani Dispensary. Guwahati, the capital city of Assam, is the medical hub of the N.E. Region. Apart from the Government Medical College, there are other Private Hospitals and Nursing Homes with modern facilities in Guwahati, which are catering to the medical needs of the people of this region. Next was the position of Tripura. The State of Tripura was having 668 number of Health Institutions and out of that, 2 are Medical Colleges, 2 District Hospitals, 579 Sub-Centres, 75 PHCs and 10 CHCs. The State was also having a total of 116 other Health Institutions, of which 1 is Ayurvedic Hospital, 40 Ayurvedic Dispensaries, 9 Homoeopathic Hospitals and 66 Homoeopathic Dispensaries. In Manipur, altogether, there were 522 Health Institutions, of which, 1 is Medical College with Post Graduation Courses, 13 are District Hospitals, 420 Sub-Centres, 72 PHCs and 16 CHCs. The State of Sikkim was though having the lowest number of 180 Health Institutions, but 1 Medical College is there in this State, besides 4 number of District Hospitals, 147 Sub-Centres, 24 PHCs and 4 CHCs. The State was also having 1 each of Ayurvedic Hospital and Dispensary, 7 Homoeopathic Hospitals and 1 Homoeopathic Dispensary.

No other State of this region was having any Medical College at that time. However, the State of Meghalaya was having a total of 530 Health Institutions and out of that, 3 are District Hospitals, 398 Sub-Centres, 103 PHCs and 26 CHCs. The State was also having 12 other Health Institutions, of which, 1 is Ayurvedic Hospital, 7 Ayurvedic Dispensaries and 4 Homoeopathic Dispensaries. Then came the position of Nagaland with 11 District Hospitals, 397 Sub-Centres, 84 PHCs and 21 CHCs, totalling to 513 number of Health Institutions. The State of Arunachal Pradesh was also having 509 Health Institutions, of which, 14 are District Hospitals, 379 Sub-Centres,

85 PHCs and 31 CHCs. Moreover, the State was also having a total of 48 other Health Institutions, and out of that, 1 is Ayurvedic Hospital, 2 Ayurvedic Dispensaries, 44 Homoeopathic Dispensaries, besides 1 Homoeopathic Hospital. The position of Mizoram was in the bottom of this group in terms of number of Health Institutions. The State was having a total of 440 Health Institutions, of which, 8 are District Hospitals, 366 Sub-Centres, 57 PHCs and 9 CHCs, besides 6 Homoeopathic Hospitals and 1 Dispensary. Further, details can be seen from Appendix-7.1.

The growth of Health Infrastructure in different States of this region during the period from Seventh Five Year Plan to Tenth Five Year Plan was very much uneven. From Appendix-7.2, it can be seen that, in case of Health Sub-Centres, the State of Arunachal Pradesh recorded the highest growth of 145.52 per cent followed by the State of Mizoram with 66.36 per cent, Nagaland with 62.70 per cent and then by Meghalaya with 46.32 per cent. The growth of Health Sub-Centres was though very slow in Tripura and Sikkim, which was 14.43 per cent and 11.36 per cent respectively, but there was no growth of Health Sub-Centres at all in the States of Assam and Manipur. In case of PHCs, Arunachal Pradesh also recorded the highest growth of 254.17 per cent followed by Nagaland with 154.54 per cent, Meghalaya with 83.93 per cent, Mizoram with 62.86 per cent and Tripura with 53.06 per cent. The growth of PHCs in other States was rather slow. In Assam, it was 35.86 per cent, Sikkim 20 per cent and in Manipur, it was the lowest of 12.50 per cent during that period.

The number of CHCs in all the States of this region, during the period from Seventh Five Year Plan to Tenth Five Year Plan, was comparatively less. The State of Assam was having the highest number of 100 CHCs only, followed by Arunachal Pradesh with 31, Meghalaya with 26, Nagaland with 21 and Manipur with 16. In all other States, the number of CHCs was 10 or less. However, the States of Meghalaya, Nagaland and Arunachal Pradesh recorded very high growth in case of CHCs. In Meghalaya, it was the highest of 766.67 per cent followed by Nagaland with 425 per cent and Arunachal Pradesh with 416.67 per cent. The growth of CHCs in Mizoram and Sikkim was also double. In Mizoram, the growth was 125 per cent and in Sikkim, it was 100 per cent. However, the growth rate in the States of Assam, Manipur and Tripura was comparatively slow. It was 66.67 per cent in Assam, 60 per cent in Manipur and only 25 per cent in Tripura during that period.

The overall growth rate of Health Infrastructure in the North Eastern Region during the period from Seventh Five Year Plan to Tenth Five Year Plan was comparatively better than the overall growth rate of the country as a whole. In case of Health Sub-Centres, the growth rate of this region was though only 10.44 per cent, and was a bit less than the all India figure of 11.61 per cent, but the growth rate of both PHCs and CHCs of N.E. Region was better than the position of the country as a whole. The overall growth of PHCs was 52.05 per cent and CHCs was 123.71 per cent as compared to the all India figures of 19.81 per cent and 111.78 per cent respectively. Further, details can be seen from Appendix-7.2.

The position of Rural Health Infrastructure in the North Eastern Region as on March, 2007 can be seen from Appendix-7.3. From this, it can be seen that, as per requirement calculated on the basis of total and tribal rural population of 2001 census, using prescribed norms, there was no shortage of Medical Institutions in the rural areas of some of the N.E. States. In case of Sub-Centres, shortage was there only in three States viz. Meghalaya, 33.33 per cent, Nagaland, 25.79 per cent and Tripura, 12.14 per cent. Whereas, in case of PHCs, shortage was there only in two States viz. Assam, 26.15 per cent and Tripura, 27.88 and in case of CHCs, shortage was also there in Assam, 51.46 per cent and in Tripura, 61.54 per cent. Further, details can be seen from Appendix-7.3.

The shortage of Health Infrastructure in the North Eastern Region was though not much, but the shortage of Health Workers and Doctors were very much there almost at every level. The Appendix-7.4 will give a clear picture of different States of this region as on March. 2007 except Assam for which, no information was available. From Appendix-7.4, it can be seen that, except Meghalaya and Sikkim, there was a shortage of Multipurpose Workers (Female/ANM) in the Sub-Centres and in the PHCs. Maximum shortage was there in Nagaland to the extent of 28.90 per cent. In case of Health Workers (Male)/MPW (M) in the Sub-Centres, there was a shortage in all the States except Manipur and Sikkim. The shortage was maximum in Arunachal Pradesh to the extent of 93.93 per cent and in Tripura to the extent of 53.71 per cent. In the PHCs, shortage of Health Assistants

(Female)/LHV was there in all the States except Mizoram. Nagaland indicated the maximum shortage of 82.14 per cent followed by Arunachal Pradesh with 81.18 per cent. Shortage of Health Assistants (Male) was also there in all the States except Mizoram and Tripura. The maximum shortage of 82.14 per cent was in Nagaland and 69.41 per cent was in Arunachal Pradesh.

In the North Eastern Region, though the shortage of Doctors was not that much, but there was an acute shortage of Specialists in this region. In the PHCs, the shortage of Doctors was there only in three States viz. Nagaland, 36.90 per cent, Mizoram, 31.58 per cent and in Arunachal Pradesh, 8.23 per cent. But in the CHCs, there were no Specialists at all, in most of the States. There was only 1 (one) Surgeon in each of the States of Manipur and Sikkim and the shortage was 93.75 per cent and 75 per cent respectively. Sikkim was also having only (one) Obstetricians/Gynaecologists, but the shortfall was 75 per cent. The States of Meghalaya and Sikkim was having 1 Physician each, but the shortfall of Meghalaya was 96.15 per cent and that of Sikkim was 75 per cent. Whereas, Tripura was having 2 Physicians but the shortfall was 80 per cent. In case of Paediatricians, the position of Sikkim was slightly better. The State was having 2 Paediatricians, though it was half of their requirement. However, it is good to see that, all the States were having Radiographers in their CHCs and there was no shortage in Mizoram and Sikkim. But maximum shortage was in Manipur to the extent of 56.25 per cent, in Nagaland, it was 47.62 per cent and in Arunachal Pradesh, 29.03 per cent.

The position of Pharmacists in PHCs and CHCs of all the States was slightly better except Sikkim. It appears that, in Sikkim, the requirement was 28, but there was no Pharmacist. However, in other States, though Pharmacists were there, but it was not adequate. The State of Arunachal Pradesh was having the maximum shortage of 73.28 per cent, Manipur, 70.45 per cent, Mizoram, 46.97 per cent, Tripura, 34.12 per cent, Nagaland, 19.05 per cent and Meghalaya, 12.40 per cent. In case of Laboratory Technicians, there was no shortage in Meghalaya and Sikkim. But Arunachal Pradesh was having the maximum shortage of 84.48 per cent followed by Nagaland with 57.14 per cent, Manipur with 53.41 per cent, Mizoram with 53.03 per cent and Tripura with 50.59 per cent. The position of Nurses and Midwives in the PHCs and CHCs was comparatively better. There was no shortage in Mizoram, Nagaland, Tripura and Sikkim. However, maximum shortage of 65.23 per cent was in Arunachal Pradesh, 38.95 per cent in Meghalaya and 8.15 per cent in Manipur. Further, details can be seen from Appendix-7.4.

The service condition in the Health Sub-Centres in many of the North Eastern States as on March, 2007 was very poor. From Appendix-7.5, it can be seen that, Sikkim is the only State, where Health Worker (F)/ANM and Health Worker (M) were there in all the Sub-Centres. In Manipur and Meghalaya, though Health Worker (F)/ANM were there in all of their Sub-Centres, but 23.57 per cent of the Sub-Centres in Manipur and 30.90 per cent in Meghalaya, were without Health Worker (M). The condition of Sub-Centres in Arunachal Pradesh was very bad. Though 26.38 per cent of the Sub-Centres were without Health Worker (F)/ANM, but 72.56 per cent of the Sub-Centres were without Health Worker (M) and the most noticeable aspect was that, 26.38 per cent of the Sub-Centres were without any Health Worker. In Assam, though 1.57 per cent of the Sub-Centres were without Health Worker (F)/ANM, but 97.81 per cent of the Sub-Centres were without Health Worker (M) and 1.57 per cent were without any Health Worker.

The condition of Tripura was also not that good. In this State, 23.66 per cent of the Sub-Centres were without Health Worker (F)/ ANM, 40.93 per cent were without Health Worker (M) and 17.62 per cent were without any Health Worker. In Nagaland, 14.86 per cent of the Sub-Centres were without Health Worker (F)/ANM and an equal percentage of Sub-Centres were without Health Worker (M) and also in the same percentage of Sub-Centres, there was no Health Worker at all. In Mizoram, there was no Health Worker (F)/ANM in 5.46 per cent of the Sub-Centres, Health Worker (M) in 13.66 per cent, and there was no Health Worker at all in 1.37 per cent of the Sub-Centres. However, on the whole, it can be seen that, though there was no much difference in the proportion of Sub-Centres working without Health Worker (F)/ANM in the N.E. Region and in the country as a whole, but in case of Health Worker (M), the difference was much more. It appears that, 74.92 per cent of the Sub-Centres of this region were functioning without Health Worker (M) as against the all India figure of 36.23 per cent. Further, details can be seen from Appendix-7.5.

The Primary Health Centres (PHCs) were also suffering from shortage of Doctors, Laboratory Technicians and Pharmacists. The Appendix-7.6 will give a clear picture of this for the States of North Eastern Region as well as for the country as a whole as on March, 2007. It can be seen that, some of the PHCs of all the States of this region were running without Doctor/Laboratory Technician/ Pharmacist. However, the condition was slightly better in Assam, Meghalaya and Sikkim, as there was at least one Doctor in each and every PHC of these States. In Assam, 4.26 per cent of the PHCs were even having four or more than four Doctors, 13.11 per cent, three Doctors, 51.48 per cent, two Doctors and 31.15 per cent of the PHCs were having one Doctor, but 30.33 per cent of the PHCs were running without any Laboratory Technician. In Meghalaya, 1.94 per cent of the PHCs were having four or more than four Doctors, 14.56 per cent, two Doctors and 83.50 per cent of the PHCs were having one Doctor. Many Lady Doctors were also there in the State of Meghalaya. It can be seen that, 46.60 per cent of the PHCs were having Lady Doctor. However, the shortage of Laboratory Technician was though not much, but 25.24 per cent of the PHCs of Meghalaya were running without Pharmacist. In Sikkim, 4.17 per cent of the PHCs were having three Doctors, 50 per cent, two Doctors and 45.83 per cent of the PHCs, were having one Doctor. Like Meghalaya, Sikkim was also having many Lady Doctors. Out of total number of PHCs in Sikkim, 79.17 per cent of them were having Lady Doctor. On the other hand, though there was no shortage of Laboratory Technician, but all the PHCs of the State were running without Pharmacist.

The position of Tripura was again different. Though 8 per cent of the PHCs of the State were running without Doctor, but 12 per cent of them were having four or more than four Doctors, 24 per cent, three Doctors, 32 per cent, two Doctors and the remaining 24 per cent of the PHCs were having one Doctor. The shortage of Laboratory Technician and Pharmacist was also there. In 53.33 per cent of the PHCs of Tripura, there was no Laboratory Technician and 26.67 per cent of the PHCs were running without Pharmacist. In Manipur, though the percentage of PHCs running without Doctor was very less, which was only 1.39 per cent, but 54.17 per cent of the PHCs were having only one Doctor and 44.44 per cent were having two Doctors. Moreover, shortage of Laboratory Technician and

Pharmacist was also very much there. In this State, 61.11 per cent of the PHCs were running without Laboratory Technician and 31.94 per cent of them were running without Pharmacist. The position of Mizoram was also not good. In this State, almost one-third i.e. 31.58 per cent of the PHCs were running without Doctor. Only 1.75 per cent of the PHCs were having two Doctors and the remaining 66.67 per cent of the PHCs were having one Doctor only. Shortage of Laboratory Technician and Pharmacist was also there. There was no Laboratory Technician in 35.09 per cent of the PHCs and 38.60 per cent of the PHCs were running without Pharmacist. In case of Arunachal Pradesh and Nagaland, the details about the availability of Doctors in the PHCs were not available. On the other hand, from the available information on Laboratory Technician and Pharmacist, it can be seen that, there was an acquit shortage of both categories of staff in the PHCs of these two States.

The overall position of the PHCs of the country as a whole was also not much different. It appears that, only 1.15 per cent of the PHCs were having four or more than four Doctors, 3.22 per cent, three Doctors, 16.88 per cent, two Doctors, 42.89 per cent, only one Doctor and 3.61 per cent of the PHCs of the country were running without any Doctor. Lady Doctor was there only in 13.90 per cent of the PHCs. Shortage of Laboratory Technician and Pharmacist was also there. More than one-third i.e. 33.78 per cent of the PHCs of the country were running without Laboratory Technician and in 13.74 per cent of them, there was no Pharmacist. Further, details can be seen from Appendix-7.6.

The position in respect of Training Schools and Health and Family Welfare Training Centres was also not good. The Appendix-7.7 will give a clear picture of the number of Training Schools and Health and Family Welfare Training Centres in different States of the North Eastern Region and in the country as a whole as on March, 2006. From this, it can be seen that, Assam is the only State, where 22 numbers of ANM/HW (F) Schools, funded by Government of India, were there. In Tripura, there were 3, in Meghalaya and Nagaland, there were 2 each and only 1 ANM/HW (F) School, funded by Government of India, was there in each of the remaining States of this region. The Government of India also established only 1 LHV/ HA (F) Promotional School in the States of Assam, Manipur, Tripura and Sikkim. As regards Health and Family Welfare, there was only 1 Health and Family Welfare Training Centre in each of the States of Assam, Manipur and Meghalaya. The States of Manipur, Mizoram and Tripura, each of them was also having 1 MPW (M) Training Centre. The country as a whole was however, having 336 ANM/HW (F) Schools, funded by Government of India, 42 LHV/HA (F) Promotional Schools, established by Government of India, 47 Health and Family Welfare Training Centres and 56 MPW (M) Training Centres, as against the number of 33, 4, 3 and 3 of the North Eastern Region as a whole, which were 9.82 per cent, 9.52 per cent, 6.38 per cent and 5.36 per cent of the figures of the country as a whole respectively. Further, details can be seen from Appendix-7.7.

The position in respect of availability of Rural Health Infrastructure and coverage of rural population in the North Eastern Region was not much different than the overall position of the country. The Appendix-7.8 will give a clear picture of each of the N.E. States and the country as a whole as on March, 2007. From this it can be seen that, amongst all the States of this region, the position in respect of availability of Health Care Infrastructure was slightly better in Tripura. In this State, for every 2 villages, there was 1 Sub-Centre, for every 12 villages, there was 1 PHC and for every 87 villages, 1 CHC was there. The position of Mizoram was not much different from Tripura. Mizoram was also having 1 Sub-Centre for every 2 villages, 1 PHC for every 14 villages and 1 CHC for every 91 villages. Then was the position of Nagaland. In this State, for every 3 villages, there was 1 Sub-Centre, for every 16 villages, there was 1 PHC and for every 63 villages, 1 CHC was there. Sikkim came after that. Sikkim was also having 1 Sub-Centre for every 3 villages, 1 PHC for every 19 villages and 1 CHC for every 113 villages.

The coverage in Manipur was also not that bad. In this State, for every 6 villages, there was 1 Sub-Centre, for every 33 villages, there was 1 PHC and for every 149 villages, 1 CHC was there. The State of Assam is though the second largest in terms of area, but it is very much densely populated and, therefore, the number of villages are much more there. Even then, there was 1 Sub-Centre for every 5 villages, 1 PHC for every 43 villages and 1 CHC for every 263 villages in Assam. In Arunachal Pradesh, for every 11 villages, there was 1 Sub-Centre, for every 48 villages, there was 1 PHC and for every

131 villages, 1 CHC was there in this State. As compared to other States of this region, the coverage in Meghalaya was less. In this State, there was 1 Sub-Centre for every 15 villages, 1 PHC for every 59 villages and 1 CHC for every 232 villages.

As regards coverage of population (as per 2001 census), Assam and Tripura were on the top position. In Assam, every Sub-Centre was covering 4544 population, every PHC was covering the highest of 38059 population and each CHC was covering 232163 population. In Tripura, the position was almost the same. In this State, each Sub-Centre was covering 4583 population, each PHC was covering 35379 population and each CHC was covering the highest of 265345 population. The coverage of population in Sikkim was also very high. In Sikkim, every Sub-Centre was covering 3272 population, every PHC was covering 20041 population and every CHC was covering 120245 population. In Manipur, the extent of population coverage was also quite high. In this State, each Sub-Centre was covering 3788 population, each PHC was covering 22095 population and each CHC was covering 99426 population. This indicates that, more number of PHCs and CHCs are required in these States to ease the workload and for providing better medical facilities to the rural people.

The coverage of population in Nagaland was also high. In Nagaland, each Sub-Centre was covering 4149 population, each PHC was covering 19610 population and each CHC was covering 78440 population. Meghalaya was also not much behind. In Meghalaya, every Sub-Centre was covering 4685 population, every PHC was covering 18104 population and every CHC was covering 71720 population. The States of Mizoram and Arunachal Pradesh are less populated and, therefore, the coverage was also less. In Mizoram, each Sub-Centre was covering 1223 population, each PHC was covering 7852 population and each CHC was covering 49730 population. And in Arunachal Pradesh, every Sub-Centre was covering 2296 population, every PHC was covering 10236 population and every CHC was covering the lowest of 28067 population.

However, comparing the position of North Eastern Region as a whole with the position of the country as a whole, it can be seen that, as regards availability of Health Care Infrastructure, the position of N.E. Region was though not at per with the position of the country, but in case of coverage of population, the position of this region was a bit better than the position of the country. It can be seen that, in N.E. Region, each Sub-Centre was covering 4204 population as against 5111, each PHC was covering 29524 population as against 33191 and each CHC was covering 151019 population as against 183558 population of the country. Further, details can be seen from Appendix-7.8.

So far, it has been found that, there was an overall shortage of Medical Institutions, Doctors, Health Workers, etc, but there was no idea about the extent of shortage of these essential amenities. The Appendix-7.9 will give an idea about these shortages in each of the North Eastern States and in the country as a whole in different years. From this, it can be seen that, amongst all the States of N.E. Region, the shortage was more in Assam. In this State, for every thousand population, there was only 0.21 Medical Institution, 0.02 Doctor, 0.06 Health Worker and 0.25 Bed. The position of Tripura was slightly better than Assam. In Tripura, for every thousand population, there was 0.22 Medical Institution, 0.26 Doctor, 0.38 Health Worker and 0.77 Bed. The average number of patients treated by a Doctor was 3045 and the average number of patients attended by a Health Worker was 2032 in the State of Tripura. The position of Nagaland was more or less similar to Tripura. In Nagaland, for every thousand population, there was 0.25 Medical Institution, 0.18 Doctor, 0.32 Health Worker and 1.05 Bed. Manipur was also very much closed to Nagaland. In Manipur, there was 0.23 Medical Institution, 0.39 Doctor, 0.48 Health Worker and 1 Bed for every thousand population of the State. Moreover, the average number of patients treated by a Doctor was 1224 and the average number of patients attended by a Health Worker was 1008 in this State.

In Meghalaya, for every thousand population, there was 0.22 Medical Institution, 0.21 Doctor, 0.79 Health Worker and 1.20 Bed. But the workload of Doctors in Meghalaya was much more. The average number of patients treated by a Doctor was 3664 and the average number of patients attended by a Health Worker was 998 in the State of Meghalaya. The position of Sikkim was slightly better than Meghalaya. In Sikkim, there was 0.32 Medical Institution, 0.33 Doctor, 1.85 Health Worker and 1.65 Bed for every thousand population. And the workload of Doctor and Health Worker was also less. The average number of patients treated by a Doctor was 2778 and the average number of patients attended by a Health Worker was 492 in Sikkim. In Arunachal Pradesh, there was 0.51 Medical Institution, 0.43 Doctor, 0.42 Health Worker and 1.80 Bed for every thousand population of the State. The position of Mizoram was also more or less similar. In Mizoram, for every thousand population, there was 0.42 Medical Institution, 0.15 Doctor, 1.17 Health Worker and 2.16 Beds.

On the whole, it can be seen that, the overall position of North Eastern Region was also poorer than the overall position of the country as a whole. In N.E. Region, for every thousand population, there was 0.23 Medical Institution, 0.10 Doctor, 0.23 Health Worker and 0.54 Bed, as against the all India figures of 0.18, 0.59, 0.78 and 0.82 respectively for every thousand population of the country. Further, details can be seen from Appendix-7.9.

The programme of Family Welfare is another important aspect of Health Care System. The rapid growth of population has become a cause of concerned not only for our country, but for the whole world. Every nation is now busy in finding the ways and means to control the growth rate and to overcome the problems posed due to overpopulation. The cause of overpopulation cannot simply be attributed to the birth rate. But the fact is that, the medical science has brought about a change in the life of human being by inventing new miraculous drugs, insecticides and new health practices, which not only reduced the death rate, but also increased the life expectancy and happiness of the people.

However, realizing the consequences of rapid growth of population, the world's nations formed many organizations and arranged conferences and seminars on population issues in different places in different times with the objective to exchange the ideas and views of the Demographers, Scientists and other Statesmen on the population problem and to find out the ways and means to face the situation and to bring down the rate of birth. Thus, the family planning became the most important factor and got the first priority to face the population explosion. According to Dr. Cillov "the family planning is the freedom of the families to have the desired number of babies when they want". The family planning was also described as the "freedom of women in having a healthy delivery" and stated that it ought to be a natural right of mothers to learn the contraceptive methods, which will make them able not to give birth to the undesired babies and by this way many poor mothers will be saved from trying the hazardous and expensive way of ending pregnancy.

Dr. John Macleod, Chief of the American Association of Anatomist, took a pioneering role and first paved the way of using the contraceptive medicine for man in 1961, and thereby Sterling Winthrop Research Institute of New York made this medicine. The Research Scholars of the Institute of Technology, Pasadena, invented a kind of vaccine, which is effective on man as well as on woman and can prevent the couple completely from giving a birth. Dr. Jack Lippes of Planned Parenthood Centre, Buffalo, U.S.A., earned the worldwide fame for his invention of Loop as a contraceptive device. Further, to bring out an improvement over the plastic Loop, the Copper-T device was invented, which showed greater potentiality and a higher rate of retention with fewer complications. Later on, the Scientists, Doctors and other Research Scholars, after intensive trial, invented improved type of Pills, Loops, Caps, Diaphragm, Creams, Jellies, etc. as contraceptive devices which are very much useful and widely in practice now-a-days. The later process of family planning came as Vasectomy, Tubectomy and Sterilisation.

The knowledge of contraceptives in some way or the other was in existence for centuries and even in the pre-historic age. India was the pioneer among all the nations of the world in the field of family planning. In Sanskrit Literature of ancient India, there were several references on this, which were termed as "contraceptive recipes" by Norman Himes. The Family Planning Programme was though launched officially in India in the year 1952 i.e. in the second year of the First Five Year Plan, but the birth control movement in the country was much older than that. The first two birth control clinics anywhere in the world were established in the State of Karnataka as far back as in 1930, but in those days, the birth control was not discussed freely. In India, as well as in the West, people belonging to the elite were only practicing it. However, at the initial stages, the Family Planning Programme was more or less exploratory in nature. To begin with, a number of Family Planning Clinics were established and advice and services were provided to the persons who wanted it. Gradually, the programme gained momentum and to popularize this, research in various fields relating to demography were taken up. Moreover, the programme of mass education and motivation, services and supplies, training of workers, association of voluntary organizations, systematic involvement of such institutions representing women etc. were also taken up.

In the year 1975-76, it was felt that, involvement of the Development Departments of both State and Central Government in the Family Planning Programme are very much necessary in order to promote and progress it at a faster pace. Thus, a comprehensive National Population Policy was developed in the month of April, 1976 and keeping in view to integrate Family Planning with the overall strategy of Socio-economic development, a number of programmes were initiated. The new population policy was welcome by all and its implementation was taken up in all the States with great sincerity and with the introduction of various kinds of incentives. This created a different atmosphere amongst the women and encouraged them to come forward with the demand that, they should have their rightful say in planning the birth of their children. Ultimately, the Family Planning Programme was integrated completely with maternal and child health care services and was treated as a vital part of the overall health strategy and later on, the programme came to be known as Family Welfare Programme instead of Family Planning Programme.

The Family Welfare Programme started in the North Eastern States along with other parts of the country in the year, 1952. But in this respect, the N.E. States are lagging much behind primarily due to its topographic condition, remoteness and non-availability of infrastructural facilities. Expansion of any plan and programme takes time to reach the common people living in the remote hilly places most of whom are of primitive type and deprived of modern and scientific ways and means of living. Moreover, there are so many social taboos and many of them still have the belief that "the children are the gift of God" and any artificial check on their birth is illegal and unethical. However, now-a-days, with the gradual expansion of education, people are becoming more and more enlightened and started realizing the need for family welfare. The Government is also trying its best to popularize the Family Welfare Programme amongst the common people by introducing different kinds of incentives and also adopting various ways and means to provide all kinds of Family Welfare facilities for their benefit. The progress of Family Welfare

Programme in each of the North Eastern States as well as in the country as a whole can be seen from Appendix-7.10 and from Appendix-7.11.

The Appendix-7.10 will give the cumulative picture of Sterilisations and Intra Uterine Device (IUD) up to the year 2002-03 and also for the year 2004-05 along with different rates. From this, it can be seen that, amongst all the North Eastern States, the progress of Family Welfare Programme in Mizoram, Assam, Tripura and Sikkim was better. The State of Mizoram could achieve the highest cumulative Sterilisation rate of 87.9 per thousand population and in case of IUD insertion, the State could achieve the second highest cumulative rate of 52.2 per thousand population up to the year 2002-03. The Conventional Contraceptive (CC) users also showed an increasing trend. The annual rate of CC users per thousand population in Mizoram was 5.2 during 2002-03, which increased to 8.6 during 2004-05 and in both the years, the rate was the third highest. The cumulative Sterilisation rate for Assam was the second highest of 68.7 per thousand population and in case of IUD insertion, the cumulative rate was 31.1 per thousand population up to the year 2002-03. The annual rate of CC users per thousand population was also increasing. It was 2.5 during 2002-03 and 2.7 during 2004-05. The position of Tripura was also quite good. The cumulative Sterilisation rate for the State was the third highest of 65.2 per thousand population and the cumulative rate in case of IUD insertion was 20 per thousand population up to the year 2002-03. The annual rate of CC users per thousand population in Tripura was the highest of 12.4 during 2002-03, but that came down to 10.2 during 2004-05, which was the second highest. Next came the position of Sikkim. The cumulative Sterilisation rate for the State was though the fourth highest having 39.7 per thousand population, but the cumulative rate in case of IUD insertion was the third highest of 50.4 per thousand population up to the year 2002-03. The annual rate of CC users per thousand population was also showed an increasing trend. During 2002-03, it was the second highest of 10, but that increased to the highest of 14.9 during 2004-05.

The position of Manipur was not that bad. The cumulative Sterilisation rate for the State was though 39 per thousand population, but the cumulative rate in case of IUD insertion was the highest of

69.9 per thousand population up to the year 2002-03. The annual rate of CC users per thousand population was also increasing. During 2002-03, it was 2.1, but that increased to 3 during 2004-05. The progress of Family Welfare Programme was rather slow in the States of Arunachal Pradesh, Meghalaya and Nagaland. In Arunachal Pradesh, the cumulative Sterilisation rate was 27.9 per thousand population and the cumulative rate of IUD insertion was 44.6 per thousand population up to the year 2002-03. The annual rate of CC users per thousand population was 2.6 during 2002-03, but it came down to 2.2 during 2004-05. The State of Meghalaya registered further slow progress. In this State, the cumulative Sterilisation rate was 15.1 per thousand population and the cumulative rate of IUD insertion was 18.8 per thousand population up to the year 2002-03. However, the annual rate of CC users per thousand population was though 2.3 during 2002-03, but it showed some increasing trend and reached to 2.6 during 2004-05. The State of Nagaland registered the lowest rate in all cases. The cumulative Sterilisation rate for the State was 12.1 per thousand population and the cumulative rate in case of IUD, insertion was only 15.7 per thousand population up to the year 2002-03. The annual rate of CC users per thousand population also showed a declining trend. During 2002-03, though it was 2.1, but it came down to the lowest of only 0.5 per thousand population during 2004-05.

The overall position of North Eastern Region as a whole was also far behind than the overall position of the country as a whole in all respects. The cumulative Sterilisation rate of N.E. Region was 59.7 per thousand population as against the figure of 124 and the cumulative rate of IUD insertion in this region was only 32.3 as against the figure of 108.2 per thousand population of the country up to the year, 2003-03. Same was the position in case of CC users also. The annual rate of CC users per thousand population of N.E. Region was only 3.4 as against 24.8 during 2002-03 and 3.5 as against 32.5 of the country as a whole, during 2004-05. Further, details can be seen from Appendix-7.10.

The Appendix-7.11 will give State-wise account of Eligible Couples along with proportion of Unsterilised and Sterilised Couples as on 31st March, 2008 and also the achievement of Sterilisation during 2007-08 and 2008-09 together with percentage changes. From this, it appears that, the programme of Sterilisation was very much effective in the States of Mizoram and Sikkim since long and even though, the rate of Sterilisation came down during 2008-09, there were, proportionately, more number of Sterilised Couples in these States as on March, 2008. In Mizoram, the percentage of Unsterilised Couples was the lowest of 56.8, which means, 43.2 per cent of the Eligible Couples were Sterilised. In Sikkim, the percentage of Unsterilised Couples was the second lowest of 73.8 and that means, 26.2 per cent of the Eligible Couples were Sterilised. In Arunachal Pradesh, though the percentage of Unsterilised Couples as on 31st March, 2008 was the third lowest of 77.5, but the rate of Sterilisation was increasing faster and it registered a growth rate of 157.4 per cent during 2008-09 over 2007-08. In Assam, even though the health care facilities are comparatively better, still the programme of Sterilisation was not that much effective. It appears that, the percentage of Unsterilised Couples in Assam was 86.8 and the percentage of Sterilised Couples was 13.2, till March, 2008. But after that, it gained momentum and increased with the highest rate of 377.3 per cent during 2008-09.

In the States of Nagaland, Meghalaya, Manipur and Tripura, the progress of Sterilisation was quite slow and it appears that, 90 per cent or more of the Eligible Couples in all these States were Unsterilised till March, 2008. In Nagaland, the percentage of Unsterilised Couples was 90 and the rate of increase of Sterilisation was only 12.4 per cent during 2008-09. In Meghalaya, the percentage of Unsterilised Couples was 90.5 and the rate of achievement in respect of Sterilisation during 2008-09 was the lowest of only 5 per cent. The position of Manipur was also more or less the same. In this State, 91.2 per cent of the Eligible Couples were Unsterilised till March, 2008 and the rate of achievement during 2008-09 was only 18.9 per cent. The Sterilisation position in Tripura was not that good up to March, 2008. Till that time, 98.3 per cent of the Eligible Couples of the State were Unsterilised and only 1.7 per cent were Sterilised. However, the achievement in respect of Sterilisation during 2008-09 was quite encouraging as it reached to a growth rate of 139.7 per cent over 2007-08.

The Appendix-7.11 will also give an idea about the Estimated Number of Couples exposed to higher order of births and the proportion of their Sterilisation. From this, it appears that, in Nagaland, the highest to the extent of 56.9 per cent of the Unsterilised Couples were exposed to 3 or more than 3 births and only 29 per 10,000 of them were Sterilised. The position of Meghalaya was almost the same. In this State, 56.8 per cent of the Unsterilised Couples were exposed to higher order of 3 or more than 3 births and 31 per 10,000 of them were Sterilised. In Arunachal Pradesh, though more than half i.e. 51.8 per cent of the Unsterilised Couples were exposed to higher order of 3 or more than 3 births, but 145 per 10,000 of them, which was the second highest proportion, were Sterilised. The position of Mizoram was not much different. In this State, 42.3 per cent of the Unsterilised Couples were exposed to higher order of 3 or more than 3 births and 136 per 10,000 of them, which was the third highest proportion, were Sterilised.

In other States, the proportion of Unsterilised Couples exposed to higher order of births, were comparatively less. In Assam, 40.9 per cent of the Unsterilised Couples were exposed to higher order of 3 or more than 3 births and 63 per 10,000 of them were Sterilised. The State of Manipur showed a different picture. In this State, though 39.6 per cent of the Unsterilised Couples were exposed to higher order of 3 or more than 3 births, but the proportion of Sterilisation per 10,000 of them was the lowest of only 5. The position of Sikkim was slightly better. In this State, 33.9 per cent of the Unsterilised Couples were exposed to higher order of 3 or more than 3 births and 53 per 10,000 of them were Sterilised. Tripura was the only State, where Unsterilised Couples exposed to higher order of births were very less. In this State, not only 24.2 per cent of the Unsterilised Couples were exposed to higher order of 3 or more than 3 births, but 148 per 10,000 of them, which was the highest proportion, were also Sterilised. That indicates, from 2007-08 onwards, the programme of Family Welfare became more effective in these States and besides Sterilisation, many of the Eligible Couples were adopting other kinds of Family Welfare measures to restrict their family size, which was a good sign for controlling population growth.

However, the overall position of North Eastern Region was far behind than the overall position of the country as a whole. It appears that, as on March, 2008, the percentage of Unsterilised Couples in N.E. Region as a whole was 87.3 as against the all India figure of

61.7. Moreover, though the achievement in respect of Sterilisation in this region during 2008-09 over 2007-08 was much more to the extent of 185.7 per cent as against 4.5 per cent of the country, but the proportion of Sterilisation per 10,000 Unsterilised Couple was much less to the extent of only 26.1 as against 57.5 of the country as a whole. However, though the percentage of Unsterilised Couples exposed to higher order of 3 or more than 3 births, was almost the same of 41 and 41.1 respectively, but the proportion of Sterilisation per 10,000 Unsterilised Couples exposed to higher order of births in N.E. Region as a whole was only 68, which was not even half of the all India figure of 140 per 10,000 Unsterilised Couples of the country exposed to higher order of 3 or more than 3 births. Further, details can be seen from Appendix-7.11.

From above, it has been found that, the Health Care facilities in North Eastern Region are quite inadequate and the programme of Family Welfare is also not that much effective in many of the States of this region. Perhaps, it will take some more time to bring about a positive change in the Health Scenario and to bring down the birth rate of this region. The Appendix-7.12 will give the State-wise picture of the estimated birth rate, death rate, natural growth rate and the infant mortality rate for the year, 2006. The same information is also available for the year, 2005 in Appendix-3.3. From these two Appendices, it appears that, there was no much positive improvement in different categories of rates of 2006. Rather, it has been found that, the birth rate had been increased for the States of Nagaland and Tripura, death rate had been increased for all the States except Assam and the infant mortality rate also had been increased in many of the States. This indicates that, there was a deficiency in the Health Care System and also in the pre- and post-natal care. However, for the country as a whole, it appears that, there was a positive improvement in all categories of rates in the year, 2006. Further, details can be seen from Appendix-3.3 and Appendix-7.12.

Housing condition is another important aspect of health care amenities and mental development. People living in a better house will definitely have better mind and better health. This is also an indicator of the economic condition of the people. The Appendix-7.13 will give an idea about the state-wise percentage distribution of households living in various types of houses as per 1991 and 2001 census. From this, it can be seen that, the overall housing condition in the North Eastern States was rather poor and there was not much improvement even after a decade. However, the housing condition in the States of Sikkim, Mizoram and Meghalaya was slightly better. As per 1991 census, in Sikkim, 26.95 per cent of households were living in pucca houses, 39.11 per cent were in semi-pucca houses and 33.94 per cent were living in kutcha houses. But during next ten years, the situation slightly improved and as per 2001 census, it could be seen that, 37.87 per cent of the households were living in pucca houses and 46.26 per cent of households were living in semi-pucca houses i.e. there was an improvement of 40.52 per cent and 18.28 per cent respectively in these two categories. Simultaneously, there was a decline of 52.65 per cent in the percentage of households living in kutcha houses.

In Mizoram, as per 1991 census, 19.10 per cent of the households were living in pucca houses, 42.52 per cent were in semi-pucca houses and 38.38 per cent were living in kutcha houses. During next ten years, much improvement was there in respect of pucca houses and it could be seen from the records of 2001 census that, 52.84 per cent of households were living in pucca houses i.e. there was an improvement of 176.65 per cent and simultaneously there was a decline in the percentage of households living in both semi-pucca and kutcha houses by 39.58 per cent and 44.06 per cent respectively. The position of Meghalaya was also more or less similar. As per 1991 census, 13.30 per cent of households were living in pucca houses, 33.72 per cent were in semi-pucca and 52.98 per cent of households were living in kutcha houses. But as per 2001 census, it could be seen that, 22.14 per cent of households were living in pucca houses and 37.49 per cent of households were living in semi-pucca houses i.e. there was an improvement of 66.47 per cent and 11.18 per cent respectively in these two categories and simultaneously there was a decline by 23.80 per cent in the percentage of households living in kutcha houses.

However, the position of the country as a whole was much better than any of the North Eastern States. As per 1991 census, 41.61 per cent of the households were living in pucca houses, 30.95 per cent were in semi-pucca houses and 27.44 per cent of the households were living in kutcha houses. But as per 2001 records, it could be seen that, 51.62 per cent of the households were living in pucca houses i.e. there was an improvement of 24.06 per cent and simultaneously there was a decline in the percentage of households living in both semi-pucca and kutcha houses by 2.65 per cent and 33.53 per cent respectively. Further, details can be seen from Appendix-7.13.

Safe drinking water is the most essential thing for maintaining good health. There are many kinds of water borne diseases and very often people become the victims of these diseases due to non-availability of safe drinking water. The Government of India has given special emphases on drinking water supply and has included this as one of the six components of Bharat Nirman Programme, which was implemented in four years from 2005-06 to 2008-09 for building rural infrastructure. Further, it was also decided that, during the Bharat Nirman Programme, 55067 uncovered habitations and about 3.31 lakh slipped-back habitations would be covered and 2.17 lakh quality-affected habitations would be addressed[5].

In the North Eastern Region, safe drinking water supply position is not good in many of the States. The Appendix-7.14 will give an idea about the state-wise position of safe drinking water supply facilities as per 2001 census and also about the coverage of habitations under rural water supply scheme as on 1st April, 2006. From this, it can be seen that, the overall position of safe drinking water facilities was very poor in the States like Manipur, Meghalaya, Mizoram and Nagaland. It appears that, the percentage of households having safe drinking water facilities was only 36 in Mizoram, 37 in Manipur, 39 in Meghalaya and 46.5 in Nagaland. The position was very poor even in the urban areas of Mizoram and Nagaland. In Mizoram only 47.8 per cent of the urban households and in Nagaland only 42.3 per cent of the urban households were having safe drinking water facilities. The overall position was comparatively better in the States of Arunachal Pradesh and Sikkim. However, the overall position of the country as a whole was much better than any of the North Eastern States.

As regards coverage of habitations under rural water supply scheme, the position was slightly better. From Appendix-7.14, it appears that, 100 per cent of the habitations were fully covered in Manipur, Tripura and Sikkim. In Meghalaya, 98.4 per cent of the habitations were fully covered and 1.5 per cent was partially covered. In Mizoram, 96.8 per cent of the habitations were fully covered and

3.2 per cent were partially covered. In Assam and Arunachal Pradesh, 93 per cent and 92 per cent of the habitations in the respective states were fully covered and 6.8 per cent and 7.2 per cent respectively were partially covered. The rural water supply position in Nagaland was not good. Only 59 per cent of the habitations were fully covered, 39.9 per cent were partially covered and 1.1 per cent of the habitations was not covered at all. Further, details can be seen from Appendix-7.14.

Sanitation is another very important aspect of human life. Clean surroundings, drainage and waste disposal system, proper toilet facilities etc. are some of the very basic human needs for leading a healthy life. The toilet facility, particularly in the rural areas of our country is quite poor. For improvement of rural sanitation and hygiene, Central and State Governments have taken up different schemes at different points of time. The Centrally Sponsored Scheme of Central Rural Sanitation Programme also been remodeled as the Total Sanitation Campaign (TSC) with the main objective of bringing about an improvement in the general quality of life in rural areas, accelerate sanitation coverage, generate demand through awareness and health education, promote hygiene behaviour among students and teachers, and endeavour to reduce water and sanitation related diseases. The sanitation coverage in 1981 was only 1 per cent, which increased to 11 per cent in 1991. By the year 2001, the access to toilets improved to 21.9 per cent of the rural population. However, in the last few years, with the launch of demand-based TSC, there has been much improvement in rural sanitation coverage in the country, which has reached to 50 per cent[6].

The Appendix-7.15 will give an idea about the availability of toilet facilities in different States of North Eastern Region as well as in the country as a whole as per 2001 census and also as per 58th round of National Sample Survey (NSS) conducted during July to December, 2002. It appears from the records of 2001 census that, the toilet facilities, both in rural and urban areas, of all the States of this region were better than the overall position of the country. However, amongst all the States of this region, position of Mizorzm, Manipur and Tripura was quite satisfactory. It can be seen that, in Mizoram, 89.02 per cent of the households were having toilet facilities. In Manipur, it was 82.03 per cent and in Tripura, 81.45 per cent of the households were having toilet facilities. From the results of NSS 58th round also, it can be seen that, the position of North Eastern States was more or less same and in some cases, it was slightly better. Even in rural areas of some of the States like Manipur, Mizoram, Nagaland and Tripura, more than 90 per cent of the households were having toilet facilities and in urban areas of these States, 100 per cent of the households were having toilet facilities. Further, details can be seen from Appendix-7.15.

The Appendix 7.16 will give an idea about the state-wise percentage distribution of households according to the type of latrine they were using, as per the results of 58th round of NSS, conducted during July to December, 2002. From this, it appears that, in rural areas of most of the States of North Eastern Region, a small portion of households were having Service latrine or Septic tank. Most of them were having other type of latrine, while a sizable portion of the households were not having any latrine. In case of Septic thank/Flush system, the position of Sikkim and Nagaland were comparatively better. In Sikkim, 47.1 per cent of the households and in Nagaland, 36.1 per cent of the households were having Septic thank/Flush system. But the position of Meghalaya and Arunachal Pradesh was not satisfactory. It is seen that, 32.2 per cent of households of Meghalaya and 28.7 per cent of households of Arunachal Pradesh were not having any latrine. But each of these percentages was however much less than the all India percentage of 76.3, of that category.

In the urban areas, people were mostly having Septic tank/Flush system. In this regard, position of Sikkim, Meghalaya, Assam and Nagaland was much better. In Sikkim, 92.3 per cent of the households and in Meghalaya, 77.7 per cent of the households were having Septic tank/Flush system. In Assam, it was 76.2 per cent and in Nagaland, it was 72 per cent. The overall position of the country as a whole was also not that bad as 70.7 per cent of the urban households were having Septic tank/Flush system. However, a major portion i.e. 51.6 per cent of the urban households of Arunachal Pradesh were having Service latrine till that time, which was not a good indication in respect of improvement of quality of life of the people. Further, details can be seen from Appendix-7.16.

NOTES

1. *Economic Survey*, 2006-07, Government of India, Ministry of Finance, New Delhi, p. 216.
2. *ibid.*, pp. 217-220.
3. *ibid.*, pp. 220-222.
4. *Website of the Ministry of Health and Family Welfare*, Government of India, New Delhi.
5. *Economic Survey*, 2007-08, Government of India, Ministry of Finance, New Delhi, p. 258.
6. *ibid.*, p. 258.

8

Power Scenario

Power or electricity plays a very vital role in the life of the people. In modern world, the people, particularly the urban people, cannot think without electricity. Electricity has become as essential to the urban people as food and water. Without electricity, activities cannot start, machineries and equipments cannot function, factories cannot run or in other words, the whole process of development comes to a grinding halt. Accelerating economic growth and achieving higher standard of living depend entirely upon the availability of adequate and reliable power at an affordable cost. But, unlike other commodities, electricity cannot be stored for future use. Its generation and consumption have to be simultaneous and instantaneous. The most commonly used power is the electric power, which is generated mainly from hydro, steam, diesel, wind and gas.

The power scenario of the North Eastern Region is not very good. Though some of the States like Arunachal Pradesh, Sikkim, Meghalaya and Mizoram are having sufficient hydro power potential, but this could not be developed and almost all the States of this region are in shortage of power. From Appendix-8.1, it can be seen that, the State of Arunachal Pradesh is having the highest quantity of 50328 MW of hydro potential, but only a small quantity of 416 MW i.e. only 8.27 per cent could be developed. However, the only hope is that, another amount of 2600 MW is under development and when it will be fully developed, the power shortage of not only Arunachal Pradesh, but of many other States of this region will go. Sikkim is though having the second highest quantity of 4286 MW of hydro potential, but only a fraction of 84 MW i.e. only 1.96 per cent could be developed. The State is of course, taking interest in development of electricity and has started the work for development of another quantity of 510 MW of hydro power.

The State of Meghalaya comes in the third position in respect of hydro power potential. Out of 2394 MW, the State could develop 185 MW i.e. 7.73 per cent, and another 84 MW is under development. In Mizoram, the hydro potential is not less, but out of 2196 MW of identified capacity, nothing could be developed and only a small quantity of 60 MW is under development. The identified hydro potential in Manipur and Nagaland is not less and are having 1784 MW and 1574 MW respectively. Manipur also could develop an amount of 105 MW and another 90 MW is under-development. On the other hand, Nagaland though could develop 99 MW, but there is nothing under-development. Identified hydro power potential in Assam and Tripura is not much. In Assam, it is 680 MW and out of that, 275 MW i.e. 40.44 per cent already developed and another 100 MW is under-development. The hydro potential in Tripura is very less. It is only 15 MW, which is already developed. But both the States of Assam and Tripura are having gas based power potential also.

In spite of so much power potentiality in the North Eastern Region, almost all the States are suffering from shortage of power. The requirement and availability of power of different States, as on March, 2005 can be seen from Appendix-8.1. From this, it can be seen that, the State of Meghalaya, though generating sufficient power and supplying it to other States, but the State itself was having a deficiency of 16.2 per cent. The deficiency in Tripura was 10.5 per cent, Assam 6.4 per cent, Mizoram 5 per cent and in Manipur, it was 2.9 per cent. Only Arunachal Pradesh and Nagaland could meet their requirements by importing power from other States. The position of the country as a whole was also not good as there was a deficiency of 7.4 per cent.

The Appendix-8.2 will give a clear picture of the type-wise installed capacity, electricity generated and consumed during 2004-05. From this, it can be seen that, though all the States of this region are having hydro power potential, but Meghalaya is the only State who generated 82.32 per cent of the total generated hydro power of the North Eastern Region. Tripura generated 8.77 per cent and Sikkim 7.61 per cent. The States of Arunachal Pradesh, Mizoram and Nagaland though generated hydro power, but the quantity of each of these States was very less. Besides hydro power, the States of Assam and Tripura are having gas. Out of the total quantity of 1390 kWh of electricity produced from gas in North Eastern Region, Assam accounted for 64.96 per cent and Tripura accounted for the remaining 35.04 per cent. As regards per capita consumption of power, Sikkim and Meghalaya were on the top. During 2004-05, the per capita consumption of electricity was the highest of 397.7 kWh in Sikkim and the second highest of 352.2 kWh in Meghalaya. The per capita consumption of electricity in Arunachal Pradesh, Mizoram and Tripura was comparatively not that less. In Arunachal Pradesh, it was 144.8 kWh, Mizoram 133.7 kWh and in Tripura, it was 113.1 kWh. In Assam, Manipur and Nagaland, per capita consumption of electricity was much less and was within 70 to 97 kWh.

During 2005-06, the position was slightly improved in all the States. The per capita consumption of electricity in Meghalaya reached to 517.5 kWh followed by Sikkim with 429.8 kWh. Arunachal Pradesh occupied third position having 297.7 kWh and Mizoram retained its fourth position with 250.2 kWh. The per capita consumption of electricity in Manipur was 215.2 kWh, Tripura was 190.6 kWh, Nagaland was 179.3 and in Assam, it was the lowest of 170.7 kWh. Compare to the position of the country as a whole, the situation in all the States of this region was bad. The per capita consumption of electricity of India was 411.1 kWh during 2004-05 and 631.4 kWh during 2005-06 and both of these figures were much higher than the corresponding consumption figures of North Eastern Region. Further, details can be seen from Appendix-8.2.

The consumption of electricity in the North Eastern States is mainly domestic. Commercial use is very less and the use of industrial power at high voltage is practically *nil* in all the States except Assam and Meghalaya, as large scale industry in these States is almost non-existent. The Appendix-8.3 will give a clear picture of the quantity of electricity sold to ultimate consumers and its percentages for different kinds of consumption during 2004-05 in each of the States of this region. From this, it can be seen that, in Arunachal Pradesh, out of the total quantity of electricity sold, 39.04 per cent was for domestic purpose, 8.11 per cent for commercial use, but however, quite a big proportion of 40.24 per cent was for miscellaneous purposes. In Assam, the highest quantity of 39.28 per cent was for domestic, 12.38 per cent for commercial use and 27.50 per cent of power at high voltage was for industrial purposes. The use of power in Manipur, Mizoram and Nagaland was mainly domestic and it was above 60 per cent. In Manipur, the domestic consumption was 63.87 per cent and 17.94 per cent was for miscellaneous purposes. In Mizoram, 67.41 per cent was for domestic use and 14.35 per cent was used for public water works and sewage pumping. In Nagaland, 65.52 per cent was for domestic and 22.02 per cent was for miscellaneous purposes.

In Meghalaya, the domestic use of power was comparatively less. It can be seen that, out of the total quantity of electricity sold during 2004-05, 20.05 per cent was for domestic use, industrial power at high voltage was 56.73 per cent and 14.94 per cent was for miscellaneous purposes. In Tripura, 39.07 per cent was for domestic use, 13.20 per cent was industrial power at low and medium voltage and 14.61 per cent was for public water works and sewage pumping. The domestic and commercial use of power in Sikkim was quite high. For domestic, it was 43.45 per cent while commercial use accounted for 24.70 per cent. The electricity used for public lighting in all the States was comparatively much less. In Meghalaya, it was the lowest of 0.17 per cent and in Sikkim, it was the highest of 19.94 per cent. The use of electricity for agriculture was almost *nil* in all the States of this region except Tripura and Assam. Tripura used quite a high proportion of 18.68 per cent and Assam used 0.78 per cent of their respective total quantity of electricity sold, for agriculture purpose. However, the consumption pattern of the country as a whole was slightly different. It can be seen that, out of the total quantity of electricity sold during 2004-05, 24.83 per cent was used for domestic purpose, 27.09 per cent as industrial power at high voltage and 22.99 per cent was used for agriculture purpose. Further, details can be seen from Appendix-8.3.

In the North Eastern States, the electricity installed capacity and generation do not follow any particular pattern. Sometimes, the installed capacity is not fully utilized and sometimes the generation is more than the installed capacity. The Appendix-8.4 will give a clear picture of the electricity installed capacity and generation from the year 1996-97 to 2005-06 for all the States of this region. From this, it can be seen that, the absolute increase in the installed capacity over a period of 9 years was not much, in all the States. However, though the percentage increase of installed capacity over that period was very high to the extent of 1216.7 in Manipur and 1616.7 in Nagaland, but the absolute increase of installed capacity was only145 MW i.e. from 12 MW to 158 MW in Manipur and 97 MW i.e. from 6 MW to 103 MW in Nagaland. The quantity of electricity generated in these two States from 1996-97 to 2004-05 was also very less and it showed many ups and downs over these years.

Assam, Meghalaya and Tripura are the only three States which have shown more or less a steady increase in the installed capacity as well as in case of generation during this period. In Assam, though the percentage increase in the installed capacity was 89.4 over a gap of 9 years, but the percentage increase in case of generation was 562.8 over a period of 8 years. In Meghalaya, the percentage increase in installed capacity was 52.4, but the percentage increase in the generation was much more to the extent of 1075.6 during the same periods. The position of Tripura was even better. The percentage increase in the installed capacity was though 218.2 over a gap of 9 years, but in case of generation, it was very high to the extent of 2763.9 per cent over a gap of 8 years in that State. These three States are the main electricity generating States in this region. However, compare to the position of the country as a whole, the percentage increase in case of generation of electricity in North Eastern Region was much less to 873.7 as against the all India figure of 1405.5 per cent, over a gap of 8 years i.e. from 1996-97 to 2004-05. Further, details can be seen from Appendix-8.4.

The consumption of electricity in most of the North Eastern States remained almost stagnant for quite a long period. In some of the States, viz. Assam and Manipur, the consumption even went down. The Appendix-8.5 will give a clear picture of the consumption pattern of electricity from 1997-98 to 2004-05 i.e. for a period of 7 years for all the States of this region as well as for the country as a whole. From this, it can be seen that, Meghalaya and Sikkim are the only two States, who could register a reasonable increase in the consumption of electricity. In Meghalaya, the consumption of electricity by the end consumers during 1997-98 was 321.4 Gwh but, it went up to 855.9 Gwh during 2004-05 registering an increase of 166.3 per cent. In Sikkim, the total consumption during 1997-98 was 92.5 Gwh but, it increased to 226.7 Gwh during 2004-05 recording a growth of 145.1 per cent. In all other States, except Assam and

Manipur, the rate of increase was very less. It was within 20 to 50 per cent. In Assam, the consumption however declined by 1.8 per cent, where as, in Manipur, the decline was much more to the extent of 44.9 per cent from 1997-98 to 2004-05 i.e. within a gap of 7 years. This obviously reflects the differential growth in economic activities. The increase in the consumption of electricity in the country as a whole was also not much. It was only 30.1 per cent during that period. Further, details can be seen from Appendix-8.5.

The condition of rural electrification in the North Eastern Region is not very good. Though all the towns of this region are electrified, but almost half of the villages of many of the States are not having electricity. From Appendix 8.6, it can be seen that, up to March, 2005, only 48.3 per cent villages of Arunachal Pradesh and 51.3 per cent of villages of Assam, were electrified. The percentage of electrified villages in Meghalaya and Tripura was almost same. In Meghalaya, it was 57.6 per cent and in Tripura, it was 57.2 per cent. The position of Nagaland was not that bad as 66.9 per cent of its villages were having electricity. The percentage of villages electrified in Mizoram and Manipur was also more or less same. In Mizoram, it was 80.6 per cent and in Manipur, it was 82.2 per cent. Amongst all the States of this region, the position of rural electrification in Sikkim was much better. Upto March, 2005, 94.4 per cent of villages of Sikkim were electrified. However, the overall position of North Eastern Region was not good. The percentage of electrified villages was only 54.3, which was much less than the overall percentage of 74.1 of the country as a whole. Further, details can be seen from Appendix-8.6.

In the North Eastern Region, though all the towns are electrified but, there are many households, even in urban areas, who do not have electricity. The condition in the rural areas is much more precarious. Even if a village is provided with electricity, there is no certainty that, all the households of that village will also have electricity. The Appendix-8.7 will give a clear picture of the availability scenario of electricity in urban and rural areas of all the States of this region. From the information of 2001 census, it can be seen that, the condition of Assam was very poor. In the urban areas, though 74.29 per cent of the household were having electricity but in rural areas, only a small proportion of 16.54 per cent of the households were having electricity. The State of Meghalaya though supplying electricity to other States but only 30.26 per cent of its households in rural and 88.14 per cent of households in urban were having electricity. Similar was the condition of Tripura. The percentage of households having electricity in rural areas was 31.75 and in urban, it was 86.36.

The proportion of electrified households in rural areas of Arunachal Pradesh and Mizoram was more or less same. In Arunachal Pradesh, it was 44.53 per cent and in Mizoram, it was 44.14 per cent. But in urban areas, the percentage of electrified households was more in Mizoram i.e. 94.42 per cent, than the percentage figure of 89.42 of Arunachal Pradesh. The condition of rural electrification in Manipur and Nagaland was slightly better. In Manipur, 52.53 per cent of the rural households were electrified and in Nagaland, it was 56.88 per cent. Whereas, in urban areas, it was not that good. In Manipur, 81.99 per cent of the urban households were having electricity and in Nagaland, it was slightly better to the extent of 90.33 per cent. Amongst all the States of North Eastern Region, the condition of Sikkim was the best both in case of rural as well as in urban. In this State, 75.02 per cent of the rural households and 97.09 per cent of the urban households were having electricity. The condition of the country as a whole was also not that good. Only 43.53 per cent of the rural households and 87.58 per cent of the urban households were having electricity till 2001.

However, as per information of 59th and 60th rounds of NSS, Assam and Manipur made considerable progress in this respect. In Assam, at the end of June, 2004, the percentage of rural households having electricity went up to 25.8 per cent and in urban, it went up to 95.9 per cent. In case of Manipur, the percentage of rural households having electricity went up to 80.9 per cent and in urban, it went up to 95.7 per cent. The percentage of urban electrified households in Mizoram reached to 99.7 till that time. The condition of the country as a whole was also improved considerably. 53.5 per cent of the households in rural areas and 92.2 per cent of the households in urban areas were having electricity at the end of June, 04. Further, details can be seen from Appendix-8.7.

It is a fact that, though the power generation in all the States of North Eastern Region has increased considerably, but they are yet to generate enough power even to meet their own requirements. There is always a shortage of power almost in all the States and that is not only affecting the normal life of the people, but also affecting the economic development of the States. The North Eastern Region has vast hydro power potential, which was estimated to 63257 MW and almost 80 per cent of this is in Arunachal Pradesh. However, due to various reasons, only about 2 per cent of the total hydro power potential of this region could be tapped so far. There is also an imbalance between hydel and thermal power, both in terms of generation and availability in this region.

At the initial stages, the North Eastern Council (NEC) played a very vital role for the development of power in this region and funded many big power projects in different States. The implementation of the projects was mostly through North East Electrical Power Corporation (NEEPCO)[1]. Later on, NEC however, restricted its funding to small power projects only.

The organizations like NHPC and PGCIL have also started their activities in the North Eastern Region. The NHPC has taken up many power projects for implementation in this region[2]. The PGCIL however, restricted its activities to inter-state transmission systems only[3]. Sub-transmission and distribution have been taken up mainly in the state sector with financial assistance from Ministry of DONER and NEC[4]. In the meanwhile, ONGC and ILFS are also in the process of setting up the 750 MW Palatana Gas Power Project in Tripura. Assam and Tripura have already entered into a MoU with ONGC/ ILFS for purchase of power[5]. Now a days the organization like NTPC is also taking up Thermal Power Project in North Eastern Region and once all this power projects are completed, there will perhaps be no shortage of power in this region instead, the North Eastern Region can supply power to other parts of the country.

NOTES

1. *North Eastern Region—VISION-2020*, Ministry of Development of North Eastern Region, North Eastern Council, Vol. II, p. 175.
2. *ibid.*, p. 176.
3. *ibid.*, p. 178.
4. *ibid.*, p. 178.
5. *ibid.*, p. 178.

9
Industrial Scenario

The Industrial scenario of our country is not bad. It is seen that, from the very ancient time, India has been famous for its industries. Even in the days of the Indus Valley Civilization, India had kept up a brisk trade with Sumar, Elam, Ur, Kish and the other advanced countries of the times, in metals, precious stones and other articles. In the mediaeval age, the wealth of India had become proverbial in far off countries and the magnificence of the court of the Great Mugal had dazzled even eyes which were accustomed to the pomp of Versailles[1]. Indian artifacts of various kinds also filled the markets of the West—gleaming brassware, embroidered shawls, iridescent silks, perfumes, pottery, gold-laced cloth, leather fabrics, gems and gem-studded ornaments and textiles excelled. Indian cotton and silk textiles by their sheer elegance and utility have continued even today, as fabrics of renown. The fabrics like Chintz, Calico and Khaki are very famous. The best Chintz were made in Golconda, Tamil Nadu and Gujarat. Calico is plainly reminiscent of Calicut and Khaki was pioneered by the veteran weavers of the west coast[2].

But, with the advent of the British, things changed. The British deliberately set out to destroy the traditional industries and therefore, India ceased to be a producer of finished goods and became, instead, a supplier of raw materials to British Industry. Western machine-made goods replaced Indian handicrafts. Moreover, the spread of railway transport and emergence of large-scale industry in India accelerated the decline of Indian cottage industries. However, after independence, it was decided to salvage this precious heritage from the junk-heap of history. Fortunately, the inherited talents of centuries lay dormant in the nooks and corners of rural India and workers skilled in practically all fields of production from weaving to metallurgy could be found again. And concerted efforts were made to develop the small scale sector and to organize these talents and re-orient them to suit modern conditions[3].

In spite of all these, the credit for modernizing Indian industry goes to the Britishers. It has been found that, the first iron-smelter was established by them in Madras in 1815, the first cotton mill near Calcutta in 1818, the first coal mine at Raniganj in 1820 and the first coffee plantation was opened in 1823. The pioneers continued to come forward even after 1850. The Jute industry, a well established cottage industry, was modernized by British entrepreneurs in 1854. The first rubber plantation was started in Kerala in 1900 and the first cement plant was set up in Madras in 1904[4].

Thereafter, a second generation of pioneers, almost all of them Indians, initiated setting up of modern industry in India. Among these pioneering ventures were Bombay Spinning and Weaving Company (1854), Bengal Iron Works (1854), Rally (Paper) Mills (1870) and Tata Iron and Steel (1907). The industrial growth at the initial stages was though slow, but by the end of First World War, India was having so many industries like coal, cotton, textiles, jute, cement, paper, iron and steel, tea and coffee, etc. The British administration also paid more attention to Indian industries and the policy of protection, started in 1922, gave a fillip to industrial growth. As a result, many new industries came up and, therefore, from 1925 to 1946, consumer industries predominated in India. From the beginning of First Five Year Plan in 1951, the country not only gave special emphasis on expanding capacities of the existing industries, but also made good beginnings in a host of other fields like heavy engineering, plant and machinery, drugs and pharmaceuticals, electrical equipments and farm inputs e.g. tractors, fertilizers and pesticides[5].

The growth of Small Scale Industries (SSI) in India during the plan periods has been described as a revolution. It assumed a distinctive role in the developmental process. The Industrial Policy resolution of 1956 says, "Government of India...stress the role of cottage, village and small scale industries in the development of the national economy. They provide immediate large scale employment; they offer a method of ensuring a more equitable distribution of the national income; and they facilitate an effective mobilization of resources of capital and skill which might otherwise remain unutilized"[6]. The small scale sector, which started with the manufacture of simple items like buckets, trunks, agricultural implements, etc., with the help of simple hand tools, has now entered into many sophisticated fields like electronics, plastics, chemicals, precision instruments, food processing and preserving, textiles, printing and many other manufacturing and servicing activities and using modern equipments and machineries.

The Indian Industry has come a long way and has passed through so many Annual Plans and Five Year Plans and now stepped into the third year of Eleventh Five Year Plan (2007-2012). During all these years, so many Acts were made/amended, policy resolutions were taken and various ways and means were adopted for the development of industry of our country as well as to assess the growth of this sector. Moreover, the Micro and Small Enterprises (MSEs) always considered as an important segment of the Indian economy. It has been found that, the MSEs have contributed around 39 per cent of the country's manufacturing output and 34 per cent of its exports in 2004-05. It also provided employment to around 29.5 million people in rural and urban areas of our country[7].

The process of economic liberalization and market reforms, while exposing the Indian MSEs to increasing levels of domestic and global competition, has also opened up attractive possibilities of access to larger markets and of stronger and deeper linkages of MSEs with larger enterprises. To cope up with such situation and to enable MSEs to enhance their competitive strength, the Government of India has taken some initiatives and measures during 2006-07, which include: (i) Enactment of the Micro, Small and Medium Enterprises Development (SMED) Act, 2006, (ii) Amendment of the Khadi and Village Industries Commission (KVIC) Act, 1956, (iii) A package for promotion of Micro and Small Enterprises to address most of the concerns in the areas e.g. credit, cluster-based development, infrastructure, technology and marketing, (iv) Setting up of an Empowered Group of Ministers (EGoM) under the Chairmanship of the External Affairs Minister to lay down a comprehensive policy for cluster-development and oversee its implementation, (v) Introduction of life insurance cover for chief promoters of units provided guarantee cover by the Credit Guarantee

Fund Trust for Small Industries (CGFTSI), under the Credit Guarantee Scheme, and (vi) De-reserved 180 items reserved for exclusive manufacture in micro and small enterprises on 16th May, 2006 and 87 such items have been de-reserved on 22nd January, 2007, after due consultation with the stakeholders[8].

The Micro, Small and Medium Enterprises Development Act, 2006 provides the first-ever legal framework for recognition of the concept of "enterprise" (both manufacturing and services) and integrating the three tiers of these enterprises, viz. micro, small and medium. Under this Act, enterprises have been categorized broadly into those engaged in (i) manufacturing, and (ii) providing/rendering of services. Both the categories have been further classified into micro, small and medium enterprises, based on their investment in plant and machinery. Under Manufacturing Enterprises; Micro Enterprises are those whose investment is up to Rs. 25 lakh. Small Enterprises are those whose investment is above Rs. 25 lakh and up to Rs. 5 crore. And the Medium Enterprises are those whose investment is above Rs. 5 crore and up to Rs. 10 crore. Under Service Enterprises; Micro Enterprises are those whose investment is up to Rs. 10 lakh. Small Enterprises are those whose investment is above Rs. 10 lakh and up to Rs. 2 crore. And the Medium Enterprises are those whose investment is above Rs. 2 crore and up to Rs. 5 crore[9].

The Act further provides for a statutory consultative mechanism at the national level with wide representation of all sections of stakeholders, particularly the three classes of enterprises, and with a wide range of advisory functions, and an Advisory Committee to assist the Board and the Centre/State Government. The other features of the Act include: (i) establishment of specific Funds for the promotion, development and enhancement of competitiveness, (ii) notification of schemes/programmes for this purpose, (iii) progressive credit policies and practices, (iv) preference in Government procurements to products and services and services of the micro and small enterprises, (v) more effective mechanism for mitigating the problems of delayed payments to micro and small enterprises, and (vi) simplification of the process of closure of business by all three categories of enterprises[10].

The Enterprises are of two types viz. (i) Organised Sector Enterprises, and (ii) Un-organised Sector Enterprises. Organised

Sector Enterprises are registered under some Factories Act, but the Un-organised Sector Enterprises are either registered under some local Authority e.g. Directorate of Industries/District Industries Centre (DIC) or are working with any other registration. To collect the Industrial statistics of the Organised Sector, the Government of India, started the Annual Survey of Industries (ASI) in the year, 1959 under the authority of the Collection of Statistics Act, 1953. The ASI covers the industrial units which are registered under Sections 2m (i) and 2m (ii) of the Factories Act, 1948 and Bidi and Cigar establishments registered under the Bidi and Cigar Workers (Conditions of Employment) Act, 1966. The survey mainly provides statistical information for assessing and evaluating objectively and realistically the change in the growth, composition and structure of the Organised Manufacturing and Servicing sector[11].

For the purpose of ASI, a Factory has been defined as, "Any Premises" wherein (i) Ten or more workers are engaged in or were engaged in carrying out any manufacturing activities with power on any day of the preceding twelve months from the date of survey, and (ii) Twenty or more workers are engaged in or were engaged in carrying out any manufacturing activities without power on any day of the preceding twelve months from the date of survey. The manufacturing activities generally include; making, altering, ornamenting, finishing, packing, oiling, washing, cleaning, breaking-up, demolishing or otherwise treating or adapting any article or substance with a view to its use, sale, transport, delivery or disposal. It also include; pumping oil, water or sewage, generating, transforming or transmitting power, printing of books, magazines, journals, etc. or service activities related to printing, constructing, reconstructing, repairing, refitting, finishing, motion picture, radio, television and other entertainment activities, other service activities like washing and dry cleaning, hair dressing and other beauty treatment, etc. In other words, it can be said that, the ASI covers all manufacturing, repairing and servicing activities, which have been classified under 3 or 4 digit level of National Industrial Classification (NIC) 1998, starting from 014 to 930[12]. The statistical information on the Un-organized sector is not always available. The National Sample Survey Organisation, however, covering this sector under their quinquennial surveys or as and when, it is needed.

The Industrial Scenario of the North Eastern Region is quite poor. It is seen that, there is hardly any registered factory in many of the North Eastern States. And the States of Arunachal Prades, Mizoram and Sikkim are not even covered under ASI. In this region, Assam is the largest industrialized State and almost 80 per cent of the registered factories of North Eastern Region are in Assam. However, the number of Large and Medium Industries are very less. The Industries of this region are mainly Small Scale Industries (SSIs) and are primarily in the un-organized sector. The activities of Sericulture, Handloom and Handicrafts, Khadi and Village Industries, etc. are also there in all the States. Some of the Handloom products like Eri and Muga shawls and the Silk Saris of Assam, Carpets of Arunachal Pradesh and the Cane and Bamboo products of Tripura are very famous.

The Appendix-9.1 will give a clear picture of the Large and Medium Industries as well as of the Small Scale Industries in different States of this region and its growth in different years from 1997-98 to 2002-03. From this, it can be seen that, Assam was having the highest of 120 number of Large and Medium Industries, which alone accounted for 56.34 per cent of the total number of Large and Medium Industries of this region. The State of Meghalaya was having the second highest of 49 numbers i.e. 23.00 per cent, while Arunachal Pradesh was having 15 numbers i.e. 7.04 per cent and Manipur was having 12 numbers i.e. 5.63 per cent of the total number of Large and Medium Industries of this region. Other States were having a very few number of Large and Medium Industries.

In case of Small Scale Industries (SSIs), the State of Assam was again on the top and it accounted for almost 64 per cent of the total number of SSIs of this region in all these years from 1997-98 to 2002-03. But the annual growth of SSIs in Assam was not much. It was ranging from 4.99 per cent to 6.84 per cent over these years. The growth of SSIs in Nagaland was very fast. Though the total number of SSIs in Nagaland was only 1.32 per cent of the total number of SSIs in 1997-98, but it increased to 3.56 per cent of the total number of SSIs of this region in 2002-03 with a high annual growth rate ranging from 15.78 per cent to 37.92 per cent over these years. The growth of SSIs was also comparatively high in Meghalaya. In 1997-98, Meghalaya was having 5.55 per cent of the total number of SSIs of this region, but in 2002-03, the State accounted for 5.97 per cent of the total number of SSIs of this region and the annual growth was ranging from 4.18 per cent to 8.87 per cent over these years. The number of SSIs in Manipur was also comparatively high and it was almost 9 per cent of the total number of SSIs of this region. But the annual growth was comparatively less. It was ranging from 1.54 per cent to 3.42 per cent over these years. Further, details can be seen from the Appendix-9.1.

The Appendix-9.2 will give an idea about the status of the Registered SSI units in different States of this region as on 2001-02. From this, it can be seen that, in case of Registered SSI units also, Assam was on the top and it accounted for 56.28 per cent of the total number of SSIs of this region. Further, it can be seen that, in most of the States, almost half and in some cases, even more than half of the SSI units were closed. The State of Assam was though having the highest number of SSI units, but interestingly, it was also having the highest proportion of closed SSI units, which was to the extent of 58.30 per cent. That followed by Tripura with 52.90 per cent, Meghalaya with 49.60 per cent and Arunachal Pradesh with 49.30 per cent. The proportion of closed SSI units was comparatively less in Nagaland and Manipur. In Nagaland, it was 18.50 per cent and in Maniput, it was 21.05 per cent.

However, though the overall proportion of closed SSI units in the North Eastern Region was slightly better than the overall proportion of the country, as the percentage of closed SSI units in this region was 38.96 as against the all India figure of 39.23 per cent, but the total number of closed units in the North Eastern Region was only 1.85 per cent of the total number of closed units of the country and the total number of working units of this region was also only 1.87 per cent of the total number of working units of the country. This indicates that, compared to the Small Scale Industrial activities of the country, the Small Scale Industrial activities of this region was very less. As regards percentage distribution of principal characteristics of the Registered SSI units e.g. number of working units, market value of fixed assets, original value of plants and machineries, employment, gross output, etc. in the North Eastern States, it was also very less compared to the overall position of the country. Further, details can be seen from Appendix-9.2.

The Appendix-9.3 will give an idea about the percentage

distribution of sick SSI units with reasons, as per census of SSI, 2001-02 and the details of State-wise Entrepreneurs Trained by Indian Institute of Entrepreneurship (IIE), Guwahati during April, 1994 to March, 2004. From this, it can be seen that, in the North Eastern Region, the sickness of the SSI units was mainly due to delay in repayment of loan and continuous declines in gross output. As regards Training of Entrepreneurs, the Indian Institute of Entrepreneurship, Guwahati took a lead role and trained 1999 Entrepreneurs within a period of 10 years and extended various supports to them for establishing SSI units and getting loans from various financial institutions. On completion of training, 997 Entrepreneurs i.e. almost 50 per cent of the trained Entrepreneurs applied for Bank finance and they could finally set-up a total number of 661 SSI units, though all were not with Bank finance. Maximum number of units were set-up in Assam, Manipur, Meghalaya and Arunachal Pradesh. The number of units set-up with Bank finance was 275, which was 27.58 per cent of the total number of Entrepreneurs applied for Bank finance. Further, details can be seen from Appendix-9.3.

The Small Scale Industries (SSIs) were primarily of three categories viz. manufacturing, repairing and maintenance and services. In most of the States, maximum number of manufacturing units, were in the rural areas, whereas the number of repairing and maintenance and the services units were mostly in the urban areas in many of the States. The Appendix-9.4 will give a clear picture of the percentage distribution of the rural-urban SSI units in each of the States of this region according to the census of SSI, 2001-02. From this, it can be seen that, in Nagaland, Manipur, Meghalaya, Assam and Sikkim, most of the manufacturing units were in rural areas, whereas, most of the Repairing and maintenance as well as the services units were in the urban areas in the States of Arunachal Pradesh, Meghalaya, Tripura and Sikkim. In case of manufacturing industries, the position of the country was also similar to the North Eastern Region i.e. most of the units were in the rural areas. But in case of repairing and maintenance as well as the services units, the position of the country was different, as these were almost equally divided amongst the rural and urban areas. However, compare to the position of the country, the output and the employment in the SSI units of the North Eastern Region was very less. The total output of this region was only 1.78 per cent and the total employment was only 3.11 per cent of the total employment in the SSI units of the country. Further, details can be seen from Appendix-9.4.

The North Eastern Region is of course quite rich in Handloom and Handicraft activities. Many people are engaged in these activities and maintaining their lively hood out of it. The Handloom and Handicraft activities of this region are though very famous not only in India, but also in abroad. But these activities, particularly in the rural areas, are suffering from absence of proper communication, non-availability of raw materials, financial help, marketing of finished products, etc. and due to that, many of the Handlooms are lying idle. The Appendix-9.5 will give an idea about the Handloom and Handicraft activities in different States of this region according to the Handloom and Handicraft census, 1995-96. From this, it can be seen that, though Handloom activities were there in all the States, but the State of Assam alone accounted for 72.13 per cent of the total Handlooms of this region. Manipur was in the second position having 13.83 per cent, followed by Tripura with 6.09 per cent, Nagaland with 3.97 per cent and Arunachal Pradesh with 2.33 per cent. Number of Handlooms was comparatively less in Meghalaya and Mizoram. But the proportion of idle looms was the highest in Mizoram. In this State, out of the total looms, 39.53 per cent were idle. Assam and Nagaland were having almost the same proportion of idle looms. In Assam, out of total looms, 7.84 per cent were idle and in Nagaland, it was 7.57 per cent. The proportion of idle looms was comparatively less in other States.

The Handicrafts of the North Eastern States are very famous. The States of Manipur, Tripura, Assam and Nagaland were having maximum number of Handicraft units. From Appendix-9.5, it can be seen that, Manipur was having 7.74 per cent of the total number of Handicraft units of the country, followed by Tripura with 6.11 per cent, Assam with 2.39 per cent and Nagaland with 1.39 per cent. North Eastern Region as a whole was having 19.22 per cent of the total number of Handicraft units of the country. As regards Artisans, Manipur alone accounted for 9.29 per cent of the total number of Artisans of the country, while Tripura accounted for 5.98 per cent, Assam, 2.45 per cent and Nagaland, 1.95 per cent. However, in terms of value of production, Nagaland was on the top with 35.98 per cent, followed by Assam with 29.72 per cent of the total value of Handicrafts production of the country. The State of Meghalaya was though having less number of Handicraft units, but the production of these units were more and it could account for 9.80 per cent of the total value of the country. The North Eastern Region as a whole, on the other hand, could account for 79.58 per cent of the total value of Handicraft products of the country. This shows the quality and popularity of the Handicraft products of the North Eastern Region. Further, details can be seen from Appendix-9.5.

Khadi and Village Industries (KVIs) have a unique capacity of utilizing locally available resources by adopting simple techniques and generating large-scale employment opportunities for the villagers at a low capital cost. These Industries also have the capacity to develop local initiatives, co-operation and the spirit of self-reliance in the economy. The Khadi and Village Industries of the North Eastern Region are quite famous and also important factors of employment generation as well as of economic development of this region. The Appendix 9.6 will give an idea about the physical performance of Khadi and Village Industries e.g. production and sale value of different items, employment generation and earnings in different States of this region during 2002-03 and 2003-04. From this, it can be seen that, though all the States were having both Khadi and Village Industries, but Village Industries were the major activities and the production and sale of goods of this sector was much more in all the States. The States of Assam, Manipur and Meghalaya were having some activities on polyester also.

The States of Assam, Manipur and Nagaland were in a better position in terms of production and sale value of goods, employment and earnings. During 2002-03, Assam was on the top with 22.98 per cent of the total production value and 19.86 per cent of the total sale value of this region. The State provided employment to 1.12 lakh persons, which was 39.16 per cent of the total employment, but in case of earnings, it was in the third position with 19.49 per cent of the total earnings of this region. During 2003-04, the situation improved further and these percentages became 26.21, 29.24, 39.23 and 23.73 respectively. The State of Manipur was in the second position with 22.67 per cent of production value, 19.62 per cent of sale value, 21.33 per cent of total employment and 21.22 per cent of the total earnings of this region, during 2002-03. During 2003-04 also, the State of Manipur could retain its second position with 19.71 per cent of production value, 17.78 per cent of sale value and 22.83 per cent of the total employment of this region. But in case of earnings, the State went down to third position with 18.52 per cent of the total sale value of the region. The State of Nagaland was though in the third position in respect of production value with 17.32 per cent, sale value with 19.09 per cent and in respect of employment with 10.49 per cent of the total employment of the region, but in case of earning, it was on the top with 24.27 per cent of the total earnings of the region during 2002-03. During 2003-04, Nagaland was also on the third position in case of production value with 15.60 per cent, sale value with 15.23 per cent and in case of employment with 9.65 per cent of the total employment of this region, but in case of earnings, it could not retain its first position and slipped down to second position with 21.72 per cent of the total earnings of the North Eastern Region. Further, details can be seen from Appendix 9.6.

The Sericulture activities are also there in all the States of North Eastern Region. Among the Sericulture activities, production of Mulberry Silk, Oak Tasar, Eri and Muga are prominent. Some of the products like Muga and Silk sarees, Endi shawls particularly of Assam are very famous. The Appendix-9.7 will give an idea about the Sericulture activities from 1999 to 2004 in different States of this region. From this, it can be seen that, Manipur and Assam are the two main Mulberry cultivating States. During 1999-2000 to 2003-2004, Manipur accounted for 44.12 per cent to 51.48 per cent of the total Mulberry cultivated area and produced 31.63 per cent to 67.58 per cent of the total production of Mulberry reeling cocoons of this region. While the State of Assam, on the other hand, accounted for 24.56 per cent to 28.83 per cent of the total cultivated area and produced 21.74 per cent to 33.42 per cent of the total production of Mulberry reeling cocoons of this region during this period.

In case of production of Eri cut cocoons, Assam was on the top and it produced 42.62 per cent to 54.26 per cent of the total production of Eri cut cocoons of this region from 1998-1999 to 2003-2004. Next to Assam was Manipur. Manipur produced 18.70 per cent to 34.75 per cent of the total, while Meghalaya accounted for 15.28 per cent to 26.36 per cent of the total production of Eri cut cocoons of this region during this period. In case of Muga, it can be seen that, Assam was the main Muga producing State and it could produce 93.73 per cent to 97.42 per cent of the total Muga reeling cccoons of this region during the period from 1998-99 to 2003-04. The Sericulture activity of Assam is very much well-known. There are many Sericulture farms in Assam and a large number of people are engaged in this activities. The Shoal Kuchi farm is very famous for its Muga and Silk sarees and Endi shawls.

In spite of all these, the overall industrial scenario of the North Eastern Region is very much dismal. The number of Large and Medium Industries are very less and there is hardly any registered Factory in many of the States. The States like Arunachal Pradesh, Mizoram and Sikkim are not even covered under Annual Survey of Industry (ASI.). The Appendix-9.8 will give an idea about the number of Factories in other five States of this region, their working capital, productive capacity, workers, emoluments, input and output and value added, etc. as per ASI, 2003-04 and 2004-05. From this, it can be seen that, almost 77 per cent of the Factories of this region were in Assam, about 13 per cent were in Tripura, little more than 5 per cent were in Nagaland and little more than 2 per cent each were in Meghalaya as well as in Manipur. But in case of fixed capital, working capital and invested capital, the State of Assam dominated the scene. The State alone accounted for almost 97 per cent of the total fixed capital, 90 per cent of the working capital and 96 per cent of the invested capital of this region. This indicates the extent of monetary investment of the State in the industrial activities of this region.

The State of Assam also provided employment to more than a lakh of people i.e. about 84 per cent of the total employed persons of this region, were in Assam. The State of Tripura also could provide employment to a good number of people, which was about 11 per cent. As regards total input, total output and net value added, Assam had the largest share. Out of the total input of the region, the share of Assam was almost 95 per cent. In case of total output and net value added, the share was almost 94 per cent in both the cases. However, from the information of ASI, 2003-04 and 2004-05, it appears that, though the State of Assam registered an increasing trend in respect of fixed capital, working capital, invested capital, employment, total input and output etc. but the State showed a declining trend in case of net value added, gross fixed capital formation and value of addition in stock. In these respects, the position of other States was also very much disappointing. This was definitely not a healthy sign.

Compared to the industrial scenario of the country, the position of the North Eastern Region was very poor in all respects. It can be seen that, the total number of factories of this region was about 1.6 per cent of the total number of factories of the country. In case of fixed capital, working capital and invested capital, it was only about 1.4 per cent in each case. The total number of persons engaged in the industrial activities in this region was only 1.7 per cent. The total amount of input and output were about 1.3 per cent each and the net value added was about 1.6 per cent of the total value added of the country. Moreover, in many cases, the North Eastern Region showed a declining trend, whereas, the overall position of the country showed an increasing trend in all respects. In some cases, the increase was even more than 100 per cent. Further, details can be seen from Appendix-9.8.

The industries of the North Eastern Region could not grow up to the expected level due to so many reasons. Infrastructure, transportation, availability of raw materials and marketing facilities for finished products, particularly in the hilly areas, are the main bottlenecks for industrial development. Non-availability of individual land in the hilly region is another problem. In the hilly States, lands are mostly community lands and therefore, at the time of leasing lands for setting up industry, non-availability of individually owned land remains a major hurdle for industrialization. Moreover, in absence of well defined land ownership, the banks are not in a position to provide industrial loans. Further, in the absence of a comprehensive industrial policy with state specific requirements and the lack of private sector investments are the other factors for slow growth of the industry. Shortage of job specific skilled labourers is another important aspect. And on the whole, the economic viability, safety and security of an industry, are the watch words for its growth.

In spite of all these, there is some hope on Handloom and Handicrafts and in the Sericulture activities of this region, which have the international reputation. Moreover, North Eastern Region is the world's largest tea growing region and it also plays an important role in the economic development of this region. However, among all the North Eastern States, Assam is having the largest tea growing area. The tea industry of Assam is not only very old, but also very famous and is the largest producer and exporter of tea in India. The tea industry of this region is also providing employment to a large number of people. Among the Handicrafts, the cane and bamboo products of Tripura, Arunachal Pradesh and Assam are very famous. It has been found that, about half of the bamboo resources of the country are in the North Eastern Region. Almost all the States of this region is having bamboo forest, but the States viz. Assam, Manipur Mizoram and Arunachal Pradesh have the maximum bamboo stock. Similarly, the State of Tripura is also famous for being the second largest producer of rubber in the country. The coal, cement and lime stone of Meghalaya are worth mentioning.

NOTES

1. *Manorama Year Book*, 1984, Manorama Publishing House, Kottayam, Kerala, p. 481.
2. *ibid.*, p. 481.
3. *ibid.*, p. 481.
4. *ibid.*, p. 474.
5. *ibid.*, p. 474.
6. *ibid.*, p. 482.
7. *Economic Survey*, 2006-07, Ministry of Finance, Government of India, New Delhi, p. 149.
8. *ibid.*, pp. 149, 150.
9. *ibid.*, p. 150.
10. *ibid.*, p. 150.
11. *Report on Annual Survey of Industries*, 2002-03, Central Statistical Organisation (Industrial Statistics Wing), Kolkata, p. II.
12. *ibid.*, pp. X, XIII.

10

Tourism Scenario

Travelling is one of the human natures, and it is as old as the humanity itself. But the objective of it gradually changes over the years. It has many purposes e.g. search for food and shelter, education and employment, duties, economic needs and business, cultural exchanges, religious purposes, to know—what is un-known, to spend holidays or leisure time, over and above—to get rid of monotonous life. Rabindranath Tagore, in one of his poems wrote, "Thou hast made me known to friends whom I knew not. Thou hast given me seats in homes not my own. Thou hast brought the distant near and made a brother to the stranger...." The poet though wrote it in a different context, but this can also have a meaning like... 'could stay in many places and could know many things—what was unknown, could make close friends—who were far away and could make brothers—who were unrelated...'. Perhaps, this could be a very good way of describing, rather explaining the importance and benefit of travelling.

Tourism has slightly different meaning. It is the organized travelling or service for tourists, especially on commercial basis. There are so many public and private sector organizations in our country, who are providing services to the tourists. The India Tourism Development Corporation (ITDC) was set up on 1st October, 1966 by amalgamating three separate undertakings then in existence, namely, the India Tourism Transport Undertaking Limited, the Hotel Corporation of India Limited and the India Tourism Corporation Limited (ITCL). The Ashoka Hotels Limited and the Janpath Hotels Limited were also merged with India Tourism Development Corporation Limited on 28th March, 1970[1]. Further, for effective and speedy fulfilment of the objectives of the

Corporation, re-orientation in the policy and planning strategy was introduced in 1980-81. The ITDC, as a public sector undertaking, took the charge of the commercial enterprises connected with tourism, e.g. construction and management of hotels, maintenance of taxi and long-distance coach services and also construction and management of motels and restaurants.

Tourism in our country is managed by the Department of Tourism, in the Ministry of Tourism and Civil Aviation. It functions under a Directorate of its own and works in close co-operation with the India Tourism Development Corporation. The Directorate is taking care of both promotional and organizational aspects of Tourism. The main objective of the Directorate is to attract both domestic as well as foreign tourists by disseminating information within India and abroad about the places of tourist interest, on one hand, and improving communication, transport facilities and hotel accommodation for the convenience and comfort of the tourists, on the other. Moreover, special emphasis has been given in the Five Year Plans on building tourists infrastructure of accommodation and transport, entertainment facilities, development of selected areas as mountain and beach resorts, development of Cultural Tourism, Wildlife Tourism, Sports Tourism, Adventure Tourism, Eco-Tourism, Circuit Tourism, etc. Further, a new orientation has also been given to the tourism policy, wherein, equal emphasis has been laid down in the Central Sector on the development of tourist facilities to benefit budget-minded tourists, both domestic and international, and the less affluent sections of the society[7]. The States are also having their own Tourism Directorate/ Department and taking all out efforts for promotion of tourism in their respective States.

The Tourism Scenario of India has changed a lot over the years. It has attained the status of hospitality industry and became the major foreign exchange earner. This sector is generating large employment and income-augmentation opportunities for all segments of people of our country both in urban as well as in the rural areas. The beauty of this sector is that, the capital costs are modest compared to large industrial investments and the gestation periods are short. The other advantage of this sector is that, the people of a particular place are getting opportunities to showcase their traditional crafts, skills, art and culture, etc. to others and generating financial benefit. Now-a-days, because of less technical skills, low capital cost and short gestation period, many Non-Governmental Organizations (NGOs) are joining in the hospitality industry and proving success in their endeavours.

From the Travel and Tourism Competitiveness Report of 2009 of the World Economic Forum, it can be seen that, India ranked 11th in the Asia Pacific Region and 62nd overall, moving up three places on the list of the world's most attractive destination. India also ranked 14th best tourists destination for its natural resources and 24th for its cultural resources, owing to many World Heritage sites, rich flora and fauna and strong creative industry. In the long-term growth, India ranked 5th and the report expected that, India will become the second largest employer in the world by the year 2019.

However, the recent global financial crisis has badly affected the tourism industry of our country. But the Tourism Ministry has indicated that, India has already started showing signs of early recovery and in December, 2009 tourist arrival grew substantially by 21 per cent registering a growth of over 8 per cent over the arrivals in December, 2007. Foreign tourist arrivals during 2009 were 5.11 million, though with a negative growth rate of (-) 3.3 per cent as compared to foreign tourist arrivals of 5.28 million and with growth rate of 4 per cent during 2008. The most noticeable thing was that, foreign tourist arrivals during the month of December, 2009 alone were 6.46 lakhs as compared to foreign tourist arrivals of 5.34 lakhs in December, 2008 and 5.97 lakhs in December, 2007[4].

The Tourism Scenario of the North Eastern Region is gaining momentum day by day eventhough, occasionally, it is getting disturbed due to various reasons. The famous Kamakhya Temple in Guwahati, Joysagar and Joydool in Sibsagar, Kaziragna and Manas Wildlife Sanctuaries in Assam, Parasuram Kund and Tawang Monastery in Arunachal Pradesh, Gangtok town, Sangu Lake, Baba Mandir and Nathu La Pass in Sikkim, the famous Shillong city and Cheerapunji in Meghalaya, Loktak Lake of Manipur, the Royal Palace of Agartala in Tripura and many other historical and religious places in other States of North Eastern Region are the major tourist attractions.

Most of the States of this region considered tourism as an important sector of their economy and felt the need to develop it for greater income generation. They also gave emphasis on Government and Private sector participation for the development of this sector in their respective States. Some of the States also gave importance for involvement of NGOs and other local people for development of tourism, particularly in the rural areas[3]. The North Eastern Council (NEC) has also come up for the development of tourism in this region and funding the tourism projects of different States. Moreover, for development of infrastructure as well as for attraction of tourists, NEC is also funding for the construction/improvement of waterways, roads and airports and for procurement of small aircrafts for better linkages within NER and between NER and the rest of the country and also with the neighbouring and other foreign countries.

Apart from the State Governments and NEC, the Union Tourism Ministry has also taken interest for the development of tourism in the North Eastern Region. The Ministry conducted a study in February, 2008 covering 50 major tourist centres and metro cities and assessed the tourist inflow and the requirement of accommodation in this region. According to this study, Narth Eastern Region is all set for a tourism boom by 2010 and the number of tourists visiting Guwahati and Shillong will increase manifold within two years. Correspondingly, the demand for luxury and normal hotel rooms will also increase. As per their assessment, by 2010, the number of domestic and foreign tourists visiting Guwahati would be 1789776 and 40980 and Shillong would be 537826 and 6758 respectively.

Further, basing on the recent growth rate, the projected demand in Guwahati for the luxury category hotel rooms will be 68 and budget hotel rooms will be 1653 per day and in Shillong, it will be 25 and 170 respectively per day in 2010. In other category of hotels, the projected demand in 2010 will be 1215 in Guwahati as against, the then demand of 855 and in Shillong, it will be 376 against 252. The study also projected that in 2015, the average demand per day for luxury hotel and budget hotel rooms in Guwahati would be 109 and 2573 respectively and in Shillong, it would be 39 and 280 respectively per day, while the daily demand for rooms in other category hotels will be 622 in Shillong in 2015. The luxury category includes hotels under heritage classification and also those classified as 4 Star, 5 Star and 5 Star Deluxe, while the budget hotels are those between 1 Star and 3 Star classifications. The other categories include hotels that are approved/licensed by the Ministry of Tourism or other authorities, but awaiting classifications[5].

For the development of adventure tourism, the Union Tourism Ministry sanctioned adventure tourism projects to various North Eastern States. The Ministry reviewed the projects sometimes in September, 2008 and in this meeting, it was decided for providing an updated list to Adventure Tour Operators Association of adventure tourism projects of the State Governments to enable them to plan activities and marketing initiatives accordingly. In the meanwhile, the Delhi based DS Group has taken a novel initiative in Assam, Meghalaya and Tripura for adventure and eco-tourism. With a view to make the community independent, they constructed a 20-room eco-lodge with bamboo walls, frond ceilings and bamboo doors to play host to travellers in Upper Assam. The Group is having similar plans for other parts of North Eastern Region. They are also involved in the revival of heritage sites and other socio-cultural activities of this region[6].

The Union Tourism Ministry has also sanctioned many state specific tourism infrastructure projects for the North Eastern States, along with the other States of the country, during the year, 2009. For Arunachal Pradesh, the Ministry has sanctioned 28 projects at a cost of Rs. 7956.54 lakhs, for Assam, 9 projects at a cost of Rs. 3379.51 lakhs, for Manipur, 18 projects at a cost of Rs. 5488.18 lakhs, for Meghalaya, 11 projects at a cost of Rs. 3341.32 lakhs, for Mizoram, 12 projects at a cost of Rs. 2886.15 lakhs, for Nagaland, 37 projects at a cost of Rs. 6087.36 lakhs, for Tripura, 20 projects at a cost of Rs. 2981.28 lakhs and for Sikkim, 63 projects at a cost of Rs. 16344.53 lakhs for constructing 3 heliports and promoting village tourism, with mega projects at Gangtok for Rs. 2390.70 lakhs[7].

The number of tourists in our country, both domestic and foreign, is continuously increasing. It can be seen from the Appendix-10.1 that, the number of domestic tourists in 1991 was 666.70 lakhs. But that was increased at a rate of 110.0 per cent and reached to 1401.20 lakhs in 1996 i.e. within a period 5 years and thereafter, increased at a higher rate of 254.7 per cent and reached to 2364.70 lakhs in 2001 i.e. within a period of 10 years and finally reached to 5265.64 lakhs in 2007 i.e. within a period of 16 years, increasing still at a higher rate of 689.8 per cent. The special feature of the domestic tourists was that, starting from 1991, their number increased every year till 2007. The corresponding higher rate of increase in the number of domestic tourists was noticed in the years 1991-92, 1992-93 and 1993-94. The growth rates in these periods were 22.2 per cent, 29.9 per cent and 20.1 per cent respectively.

However, in case of foreign tourists, though their number increased considerably, but there were some rise and fall in their numbers, in the subsequent years, starting from 1991. In 1991, the number of foreign tourists was 31.47 lakhs, but that was increased to 50.30 lakhs in 1996, growing at a rate of 59.8 per cent. In 2001 i.e. within a period of 10 years, it reached to 54.36 lakhs, with a growth rate of 72.7 per cent and finally reached to 132.31 lakhs in 2007 i.e. within a period of 16 years, growing at a very high rate of 320.0 per cent. The corresponding decrease in the growth rate of foreign tourists was noticed in 1991-92, which was –1.6 per cent, in 2000-01, it was –7.8 per cent and in 2001-02, it was –5.1 per cent. But on the other hand, the higher corresponding growth rate was noticed in the years 2002-03 and 2003-04, which was 30.1 per cent and 24.6 per cent respectively. Further, details can be seen from Appendix-10.1.

The tourist inflow into the North Eastern States is gradually increasing and Assam, Meghalaya, Tripura and Sikkim are the main attraction. The Appendix-10.2 will give a clear picture of the numbers of domestic and foreign tourists visited different States of this region from 2001 to 2007. From this, it can be seen that, out of total number of tourists visited North Eastern States, Assam accounted for about 68 per cent of them, Meghalaya around 10 per cent, Tripura around 8 per cent and Sikkim around 7 per cent in all these years. In case of domestic tourists, these four States also maintained almost the same percentages. But, in case of foreign tourists, Sikkim maintained a unique record of highest number of foreign tourists registering alone about 46 per cent of the total number of foreign tourists visited this region, during this period. However, Assam maintained another unique record of increasing tourist inflow, in every subsequent year, both in case of domestic as well as foreign, from the year 2001 to 2007. While in all other States, the growth rate of tourists was uneven, both in case of domestic and foreign tourists, during these years.

The nature of growth of tourists in the North Eastern States during the period from 2001-02 to 2006-07 can be seen from Appendix-10.3. From this, it can be seen that, the State of Assam witnessed the highest growth of 92.79 per cent, 93.33 per cent domestic and 3.86

per cent foreign tourists during 2001-02 and the second highest of 32.33 per cent, 32.46 per cent domestic and 3.42 per cent foreign tourists during 2005-06. The overall growth of tourists in Assam within a gap of 6 years i.e. from 2001 and 2007 was 239.27 per cent, 240.06 per cent domestic and 109.03 per cent foreign tourists, which was a very good sign. Meghalaya had the highest growth of 50.07 per cent, 50.32 per cent domestic and 31.63 per cent foreign tourists during 2001-02 and the second highest of 39.19 per cent, 38.47 per cent domestic and 100.38 per cent foreign tourists during 2002-03. The overall growth of tourists in Meghalaya within a gap of 6 years i.e. from 2001 and 2007 was 155.65 per cent, 156.12 per cent domestic and 120.38 per cent foreign tourists. Meghalaya however, witnessed the negative growth of –14.56 per cent, –13.29 per cent domestic and –58.90 per cent foreign tourists during the period 2004-05.

The State of Tripura though attracted third highest number of tourists of this region, but the growth rate in subsequent years was not uniform. The State rather witnessed a high negative growth of –17.07 per cent, –17.08 per cent domestic and –15.58 per cent foreign tourists during 2004-05. The overall growth of domestic tourists also came down to –3.97 per cent within a gap of 6 years i.e. from 2001 and 2007. But the growth of foreign tourists showed a very good sign registering a growth rate of 110.38 per cent during that period. In case of Sikkim, the highest growth rate of tourists was in the period 2003-04, which was 28.04 per cent, 28.42 per cent domestic and 22.40 per cent foreign tourists. But at the same time, the State also witnessed negative growth of –28.35 per cent, –21.62 per cent domestic and –72.39 per cent foreign tourists during 2001-02. The overall growth of domestic tourists within a gap of 6 years i.e. from 2001 and 2007 was though 61.86 per cent, but there was a negative growth of –43.61 per cent in case of foreign tourists during that period, which was not a positive sign.

In Arunachal Pradesh, though there was a negative growth of –31.67 per cent, –31.14 per cent domestic and –42.10 per cent foreign tourists during 2001-02 and also a negative growth of –49.16 per cent, –49.79 per cent domestic and –34.22 per cent foreign tourists during 2002-03, but the State could contain the negative growth from 2003-04 and started attracting more and more tourists towards it. During 2003-04, Arunachal Pradesh registered a growth rate of 116.09

per cent, 115.95 per cent domestic and 118.70 per cent foreign tourists during that period. And within a gap of 6 years i.e. from 2001 and 2007, the overall growth rate reached to 1298.56 per cent, 1334.87 per cent domestic and 584.83 per cent foreign tourists. The tourist inflow into the other States viz. Manipur, Mizoram and Nagaland was comparatively much less and the growth rates in different years were also showed ups and downs during the period from 2001 to 2007. However, within a gap of 6 years i.e. from 2001 and 2007, Manipur could register a growth rate of 32.81 per cent, Mizoram 51.54 per cent and Nagaland 111.71 per cent. In spite of all these, the tourist inflow into the North Eastern Region was very less as compared to the position of the country as a whole. It can be seen that, the percentage of total number of tourists visited this region, was not even 1 per cent of the total number of tourists visited our country, in any of the year from 2001 to 2007 except 2002. In 2002, the percentage was only 1.02. Further, details can be seen from Appendix-10.2 and Appendix-10.3. The tourism industry of the North Eastern Region will have to go a long way in order to achieve its goal.

NOTES

1. *Manorama Year Book*, 1984, Manorama Publishing House, Kottayam, Kerala, p. 572.
2. *ibid.*, p. 572.
3. *North Eastern Region—VISION-2020*, Ministry of Development of North Eastern Region, North Eastern Council, Vol. II, p. 133.
4. *The Indian Express* (Best of India), dated 10-14 March, 2010.
5. *The Times of India*, Guwahati, dated 3rd June, 2008.
6. *The Shillong Times*, Shillong, dated 6th September, 2008.
7. *The Indian Express*, *op. cit.*

11

Employment Scenario

The employment scenario of the North Eastern Region is not very good. It is a fact that, the number of job seekers is increasing day-by-day, but the employment opportunities are very much limited and are not increasing in a proportionate way and therefore, there is, always a surplus in the number of job seekers. The North East economy is primarily agrarian and there is no much scope of employment for the educated youths. The educated youths generally prefer to go for the 'white collar' jobs. The industrial sector of this region could not grow much due to resource deficiency and infrastructural inadequacy. And on the other hand, private sector participation is also affected due to various socio-political reasons, and therefore, the pressure is on the public sector. But the opportunities of employment in the Government offices have almost reached to its saturation point and there is hardly any scope for increase in the number of posts in different cadres. On the other hand, the Colleges and the Universities are producing increasing number of graduates and post-graduates every year, both in general and technical disciplines, without thinking much on their employment opportunities. In addition to educated job seekers, there are uneducated or less educated or skilled job seekers, who on many occasions, go un-noticed. There is another group of persons, who are underemployed and very often try to get a better job as per their educational qualification or up to their satisfaction. All these make the employment/unemployment scenario more complex and go beyond the scope of assessment.

Employment is a basic necessity. Without employment one cannot survive. Presently, the Government of India is in the process of implementing the "Right to Education Act". It is definitely a welcome move, though many of the States have many apprehensions and reservations about the implementation of the Act. Perhaps that apprehensions and reservations can be sorted out at the time of actual implementation, and in course of time, there will be no illiterate children and one day, India will attain the glory of cent per cent educated country. But, is it the only thing we want to content with?—Perhaps not. A person literate or illiterate, needs something to do, not only for his or her livelihood, but also for keeping himself engaged and to utilize his or her knowledge for the development of the society or of the country and for the betterment of its people. An educated person without a job, instead of becoming a matter pride for the country—turns out to be a liability in no time. Not only that, unemployed or underemployed persons always suffer from mental frustration and many a time that leads them to unlawful activities, madness or even push them for ending their lives. Therefore, like "Right to Education Act", the Government of India can think for implementing "Right to Employment Act" so that, one day, there will be no unemployed person in our country. The whole employment system may be reorganized and sufficient employment generating plans may be taken up so that the right person can be placed in the right job and there will be no frustration and no wastage of knowledge. Initially, it may be a utopian dream, but if every one is sincere, a day may come, it may turn out to be a reality.

Our country is still suffering from the problem of employment and unemployment to a great extent. But some recent studies showed a ray of hope and indicated that, the annual growth rate of employment has been accelerated and unemployment has gone up not because of the high growth, but because growth was not high enough[1]. In the Tenth Five Year Plan, special emphasis was given for increasing employment by promoting growth oriented sectors and activities and aimed to create approximately 50 million employment opportunities—30 million from the normal process of growth and additional 20 million from special initiatives[2]. The National Sample Survey Organization (NSSO), in their quinquennial surveys collects information on employment and unemployment. And on the basis of the results of different rounds, Appendix-11.1 has been prepared to illustrate the employment and unemployment position and its growth, at different points of time. From the results of the 61st round of NSS, conducted during July, 2004 to June, 2005, it can be seen that, the annual growth rate of labour force has not only accelerated from 1.60 per cent during 1993-2000 to 2.54 per cent during 1999-2005, but crossed the 2.06 per cent mark recorded during 1983-1994. However, on the other hand, it can be seen that, more than 47 million persons were provided employment during 1999 to 2005. Further, the net annual addition to employment on Usual Principal Status (UPS) basis went up from 5.47 million during 1993-2000 to 9.58 million during 1999-2005. Simultaneously, though the annual growth rate of workforce increased from 1.57 per cent during 1993-2000 to 2.48 per cent during 1999-2005 and even crossed the 2.09 per cent mark recorded during 1983-1994, still the annual labour force growth was higher at 2.54 per cent during 1999-2005. As a result, despite the faster growth of employment, unemployment was higher at 3.06 per cent of the labour force in 2004-05 compared to 2.78 per cent in 1999-2000. However, the incidence of unemployment had come down from 2.88 per cent in 1983 (38th round) to 2.62 per cent in 1993-94 (50th round)[3]. Further, details can be seen from Appendix-11.1.

From Appendix-11.2, it can be seen that, the increase in unemployment between 55th and 61st round of NSS, i.e. between 1999-2000 and 2004-2005, was primarily because of an increase in unemployment in all categories i.e. Usual Principal Status (UPS), Current Weekly Status (CWS) and Current Daily Status (CDS) for females, both in rural and urban areas. And in addition, while unemployment among males declined in terms of UPS and CWS, it increased in terms of CDS, both in rural and urban areas. Further, details can be seen from the Appendix-11.2.

The reversal of the declining trend in employment growth—from 2.09 per cent in the ten years ending 1993-94 to 1.57 per cent in the five years ending in 1999-2000 to 2.48 per cent in the five years ending in 2004-05 is an encouraging development. There is actually a need for faster employment growth, not only for absorbing the addition to the labour force, particularly with the ongoing demographic changes, but reducing the unemployment rate. The share of agriculture in total employment has come down from 61.67 per cent in 1993-94 to 58.54 per cent in 1999-2000, and further to 54.19 per cent in 2004-05. With the declining share of agriculture in GDP, the scope for absorbing substantial additional labour force in agriculture appears limited. However, construction and services, particularly transport, storage and communication, contributed in maintaining employment growth in the economy though employment growth in manufacturing fell short of its potential[4].

Employment growth in the organized sector, public and private combined, declined during nineties. Annual employment growth in establishments covered by Employment Market Information System of Ministry of Labour decelerated from 1.20 per cent during 1983-1994 to –0.38 per cent per annum during 1994-2004. This deceleration happened in spite of an acceleration in annual employment growth in the private sector from 0.44 per cent to 0.61 per cent during the reference periods, as this acceleration was not enough to make up for the corresponding decline of employment from 1.53 per cent to –0.80 per cent in the public sector during that period[5].

In the North Eastern Region, maintenance of employment statistics suffers from various short comings and deficiencies. Even now, many of the States of this region do not have separate Employment Exchange Offices or Employment Officers who can maintain proper records of employment and unemployment. These works are being done by other officers in addition to their own duties in many of the States. Moreover, the Government offices are generally located in the urban or semi-urban areas, and it is not very easy to maintain the records of unemployed youths or job seekers, who are residing in the hilly and remote rural areas. On the other hand, many of the job seekers are also not well aware about the procedure of the Employment Exchanges. Absence or inadequacy of electronic and print media is another short coming in the rural areas.

However, the Appendix-11.3 will give an idea about the position of Employment Exchanges and the details of job seekers of different States of this region for the year 2000 and 2005. From this, it can be seen that, all together there were 99 Employment Exchanges at the end of 2005 in the North Eastern Region and out of this, 52 i.e. 52.52 per cent were in Assam alone. In other States, the number of Employment Exchange was very less. Mizoram was having the lowest of only 3, while Manipur and Meghalaya were having the highest of 11 each. The State of Assam registered the highest number of 2.18 lakhs of persons in 2005, which was 63.51 per cent of the total registration of this region in that year. The next highest registration was in Manipur. In 2000, total number of registration in Manipur was 0.11 lakh and that reached to 0.76 lakh in 2005, with a growth rate of 624.76 per cent. In Assam, the growth of registration from the year, 2000 to 2005, was also quite high to the extent of 59.18 per cent. In Tripura, there was a nominal increase of only 4.62 per cent in the number of registration during the period from 2000 to 2005. In all other States, there was a considerable decline in the number of registration, which is quite unusual.

As per live register, a total of 23.20 lakhs job seekers were there in the North Eastern Region at the end of the year, 2000, which increased to 28.35 lakhs in 2005 i.e. there was a net increase of 5.14 lakhs in 5 years. Out of the total number of job seekers in North Eastern Region, Assam accounted for 62.2 per cent in the year, 2000 and almost the same of 62.1 per cent in the year, 2005. The position of placement to submission was not at all encouraging. Tripura is the only State which showed some meaningful results. In this State, placement to submission was 25.0 per cent in 2000 and 11.8 per cent in 2005. The position of other States is not worth mentioning. However, the position of placement to submission of the North Eastern Region as a whole was, 3.4 per cent in 2000 and only 0.5 per cent in 2005.

Comparing the position of this region with the country as a whole, we can find that, the total number of registration was only 3.56 per cent in 2000 and 6.32 per cent in 2005. Total number of job seekers in North Eastern Region was only 5.61 per cent of the total job seekers of the country in 2000 and that was 7.23 per cent in the year 2005. As regards placement to submission, it was 7.7 per cent in 2000 and 7.2 per cent in 2005 in the country, as against 3.4 per cent and 0.5 per cent in this region, in the corresponding years. Further, details can be seen from Appendix-11.3.

The Appendix-11.4 shows the age group-wise job seekers in the year 1999 and in 2004 in different States of this region. As we have seen that, as per live register, job seekers were more in Assam, Manipur and Tripura, or in other words, it can be said that, more number of persons were registering their names with the Employment Exchanges in these States. From Appendix-11.4, it appears that, more than half of the total job seekers of the respective States except Tripura, were in the age group 20-29 years. In Assam and Manipur, around 20 per cent of the job seekers were up to the age of 19 years and almost the same percentage of job seekers were also in the age group 30-39 years, at the end of both the years 1999 and 2004. From the information of Tripura, it appears that, comparatively, more number of persons registered their names with the Employment Exchanges at an early age. Out of the total number of job seekers in Tripura, almost 36 per cent were up to the age of 19 years, around 40 per cent were in the age group 20-29 years and about 18 per cent were in the age group 30-39 years. Job seekers in the age group 40 years and above were much less and there were no job seekers in the age of 60 years and above in any of the States except Assam and Manipur. In Assam, quite a good number of job seekers i.e. about 8000 were there in 1999 and about 400 were in 2004 in the age group 60 years and above. In Manipur, it was much less to the extent of less than 50 in 1999 and about 100 in 2004 in that category.

Comparing the position of job seekers of the North Eastern Region with the job seekers of the country as a whole, it can be seen that, the proportion of job seekers in this region was a bit high at the early age at the end of both the years 1999 and 2004. Out of the total number of job seekers of the North Eastern Region, 22.04 per cent in 1999 and 24.66 per cent in 2004 were in the age upto 19 years as against the all India figure of 20.51 per cent and 21.79 per cent respectively. Further it appears that, in case of North Eastern Region, 52.04 per cent in 1999 and 51.71 per cent in 2004 were in the age group 20-29 years as against the all India percentage of 51.48 and 49.31 respectively at the end of these two years. However, the position was reversed in the age group 30-39 years. In North Eastern Region, the percentage of job seekers was 19.12 in 1999 and 19.32 in 2004 as against the all India figures of 23.27 per cent and 23.34 per cent respectively in that age group. Finally, it can be seen that, job seekers were there even at the age of 60 years and above, though their proportion was much less, both in this region as well as in the country as a whole. Further, details can be seen from the Appendix-11.4.

The Appendix-11.5 will give an idea about the women job seekers in different States of this region at the end of the year 2000 and 2005. From this, it can be seen that, proportionately, more number of women in Assam, Manipur and Tripura, registered their names with the

Employment Exchanges and their number in 2000 increased many fold in 2005. In all other States, there was a negative growth in the number of registration of women job seekers. Further, it can be seen that, out of the total number of women registration in North Eastern Region at the end of 2000 and 2005, Assam accounted for 56.50 per cent and 66.64 per cent respectively. Manipur accounted for 3.88 per cent and 18.66 per cent, while Tripura recorded for 13.79 per cent and 7.52 per cent respectively in these two years.

From Appendix-11.3 and Appendix-11.5, it can be seen that, the proportion of women job seekers was comparatively high both at the end of 2000 and 2005 in Meghalaya, Tripura, Arunachal Pradesh and Mizoram. As per the record of Live Register, out of the total number of job seekers in Meghalaya, the highest of 41.24 per cent in 2000 and 40.26 per cent in 2005 were women job seekers. The second highest proportion of women job seekers was in Tripura. It was 37.71 per cent in 2000 and 36.60 per cent in 2005. Then came the position of Arunachal Pradesh with 33.33 per cent in 2000 and 31.07 per cent in 2005. In Mizoram, though the percentage of women job seekers was a bit less to the extent of 29.42 per cent at the end of 2000, but it increased to 36.05 per cent at the end of 2005.

However, the overall percentage of women job seekers in the North Eastern Region as a whole was 25.17 per cent and 25.73 per cent at the end of 2000 and 2005 respectively, as against the national figures of 25.29 per cent and 26.95 per cent respectively at the end of these two years. This indicates that, the proportion of women job seekers in the North Eastern Region and in the country as a whole was more or less same in both the years. But in case of women job seekers, the percentage of Placement to Registration was much less in this region, which was only 1.4 in 2000 and 0.3 in 2005 as against the all India figure of 2.2 per cent and 2 per cent respectively. This indicates that, proportionately, less number of women of the North Eastern Region were getting job through Employment Exchanges. Further, details can be seen from Appendix-11.5.

The Appendix-11.6 will give a clear picture of the castewise job seekers in different States of North Eastern Region in 2000 and 2004. From this, it can be seen that, in all the States, except Assam, Manipur and Tripura, Scheduled Caste (SC) job seekers were very less. From Appendix-11.4 and Appendix-11.6, it can be seen that, out of the total number of job seekers in Assam, 6.21 per cent at the end of 1999 and 6.30 per cent at the end of 2004 were Scheduled Caste (SC). In Manipur, it was 1.53 per cent and 1.44 per cent, whereas, in Tripura, the percentage of SC job seekers was the highest of 15.19 per cent at the end of 1999 and 17.12 per cent at the end of 2004. The North Eastern States except Assam, Manipur and Tripura, are Scheduled Tribe (ST) dominated States, and as such, job seekers are mostly ST in these States. The highest proportion of ST job seekers, were in Nagaland. Out of the total number of Job seekers, 95.62 per cent at the end of 1999 and 98.63 per cent at the end of 2004 were ST in that State. In Mizoram, ST job seekers were more than 80 per cent. Proportion of ST job seekers in Meghalaya was also very high. Out of the total number of job seekers, 79.50 per cent at the end of 1999 and 76.68 per cent at the end of 2004 were ST in Meghalaya. Number of ST job seekers in Arunachal Pradesh were comparatively a bit less. Out of the total number of job seekers in 1999, 40.25 per cent were ST and in 2004, the percentage of ST job seekers was 53.54 in Arunachal Pradesh.

The information on Other Backward Class (OBC) job seekers was not much available. However, from the available information of Live Register, it can be seen that, in case of Assam, out of the total number of job seekers, 11.73 per cent at the end of 1999 and 13.95 per cent at the end of 2004, were OBC. In case of Tripura, it was 0.66 per cent in 1999 and 3.15 per cent in 2004. However, comparing the position of North Eastern Region with the position of the country as a whole, it can be seen that, SC job seekers in this region was much less. It was 6.08 per cent at the end of 1999 and 6.73 per cent at the end of 2004 as against the all India figure of 14.73 per cent and 15.99 per cent respectively. Similar was the case of OBC job seekers. In North Eastern Region, the percentage of OBC job seekers was 7.56 at the end of 1999 and 9.22 at the end of 2004, as against 16.94 per cent and 20.28 per cent of the country respectively. But in case of ST job seekers, the position was different. In North Eastern Region, out of the total number of job seekers, 19.65 per cent at the end of 1999 and 19.89 per cent at the end of 2004 were ST job seekers as against the corresponding figures of 4.36 per cent and 5.48 per cent of the country respectively. In case of placement to registration, the position of North Eastern Region was very poor in all these three categories.

In case of SC, it was 0.8 per cent in 1999 and 0.7 per cent in 2004, against the all India percentage of 3.8 and 2.2 respectively. In case of ST, it was 0.9 per cent and 0.4 per cent as against 6.4 per cent and 3 per cent of the country. Similar was the case with OBC. The percentage of OBC placement to registration in North Eastern Region was 1.1 per cent in 1999 and in the country, it was 2.6 per cent in 1999 and 1.4 per cent in 2004. Further, details can be seen from Appendix-11.6.

The Appendix-11.7 will give an idea about the total number of workers and total number of non-workers and their percentages as per 2001 census in different States of North Eastern Region. From this, it can be seen that, amongst all the States, Mizoram was having the highest proportion of workers. In this State, out of the total population, 52.57 per cent were workers and 47.43 per cent were non-workers. That indicates that, proportionately, non-workers were less in Mizoram. In rural areas, the percentage of workers was even higher to the extent of 57.21 per cent and in urban, it was 47.87 per cent. Sikkim is though the smallest State in this region with smallest population, but it came in the second highest position in terms of employment. Out of the total population, the percentage of workers was 48.64 and the percentage of non-workers was 51.36. On the other hand, the State of Assam was though having more than two-third population of this region, but the percentage of workers to total population of the State was only 35.78, which was the lowest and the percentage of non-workers was 64.22, which was the highest amongst all the States of this region. The percentage of non-workers was also quite high in Tripura. Out of total population of the State, the percentage of workers was only 36.25 and the percentage of non-workers was the second highest of 63.75 per cent. In all other States, the percentage of workers to total population of the respective States was within 41 to 44 per cent and that of non-workers was 56 to 59 per cent. This indicates that, except Mizoram, the non-worker population was much more than the worker population in all the States. The overall position of the North Eastern Region was also not better than the overall position of the country. The percentage of workers of the North Eastern Region was 37.76 and that of non-workers was 62.24, as against 39.10 per cent and 60.90 per cent of the country respectively.

Further, it can be seen that, in all the States, the male workers were more than the female workers, both in rural and urban. Moreover, the percentage of male as well as of female workers was more in the rural areas in all the States with the exception of Assam and Tripura, in respect of male workers. In Assam, the percentage of male workers to total male population was 49.41 in rural, but it was 52.90 in urban. While in Tripura, the percentage of male workers to total male population was 50.42 in rural, but it was 51.64 in urban. This indicates that, in the urban areas of Assam and Tripura, male workers were proportionately more. In other words, it can be said that, male people were getting more job opportunities in the urban areas of Assam and Tripura.

The female workers of Mizoram showed another unique character. Amongst all the States, the percentage of female workers to total female population was the highest in both rural and urban areas. In rural, it was 54.55 per cent and in urban, it was 40.52 per cent. The State of Manipur was also having almost the same characteristic. In this State, the percentage of female workers to total female population was 41.53 in rural and 32.25 in urban, which were the second highest proportions among all the States of this region. The position of Sikkim and of Meghalaya was also not lagging much behind. In Sikkim, the percentage of female workers to total female population was 40.60 in rural and 21.67 in urban, while in Meghalaya, it was 38.62 per cent in rural and 20.98 per cent in urban. This indicates that, in these four States, the females were economically more active, both in rural as well as in urban areas. However, comparing the position of North Eastern Region with the position of the country, it can be seen that, the percentage of male workers to total male population in North Eastern Region was a bit less to the extent of 49.68 per cent as against 52.11 per cent in rural, while in urban, it was slightly more to the tune of 50.97 per cent as against 50.60 per cent of the country.

In case of non-workers, it can be seen that, the percentage of non-workers to total population, in case of both male and female, was more in urban in all the States except Assam and Tripura, where the percentage of male non-workers was more in rural. In Assam, the percentage of male non-workers to total male population was 50.59 in rural and 47.10 in urban and in Tripura, it was 49.58 per cent in rural and 48.36 per cent in urban. However, amongst all the States of this region, the percentage of male non-workers to total male population was the highest in Nagaland, both in rural as well as in urban. In rural, it was 52.68 per cent and in urban, it was 56.19 per cent. The position of Meghalaya was very much close to Nagaland. In Meghalaya, the percentage of male non-workers to total male population was 50.57 in rural and 56.18 in urban.

However, in case of female, the percentage of female non-workers to total female population was more in urban in all the States. Further, it can be seen that, the proportion of female non-workers was the highest in Assam and the second highest in Tripura, both in case of rural as well as in urban. In Assam, it was 77.85 per cent in rural and 89.39 per cent in urban, where as in Tripura, it was 77.13 per cent in rural and 87.55 per cent in urban. The proportion of female non-workers was also quite high in Meghalaya, both in rural and urban areas. It was 61.38 per cent in rural and 79.02 per cent in urban.

The overall position of non-workers in the North Eastern Region was poorer than the position of the country, particularly in rural areas, both for male and female non-workers. The proportion of male non-workers to total male population of North Eastern Region was 50.32 against 47.89 per cent and for female non-workers, it was 73.68 per cent against 69.21 per cent in rural. But in urban, it was slightly better at 49.03 per cent against 49.40 per cent for male non-workers and 83.40 per cent against 88.12 per cent of the country for female non-workers. This indicates that, in the North Eastern Region, proportionately, more number of males in the rural areas, were without any job. However, non-workers include all children, students, house wives, pensioners, renters, old and sick people, baggers, etc. and that is why, total number of non-workers does not give the actual picture of total number of job seekers at any point of time. Further, details can be seen from Appendix-11.7.

The job seekers are generally of the age group 15-29 years. Out of these, those who want to enter into service after class-X will be of the age group 15-19 years and those who want to enter into service after class-XII or graduation and post-graduation will be of the age group 20-29 years. Therefore, the population of the age group 15-29 years or the youths, are very vital and they are the future of the nation. They need proper nourishment and guidance, provisions for education for making their career and employment for livelihood. The youths occupy a large portion of our population. The Appendix-11.8 will give an idea about the youths in the age group 15-29 years and their percentage to total population in different States of North Eastern Region as well as of the country as a whole, as per 2001 census. From this, it can be seen that, the youths of this region, in the age group 15-29 years, occupied 27.75 per cent of the total population and this was even more than the national figure of 26.58 per cent. That means, proportionately, youths are more in this region. In some of the North Eastern States, this proportion was very high. In Nagaland, the percentage of youths in the age group 15-29 years was the highest of 32.13 per cent. The States like Sikkim, Mizoram and Manipur, all were having more than 30 per cent of their population in the age group 15-29 years. And therefore, the job seekers or in other words, employment opportunities, will have to be more in these States. Further, details can be seen from Appendix-11.8.

It is a fact that, in the North Eastern Region, more than 80 per cent of the population is living in the villages and agriculture is the main stay of their livelihood. In the villages, almost all households are having some cultivable land for growing crops and in case of need, some of them even working as agricultural labourers also. The Appendix-11.9 and Appendix-11.10 will give an idea about the percentage of workers worked as cultivators, agricultural labourers and other workers, and the changes that have taken place over the three consecutive population censuses of 1981 to 2001 in different States of this region. From this, it can be seen that, along with the other parts of the country, there was a sharp decline in the proportion of cultivators in all the States of this region. The change in the rate of decline within a period of 20 years was very high to the extent of 23.4 per cent in Manipur. This followed by 16.3 per cent in Tripura, 15.7 per cent in Mizoram, 14.5 per cent in Meghalaya, 13.5 per cent in Arunachal Pradesh and 10.2 per cent in Sikkim, as against the national figure of 9.9 per cent.

But on the other hand, there was an increase in the proportion of agricultural labourers in all the States except Tripura. The rate of increase within a period of 20 years was the highest of 7.7 per cent in Meghalaya, 7.0 per cent in Manipur, 3.2 per cent each in Mizoram and Sikkim, 2.9 per cent in Nagaland and 1.4 per cent in Arunachal

Pradesh, against the national increase of 1.6 per cent. The reason of such changes i.e. from cultivators to agricultural labourers might be attributed to the fact that, in the rural areas, gradually the family size was increasing and separating and accordingly the household land was getting divided. And in some cases, the small piece of land, one was getting after division, was not enough for maintaining his livelihood and that forced him to work as agricultural labourer in others land.

Another aspect of this was that, there was an increase in the proportion of other workers that means, the non-farm sector was growing and that was definitely a good sign for the economic development of any State. It can be seen that, the proportion of other workers increased in all the States of this region along with the national increase in 2001. The highest increase was of the order of 46.1 per cent in Tripura, followed by 44.0 per cent in Assam and 42.0 per cent in Sikkim. The increase was little more than 37 per cent each in the States of Mizoram, Manipur and Arunachal Pradesh. The lowest increase was 29.0 per cent in Nagaland. The change in the rate of increase over a period of 20 years was the highest of 13.4 per cent in Tripura. It was also quite high to the extent of 11.0 per cent in Mizoram, 10.7 per cent in Arunachal Pradesh. In other States like Meghalaya, Sikkim and Manipur, it was within 4 to 6 per cent. The State of Nagaland recorded the lowest change of 2.1 per cent. Further, details can be seen from Appendix-11.9 and Appendix-11.10.

The Appendix-11.11 (a) and the Appendix-11.11 (b) will give an idea about the percentage distribution of usually employed persons by category of employment in rural and urban areas of all the States of North Eastern Region for three different periods of 1993-94, 1999-2000 and 2004-05. From Appendix-11.11 (a), it can be seen that, in rural areas of almost all the States, the proportion of self-employment, that means, mostly the agriculture and allied activities, was gradually increasing. This indicates that, the rural people are becoming self-dependent, and that is definitely a good sign towards the solution of rural un-employment problem. The percentage of self-employed persons was the highest of 91.1 per cent in Mizoram during the period of 1993-94, which though came down to 89.0 per cent in 1999-2000, but it again increased to 91.4 per cent during 2004-05. The second highest percentage was in Nagaland. In 1993-94, the percentage of self-employed persons was 78.1, but it reached to 82.1 per cent in 1999-2000 and finally reached to 88.3 per cent in 2004-05. In Manipur, the percentage of self-employed persons was also quite high though there was slight decline in the middle. In 1993-94, it was 83.0 per cent, but it came down to 80.0 per cent in 1999-2000 and then again it reached to 85.1 per cent in 2004-05, which was the third highest. In Arunachal Pradesh and Tripura, though there was a declining trend in the percentage of self-employed people, but it was quite marginal. In Arunachal Pradesh, it was 85.4 per cent in 1993-94 and it came down to 79.3 per cent in 1999-2000, but it recovered to some extent and reached to 83.3 per cent in 2004-05. Similar was the situation in Tripura. In 1993-94, the percentage of self-employed people was 56.9 and it came down to 47.2 per cent in 1999-2000 and then again reached to 52.8 per cent in 2004-05.

In rural areas, the scope for regular and casual employment was quite limited and both were showing declining trend almost in all the States. In case of regular employment, the declining trend in Nagaland and Assam was very sharp. In Nagaland, the percentage of regularly employed persons was 19.2 in 1993-94, but it decreased to 16.6 per cent in 1999-2000 and then to 11.0 per cent in 2004-05. In case of Assam, it was 14.4 per cent in 1993-94, but it reached to 16.6 per cent in 1999-2000 and then came down to only 9.1 per cent in 2004-05. However, the proportion of regularly employed persons in Sikkim was the highest, though there was a slow decline on this over the years. The percentage of regularly employed persons in the rural areas of Sikkim was 27.0 in 1993-94, but it came down to 26.1 per cent in 2999-2000 and finally reached to 25.2 per cent in 2004-05.

The scenario of casual labourers was slightly different. It can be seen that, except Assam, Nagaland and Sikkim, all other States, showed an increasing trend in the proportion of casual labourers during the period from 1993-94 to 1999-2000 and then all the States showed a declining trend, and in case of some of the States, decline was very sharp. In Assam, the percentage of casual labourers was 25.2 in 1999-2000, but it came down to 19.9 per cent in 2004-05. In Manipur, it was 10.0 per cent in 1999-2000 and it came down to almost half i.e. to 5.4 per cent in 2004-05. The decline was also quite noticeable in Sikkim and Tripura. In Sikkim, it came down from 11.9 per cent to 7 per cent. The percentage of casual labourers in Tripura was the highest of 41.7 per cent in 1999-2000, but it came down to 37.0 per cent in 2004-05.

The situation in the country as a whole was also more or less similar to North Eastern States, in case of self-employment and casual employment, but it was quite opposite, in case of regular employment. It can be seen that, the percentage of self-employed people in the country was though 58.1 per cent in 1993-94, but it came down to 55.8 per cent in 1999-2000 and then again reached to 60.2 per cent in 2004-05. Similarly, the percentage of casual labourers, which was 35.3 per cent in 1993-94, first increased to 37.4 per cent in 1999-2000, and then came down to 32.8 per cent in 2004-05. This indicates that, there is no stability in such employment and it mostly depend on opportunities. But, the regularly employed people of the country showed a different trend. The percentage of regularly employed people registered a gradual increase from 6.6 per cent in 1993-94 to 6.8 per cent in 1999-2000 and finally reached to 7.1 per cent in 2004-05. This indicates that, in other parts of the country, regular employment opportunities, in the rural areas, were gradually increasing. That is definitely the indication of rural development, which is very much essential for uplifting the economic status of the rural people as well as to contain the outflow of rural people to cities, which are already over-crowded. Further, details can be seen from Appendix-11.11 (a).

The employment scenario in the urban areas is different from that of the rural areas. In urban areas, self-employment and the regular employment or in other words, regular salaried people are more as the shops, business establishments, offices, institutions, organizations, factories, etc. are generally located in the urban areas. The Appendix-11.11 (b), will give an idea about the pattern of employment in urban areas of all the North Eastern States for three different periods of 1993-94, 1999-2000 and 2004-05. From this, it can be seen that, the percentage of self-employment, and the percentage of regular salaried employment, were inversely proportional almost in all the States and the difference between these two percentages was quite big in some cases. That indicates that, all the urban centres of different States were not equally developed in respect of both the activities. That means, in some urban centres, proportionately, the self-employment activities were more and the regular salaried activities were less, and in some other centres, the situations were the opposite. However, the urban centres of Assam, more or less had equal shares in both the activities and their proportions were not varying largely. In case of urban areas of Assam, it can be seen that, the percentage of self-employment and the percentage of regular employment were 45.3 and 43.1 respectively in 1993-94, but it came down to 44.7 and 42.9 in 1999-2000 and finally reached to 42.3 and 45.1 respectively in 2004-05.

But in urban areas of all other States, this difference was quite large. The percentage of self-employed people was the highest of 63.9 per cent in Manipur in 1993-94, whereas the percentage of regular employment was 33.3 at that time. And in 1999-2000, these were 60.3 per cent and 30.6 per cent and in 2004-05, these were 65.4 per cent and 29.9 per cent. Similar was the case in Mizoram. During 1993-94, the percentage of self-employed people in the State was the second highest of 61.0 per cent and the percentage of regular employment was 33.1 per cent. In 1999-2000, these were 49.5 per cent and 33.8 per cent and in 2004-05, these were 59.0 per cent and 34.1 per cent respectively. In Arunachal Pradesh, the situation was different. In 1993-94, the percentage of self-employment was the lowest of 22.0 per cent, whereas, the percentage of regular employment at that time was 69.5 per cent. In 1999-2000, these were 24.1 per cent and 59.0 per cent and in 2004-05, it came very closer to 42.7 per cent and 48.8 per cent respectively. The situation of the country as a whole was similar to Assam. In 1993-94, the percentage of self-employment in the country was 42.4 and the percentage of regular employment was 39.5. In 1999-2000, these were 42.2 per cent and 40.0 per cent and in 2004-05, these were 45.4 per cent and 39.5 per cent respectively.

The casual employment showed some irregular movement in all the States except Assam. In Assam, casual employment registered an increasing trend. The percentage of casual employment, which was 11.6 in 1993-94, increased to 12.4 per cent in 1999-2000 and finally reached to 12.6 per cent in 2004-05. The proportion of casual employment was quite high in Tripura. In 1993-94, the percentage of casual labourers was 12.9, which increased to 15.7 per cent in 1999-2000 and then again came down to 13.3 per cent in 2004-05. Similar was the case in Meghalaya. In 1993-94, the percentage of casual labourers was 10.1 and it increased to 17.3 per cent in 1999-2000 and then came down to 9.1 per cent in 2004-05. The situation in the country was different and it showed a declining trend over the years. In 1993-94, the percentage of casual labourers was 18.1 and it came down to 17.8 per cent in 1999-2000 and then further declined to 15.0 per cent in 2004-05. Further, details can be seen from Appendix-11.11 (b).

The regular employment in the North Eastern Region is mainly in the Public Sector, as the Private Sector has not been developed properly in any of the States of this region except Assam. This region witnessed a rapid expansion of employment in the Public Sector in 1980s and 1990s due to formation of new States, shifting of capitals and establishment of administrative machinery for them in one hand, and on the other, to compensate for the lack of employment opportunities from the private investment. The Appendix-11.12 will give an idea about the employment scenario in different States of this region from 1981 to 2002. From this, it can be seen that, in Mizoram, more than 97 per cent of employment was in the Public Sector and the rate of increase of the Public Sector employment from 1981 to 2002 was the highest of 166.67 per cent. In Manipur and Nagaland, more than 96 per cent of employment was in the Public Sector and the rate of increase of employment in the Public Sector was also much higher to the extent of 122.22 per cent in Manipur and 89.74 per cent in Nagaland during that period. The position of Meghalaya and Tripura was more or less same and both of them were having more than 89 per cent of the employment in the Public Sector. However, the rate of increase of Public Sector employment from 1981 to 2002 was more in Tripura to the extent of 77.42 per cent and in Meghalaya, it was 65.91 per cent respectively.

The situation in Assam was completely different. It can be seen that, Assam accounted for almost 60 per cent of the Public Sector employment and almost 95 per cent of the Private Sector employment of the North Eastern Region in all these years from 1981 to 2002. However, the rate of increase of the Public Sector employment in Assam was not as high as it was in other States. It was 46.93 per cent during that period. The Private Sector of Assam was though having more number of employees every year, but the rate of increase of Private Sector employment was much slower to the tune of only 7.82 per cent after a gap of 21 years i.e. from 1981 to 2002. That means, the expansion or the new investment in the Private Sector of Assam was much less and the reason of such slow growth might be due to socio-political reasons. However, in Public Sector, the total number of persons in 1981 was 3.58 lakhs, which increased to 5.26 lakhs in 2002, whereas, in Private Sector, it was 4.99 lakhs in 1981 and it reached to 5.38 lakhs in 2002 i.e. after a gap of 21 years.

However, comparing the position of North Eastern Region with the position of the country as a whole, it can be seen that, though the total number of employment in the Public Sector of this region increased at a rate of 63.00 per cent within a gap of 21 years i.e. from 1981 to 2002, as against the all India increase of 21.10 per cent during that period, even than, the total number of Public Sector employment of this region was only 4.81 per cent of the total Public Sector employment of the country. In case of Private Sector, the rate of increase of employment was though slow in both North Eastern Region and the country, still the position of the country was better. The Private Sector employment of the country increased at a rate of 14.02 per cent from 1981 to 2002, whereas, the rate of increase in this region was 10.72 per cent during that period and the total employment was only 6.74 per cent of the total Private Sector employment of the country. Further, details can be seen from Appendix-11.12.

The unemployment position in different States of this region for three different periods of 1983, 1993-94 and 1999-2000 can be seen from Appendix-11.13. From this, it can be seen that, though the unemployment was increasing in almost all the States, but the State of Assam experienced the highest proportion of unemployment during these periods. Out of the total number of labour force, 2.2 per cent was unemployed in 1983, which increased to 5.6 per cent in 1993-94 and then slowed down a bit and came to 4.6 per cent. The proportion of unemployment amongst females was much higher than males. It was 2.4 per cent in 1983 and then reached to 9.5 per cent in 1993-94 and then of course came down to 8.0 per cent in 1999-2000. That means, though the proportion of unemployment in Assam was the highest amongst all the States, still there was a positive indication of slowing down of unemployment rate from 1999-2000.

The State of Tripura showed slightly different trend. The proportion of unemployed labour force was 3.9 per cent in 1983, which came down to 3.4 per cent in 1993-94 and then further declined to 1.9 per cent in 1999-2000. But the proportion of unemployed females maintained a similar trend like Assam. The proportion of unemployed females was quite high in Tripura. In 1983, it was 7.7 per cent, which increased to 8.4 per cent in 1993-94 and then slowed down a bit and reached to 4.5 per cent in 1999-2000. In the States like Arunachal Pradesh, Manipur, Meghalaya, Mizoram, Nagaland and Sikkim, proportionately, female unemployment was less than male. This perhaps indicates that, in the hilly States of North Eastern Region, proportionately, female workers were more. That means, in the hilly areas of this region, proportionately, more number of women were economically active and unemployment problem amongst them was less. The position of the country as a whole was not very alarming. The overall unemployment amongst the labour force, which was 2 per cent in 1983, reached to 2.3 per cent in 1999-2000. That means, it increased by a meager amount of 0.3 per cent within a period of 17 years. However, the unemployment proportion of both males and females, registered an increasing trend. In case of male labour force, the percentage of unemployed male was 2.3 in 1983, but it reached to 2.5 per cent in 1999-2000. Similarly, the percentage of unemployed female labour force, which was 1.3 per cent in 1983, reached to 1.8 per cent in 1999-2000. Further, details can be seen from Appendix-11.13.

The job seekers, particularly, the first time job seekers, are the youths, and they are generally coming under three age groups. The first group, that means, those who want to enter into service after class-X, are coming within 15-19 years and the second group, that means, those who want to enter into service after class-XII, are coming within 20-24 years and the third group, that means, those who want to enter into service after graduation and post-graduation, are coming within 25-29 years. Therefore, the youths, within the age group 15-29, are the vulnerable group to employment. But, it is not always possible to provide employment to all of them at a time and therefore, some of them remained unemployed. The unemployment scenario among the youths at two different periods of 1999-2000 and 2004-05 in all the States of this region can be seen from Appendix-11.14 for the rural areas and from Appendix-11.15 for urban areas. From Appendix-11.14, it appears that, in 1999-2000, the percentage of unemployment amongst the rural youths of Assam was more. In Assam, the percentage of unemployment amongst the rural youths in the age group 15-29 years was the highest of 12.5 per cent. Amongst males, it was 10.2 per cent and amongst females, it was 24.5 per cent. From this, it also appears that, job seekers were more in the age group 20-24 years and the unemployment rate amongst them was also more. In case of males, it was 13.8 per cent and in case of females, it was 32.9 per cent. But in 2004-05, the unemployment rate amongst the rural youths of Assam came down to 9.7 per cent, for males, it came down to 8.5 per cent and for females, it came down to 15.3 per cent. However, the unemployment rate amongst the males was though high to the extent of 11.1 per cent in the age group 20-24 years, but amongst the females, it was high to the tune of 19.1 per cent in the age group 15-19 years during 2004-05.

Similar was the rural position of Nagaland in 1999-2000. The unemployment rate amongst the rural youths of Nagaland in the age group 15-29 years was the second highest of 10 per cent. The unemployment rate amongst the youths of the age group 20-24 was also high. In case of males, it was 15.3 per cent and in case of females, it was 14.5 per cent. But in 2004-05, the situation changed and unemployment rate amongst the youth went upto 14.9 per cent. Amongst males, the unemployment rate was as high as 26.9 per cent in the age group 20-24 years, whereas, in case of females, it was also more with 15 per cent in the same age group. Sikkim and Manipur showed slightly different picture. In 1999-2000, the unemployment rate amongst the rural youths of Sikkim was the third highest of 8.4 per cent. In case of males, it was more to the extent of 13.1 per cent in the age group 25-29 years, whereas, in case of females, it was more to the tune of 10.3 per cent in the age group 20-24 years. But in 2004-05, the unemployment rate amongst the youths came down to 7 per cent. However, the unemployment rate for both males and females in the age group 20-24 years was more. In case of males, it was 13 per cent and in case of females, it was 6.4 per cent.

In 1999-2000, the unemployment rate amongst the rural youths of Manipur was 5.8 per cent. But in case of males, it was more with 6.4 per cent in the age group 15-19 years, whereas, in case of females, it was more to the extent of 10.7 per cent in the age group 20-24 years. But in 2004-05, the unemployment rate amongst the rural youths of Manipur came down to 3.9 per cent, amongst males, it was 5.1 per cent and amongst females, it was as low as 2.3 per cent. The State of Tripura showed an unusual picture. In 1999-2000, the unemployment rate amongst the rural youths was as low as 3.9 per cent, but in 2004-05, it went up to 33 per cent, which was the highest among all the States of this region. The unemployment rate amongst the males in the age group 15-19 years was more to the extent of 33.6 per cent, but in case of females, it was as high as 67.1 per cent in the age group 20-24 years.

The unemployment rate amongst the rural youths of the country as a whole was not much. In 1999-2000, it was 4.6 per cent, but amongst male, it was more to the extent of 6.5 per cent in the age group 15-19 years, whereas, in case females, it was more to the tune of 4.9 per cent in the age group 20-24 years. However, in 2004-05, the unemployment rate amongst the rural youths of the country went up a bit and reached to 5.7 per cent. In case of males, it was more to the tune of 7.9 per cent in the same age group of 15-19 years, whereas, in case of females, it was more to the extent of 9.3 per cent also in the age group of 20-24 years. Further, details can be seen from Appendix 11. 14.

From Appendix-11.15, it appears that, the unemployment rate amongst the urban youths of Tripura was quite high to the extent of 21.4 per cent in 1999-2000 and it was very high to the extent of 61.4 per cent in 2004-05. In 1999-2000, the unemployment rate was more in the age group 20-24 years for both males and females. For males, it was 35.2 per cent and in case of females, it was almost same with 35.3 per cent. But in 2004-05, the unemployment rate amongst males was more to the extent of 55.4 per cent in the age group 15-19 years, whereas, in case of females, it was very high to the tune of 94.8 per cent. There might be so many reasons for such increase in the unemployment rate amongst the youths, which are not easily understandable. However, to some extent, the reasons for increasing the rate of unemployment amongst the rural as well as the urban youths, might had been, due to insurgency and other socio-political reasons.

The unemployment rate amongst the urban youths of Assam and Nagaland was also quite high. In Nagaland, the rate of unemployment amongst the urban youths was 28.3 per cent in 1999-2000. The rate was more in the age group 20-24 years for both males and females. In case of males, it was 34.0 per cent and in case of females, it was 55.5 per cent. But in 2004-05, the unemployment rate slowed down to 27.7 per cent. However, this time also, unemployment rate was high in the same age group of 20-24 years for both males and females.

For males, it was 33.2 per cent and for females, it was almost the same of 55.2 per cent.

The State of Assam also registered a declining trend in the rate of urban unemployment. In 1999-2000, the unemployment rate amongst the youths was 26.6 per cent and the rate was high in the age group of 20-24 years for both males and females. In case of males, it was 34.4 per cent and in case of females, it was quite high to the extent of 70.5 per cent. But in 2004-05, the unemployment rate reduced to 23.3 per cent. However, high rate of unemployment remained in the same age group of 20-24 years for both. For males, it was 26.9 per cent and for females, it was 50.0 per cent. The urban unemployment rate amongst the youths in Manipur, Meghalaya and Sikkim was though in the higher side, but it was showing a declining trend. In Manipur, it was 23.1 per cent in 1999-2000, bit it came down to 19.3 per cent in 2004-05. In Meghalaya, it was 14.3 per cent in 1999-2000 and it came down to 12.5 per cent in 2004-05. Similarly, the percentage of unemployment in Sikkim, which was 19.0 per cent in 1999-2000, reduced to 8 per cent in 2004-05, which was definitely a good indication towards the solution of unemployment problem.

The unemployment rate among the urban youths of the country as a whole was less than most of the States of North Eastern Region and it was also showing a declining trend. In 1999-2000, it was 12.4 per cent. For males, it was more to the extent of 15.4 per cent in the age group 15-19 years, whereas, in case of females, it was more with 22.6 per cent in the age group 20-24 years. In 2004-05, the rate came down to 11.9 per cent. However, in case of males, the rate remained high with 14 per cent in the same age group of 15-19 years and in case of females, it was high to the extent of 25.8 per cent also in the same age group of 20-24 years. Further, details can be seen from Appendix-11.15.

NOTES

1. *Economic Survey*, 2006-07, Ministry of Finance, Government of India, New Delhi, p. 15.
2. *ibid.*, p. 208.
3. *ibid.*, p. 208, 210.
4. *ibid.*, p. 210, 211.
5. *ibid.*, p. 211.

12

Economic Scenario

The economic scenario of the North Eastern Region is very poor. It is basically an under developed and unbalanced agrarian economy with very weak industrial sector. There are wide differences among the States of this region in terms of resource endowments, level of industrialization and infrastructure facilities. The resources of some of the States of this region are primarily forest based. But due to the Supreme Court's ban on felling of trees, the economy of the States has affected very badly. In Assam, the industrial sector has developed mainly around tea and oil. The other industrial units like sugar mills, jute mills, paper mills and even food processing units have not been very much successful. In Meghalaya, some coalmines are there, but these are small and located only in Jaintia Hills District. Moreover, though the cottage industries are there in all the States, but these are localized and mostly for own consumption. The income generation from this is very less. The hilly States are also suffering from marketing facility, road and other communication system, and this has become a stumbling block for the industrialization *vis-à-vis* economic development. Therefore, still now, the economy of this region is primarily depending on agriculture.

But again, the full potential of this sector could not have been exploited. This is because of the age-old practice of *Jhum*/shifting cultivation in the hilly States and even in the hilly regions of the plane State like Assam. The scope for settled cultivation in the hills is very limited. However, people have started terrace cultivation on the hill slopes, wherever possible. The shifting cultivation is largely of mono-cropping and it is also getting affected sometimes by rain and sometimes by wild animals. Moreover, in many areas, there are social taboos about the use of chemical fertilizer. They rather prefer to use compost manure instead of chemical fertilizer. All these factors contributed to the low yield rate and as a result, the region is not in a position to produce enough food for meeting the needs of its people. The States rather, importing foodgrains worth crores of rupees every year from out side. Since agriculture and industry has not really taken off, and not contributing much towards the State Domestic Product (SDP), the pressure for employment is on service sector and as such, this sector has expanded disproportionately. Due to low economic activity, the States of this region are resource deficit, and a large portion of these limited resources are being spent mainly to maintain the service sector.

The State Domestic Product or the State Income is the main indicator for measuring the growth as well as the level of development and also to study the structural changes that are taking place in the economy of a State. Moreover, this is also used to measure the regional disparities. The SDP measures, in money terms, all goods and services that an economy produces, without duplication within a given period of time, which is generally a fiscal year. For estimating SDP, it is essential to take into account, all goods and services produced during the period, irrespective of their uses i.e. whether these are marketed or bartered or used for self-consumption. The estimates of SDP are generally prepared basing on income-generating approach. That means, it measures the income generated due to factors of production physically located within the geographical boundaries of the State and the volume of goods and services produced within the State. The estimates of SDP are prepared, both at current price and constant price. The estimates at current price indicate the value of output at the prevailing market prices during a particular year, while at constant price or at the base year price, the estimates indicate the relative change in the value of output in the subsequent years, which actually measure or indicate the real growth of an economy.

The SDP has basically three components viz., (i) Primary sector, which broadly covers all land-based products, (ii) Secondary sector, which broadly covers all man made products, and (iii) Tertiary sector, which generally covers all service activities. The economy of the North Eastern Region is though basically agrarian, but the contribution of agriculture and its allied activities, that means, of the primary sector, towards SDP is not much in respect of all the States of this region. The Appendix 12.1 will show the composition of Gross State Domestic Product (GSDP) (based on the averages for the period from 2000-01 to 2004-05) for all the States of this region.

From this, it can be seen that, the primary sector of Assam was comparatively better and its contribution towards GSDP was the highest of 38.5 per cent. In the primary sector, the main activities were agriculture, mining and quarrying and their contribution was 28.3 per cent and 6.2 per cent respectively. The secondary sector of Assam was not that strong and its contribution towards GSDP was only 15.0 per cent. However, the only positive side of this was that, the manufacturing part was comparatively much better. There were a good number of registered manufacturing units and the contribution of manufacturing alone was 9.4 per cent, which was the highest amongst all the North Eastern States. The contribution of tertiary sector of Assam towards GSDP was 46.5 per cent. In the tertiary sector of the State, the prominent activities were trade, hotel and restaurant i.e. tourism activities, which contributed 15.4 per cent, public administration, which contributed 7.0 per cent, and other services, the contribution of which was 10.0 per cent.

The contribution of primary sector towards GSDP was second highest of 36.3 per cent in Nagaland. The position of agriculture was comparatively better and it alone contributed 33.1 per cent. The secondary sector of Nagaland was rather poor and its contribution towards GSDP was only 12.1 per cent. Construction was the main contributor in the secondary sector and it alone contributed 10.9 per cent. In the tertiary sector of Nagaland, road transport played an important role and amongst all the States of this region, transport sector of Nagaland contributed the highest of 17.0 per cent towards GSDP. This followed by public administration with 12.1 per cent and real estate with 8.7 per cent. However, the total contribution of tertiary sector of the State towards GSDP was 51.6 per cent.

In Meghalaya, the primary sector had two main components viz. agriculture and mining and quarrying. The Jaintia Hill District of Meghalaya is very rich in coal mines and it has become a major contributing factor towards the state economy. In Meghalaya, the contribution of primary sector towards GSDP was 31.8 per cent, and out of this, 21.3 per cent was from agriculture and 8.7 per cent was from mining and quarrying, which was the highest amongst all the North Eastern States. The contribution of secondary sector was much less to the extent of only 15.2 per cent and out of this, 9.5 per cent was from construction alone. The tertiary sector of Meghalaya was strong in trade, hotel and restaurant—that means tourism activities and in public administration. The contribution of tertiary sector of Meghalaya towards GSDP was though 53.0 per cent, but the contribution of trade, hotel and restaurant was 14.7 per cent, public administration was 13.6 per cent and 9.0 per cent was from real estate.

The contribution of primary sector of Arunachal Pradesh towards GSDP was the fourth highest of 31.3 per cent. The primary sector had two main components viz. agriculture, the contribution of which was 25.2 per cent and forestry and logging, the contribution of which was 3.5 per cent. In the secondary sector, construction was the main activities and out of the total contribution of 23.2 per cent of secondary sector, 16.0 per cent was from construction alone. In the tertiary sector, public administration and other services were the main activities in Arunachal Pradesh. The contribution of tertiary sector towards GSDP was the lowest of 45.5 per cent, amongst all the States of this region, and out of this, 17.3 per cent was from public administration and 11.7 per cent was from other services.

The primary sector of Manipur consisted mainly of agriculture and fishing. The total contribution of the primary sector towards GSDP was 27.1 per cent and out of this, 22.3 per cent was from agriculture and 3.0 per cent was from fishing. In the secondary sector, manufacturing and construction were the main activities. The contribution of secondary sector towards GSDP was 23.5 per cent, 8.7 per cent was from manufacturing and 12.5 per cent was from construction. The major contributing factors of tertiary sector of Manipur were trade, hotel and restaurant, public administration and other services. The total contribution of tertiary sector towards GSDP was 49.4 per cent and out of this, 16.9 per cent was from public administration, 11.6 per cent was from other services and 9.7 per cent was from trade, hotel and restaurants.

The main component of primary sector of Tripura was agriculture. Out of total contribution of 23.7 per cent of primary sector towards GSDP, agriculture alone accounted for 19.6 per cent. Fishing contributed only 1.9 per cent while forestry and logging contributed a meagre amount of 1.4 per cent. The secondary sector was based mainly on construction. However, some registered and unregistered manufacturing units were there. The total contribution of the secondary sector towards GSDP was 24.6 per cent and out of this, 19.3 per cent was from construction and 2.8 per cent was from manufacturing. The contribution of tertiary sector towards GSDP of Tripura was quite high to the extent of 51.7 per cent. But the main contributing factors of tertiary sector were trade, hotel and restaurants, which contributed 12.3 per cent, public administration, which contributed the maximum of 15.1 per cent, and other services, the contribution of which was 13.1 per cent.

The primary sector of Mizoram was also consisted mainly of agriculture. The total contribution of primary sector towards GSDP was 22.5 per cent and out of this, 20.4 per cent was from agriculture. Like Tripura, the main component of secondary sector was construction. The total contribution of secondary sector towards, GSDP was 14.4 per cent and out of this, 11.5 per cent was from construction. Amongst all the States of this region, the contribution of tertiary sector of Mizoram was the highest of 63.1 per cent. The major contributing factors of tertiary sector were trade, hotels and restaurants, real estate, public administration and other services and their contributions were 9.1 per cent, 14.0 per cent, 21.0 per cent and 13.1 per cent respectively.

The contribution of primary sector towards GSDP of Sikkim was the lowest of 19.0 per cent, amongst all the North Eastern States. The main component of primary sector was agriculture and its contribution was 16.9 per cent. But on the other hand, the contribution of secondary sector was the highest amongst all the States, to the extent of 25.5 per cent. The construction side of secondary sector was quite strong and it contributed the maximum of 17.9 per cent. Moreover, there were a number of registered manufacturing units, which contributed 2.9 per cent and even the electricity also contributed a high amount of 4.7 per cent towards the GSDP of the State. The contribution of tertiary sector towards the GSDP of Sikkim was 55.5 per cent, which was the second highest amongst all the states of this region. The primary contributing factors of tertiary sector was trade, hotels and restaurants, which contributed 7.1 per cent, public administration which contributed 17.5 per cent and other services, the contribution of which was the highest of 20.6 per cent.

From Appendix-12.1, it appears that, in all the States, the main contributing factor towards GSDP was agriculture in case of primary sector, construction in case of secondary sector, but in case of tertiary sector, public administration and other services were the main contributing factors. However, the contribution of primary sector of the North Eastern Region as a whole towards GSDP was more to the extent of 34.2 per cent as against the corresponding figure of 24.3 per cent of the country as a whole. But the contribution of secondary as well as of tertiary sectors of North Eastern Region was less than the corresponding figures of the country as a whole. The total contribution of secondary sector of this region was 16.8 per cent as against 23.5 per cent and the contribution of tertiary sector was 49.0 per cent as against 52.2 per cent of the country.

The main contributing factor of the secondary sector of the country was manufacturing and its contribution was 15.2 per cent which was much more than the corresponding figure of 6.7 per cent of this region. In tertiary sector, the main contributing factor of the country was trade, hotels and restaurants and its contribution was 15.2 per cent, which was also more than the corresponding figure of 13.0 per cent of this region. In tertiary sector of North Eastern Region, the major contribution towards GSDP was from public administration and other services, and these two together, contributed 21.1 per cent, which was much more than the all India combined figure of 14.6 per cent for these two items. All these indicated that the North Eastern Region was resource deficit and as such the economic activities were less. And on the other hand, the pressure was on service sector and a large portion of the limited resources were spent on public administration and other services.

The Appendix-12.2 will further illustrate the sector-wise composition of GSDP for the years 1995-96, 2000-01 and 2004-05 and the coefficient of variations for all the States as well as the region as a whole. From this, it can be seen that, there had been a gradual decline in the contribution of primary sector towards GSDP, over the time, almost in all the States except Nagaland. Decline in the share of secondary sector was also there in most of the States except Manipur, Tripura and Sikkim. However, there had been a gradual increase in the share of tertiary sector in Arunachal Pradesh, Assam, Manipur, Meghalaya and Mizoram. Further, details can be seen from Appendix-12.2.

The state-wise and year-wise Net State Domestic Product (NSDP) at current price and its growth from 1999-00 to 2005-06 can be seen from Appendix-12.3. From this, it can be seen that, there had been a continuous growth in the NSDP in all the States except Arunachal Pradesh and Manipur. In the year 2002-03, Arunachal Pradesh experienced a negative growth of 1.6 per cent and in 2000-01, Manipur registered a negative growth of 4.7 per cent. The growth of NSDP over the years was however, not uniform in any of the State. The State of Arunachal Pradesh registered the highest growth of 17.8 per cent in 2001-02, Assam, 12.4 per cent in 2005-06, Manipur, 27.4 per cent in 2004-05, Meghalaya, 14.2 per cent in 2001-02, Mizoram, 11.8 per cent in 2001-02, Nagaland, 28.6 per cent in 2000-01, Tripura, 15.2 per cent in 2001-02, Sikkim, 12.8 per cent in 2002-03 and the nation registered the highest growth of 13.8 per cent in 2005-06. Further, details can be seen from Appendix-12.3.

The per capita NSDP or the per capita State income is an indicator of the economic status of the people of a State. The Appendix-12.4 will give a clear picture of the per capita NSDP and its growth from the Year 1999-00 to 2005-06 for different States of North Eastern Region. From this, it can be seen that, the per capita NSDP was the highest in Mizoram in most of the years. The per capita NSDP was also high in Nagaland, Tripura and Sikkim, but it was quite low in Assam and Manipur. It can also be seen that, the national per capita NSDP was more than the per capita NSDP of many of the States of this region in most of the years. Further, it can be seen that, similar to NSDP, the per capita NSDP was increasing over the years in all the States except Arunachal Pradesh and Manipur. Arunachal Pradesh recorded a negative growth of 2.6 per cent in 2002-03 while Manipur registered a negative growth of 6.7 per cent in 2000-01. Further, details can be seen from Appendix-12.4.

The state-wise and year-wise NSDP and its growth at 1993-94 price can be seen from Appendix-12.5 for all the North Eastern States from the years 1993-94 to 2002-03. From this, it appears that, the growth of NSDP over the years was not positive and uniform always. Except the State of Meghalaya, all other States registered negative growth at least once during this period. The State of Arunachal Pradesh though registered a high positive growth of 14.95 per cent in 1995-96 and 14.43 per cent in 2000-01, but there was a negative growth of 6.01 per cent in 1996-97, 0.22 per cent in 1999-2000 and 0.19 per cent in 2001-02. The highest growth of Assam was of 7.25 per cent in 1996-97, but it showed a negative growth of 0.88 per cent in 1998-99. The State of Manipur registered the highest growth of 13.25 per cent in 1999-00, but there was a negative growth of 2.72 per cent in 1994-95 and 1.83 per cent in 2000-01. In Meghalaya, the highest growth was of 11.45 per cent in 1995-96 and there was no negative growth. The State of Nagaland registered a very high growth of 36.17 per cent in 2000-01, but on the other hand, it registered a negative growth of 4.69 per cent in 1998-99. The highest growth in Tripura was of 18.44 per cent in 2000-01, but there was a negative growth of 1.11 per cent in 1994-95. In Sikkim, the highest growth was of 14.91 per cent in 1997-98, but there was a negative growth of 2.37 per cent in 1994-95. The country as a whole, however, registered a positive growth over these years and the highest growth was of 7.79 per cent in 1996-97. Further, details can be seen from Appendix-12.5.

The position of per capita NSDP at 1993-94 price for all the States from 1993-94 and its growth over the years can be seen from Appendix-12.6. Similar to NSDP at constant price, per capita NSDP at constant price also showed many ups and downs in its growth. In this case also except Meghalaya, all other states registered negative growth at least once. In case of Arunachal Pradesh, the highest negative growth was of 8.15 per cent in 1996-97, in Assam, it was 2.28 per cent in 1998-99, in Manipur, it was 5.23 per cent in 1994-95. Nagaland registered the highest negative growth of 11.36 per cent in 1998-99, Tripura, 3.07 per cent in 1994-95 and Sikkim, 5.79 per cent also in 1994-95. In case of per capita NSDP, the country also registered positive growth in all these years, though there were ups and downs in the growth rates.

The actual growth of economy can be seen from Appendix-12.3, which shows the NSDP at current price and Appendix-12.5, which shows the NSDP at constant price. From the available information of 1999-2000 to 2002-2003 in both Appendices, it can be seen that, compared to the NSDP at constant price, the NSDP at current price, increased from 62.27 per cent to 91.51 per cent in Arunachal Pradesh during this period. This increase was the highest in Assam and was from 112.08 per cent to 134.73 per cent and it showed a uniform increase over these years. In Manipur, the NSDP at current price registered an increase of 81.31 per cent to 86.84 per cent, in Meghalaya, it was from 63.45 per cent to 89.90 per cent and in Tripura, the increase was from 70.52 per cent to 77.57 per cent. The country also registered a uniform increase of 57.06 per cent to 72.10 per cent in these years.

Similarly from the available information in both Appendix-12.4, which shows per capita NSDP at current price and Appendix-12.6, which shows per capita NSDP at constant price, it can be seen that, compared to the per capita NSDP at constant price, the per capita NSDP at current price increased from 61.38 per cent to 90.09 per cent during the period from 1999-2000 to 2002-2003 in Arunachal Pradesh. The increase was also the highest in Assam to the extent of 112.08 per cent to 134.73 per cent, and it also showed a uniform increase over these years. The State of Manipur registered an increase of 88.18 per cent to 93.20 per cent, Meghalaya, 62.29 per cent to 92.82 per cent, Nagaland, 47.33 per cent to 58.36 per cent and in Tripura, the increase was 70.09 per cent to 79.11 per cent. In this case also the nation registered a uniform growth and it was from 57.27 per cent to 72.37 per cent from the period from 1999-2000 to 2002-2003.

However, from all these, one think is clear that, the growth of per capita NSDP at current price as well as the growth of per capita NSDP at constant price was not uniform in any of the North Eastern States rather, almost all the States registered a negative growth at least once over the years. This is not a healthy sign for a growing economy. Moreover, the national per capita NSDP either at current price or at constant price was more than the corresponding per capita NSDP of many of the States in different years. This indicates that, the North East economy will have to grow with a positive and higher rate to catch up with the national economy. For this purpose, the contribution of the secondary sector towards SDP will have to increase. That means, the secondary sector, particularly the manufacturing sector will have to grow further for generating employment opportunities, which will in turn, ease the burden on tertiary sector, particularly the spending on maintenance of public administration and other services.

13

Poverty Alleviation Scenario

There is a saying—"all rich are rich alike but, all poors are poor in their own ways". Poverty and backwardness in the world over is due to various factors and the consequences are more or less same everywhere. Poverty has been extolled by poets, prescribed by saints, and welcomed by philosophers. Again and again, it was said that, the poor are blessed, for they are free from the cares of riches, free from temptations of wealth; they live plainly but their mind is filled with noble thoughts. But, on the other hand, it always remained a question mark in the mind of common people as to, what poverty these noble people wanted to mean, whether they know what poverty really means, or they are simply carried away by an unrealistic imagination. It is hard to believe that, the man who cannot sleep due to hunger, want of a shelter, medicine in sickness, can be content with and can have noble thoughts in his mind. However, noble people are always noble and it is better not to question on their thoughts and expressions.

The poverty what we can think of, means want of food for a growing family, clothes in the season of cold, a shelter against the in clemencies of weather, medical help in sickness, means to carry on one's studies, etc. It is said that, poverty has no temptation to vice. But on the contrary, it can be found that, poverty is one long temptation to crimes of all kinds. Very often people commit crimes under the pressure of poverty rather than under any other single factor. It can be said that, poverty is really a curse; and due to poverty, there are sufferings, people are loosing their morals and many crimes are taking place in the society.

It is believed that, poverty is the curse of a capitalist society where there is very little economic justice, where those who are willing, do not get work and those who work do not eat. It is also believed that, had there been equitable distribution of national wealth, poverty and want, starvation and diseases, illiteracy and unemployment, would have been eliminated to a great extent. Capitalism increases the gulf between rich and poor and the ugliness of poverty becomes too palpable. Poverty and backwardness are also due to caste system, untouchability, exclusion, etc. It is a fact that, the Scheduled Castes are so due to continued exploitation and domination by the higher castes. The Scheduled Tribes are so due to their isolation and exclusion. And there are people, who are poor due to their own habit. Over and above, it is a fact that, economically weaker section of people, are also suffering in the hands of landlords and moneylenders.

The poverty has two aspects; one is comparative poverty and the other is genuine poverty. The man comparatively poor has hope of not being so poor; it gives him the energy to struggle, the zest for action. But the genuinely poor man is in a pitiable condition. He does not know where to go, what to do, or to whom to turn. Social conditions are not favourable for him. He loses human dignity and self-respect. He borrows, begs and steals, and one day finds release in death. Very often, it is seen that, many of the genuinely poor people are the victims of circumstances. Nobody wants to know the reason of their fates, nobody bothers for them, sometimes people laugh at them, and sometimes people wants to get rid of them by giving a handful of rice or at best a coin. This is really sad. Will a time come? Will some one think for them? Will some one feel for them? Will some one save them from their miseries? That's remained to be seen.

When we talk about poverty, we mean comparative poverty, and when we talk about alleviation of poverty, we mean making the poverty less severe, by way of providing ways and means for economic development, raising standard of living, education and employment opportunities and on the whole, for a decent way of living. It is a fact that, everywhere, rural population is more than the urban population and poverty is also more in the rural areas. In our country, even now, more than 80 per cent of our people are living in rural areas and producing the most essential things like food and vegetable for themselves as well as for the people living in the urban areas.

Therefore, the economic development of our country lies in the economic development of the rural areas and the socio-economic status of the rural people. Development of our rural areas, therefore, has always been a cause of concern, but a systematic beginning could only be made from the early fifties with introduction of Community Development Programme.

This programme first helped to establish a network of basic extension and development services in the villages, thereby, creating awareness among the rural communities about the potentials and means of development. Which in turn was helpful for quicker adoption of new technological advancement. Later on, with the abolition of landlords and reform of land tenure system, adoption of various development programmes and investment in the successive Five Year Plans, paved the way for creation of essential physical and institutional infrastructure of socio-economic development in rural areas. The main development programmes were—Small Farmers Development Agencies (SFDA), Drought Prone Area Programme (DPAP), Command Area Development (CAD), etc. However, none of these programmes covered the whole country and on the other hand, many of the Community Development Blocks were having more than one such programmes in operation. Therefore, to put an end of such multiplicity of programmes operated through a multiplicity of agencies, a single alternative programme, viz. Integrated Rural Development Programme (IRDP), operative throughout the country was proposed in the Central Budget of 1976-77 and a beginning was made with the intention to assist the rural population to derive economic benefits from the developmental assets of the area.

The IRDP had been conceived essentially as an anti-poverty scheme and was decided to implement in different States as a Centrally Sponsored Scheme with equal matching funding pattern between Centre and State. The main objective of the scheme was to evolve operationally integrated strategy for the purpose of increasing production and productivity in agriculture and allied sectors based on better use of land, water and sunlight and also of the resource and income development of vulnerable section of population in all the Development Blocks of the country. In addition to that, various other anti-poverty programmes, like Assistance to Small and Marginal Farmers (ASMF), National Rural Employment Programme (NREP),

Rural Landless Employment Guarantee Programme (RLEGP), Integrated Child Development Services (ICDS), Training of Youth for Self-Employment (TRYSEM), etc. were implemented for raising the socio-economic status of the needy people.

Poverty has many levels, and in recognition of the various levels of poverty that exist in the society, the Government of India initiated a pioneering task in the form of household survey in early eighties, to identify the families living below a specific income level, what is came to be known as the Poverty Line. For this purpose, the Poverty Line was drawn at the annual income of Rs. 3500 for a family of 5 persons, and all families below this line were termed as families Below Poverty Line (BPL) and were considered as the target group. Amongst the people living below the poverty line, there were again poorest of the poor and other vulnerable sections of society. Therefore, the Government of India took special care of the poorest of the poor and of the vulnerable section of people and implemented the IRDP in all the districts of our country through a district level authority known as Rural Development Agency. Moreover, some of the schemes were also modified suited to the local condition. In addition to that, many other developmental programmes/schemes were taken up time to time for the benefit of the poor people for their upliftment and socio-economic development.

The major anti-poverty programmes are—(i) Swarnajayanti Gram Swarozgar Yojana (SGSY). This was launched in April,1999 after restructuring the IRDP and allied programmes. It is the only Self-Employment Programme being implemented for the rural poor on cost sharing basis of 75:25 between the Centre and States. The objective of the SGSY is to bring the assisted *swarozgaris* above the poverty line by providing them income generating assets through bank credit and Government subsidy, (ii) Pradhan Mantri Gram Sadak Yojana (PMGSY). This was launched on 25th December, 2000 as a 100 per cent Centrally Sponsored Scheme with the primary objective of providing all-weather connectivity to the eligible unconnected habitations in the rural areas, (iii) Sampoorna Grameen Rozgar Yojana (SGRJ). This programme was launched on 25th September, 2001. The objective of the programme is to provide additional wage employment in the rural areas as also food security, alongside creation of durable community, social and economic infrastructure in rural areas, (iv) Indira Awas Yojana (IAY). This scheme aims at providing dwelling units, free of cost, to the poor families of the Scheduled Castes, Scheduled Tribes, freed bonded labourers and also the non-SC/ST persons below the poverty line in rural areas. The scheme is funded on a cost sharing basis of 75:25 between the Centre and the States, (v) Swarna Jayanti Shahari Rozgar Yojana (SJSRY). This is an urban self-employment programme funded on a cost sharing basis of 75:25 between the Centre and the States. The objective of this programme is to provide employment to the unemployed youths, group employment to the women members and generation of man-days in the form of Development of Women and Children in Urban Areas (DWCUA), (vi) Valmiki Ambedkar Awas Yojana (VAMBAY). This programme was launched in December, 2001 to facilitate the construction and up-gradation of dwelling units for slum dwellers and to provide a healthy environment through community toilets under Nirmal Bharat Abhiyan, (vii) Rashtriya Swasthya Bima Yojana (RSBY). This programme was formally launched on 1st October, 2007. All workers in the unorganized sector who come in the category of Below Poverty Line (BPL) and their families are being covered under this scheme. This scheme also has a provision of smart card for the beneficiaries to enable cashless transaction for health care[1].

The poverty alleviation programmes, along with the other parts of our country, were also taken up in all the States of North Eastern Region. It can be seen from Appendix-13.1 that, at the initial stage i.e. before taking up the IRDP (during 1973-74), more than half of the people of all the States of this region as well as half the people of our country, were poor and the poverty ratio was much higher in rural than in urban. The combined poverty ratio of this region as a whole was about 50.79 per cent, which was of course less than the national average of 54.88 per cent. But after taking up various poverty alleviation programmes, the poverty of this region came down to about 34.60 per cent during 1993-94, which was also less than the national average of 35.97 per cent. The poverty ratio of N.E. Region further came down to about 29.16 per cent during 1999-2000, which was, however, a bit more than the national average of 26.10 per cent at that time. The details of state-wise rural and urban poverty position for each of the North Eastern States along with the national position for all these three years can be seen from Appendix-13.1.

From the results of the 61st round of National Sample Survey (NSS), it can be seen that, on the basis of Uniform Recall Period (URP) consumption distribution data, the poverty ratio was 28.3 per cent in rural areas, 25.7 per cent in urban areas and 27.5 per cent for the country as a whole during 2004-05. The corresponding poverty ratio from the Mixed Recall Period (MRP) consumption distribution data was 21.8 per cent for rural areas, 21.7 per cent for urban areas and 21.8 per cent for the country as a whole. The URP consumption data used 30-day recall/reference period for all items of consumption, while the MRP used 365-day recall/reference period for five infrequently purchased non-food items viz. clothing, footwear, durable goods, education and institutional medical expenses and 30-day recall/reference period for remaining items[2].

The poverty ratio in the North Eastern Region, in terms of the mixed recall data, was estimated to 14 per cent during 2004-05, which was much lower than the national figure of 21.8 per cent of the same period. But the general feeling in the region, both among governments and the people was that, the measures adopted, grossly underestimated the true extent of poverty in the region. It was also widely believed, in academic and popular circles that, wide inter and intra-state variations in the socio-economic conditions have not been adequately taken into account. Further, the adoption of one poverty line (rural and urban) for all N.E. States needs re-examination. The lower value for the urban poverty line as compared to the rural poverty line is not consistent with ground realities. There are also significant variations in the cost of living in different states that have not been adequately taken into account in determining levels of poverty[3].

The poverty scenario of the North Eastern Region is different from the other parts of the country in many ways. This is even vary from State to State of this region, as the proportion of rural-urban population and the basic amenities like communication, health, education, electricity, water supply, sanitation, job opportunity and on the whole, the cost of living, are different in different States. The proportion of rural-urban population is very much different in different States. It varies from 88.93 : 11.07 of Sikkim to 50.37 : 49.63 of Mizoram. The topographic condition of each State, basically, made the socio-economic life of its people different. The rural people of the hilly region are primarily agriculturists and are pursuing the age old method of Jhum cultivation, where the yield rate is very low. Scope for other kinds of employment is also very much limited in the hilly region. It is seen that, the poverty is largely amongst the agriculturists in rural areas and it is amongst the self employed persons and casual labourers in urban areas.

It is also a fact that, the educational facilities in different States are very much different. The people of different States are not equally literate and the gender literacy disparity is also very much prominent. In some States, though the literacy rate is high, but the skill development is low. The poor people are mostly illiterate and lack of skill. For economic development and up-gradation of quality of life, both knowledge and skill are very much required. Actually, there are multiple deprivations associated with the poverty of each States of this region and to measure its levels, special methods are required to be adopted.

However, for poverty alleviation in the North Eastern Region, there is a need for understanding the root cause(s) separately for each State, and to address them properly while formulating the plans and to adopt remedial measures at the implementation stage for alleviating poverty levels in a phased manner and finally to eradicate poverty of this region, for good.

NOTES

1. *Economic Survey*, 2007-08, Ministry of Finance, Government of India, New Delhi, pp. 240, 246.
2. *ibid.*, p. 243.
3. *North Eastern Region—VISION-2020*, Ministry of Development of North Eastern Region, North Eastern Council—Vol. II and III, May, 2008, p. 32.

14

Human Development Scenario

The concept of human development is very wide and complex. It is not very easy to define or to give a clear idea about the meaning of human development, as it is a qualitative aspect and is associated with so many factors. Ordinarily, it can be said that, human development is a process of enlarging people's choices. In principle, these choices can be infinite and change over time. But, at all levels of development, the three essential ones are: for people to lead a long and healthy life, to acquire knowledge and to have access to resources needed for a decent standard of living. If these essential choices are not available, many other opportunities remain inaccessible. However, human development does not end there. Additional choices, highly valued by many people ranging from political, economic and social freedom to opportunities for being creative and productive, and enjoying personal self-respect and guaranteed human right i.e. the principle of "live and let live" are also important to it.

Human development has two sides: the freedom of human capabilities—such as improved health, knowledge and skills—and the use people make of their acquired capabilities for leisure, productive purposes or being active in cultural, social and political affairs. If the scale of human development does not finally balance the two sides, considerable human frustration may result.

According to this concept of human development, income is clearly only one option that people would like to have albeit an important one. But, it is not the sum total of their lives. Development must therefore, be more than just the expansion of income and wealth. Its focus must be people[1].

The human development is concerned with developing human capabilities and using them productively. It also means development for people, including the creation of economic opportunities for all. The human development goals can range from the most basic ones of human survival to the most advanced human agenda of modern science and technology.

The Human Development Report, 1992 stated that, "Human Development is a broad and comprehensive concept. It covers all human choices in all societies at all stages of development. It broadens the development dialogue from a discussion of mere means (GNP growth) to a discussion of the ultimate ends. It is as concerned with the generation of economic growth as with its distribution, as concerned with basic needs as with the entire spectrum of human aspirations, as concerned with the human dilemmas of the north as with the human development in the south. The concept of human development does not start with any predetermined model. It draws its inspiration from the long-term goals of a society. It weaves development around people, not people around development"[2]. The report furthered the exploration of human development by considering the interaction between people and their natural environment. If the objective of development is to improve people's choices then, it must do so, not only for the well being of the present generation but also for future generations. In other words, development must be sustainable.

Human development and sustainability are essential components of the same ethics of universalism of life claims. There is no tension between the two concepts, for they are a part of the same overall design. In such a conceptual framework, sustainability is, in a broad sense, a matter of distributional equity of sharing development opportunities between the present and the future generations. There would, however, be something distinctly odd if we were deeply concerned for the well-being of future generations, as yet unborn generations, while ignoring the plight of the poor today. The ethics of universalism clearly demands both intra and intergenerational equity. This equity of opportunities is necessarily not the final achievements, however, it is decidedly the essential requirement for proper human development. Each individual is entitled to just opportunities for making the best use of his/her capabilities. So is each generation. How they actually use these opportunities? What are the possible results they are likely to realize? etc. are a matter of their own choice. They must have such choice now and in future[3].

The problems of human development is not the same everywhere. It is different in countries having different historical experiences. A country may have large potentials of human resources but, lack of proper planning can reduce these vital resource potentials into equally large liabilities. If anything has to be gained meaningfully, it is necessary to plan for human development.

Human development is a qualitative aspect and it is not very easy to measure. Its concept is much broader and more complex. There is no specific indicator(s) for measuring the level of human development. However, many economists put forward the concept that, national income is a good indicator of human well-being, as it is evident that, there is a strong relationship, since economic growth is an important means to human development. But human outcomes do not depend on economic growth and levels of national income alone. They also depend on how the resources are used—whether for developing weapons or producing food, building palaces or providing clean water. Human outcomes such as democratic participation in decision-making or equal rights for men and women, life expectancy, literacy rate, the gaps between men and women in schooling do not depend on income[4].

The Human Development Reports, since inception, have published the Human Development Index (HDI). These reports have been complemented and enriched time to time by taking into account various aspects of human life and presenting an extensive set of indicators. The HDI focuses mainly on three measurable dimensions of human development: living a long and healthy life, being educated and having a decent standard of living. It combines measures of life expectancy, school enrolment, literacy and income to allow a broader view of a country's development than does income alone[5].

The level of human development of our country is not very satisfactory. From the UNDP's Global Human Development Report (HDR) 2007, it can be seen that, in spite of the absolute value of the Human Development Index (HDI) for India improving from 0.577 in 2000 to 0.611 in 2004 and further to 0.619 in 2005, the relative ranking of India has not changed much. India ranks at 128 among the countries with medium human development out of 177 countries of the world as against 126 in the previous year. In terms of Gender Development Index (GDI), India ranks 113 out of 157 countries ranked on the basis of their GDI value. However, the country has done better in terms of per capita income than in other components of human development[6].

The human development scenario of the North Eastern Region is not very satisfactory. The first and foremost aspect of human development is education, and this region is very much lacking in that respect. The overall literacy rate of this region, as per 2001 census, was only 65.07 per cent. From Appendix-14.1, it can be seen that, the female literacy was quite low and the literacy gap was as high as 20.30 per cent in the State of Arunachal Pradesh and 19.80 per cent in the State of Manipur. The enrolment ratio of females, as on September, 2004, at the High/Post Basic Schools (i.e. class IX-X) was though good in Meghalaya, Sikkim and Mizoram but, in Pre-Degree Junior Colleges/Higher Secondary Schools (i.e. class XI-XII), it was quite low in all the States. As regards male-female teachers ratio, it can be seen that, the ratio of female teachers in High/Post Basic Schools (i.e. class IX-X) was very low in all the States except Meghalaya, Manipur and Nagaland. In Pre-Degree Junior colleges/ Higher Secondary Schools (i.e. class XI-XII), it was also very low in all the States except Meghalaya, Nagaland and Mizoram. The educational sector of this region is lagging much behind due to various factors. Though there is not much shortage of schools, but high quality schools are very few. Moreover, many of the schools suffer from shortage of teachers. Also, there is an acute shortage of trained teachers and infrastructure in the educational institutions. As regards higher and technical education, it can be mentioned that, some of the States of this region do not have a single Medical or Engineering College. The other important factors are—the plan allocation for the education sector is comparatively less and the teachers are ill paid. The male-female workers ratio was very much unsatisfactory in some of the States of this region. It was as low as only 39 female per 100 male workers in the States of Assam and Tripura.

The living condition of people of this region is quite poor. It is seen from the results of 2001 census that, the percentage of people living in pucca/permanent houses was ranging from 8.39 per cent of

Manipur to 22.14 per cent of Meghalaya. However, the condition was slightly better in Sikkim and Mizoram. In sikkim, it was 37.87 per cent and in Mizoram, it was 52.84 per cent. The availability of the most essential item like drinking water was very bad in almost all the States except Sikkim and Arunachal Pradesh, where the position was slightly better. The percentage of households having safe drinking water was varying from 36 of Mizoram to 58.8 of Assam. In Sikkim, the percentage was 70.7 and in Arunachal Pradesh, it was 77.5. As regards toilet facility, it appears that, most of the households in all the States were having some kind of toilet facility. But, the provision of septic tank/flash was very less, particularly in the rural areas.

The other important indicators for human development are—use of electricity and telephone. It is seen from the information of 2001 census and of 2004-05 that, in most of the States, the percentage of households having electricity was ranging from 41 to 77 per cent. The maximum number of households having electricity was in Sikkim and their percentage was 77.76. The per capita consumption of electricity was also a bit more there, to the extent of 397.7 kWh. The per capita consumption of electricity in Meghalaya was also comparatively high and was of the order of 352.2 kWh. In Assam, the percentage of households having electricity was only 24.90 and the per capita consumption was also very less to the extent of 85.3 kWh. Moreover, on the whole, the per capita consumption of electricity in this region was much less than the all India per capita figure of 411.1 kWh. The Tele density in this region, as on December, 2004 was very low. Except Mizoram and Arunachal Pradesh, in all other States, it was within 2.41 to 3.37 per 100 persons. In Mizoram, the Tele density was 7.13 and in Arunachal Pradesh, it was 6.22.

In case of health indicators, the scenario is not that good. From the reports of 2006 and 2007, it appears that, the birth rate in both the States of Assam and Meghalaya was the highest and was of the order of 24.6 and 24.7 respectively, which were also more than the national rate of 23.5. The birth rate in other States was ranging from 13.4 of Manipur to 19.2 of Sikkim. Interestingly, the death rate was also more in the same two States of Assam and Meghalaya and was of the order of 8.7 and 8.0 respectively, which were also more than the national rate of 7.5. The death rate in other States was between 4.5 of Manipur to 7.3 of Arunachal Pradesh. In case of infant mortality rate, Assam was again on the top having the figure of 66, and close to that was Arunachal Pradesh having the rate of 61. The availability of Doctor as well as the Bed was very poor. The number of Doctor per 1000 population was the lowest of 0.02 of Assam to the highest of 0.43 of Arunachal Pradesh, which was much less than the national figure of 0.59. The availability position of Bed per 1000 population was again the lowest of the order of 0.25 in Assam. The position was comparatively a bit better in Mizoram. The State was having 2.16 numbers of Beds per 1000 population and this was of course higher than the national figure of 0.82. However, all these indicate that, the health care facilities in the North Eastern Region are not at all satisfactory. The position though slightly better in the urban areas, but the rural people, that means, more than 80 per cent of people of this region are not getting adequate health coverage.

In case of per capita Net State Domestic Product (NSDP), all the States of this region, except Sikkim, are lagging behind the national NSDP figure of Rs. 25716. In this respect also, Assam was in the lowest position having per capita NSDP of Rs. 18598 only. Further, details can be seen from Appendix-14.1.

From the above scenario, it can be concluded that, the North Eastern Region will have to go a long way in respect of its Human Development.

NOTES

1. *Human Development Report*, 1990, United Nations Development Programme (UNDP), Oxford University Press, p. 10.
2. *Human Development Report*, 1992, UNDP, p. 2.
3. *Human Development Report*, 1994, UNDP, p. 13.
4. *ibid.*, p. 127.
5. *ibid.*, p. 127.
6. *Economic Survey, 2007-08*, Ministry of Finance, Government of India, New Delhi, pp. 239, 240.

15

Conclusions

The socio-economic scenario of the North East India is not very complacent and there are so many reasons for that. This region is in the North East extremity of our country and is consisting mostly of hilly States. The international boundaries are there almost in all sides of this region except a small portion of land in its western side. This is actually a land-locked area and is connected to the rest of the country through the narrow 28 kms. Siliguri corridor. The region is though strategically very important, but in respect of infrastructure, it is very poor and as such the country is facing various problems, very often. The hilly terrains are very much un-hospitable for building up road communication and for development of other infrastructural system. This not only created communicational and economical problems, but also isolated the hill people from the main stream, to certain extent. And that is hampering the educational and socio-cultural growth of the hill people.

The North East Economy is basically agrarian and the hill people are pursuing the age old method of Jhum cultivation, in which, the yield rate is very low. The region is still not in a position to produce enough food for its people and have to import it from other parts of the country every year. Due to lack of infrastructure and in absence of marketing facilities, other economic activities could not take place, particularly in the rural areas and people remained mostly poor and below the poverty line. Their living condition is also very poor. Almost half of the rural people of this region are living in kutcha houses with poor sanitation. Except Assam, industrial activities are very much limited in this region and the people are largely depending upon public sector employment which has almost reached to the saturation point and as such unemployment problem is gradually increasing.

The educational scenario of this region is not very satisfactory. Though there is not much shortage of schools and colleges, but most of the schools are in shortage of proper infrastructure and there is an acquit shortage of trained teachers. The schools in the rural areas are the worst sufferers due to so many factors. In the interior places, the schooling habit among the children is lacking and sometimes their parents also do not feel the urge of sending their children to the schools. Moreover, the dropout ratio is very high due to the fact that, sometimes the students are not interested for further studies, sometimes higher educational facilities are not available at the place of residence or nearby, and sometimes for the necessity of joining household duties, etc. On the other hand, due to lack of communication and other basic amenities, very often, teachers are reluctant to go and stay in the interior places. Besides these, there is also a problem of overseeing the functioning and performance of the schools time to time. The overall literacy rate of this region is not that good. The literacy rate of some of the States like Arunachal Pradesh, Assam and Meghalaya is even less than the overall literacy rate of the country. The male-female literacy gap is also quite high in most of the States of this region. That means, the females are lagging much behind in respect of education in these States. This needs proper attention and the position should be improved. It should also be kept in mind that, literacy rate alone cannot be an indicator of development. Level of education, efficiency and skill are always considered as the guiding factors of success in this field.

In the higher level, particularly in the field of technical and professional education, many of the States are lagging much behind. In some of the States, facilities for science education, particularly the subjects like physics, chemistry, mathematics and statistics, etc. are very much limited and for studying engineering or medical, they have to depend entirely on the other States. Quality education, which is very much necessary for building up character, generating aptitude and skill and making competitive mind etc, is very much lacking in this region. This is the age of competition and there is hardly any good institution or coaching centre in this region who can properly train up the students for sitting in the highly competitive examination like IIT, MBA, IAS, IPS or in the fields of Engineering and Medical, etc. It is high time to find the ways and means to remove the deficiencies and to bring about the reform in the education sector for the betterment of this region. Education is one of the most essential requirements for building up the future of not only a person, but also of the nation. Therefore, it should be looked at in a broader perspective and with a pure mind and an honest soul, and there should not be any compromise with the quality at any stage, at any time.

The Healthcare scenario of the North Eastern Region, particularly of the rural areas is not very satisfactory. In spite of physical expansion of healthcare facilities, access to quality health services remained a distant dream in the remote areas and even in urban areas of many of the States of this region. People still need to travel long distances to come to Guwahati or to go to other part of the country for consulting doctors or specialists or for diagnostic or therapeutic treatment. Rural healthcare services are very poor due to acquit shortage of skilled medical and paramedical staff, specialized doctors, essential equipments and medicines. The reason for poor healthcare services in the rural areas is not only the absence of proper communication and other infrastructure, but it has other reasons also, and these are—social taboos, reluctance in allopathic medicines and under use of healthcare facilities. Rural people have the preference towards traditional methods of treatment and local medicines. Therefore, for improvement of rural healthcare, it is very much essential to make the rural people aware about the benefit of allopathic treatment and to increase their willingness towards this.

The North Eastern Region is though called the store house of power potentials, but at present, almost all the States are deficit in power and are importing it from the neighbouring States who are also deficit. The region is having more than 63 thousand MW of hydro-power potential, but only a fraction of it i.e. 1.86 per cent of this has so far been developed and 5.45 per cent of it is under development. This is not enough for meeting the requirement of this region. Therefore, among other factors, load—shading has also became a regular phenomenon in many of the States of this region. The industrial and commercial use of power is very less and agricultural use of power in most of the States is non-existent. The per capita consumption of power in all the States is much less than the overall per capita consumption of power of the country. In some of the States, it is even 1/3rd of the national consumption figure. The shortage of power is hampering the industrial growth to some extent. Position of rural electrification is also not good. In many of the States, almost ½ of the villages are not electrified. The percentage of households having electricity in the rural areas is very less. Therefore, there is an urgent need of developing the power sector and providing power to the ultimate consumer for all-round development of this region.

The scenic beauty of many of the places of North Eastern Region is very good and these are always attracting people. The famous Shillong city, capital of Meghalaya, which is called the Scotland of the East, is a hub for the tourists. Little away from Shillong is excellent Cheerapunji and the world famous Mawsynram, the place of world's heaviest rainfall. The spectacular township of Bomdila and Tawang, Sela-Pass and the Tawang Monastery in Arunachal Pradesh are worth seeing. Apart from this, the famous Kamakhya temple in Guwahati, Kaziranga Wildlife Sanctuary and many other important places and religious temples of this region are the attractions of tourists. But so long, the tourism industry could not develop in a well organized manner in this region. The beauty of the hospitality industry is that, it requires less capital cost, short gestation period and generates maximum profit. It creates employment and economic benefit for all sections of society—rich or poor—literate or illiterate, directly or indirectly. But the growth of hospitality industry requires, as the name implies, a very much cordial and congenial atmosphere, proper infrastructure and most importantly, the safety and security of the tourists. If it can be looked at in that perspective and need based schemes are taken up for development of required infrastructure for the tourists, this can be a boon for this region.

The economic condition of this region is not very satisfactory. The State Domestic Product (SDP) of almost all the States is largely depending upon Service Sector. The Primary Sector is consisting mainly of agriculture and the contribution of this sector is around 30 per cent and it is gradually showing a decreasing trend. The contribution of Secondary sector is also very less and is around 20 per cent only. Therefore, the major portion of SDP is coming from Tertiary Sector, particularly from public administration and other services, which is already over burdened. The per capita Net State Domestic Product (NSDP) of all the States of this region is also less than the overall per capita NSDP of the country. That means, the economic status of the people of this region is below the national average. That is definitely not a good indication.

The North Eastern States are resource deficit and are depending mostly on central funding. This cannot continue for long. States should find out the ways and means to generate their own resources. Manufacturing, trade and commerce, hotel and restaurants and industrialization are some of the areas, which can generate maximum employment and economic benefit. It is not at all good to see that, many of the North Eastern States do not have any registered factory/industry and not covered by Annual Survey of Industries (ASI). Special attention may be given for creating a congenial atmosphere for private investment and building up public-private partnership wherever required for the economic boost of this region.

For manufacturing activities and industrialization, it is not always necessary to have the physical resource at a particular place. The physical resource can be transported or imported from other places whenever required. What is always required is educated and skilled human resource. This can be hired on a short term basis, but it cannot be a permanent solution and it is not economical also. This is to be produced or generated from within. There is no dearth of human resource in the North Eastern States. Only they are to be educated and trained properly to shoulder that responsibility. It is a well-known fact that, though technology plays a vital role in the economic development, but the pace of development is always determined and sustained by the level of education and skill of the persons involved in it. Keeping that in mind, a new initiative may be taken up to bring about a change, without compromising the quality, in the system of education and employment and also in the plan formulation and implementation, in order to speed up and to sustain the process of overall development of the North Eastern Region.

APPENDICES

Appendix 3.1

State-wise Distribution of Area, Total Population, Scheduled Tribe (ST) Population and Density of Population as per 2001 census

Sl. No.	Name of the State/NER/India	Notional Area (sq. km)	Total No. of Districts	Total No. of Towns	Total No. of Villages	Total Population	Percentage over Total Population of NER/India	Density of Population	Total Scheduled Tribe (ST) Population	Percentage over Total ST Population of NER/India	Density of ST Population	Percentage of ST Population over Total Population of State/NER/India
1	2	3	4	5	6	7	8	9	10	11	12	13
1.	Arunachal Pradesh	83743	13	17	4065	1097968	2.82	13	705158	6.74	8	64.22
2.	Assam	78438	23	125	26312	26655528	68.60	340	3308570	31.61	42	12.41
3.	Manipur*	22327	9	33	2391	2166788	5.58	97	741141	7.08	33	34.20
4.	Meghalaya	22429	7	16	6026	2318822	5.97	103	1992862	19.04	89	85.94
5..	Mizoram	21087	8	22	817	888573	2.29	42	839310	8.02	40	94.46
6.	Nagaland	16579	8	9	1317	1990036	5.12	120	1774026	16.95	107	89.15
7.	Tripura	10492	4	23	870	3199203	8.23	305	993426	9.49	95	31.05
8.	Sub-Total, NER	255095	72	245	41798	38316918	98.61	150	10354493	98.93	41	27.02
9.	Sikkim	7096	4	9	452	540851	1.39	76	111405	1.07	16	20.60
10.	Grand Total, NER	262191	76	254	42250	38857769	3.78	148	10465898	12.41	40	26.93
11.	India*	3287263	593	5161	638588	1028610328	100.00	313	84326240	100.00	26	8.20

Note: * Population figures for three sub-divisions viz. Mao Maran, Paomata and Purul of Senapati District of Manipur are not included as Census results were cancelled in these three sub-divisions due to technical and administrative reasons.

Appendix 3.2

State-wise Distribution of Household, Population, Household Size, Sex Ratio, Scheduled Tribe (ST) Population and their Percentage with Sex and Rural-Urban Break-up as per 2001 census

Sl. No	Name of the State/NER/ India	Total/ Rural/ Urban	Population			Total Number of House-holds	House-hold size	Sex ratio	ST Population			Percentage of ST Population		
			Total	Male	Female				Total	Male	Female	Total	Male	Female
1	2	3	4	5	6	7	8	9	10	11	12	13	14	15
1.	Arunachal Pradesh	T	1097968	579941	518027	215574	5.09	893	705158	352017	353141	64.22	60.70	51.80
		R	870087	454680	415407	166468	5.23	914	606278	303072	303206	69.60	66.65	72.99
		U	227881	125261	102620	49106	4.64	819	98880	48945	49935	43.39	39.07	48.66
2.	Assam	T	26655528	13777037	12878491	4914823	5.42	935	3308570	1678117	1630453	12.41	12.18	12.66
		R	23216288	11939945	11276343	4203976	5.52	944	3154546	1598267	1556279	13.59	13.39	13.89
		U	3439240	1837092	1602148	710847	4.84	872	154024	79850	74174	4.48	4.35	4.63
3.	Manipur	T	2166788	1095634	1071154	375095	5.78	978	741141	374319	366822	34.20	34.16	34.25
		R	1590820	808953	781867	273098	5.83	967	705912	357052	348860	44.37	44.14	44.62
		U	575968	286681	289287	101997	5.65	1009	35229	17267	17962	6.12	6.02	6.21
4.	Meghalaya	T	2318822	1176087	1142735	418850	5.54	972	1992862	996567	996295	85.94	84.74	87.19
		R	1864711	946999	917712	333119	5.60	969	1682670	846830	835840	90.24	89.42	91.08
		U	454111	229088	225023	85731	5.30	982	310192	149737	160455	68.31	65.36	71.31
5.	Mizoram	T	888573	459109	429464	176134	5.04	935	839310	422963	416347	94.46	92.13	96.95
		R	447567	232726	214841	86951	5.15	923	430883	219919	210964	96.27	94.50	98.20
		U	441006	226383	214623	89183	4.94	948	408427	203044	205383	92.61	89.69	95.69
6.	Nagaland	T	1990036	1047141	942895	328057	6.07	900	1774026	913203	860823	89.15	87.21	91.30
		R	1647249	859716	787533	263129	6.26	916	1544022	795008	749014	93.73	92.47	95.11
		U	342787	187425	155362	64928	5.28	829	230004	118195	111809	67.10	63.06	71.97
7.	Tripura	T	3199203	1642225	1556978	664334	4.82	948	993426	504320	489106	31.05	30.71	31.41
		R	2653453	1363638	1289815	539713	4.92	946	967997	491080	476917	36.48	36.01	36.98
		U	545750	278587	267163	124621	4.38	959	25429	13240	12189	4.66	4.75	4.56
8	Sub-Total, NER	T	38316918	19777174	18539744	7092867	5.40	937	10354493	5241506	5112987	27.02	26.50	27.58
		R	32290175	16606657	15683518	5866454	5.50	944	9092308	4611228	4481080	28.16	27.77	28.57
		U	6026743	3170517	2856226	1226413	4.91	901	1262185	630278	631907	20.94	19.88	22.12

(Contd.)

Appendix-3.2 (*Contd.*)

1	2	3	4	5	6	7	8	9	10	11	12	13	14	15
9	Sikkim	T	540851	288484	252367	114223	4.74	875	111405	56940	54465	20.60	19.74	21.58
		R	480981	255774	225207	101225	4.75	880	101909	52249	49660	21.19	20.43	22.05
		U	59870	32710	27160	12998	4.61	830	9496	4691	4805	15.86	14.43	17.69
10	Total, NER	T	38857769	20065658	18792111	7207090	5.39	937	10465898	5298446	5167452	26.93	26.41	27.50
		R	32771156	16862431	15908725	5967679	5.49	943	9194217	4663477	4530740	28.06	27.66	28.48
		U	6086613	3203227	2883386	1239411	4.91	900	1271681	634969	636712	20.89	19.82	22.08
11	All India	T	1028610328	532156772	496453556	193579954	5.31	933	84326240	42640829	41685411	8.20	8.01	8.40
		R	742490639	381602674	360887965	137747384	5.39	946	77338597	39045650	38292947	10.42	10.23	10.61
		U	286119689	150554098	135565591	55832570	5.12	900	6987643	3595179	3392464	2.44	2.39	2.50

Appendix 3.3

State-wise Estimated Birth Rate, Death Rate, Natural Growth Rate and Infant Mortality Rate, 2005 (As per SRS Bulletin, October, 2006)

Sl. No.	*Name of the State/NER/India*	*Birth Rate*			*Death Rate*			*Natural Growth Rate*			*Infant Mortality Rate*		
		Total	*Rural*	*Urban*	*Total*	*Rural*	*Urban*	*Total*	*Rural*	*Urban*	*Total*	*Rural*	*Urban*
1	2	3	4	5	6	7	8	9	10	11	12	13	14
1.	Arunachal Pradesh	23.3	24.4	18.7	5.0	5.5	2.8	18.3	18.9	15.9	37	39	17
2.	Assam	25.0	26.6	15.3	8.7	9.2	5.6	16.3	17.4	9.6	68	71	39
3.	Manipur	14.7	14.5	15.5	4.1	4.0	4.4	10.7	10.5	11.1	13	12	14
4.	Meghalaya	25.1	27.3	15.1	7.5	7.9	6.0	17.5	19.4	9.1	49	50	42
5.	Mizoram	18.8	23.2	14.4	5.1	6.2	4.1	13.7	17.1	10.3	20	26	10
6.	Nagaland	16.4	16.5	16.1	3.8	4.0	3.1	12.6	12.5	13.1	18	17	22
7.	Tripura	16.0	16.5	13.8	5.7	5.7	5.8	10.3	10.7	8.0	31	31	29
8.	Sikkim	19.9	20.2	18.0	5.1	5.2	4.8	14.8	15.0	13.2	30	31	15
9.	All India	23.8	25.6	19.1	7.6	8.1	6.0	16.3	17.5	13.1	58	64	40

Appendix 3.4

State-wise Distribution of Population of the Age Group 0-6 Years and their Percentage, Literacy with Sex and Rural-Urban Break-up, as per 2001 census

Sl. No.	Name of the State/NER/India	Total/Rural/ Urban	Population (0-6 years)			% of population of 0-6 Years over Total Population			Literate Population			% of Literacy of Total Population (Excluding Population of 0-6 years)		
			Total	Male	Female	Total	Male	Female	Total	Male	Female	Total	Male	Female
1	2	3	4	5	6	7	8	9	10	11	12	13	14	15
1.	Arunachal Pradesh	T	205871	104833	101038	18.75	18.08	19.50	484785	303281	181504	54.34	63.83	43.53
		R	169029	86230	82799	19.43	18.96	19.93	335284	212415	122869	47.83	57.65	36.94
		U	36842	18603	18239	16.17	14.85	17.77	149501	90866	58635	78.26	85.19	69.49
2.	Assam	T	4498075	2289116	2208959	16.87	16.61	17.15	14015354	8188697	5826657	63.25	71.28	54.61
		R	4104407	2086499	2017908	17.68	17.47	17.90	11416293	6721956	4694337	59.73	68.22	50.70
		U	393668	202617	191051	11.45	11.03	11.92	2599061	1466741	1132320	85.34	89.74	80.24
3.	Manipur	T	308585	157682	150903	14.24	14.39	14.09	1310534	753466	557068	70.53	80.33	60.53
		R	233675	119486	114189	14.69	14.77	14.60	913282	533038	380244	67.29	77.31	56.95
		U	74910	38196	36714	13.01	13.32	12.69	397252	220428	176824	79.28	88.64	70.01
4.	Meghalaya	T	467979	237215	230764	20.18	20.17	20.19	1157875	614272	543603	62.56	65.34	59.61
		R	400563	202981	197582	21.48	21.43	21.53	824173	440755	383418	56.29	59.24	53.24
		U	67416	34234	33182	14.85	14.94	14.75	333702	173517	160185	86.30	89.05	83.50
5.	Mizoram	T	143734	73176	70558	16.18	15.94	16.43	661445	350105	311340	88.80	90.72	86.75
		R	80466	40947	39519	17.98	17.59	18.39	298339	162880	135459	81.27	84.93	77.26
		U	63268	32229	31039	14.35	14.24	14.46	363106	187225	175881	96.13	96.43	95.80
6.	Nagaland	T	289678	147524	142154	14.56	14.09	15.08	1132323	640201	492122	66.59	71.16	61.46
		R	241197	122519	118678	14.64	14.25	15.07	882926	498181	384745	62.79	67.58	57.52
		U	48481	25005	23476	14.14	13.34	15.11	249397	142020	107377	84.74	87.44	81.42

(Contd.)

Appendix-3.4 (*Contd.*)

1	2	3	4	5	6	7	8	9	10	11	12	13	14	15
7.	Tripura	T	436446	222002	214444	13.64	13.52	13.77	2022099	1150707	871392	73.19	81.02	64.91
		R	383177	194660	188517	14.44	14.27	14.62	1582775	916514	666261	69.72	78.40	60.50
		U	53269	27342	25927	9.76	9.81	9.70	439324	234193	205131	89.21	93.21	85.03
8.	Sub-Total. NER	T	6350368	3231548	3118820	16.57	16.34	16.82	20784415	12000729	8783686	65.02	72.53	56.96
		R	5612514	2853322	2759192	17.38	17.18	17.59	16253072	9485739	6767333	60.92	68.97	52.36
		U	737854	378226	359628	12.24	11.93	12.59	4531343	2514990	2016353	85.68	90.07	80.76
9.	Sikkim	T	78195	39842	38353	14.46	13.81	15.20	318335	189060	129275	68.81	76.04	60.40
		R	72017	36627	35390	14.97	14.32	15.71	273282	163161	110121	66.82	74.45	58.01
		U	6178	3215	2963	10.32	9.83	10.91	45053	25899	19154	83.91	87.81	79.16
10.	Total, NER	T	6428563	3271390	3157173	16.54	16.30	16.80	21102750	12189789	8912961	65.07	72.58	57.01
		R	5684531	2889949	2794582	17.35	17.14	17.57	16526354	9648900	6877454	61.01	69.06	52.44
		U	744032	381441	362591	12.22	11.91	12.58	4576396	2540889	2035507	85.66	90.04	80.75
11.	India	T	163819614	84999203	78820411	15.93	15.97	15.88	560687797	336533716	224154081	64.84	75.26	53.67
		R	126470497	65407648	61062849	17.03	17.14	16.92	361870817	223551641	138319176	58.74	70.70	46.13
		U	37349117	19591555	17757562	13.05	13.01	13.10	198816980	112982075	85834905	79.92	86.27	72.86

Appendix 3.5

Population Trends in the North Eastern Region

(*In thousand Persons*)

Census Year	Name of the North Eastern States/NER										India @**#
	Arunachal Pradesh*	Assam @	Manipur	Meghalaya	Mizoram	Nagaland	Tripura	Sub-Total, NER	Sikkim	Total, NER	
1	2	3	4	5	6	7	8	9	10	11	12
1901	0	3290	284	341	82	102	173	4272	59	4331	238396
1911	0	3849	346	394	91	149	230	5059	88	5147	252093
1921	0	4637	384	422	98	159	304	6004	82	6086	251321
1931	0	5560	446	481	124	179	382	7172	110	7282	278977
1941	0	6695	512	556	153	190	513	8619	122	8741	318661
1951	0	8029	578	606	196	213	639	10261	138	10399	361088
1961	337	10837	780	769	266	369	1142	14500	162	14662	439235
1971	468	14625	1073	1012	332	516	1556	19582	210	19792	548160
1981	632	18041	1421	1336	494	775	2053	24752	316	25068	683329
1991	865	22414	1837	1775	690	1210	2757	31548	406	31954	846421
2001#	1098	26656	2294	2319	889	1990	3199	38445	541	38986	1028737

Notes

* Census in Arunachal Pradesh for the first time in 1961

@ The 1981 Census could not be held in Assam. The population figure for 1981 has been worked out by interpolation.

** The 1991 Census was not held in Jammu & Kashmir. The population figure for 1991 has been worked out by interpolation.

\# India and Manipur figures include estimated figures for three sub-divisions viz. Mao Maran, Paomata and Purul of Senapati District of Manipur as census results of 2001 were cancelled in these sub-divisions due to technical and administrative reasons.

Appendix 3.6

Decadal Variation in Population, Change in Decadal Variation and Average Exponential Growth Rate of Population

Sl. No.	Name of the State/India	Decadal Growth Rate of Population (%)			Change in the Growth Rate		Average Annual Exponential Growth Rate (%)		
		1971-1981	1981-1991	1991-2001	Col.4-col.3	Col.5-col.4	1971-1981	1981-1991	1991-2001
1	2	3	4	5	6	7	8	9	10
1.	Arunachal Pradesh	35.15	36.83	27.00	1.68	-9.83	3.01	3.14	2.39
2.	Assam	23.36	24.24	18.92	0.88	-5.32	2.10	2.17	1.73
3.	Manipur	32.46	29.29	24.86	-3.17	-4.43	2.81	2.57	2.22
4.	Meghalaya	32.04	32.86	30.65	0.82	-2.21	2.78	2.84	2.67
5.	Mizoram	48.55	39.70	28.82	-8.85	-10.88	3.96	3.34	2.53
6.	Nagaland	50.05	56.08	64.53	6.03	8.45	4.06	4.45	4.98
7.	Tripura	31.92	34.30	16.03	2.38	-18.27	2.77	2.95	1.49
8.	Sikkim	50.77	28.47	33.06	-22.30	4.59	4.11	2.51	2.86
9.	All India	24.66	23.87	21.54	-0.79	-2.33	2.20	2.14	1.95

Source: Registrar General of India, New Delhi.

Note: Growth rates of India and Manipur during 1991-2001 are based on the estimated population of census 2001 as these include the estimated population of the three sub-divisions of Senapati District of Manipur where census results were cancelled due to technical and administrative reasons.

Appendix 3.7

State-wise Projected Population of North Eastern Region and India upto 2025

Year	Name of the North Eastern States/NER										India *
	Arunachal Pradesh	Assam	Manipur *	Meghalaya	Mizoram	Nagaland	Tripura	Sub-Total, NER	Sikkim	Total, NER	
1	2	3	4	5	6	7	8	9	10	11	12
2001	1097968	26655528	2294000	2318822	888573	1990036	3199203	38444130	540851	38984981	1028737540
2002	1124209	27116669	2344927	2380735	911054	2079508	3246871	39203973	556319	39760292	1048797921
2003	1151078	27585787	2396984	2444300	934104	2173003	3295250	39980506	572230	40552736	1069249481
2004	1178589	28063021	2450197	2509563	957736	2270701	3344349	40774156	588596	41362752	1090099845
2005	1206757	28548511	2504592	2576568	981967	2372792	3394180	41585367	605430	42190797	1111356792
2006	1235599	29042401	2560194	2645363	1006811	2479472	3444753	42414593	622745	43037338	1133028249
2007	1265129	29544834	2617030	2715994	1032283	2590949	3496080	43262299	640555	43902854	1155122300
2008	1295366	30055960	2675128	2788511	1058400	2707438	3548171	44128974	658875	44787849	1177647184
2009	1326325	30575928	2734516	2362964	1085177	2829165	3601039	45015114	677719	45692833	1200611304
2010	1358024	31104892	2795222	2939405	1112632	2956364	3654694	45921233	697102	46618335	1224023224
2011	1390481	31643006	2857276	3017887	1140782	3089282	3709149	46847863	717039	47564902	1247891677
2012	1423714	32190431	2920707	3098465	1169644	3228176	3764416	47795553	737546	48533099	1272225564
2013	1457740	32747325	2985547	3181194	1199236	3373315	3820506	48764863	758640	49523503	1297033962
2014	1492580	33313854	3051826	3266132	1229576	3524979	3877431	49756378	780337	50536715	1322326124
2015	1528253	33890183	3119577	3353338	1260685	3683463	3935205	50770704	802655	51573359	1348111483
1016	1564778	34476484	3188831	3442872	1292580	3849071	3993839	51808455	825611	52634066	1374399657

(Contd.)

Appendix-3.7 (*Contd.*)

1	2	3	4	5	6	7	8	9	10	11	12
1017	1602177	35072927	3259624	3534796	1325282	4022125	4053348	52870279	849223	53719502	1401200450
1018	1640469	35679689	3331987	3629175	1358812	4202960	4113742	53956834	873511	54830345	1428523858
1019	1679676	36296947	3405957	3726074	1393190	4391925	4175037	55068806	898494	55967300	1456380073
1020	1719820	36924884	3481570	3825561	1428438	4589386	4237245	56206904	924191	57131095	1484779484
2021	1760924	37563685	3558860	3927703	1464577	4795725	4300380	57371854	950622	58322476	1513732683
2022	1803010	38213537	3637867	4032573	1501631	5011341	4364456	58564415	977810	59542225	1543250470
2023	1846102	38874631	3718628	4140242	1539622	5236650	4429486	59785361	1005776	60791137	1573343854
2024	1890224	39547162	3801181	4250787	1578575	5472090	4495486	61035505	1034541	62070046	1604024059
2025	1935400	40231328	3885568	4364283	1618513	5718115	4562468	62315675	1064129	63379804	1635302528

* Population figures of Manipur and India for the year 2001 include the estimated population of the three sub-divisions viz. Mao Maran, Paomata and Purul of Senapati District of Manipur as the results of 2001 census were cancelled in these sub-divisions due to technical and administrative reasons.

Appendix 4.1
State-wise Classification of Forest Area

(Area in sq. km)

Sl. No.	Name of the State/NER/India	Geographic Area (GA)	Total Forest Area as in State Forest Report (SFR), 2001	Recorded Forest Area (2003)				Percent of GA	Change w.r.t. SFR, 2001
				Reserved Forest (RF)	Protected Forest (PF)	Unclassed Forest (UF)	Total Forest Area		
1	2	3	4	5	6	7	8	9	10
1.	Arunachal Pradesh	83743	51540	10178	9536	31826	51540	61.55	0
2.	Assam	78438	27018	18060	0	8958	27018	34.45	0
3.	Manipur	22327	17418	1467	4171	11780	17418	78.01	0
4.	Meghalaya	22429	9496	1112	12	8372	9496	42.34	0
5.	Mizoram	21087	15935	7909	3568	5240	16717	79.30	782
6.	Nagaland	16579	8629	308	508	7813	8629	52.05	0
7.	Tripura	10492	6293	3588	664	2041	6293	60.01	0
8.	Sub-Total, NER	255095	136329	42622	18459	76030	137111	53.75	782
9.	Sikkim	7096	5765	5452	389	0	5841	82.31	76
10.	Total NER	262191	142094	48074	18848	76030	142952	54.52	858
11.	India	3287263	768436	399919	238434	136387	774740	23.57	6304

Source: State Forest Report, 2003, Forest Survey of India (Ministry of Environment and Forest), Dehradun.

Appendix 4.2

State-wise Area under Forest Cover

(Area in sq. km)

Sl. No.	Name of the State/NER/India	Geographic Area (GA)	Area under Forest Cover				Percent of GA	Scrub
			Very Dense Forest	Moderately Dense Forest	Open Forest	Total Forest Area		
1	2	3	4	5	6	7	8	9
1.	Arunachal Pradesh	83743	13907	39604	14508	68019	81.22	116
2.	Assam	78438	1684	11358	14784	27826	35.48	219
3.	Manipur	22327	720	5818	10681	17219	77.12	74
4.	Meghalaya	22429	168	6323	10348	16839	75.08	169
5.	Mizoram	21087	84	7404	10942	18430	87.42	274
6.	Nagaland	16579	57	5650	7902	13609	82.09	231
7.	Tripura	10492	58	4988	3047	8093	77.18	1
8.	Sub Total, NER	255095	16678	81145	72212	170035	66.66	1084
9.	Sikkim	7096	458	1904	900	3262	45.97	360
10.	Total NER	262191	17136	83049	73112	173297	66.10	1444
11.	India	3287263	51285	339279	287769	678333	20.64	40269

Source: State Forest Report, 2003, Forest Survey of India (Ministry of Environment and Forest), Dehradun.

Appendix 4.3

State-wise Change in Forest Cover Since 2001 Assessment

(Area in sq. km)

Sl. No.	Name of the State/NER/India	2001 Assessment			2003 Assessment			Change		
		Dense	Open	Total	Dense	Open	Total	Dense	Open	Total
1	2	3	4	5	6	7	8	9	10	11
1.	Arunachal Pradesh	53932	14113	68045	53511	14508	68019	–421	395	–26
2.	Assam	15830	11884	27714	13042	14784	27826	–2788	2900	112
3.	Manipur	5710	11216	16926	6538	10681	17219	828	–535	293
4.	Meghalaya	5681	9903	15584	6491	10348	16839	810	445	1255
5.	Mizoram	8936	8558	17494	7488	10942	18430	–1448	2384	936
6.	Nagaland	5393	7952	13345	5707	7902	13609	314	–50	264
7.	Tripura	3463	3602	7065	5046	3047	8093	1583	–555	1028
8.	Sub–Total, NER	98945	67228	166173	97823	72212	170035	–1122	4984	3862
9.	Sikkim	2391	802	3193	2362	900	3262	–29	98	69
10.	Total NER	101336	68030	169366	100185	73112	173297	–1151	5082	3931
11.	India	416809	258729	675538	390564	287769	678333	–26245	29040	2795

Source: State Forest Report, 2003, Forest Survey of India (Ministry of Environment and Forest), Dehradun.

Appendix 4.4

State-wise Land Utilization Pattern—2003-04 (Provisional)

('000 Hectares)

Sl. No.	Name of the State/NER/India	Geographical Area	Reporting Area for Land Utilization Statistics	Classification of Reporting Area Excluding Fallow Land				
				Forests	Not Available for Cultivation			
					Area put to non-Agricultural Use	Barren & Uncultivable Land	Total (6+7)	Permanent Pastures & Other Grazing Lands
1	2	3	4	5	6	7	8	9
1.	Arunachal Pradesh	8374	5498	5154	5	21	26	4
2.	Assam	7844	7850	1933	1081	1453	2533	160
3.	Manipur	2233	1945	1693	26	1	27	1
4.	Meghalaya	2243	2227	951	87	128	215	0
5.	Mizoram	2108	2085	1594	125	9	134	6
6.	Nagaland	1658	1583	863	75	0	75	0
7.	Tripura	1049	1049	606	131	3	134	0
8.	Sub-total, NER	25509	22237	12794	1530	1615	3144	171
9.	Sikkim	710	672	265	143	107	250	4
10.	Total NER	26219	22909	13059	1673	1722	3394	175
11.	India	328726	305843	69700	24485	17733	42218	10455

Note: ' 0 ' denotes no reporting of data.

Source: Fertilizer Statistics, 2005-06, the Fertilizer Association of India, New Delhi.

Appendix 4.4 (Contd.)

State-wise Land Utilization Pattern—2003-04 (Provisional)

('000 Hectares)

Sl. No.	Name of the State/NER/India	Classification of Reporting Area Excluding Fallow Land — Other Uncultivated Land: Land under Misc. Tree Crops & Groves not Included in net Area Sown	Cultivable Waste Land	Total (9+10+11)	Fallow land: Fallow Lands Other than Current Fallows	Current Fallows	Total (13+14)	Net Area Sown	Area Sown More than Once	Total Cropped Area (16+17)	Percentage of Net Area Sown Over Total Reporting Area
1	2	10	11	12	13	14	15	16	17	18	19
1.	Arunachal Pradesh	36	37	77	47	30	77	164	99	263	2.98
2.	Assam	209	77	445	66	99	164	2774	1188	3962	35.34
3.	Manipur	6	1	8	–	–	–	217	–	217	11.16
4.	Meghalaya	161	441	605	167	63	229	227	46	272	10.19
5.	Mizoram	15	6	27	194	38	233	98	0	98	4.70
6.	Nagaland	122	58	179	76	84	160	305	65	370	19.27
7.	Tripura	27	1	28	1	1	2	280	53	333	26.69
8.	Sub total, NER	576	621	1369	551	315	865	4065	1451	5515	18.28
9.	Sikkim	5	2	12	30	5	35	110	11	121	16.37
10.	Total NER	581	623	1381	581	320	900	4175	1462	5636	18.22
11.	India	3369	13176	26999	11238	14805	26043	140883	49761	190644	46.06

Note: '–' means area is less than 500 hectares.

Source: Fertilizer Statistics, 2005-06, the Fertilizer Association of India, New Delhi.

Appendix 4.5

State-wise Gross Cropped and Irrigated Area and Area under Foodgrains with Cropping Intensity, 2003-04 (Provisional)

(Area in '000 Hectares)

Sl. No.	Name of the State/NER/India	Cultivated Area		Cropping Intensity (%)	Irrigated Area		Percentage of Net Irrigated Area to Net Cultivated Area	Area under Foodgrains	Share of Area under Foodgrains to Total Cropped Area (%)
		Net	Gross		Net	Gross			
1	2	3	4	5	6	7	8	9	10
1.	Arunachal Pradesh	164	263	160.4	42	43	25.6	191	72.6
2.	Assam	2774	3962	142.8	172	215	6.2	2742	69.2
3.	Manipur	217	217	100.0	40	40	18.4	166	76.5
4.	Meghalaya	227	272	119.8	60	82	26.4	135	49.6
5.	Mizoram	98	98	100.0	16	18	16.3	75	76.5
6.	Nagaland	305	370	121.3	67	104	22.0	263	71.1
7.	Tripura	280	333	118.9	40	52	14.3	250	75.1
8.	Sub total, NER	4065	5515	135.7	437	554	10.8	3822	69.3
9.	Sikkim	110	121	110.0	9	15	8.2	72	59.5
10.	Total NER	4175	5636	135.0	446	569	10.7	3894	69.1
11.	India	140883	190644	135.3	55105	76820	39.1	123447	64.8

Source: Fertilizer Statistics, 2005-06, the Fertilizer Association of India, New Delhi.

Appendix 4.6

State-wise Net Area Irrigated by Source—2003-04 (Provisional)

('000 Hectares)

Sl. No.	Name of the State/NER/India	Canals			Tanks	Wells			Total Net Irrigated Area
		Govt.	Private	Total		Tube Wells	Other Wells	Other Source	
1	2	3	4	5	6	7	8	9	10
1.	Arunachal Pradesh	0	0	0	0	0	0	42	42
2.	Assam	150	0	150	0	2	0	20	172
3.	Manipur	0	0	0	0	0	0	40	40
4.	Meghalaya	15	45	60	0	0	0	0	60
5.	Mizoram	6	10	16	0	0	0	0	16
6.	Nagaland	0	0	0	0	0	0	67	67
7.	Tripura	12	0	12	2	0	2	24	40
8.	Sub-total, NER	183	55	238	2	2	2	193	437
9.	Sikkim	0	0	0	0	0	0	9	9
10.	Total NER	183	55	238	2	2	2	202	446
11.	India	14941	205	15145	1943	24169	11096	2752	55105

Note: ' 0 ' denotes no reporting of data.

Source: Fertilizer Statistics, 2005-06, the Fertilizer Association of India, New Delhi.

Appendix 4.7

State-wise Area, Production and Average Yield per Hectare of Principal Crops—2004-05 (Provisional)

Sl. No.	Name of the State/NER/India	Area/Production/ Yield	Rice	Wheat	Jowar	Bajra	Maize	Ragi	Small Millets	Barley	Total Cereals
1	2	3	4	5	6	7	8	9	10	11	12
1.	Arunachal Pradesh	A	121.6	4.3	0	0	37.8	0	22.4	0	186.1
		P	135.0	8.7	0	0	55.0	0	21.4	0	220.1
		Y	1110	2023	0	0	1455	0	955	0	1183
2.	Assam	A	2376.8	63.9	0	0	19.2	0	8.0	0	2467.9
		P	3470.7	68.1	0	0	13.9	0	4.1	0	3556.8
		Y	1460	1066	0	0	724	0	513	0	1441
3.	Manipur	A	176.3	0	0	0	3.2	0	0	0	179.5
		P	435.9	0	0	0	8.9	0	0	0	444.8
		Y	2472	0	0	0	2781	0	0	0	2478
4.	Meghalaya	A	111.5	0.9	0	0	16.9	0	2.6	0	131.9
		P	193.7	1.6	0	0	24.0	0	2.3	0	221.6
		Y	1737	1778	0	0	1420	0	885	0	1680
5.	Mizoram	A	54.8	0	0	0	7.5	0	0	0	62.3
		P	104.1	0	0	0	15.7	0	0	0	119.8
		Y	1900	0	0	0	2093	0	0	0	1923

(Contd.)

Appendix 4.7 (*Contd.*)

1	2	3	4	5	6	7	8	9	10	11	12
6.	Nagaland	A	153.0	8.2	2.5	2.7	46.4	0	7.0	4.4	224.2
		P	259.8	13.0	4.0	4.0	83.5	0	7.0	7.0	378.3
		Y	1698	1585	1600	1481	1800	0	1000	1591	1687
7.	Tripura	A	242.6	1.1	0	0	2.8	0	0	0	246.5
		P	545.1	2.8	0	0	3.0	0	0	0	550.9
		Y	2247	2545	0	0	1071	0	0	0	2235
8.	Sub-total, NER	A	3236.6	78.4	2.5	2.7	133.8	0	40.0	4.4	3498.4
		P	5144.3	94.2	4.0	4.0	204.0	0	34.8	7.0	5492.3
		Y	1589	1202	1600	1481	1525	0	870	1591	1570
9.	Sikkim	A	14.7	5.7	0	0	36.7	4.5	4.2	1.2	67.0
		P	21.6	8.3	0	0	58.2	4.1	3.6	1.5	97.3
		Y	1469	1456	0	0	1586	911	867	1250	1452
10.	Total NER	A	3251.3	84.1	2.5	2.7	170.5	4.5	44.2	5.6	3565.4
		P	5165.9	102.5	4.0	4.0	262.2	4.1	38.4	8.5	5589.6
		Y	1589	1219	1600	1481	1538	911	869	1518	1568
11.	India	A	41906.7	26382.9	9092.3	9232.9	7430.4	1552.7	1100.6	616.5	97315.0
		P	83131.7	68636.9	7244.3	7931.7	14172.0	2432.4	477.6	1207.1	185233.3
		Y	1984	2602	797	859	1907	1567	434	1958	1903

A = Area in ' 000 hectares; P = Production in ' 000 tonnes; Y = Yield in kg/hectare; ' 0 ' denotes no reporting of data.

Source: Fertilizer Statistics, 2005-06, The Fertilizer Association of India, New Delhi

Appendix 4.7 **(Contd.)**

State-wise Area, Production and Average Yield per Hectare of Principal Crops—2004-05 (Provisional)

Sl. No.	Name of the State/NER/India	Area/ Produc-tion/ Yield	Gram	Tur (Arhar)	Total Pulses	Total Food-grains	Ground-nut	Soya-bean	Total Oil Seeds	Sugar-cane	Cotton*	Jute**
1	2	3	13	14	15	16	17	18	19	20	21	22
1.	Arunachal Pradesh	A	0	0.5	6.5	192.6	0	3.2	25.9	0.7	0	0
		P	0	0.4	6.8	226.9	0	4.3	27.0	14.1	0	0
		Y	0	800	1046	1178	0	1344	1042	20143	0	0
2.	Assam	A	2.1	6.7	107.6	2575.5	0	0	277.4	23.9	1.0	58.0
		P	1.1	4.8	61.4	3618.2	0	0	146.8	883.9	1.0	410.4
		Y	524	716	571	1405	0	0	529	36983	170	1274
3.	Manipur	A	0	0	7.9	187.4	0	0	1.8	0.6	0	0
		P	0	0	3.0	447.8	0	0	0.8	21.8	0	0
		Y	0	0	380	2390	0	0	444	36333	0	0
4.	Meghalaya	A	0.5	0.8	2.6	134.5	0	1.0	9.8	0.1	7.2	4.0
		P	0.3	0.6	3.6	225.2	0	0.9	6.5	0.2	7.8	20.2
		Y	600	750	1385	1674	0	900	663	2000	184	909
5.	Mizoram	A	0	0.2	3.7	66.0	0	1.5	7.3	1.2	0.5	0
		P	0	0.2	4.8	124.6	0	1.6	5.6	5.7	1.3	0
		Y	0	1000	1297	1888	0	1067	767	4750	442	0

(Contd.)

Appendix 4.7 (*Contd.*)

1	2	3	13	14	15	16	17	18	19	20	21	22
6.	Nagaland	A	1.0	6.4	31.6	255.8	5.5	30.0	70.3	3.0	1.5	2.0
		P	1.0	6.0	25.2	403.5	7.0	48.0	81.9	142.1	0.2	6.7
		Y	1000	938	797	1577	1273	1600	1165	47367	23	603
7.	Tripura	A	0.4	1.2	8.9	255.4	0.9	0	5.4	1.1	1.1	1.3
		P	0.2	0.8	5.5	556.4	0.9	0	3.9	52.4	1.5	10.7
		Y	500	667	618	2179	1000	0	722	47636	232	1482
8..	Sub-total, NER	A	4.0	15.8	168.8	3667.2	6.4	35.7	422.5	30.6	11.3	65.3
		P	2.6	12.8	110.3	5602.6	7.9	54.8	272.5	1120.2	11.8	448.0
		Y	650	810	653	1528	1234	1535	645	36608	178	1235
9.	Sikkim	A	0	0	6.9	73.9	0	3.9	9.9	0	0	0
		P	0	0	6.6	103.9	0	3.3	7.6	0	0	0
		Y	0	0	957	1406	0	846	768	0	0	0
10.	Total NER	A	4.0	15.8	175.7	3741.1	6.4	39.6	432.4	30.6	11.3	65.3
		P	2.6	12.8	116.9	5706.5	7.9	58.1	935.0	1120.2	11.8	448.0
		Y	650	810	665	1525	1234	1467	2162	36608	178	1235
11.	India	A	6714.6	3518.5	22763.0	120078.0	6640.4	7571.2	27523.3	3661.5	8786.6	773.9
		P	5469.4	2346.9	13129.5	198362.8	6774.4	6876.3	24353.5	237088.4	16428.6	9399.3
		Y	815	667	577	1652	1020	908	885	64752	318	2186

A = Area in ' 000 hectares; P = Production in ' 000 tonnes; Y = Yield in kg/hectare; * = ' 000 bales Of 170 kg each; ** = ' 000 bales of 180 kg each; ' 0 ' denotes no reporting of data.

Source: Fertilizer Statistics, 2005-06, the Fertilizer Association of India, New Delhi.

Appendix 4.8

State-wise Area, Production and Yield Rate of Fruits—2000-01 to 2002-03 (Provisional)

Sl. No.	Name of the State/NER/India	Area (' 000 hectares)			Production (' 000 tonnes)			Yield Rate (kg/hectare)		
		2000-01	2001-02	2002-03	2000-01	2001-02	2002-03	2000-01	2001-02	2002-03
1	2	3	4	5	6	7	8	9	10	11
1.	Arunachal Pradesh	51.1	41.6	40.8	123.1	124.9	82.1	2409	3002	2012
2.	Assam	107.0	110.8	91.8	1293.8	1335.1	1126.5	12092	12050	12271
3.	Manipur	24.7	26.1	26.7	118.7	134.0	137.8	4806	5134	5161
4.	Meghalaya	24.1	24.0	15.3	186.9	186.9	153.3	7755	7788	10020
5.	Mizoram	18.0	19.0	17.2	66.7	63.4	55.0	3706	3337	3198
6.	Nagaland	24.7	25.0	8.5	290.4	302.0	65.9	11757	12080	7753
7.	Tripura	28.9	28.3	28.4	450.8	452.1	459.1	15599	15975	16165
8.	Sub-total, NER	278.5	274.8	228.7	2530.4	2598.4	2079.7	9086	9456	9094
9.	Sikkim	9.4	12.3	10.0	10.0	10.3	8.1	1064	837	810
10.	Total NER	287.9	287.1	238.7	2540.4	2608.7	2087.8	8824	9086	8747
11.	India	3869.0	4010.2	3787.9	43138.1	43000.9	45203.1	11150	10723	11934

Source: Fertilizer Statistics, 2005-06, the Fertilizer Association of India, New Delhi.

Appendix 4.9

State-wise Area, Production and Yield Rate of Vegetables—2000-01 to 2002-03 (Provisional)

Sl. No.	Name of the State/NER/India	Area (' 000 hectares)			Production (' 000 tonnes)			Yield Rate (kg/hectare)		
		2000-01	2001-02	2002-03	2000-01	2001-02	2002-03	2000-01	2001-02	2002-03
1	2	3	4	5	6	7	8	9	10	11
1.	Arunachal Pradesh	21.0	20.8	20.5	83.7	83.9	81.5	3986	4034	3976
2.	Assam	238.3	237.4	232.0	2693.1	2935.2	2464.4	11301	12364	10622
3.	Manipur	9.7	10.6	11.6	67.4	66.1	71.9	6948	6236	6198
4.	Meghalaya	37.7	35.7	38.1	303.6	265.9	338.9	8053	7448	8895
5.	Mizoram	7.9	6.8	4.3	47.3	44.1	31.9	5987	6485	7419
6.	Nagaland	26.9	26.3	6.7	253.6	286.0	78.5	9428	10875	11716
7.	Tripura	31.8	31.3	31.6	328.1	353.2	360.3	10318	11284	11402
8.	Sub-total, NER	373.3	368.9	344.8	3776.8	4034.4	3427.4	10117	10936	9940
9.	Sikkim	13.5	14.2	14.1	59.7	60.0	59.1	4422	4225	4191
10.	Total NER	386.8	383.1	358.9	3836.5	4094.4	3486.5	9918	10687	9714
11.	India	6250.1	6155.7	6091.8	93849.8	88622.0	84815.0	15016	14397	13923

Source: Fertilizer Statistics, 2005-06, the Fertilizer Association of India, New Delhi.

Appendix 4.10

State-wise/Season-wise Consumption of N, P_2O_5 & K_2O and Total (2004-05 and 2005-06)

Sl. No.	Name of the State/NER/India	Nutrient	Consumption (' 000 tonnes)					
			2004-05			2005-06 (Provisional)		
			Kharif	Rabi	Total	Kharif	Rabi	Total
1	2	3	4	5	6	7	8	9
1.	Arunachal Pradesh	N	0.26	0.19	0.45	0.25	0.19	0.44
		P_2O_5	0.05	0.15	0.20	0.05	0.15	0.20
		K_2O	0.04	0.07	0.11	0.04	0.07	0.11
		Total	0.35	0.41	0.76	0.34	0.41	0.75
2.	Assam	N	36.46	41.48	77.94	42.28	51.23	93.51
		P_2O_5	22.35	28.57	50.92	25.48	30.56	56.04
		K_2O	18.44	18.60	37.04	21.25	27.32	48.57
		Total	77.25	88.65	165.90	89.01	109.11	198.12
3.	Manipur	N	11.13	5.92	17.05	9.51	2.58	12.09
		P_2O_5	1.65	0.75	2.40	1.01	0.37	1.38
		K_2O	0.41	0.54	0.95	0.47	0.26	0.73
		Total	13.19	7.21	20.40	10.99	3.21	14.20

(Contd.)

Appendix-4.10 (*Contd.*)

1	*2*	*3*	*4*	*5*	*6*	*7*	*8*	*9*
4.	Meghalaya	N	1.55	1.30	2.85	1.79	1.20	2.99
		P_2O_5	1.15	0.75	1.90	0.86	0.84	1.70
		K_2O	0.05	0.13	0.18	0.11	0.11	0.22
		Total	2.75	2.18	4.93	2.76	2.15	4.91
5.	Mizoram	N	0.34	0.27	0.61	0.55	0.42	0.97
		P_2O_5	0.28	0.23	0.51	0.46	0.37	0.83
		K_2O	0.18	0.12	0.30	0.24	0.24	0.48
		Total	0.80	0.62	1.42	1.25	1.03	2.28
6.	Nagaland	N	0.17	0.14	0.31	0.18	0.15	0.33
		P_2O_5	0.12	0.10	0.22	0.13	0.09	0.22
		K_2O	0.03	0.04	0.07	0.04	0.03	0.07
		Total	0.32	0.28	0.60	0.35	0.27	0.62

Source: Fertilizer Statistics, 2005-06, the Fertilizer Association of India, New Delhi.

Appendix 4.10 (Contd.)

State-wise/Season-wise Consumption of N, P_2O_5 & K_2O and Total (2004-05 and 2005-06)

Sl. No.	Name of the State/NER/India	Nutrient	Consumption (' 000 tonnes)					
			2004 - 05			2005 - 06 (Provisional)		
			Kharif	Rabi	Total	Kharif	Rabi	Total
1	2	3	4	5	6	7	8	9
7.	Tripura	N	4.08	5.25	9.33	4.08	5.85	9.93
		P_2O_5	0.92	1.66	2.58	1.22	1.68	2.90
		K_2O	0.63	0.90	1.53	1.09	1.25	2.34
		Total	5.63	7.81	13.44	6.39	8.78	15.17
8.	Sub-total, NER	N	53.99	54.55	108.54	58.64	61.62	120.26
		P_2O_5	26.52	32.21	58.73	29.21	34.06	63.27
		K_2O	19.78	20.40	40.18	23.24	29.28	52.52
		Total	100.29	107.16	207.45	111.09	124.96	236.05
9.	Sikkim	N	0.31	0.13	0.44	0.11	0.10	0.21
		P_2O_5	0.11	0.07	0.18	0.05	0.06	0.11
		K_2O	0	0	0	0	0.03	0.03
		Total	0.42	0.20	0.62	0.16	0.19	0.35

(Contd.)

Appendix 4.10 (*Contd.*)

1	2	3	4	5	6	7	8	9
10.	Total NER	N	54.30	54.68	108.98	58.75	61.72	120.47
		P_2O_5	26.63	32.28	58.91	29.26	80.06	109.32
		K_2O	19.78	20.40	40.18	23.24	29.31	52.55
		Total	100.71	107.36	208.07	111.25	171.09	282.34
11.	India	N	5503.64	6210.27	11713.91	6028.21	6695.11	12723.32
		P_2O_5	1920.96	2702.83	4623.79	2150.97	3052.71	5203.68
		K_2O	923.64	1137.02	2060.66	1018.48	1394.83	2413.31
		Total	8348.24	10050.12	18398.36	9197.66	11142.65	20340.31

Source: Fertilizer Statistics, 2005-06, the Fertilizer Association of India, New Delhi.

Appendix 5.1

State-wise Details of Roads as on 31st March, 2002

(Length in kms)

Sl. No.	Name of the State/ NER/India	Length of Total Roads			Length of Highways			Length of National Highways (NH)		
		Total	Surfaced	Un-surfaced	Total	Surfaced	Un-surfaced	Total	Surfaced	Un-surfaced
1	2	3	4	5	6	7	8	9	10	11
1.	Arunachal Pradesh	18365	5689	12676	17218	5612	11606	392	381	11
2.	Assam	89486	12882	76604	78471	10382	68089	2836	2836	0
3.	Manipur	11434	3863	7571	10882	3782	7100	954	954	0
4.	Meghalaya	9565	6560	3005	8165	6383	1782	717	717	0
5.	Mizoram	5075	2877	2198	4826	2867	1959	927	894	33
6.	Nagaland	21021	6451	14570	20180	6332	13848	369	369	0
7.	Tripura	16296	4393	11903	14740	4195	10545	400	400	0
8.	Sub-Total, NER	171242	42715	128527	154482	39553	114929	6595	6551	44
9.	Sikkim	2019	1546	473	1918	1509	409	62	62	0
10.	Total NER	173261	44261	129000	156400	41062	115338	6657	6613	44
11.	India	2456647*	1420489	1036158	1981409	1175353	806056	58112	58006	106

*excludes 26697 kms. of PMGSY roads.

Source: Basic Road Statistics of India, Ministry of Shipping, Road Transport and Highways, Government of India, New Delhi, Oct, 2004.

Appendix 5.2

State-wise Details of Highways by Type of Surface as on 31st March, 2002

(Length in kms)

Sl. No.	Name of the State/NER/India	Total	Surfaced				Un-surfaced		
			Total	Water Bound Macadam (WBM)	Black Top (B.T)	Cement Concrete (C.C)	Total	Motorable	Non-Motor-able
1	2	3	4	5	6	7	8	9	10
1.	Arunachal Pradesh	17218	5612	981	4631	@	11606	3032	8574
2.	Assam	78471	10382	936	9445	1	68089	48734	19355
3.	Manipur	10882	3782	949	2777	56	7100	5662	1438
4.	Meghalaya	8165	6383	2188	4195	@	1782	1758	24
5.	Mizoram	4826	2867	@	2867	@	1959	1959	@
6.	Nagaland	20200	6352	2930	3402	20	13848	12418	1430
7.	Tripura	14740	4195	1505	2690	@	10545	5101	5444
8.	Sub Total, NER	154502	39573	9489	30007	77	114929	78664	36265
9.	Sikkim	1918	1509	489	1020	@	409	409	@
10.	Total NER	156420	41082	9978	31027	77	115338	79073	36265
11.	India	1981409	1175353	298451	874380	2522	806056	536184	269872

Note: @ = Not Available.

Source: Basic Road Statistics of India, Ministry of Shipping, Road Transport and Highways, Government of India, New Delhi, Oct, 2004.

Appendix 5.3

State-wise Details of other PWD Roads by Type of Surface as on 31st March, 2002

(Length in kms.)

Sl. No.	Name of the State/NER/India	Total	Surfaced				Un-surfaced		
			Total	Water Bound Macadam (WBM)	Black Top (BT)	Cement Concrete (CC)	Total	Motorable	Non-Motorable
1	2	3	4	5	6	7	8	9	10
1.	Arunachal Pradesh (e)	12169	5231	981	4250	@	6938	3021	3917
2.	Assam (b)	26416	4733	0	4733	@	21683	16995	4688
3.	Manipur (e)	6638	1814	830	984	@	4824	3386	1438
4.	Meghalaya	6013	4914	2151	2763	@	1099	1099	0
5.	Mizoram	3730	1829	0	1829	@	1901	1901	0
6.	Nagaland (c)	6273	945	0	945	@	5328	4922	406
7.	Tripura (c)	5569	3659	1505	2154	@	1910	1910	0
8.	Sub-Total, NER	66808	23125	5467	17658	@	43683	33234	10449
9..	Sikkim	1670	1261	489	772	@	409	409	0
10.	Total NER	68478	24386	5956	18430	@	44092	33643	10449
11.	India	725425	603358	105244	497922	192	122067	91077	30990

Note: (b) — As on 31st March, 1995, (c) - As on 31st March, 1996 and (e) - As on 31st March, 1999, and @ - Not Available.

Source: Basic Road Statistics of India, Ministry of Shipping, Road Transport and Highways, Govt. of India, New Delhi, Oct, 2004.

Appendix 5.4

State-wise Details of Roads under Forest Department by Type of Surface as on 31st March, 2002

(Length in kms.)

Sl. No.	Name of the State/NER/India	Total	Surfaced				Un-surfaced		
			Total	Water Bound Macadam (WBM)	Black Top (BT)	Cement Concrete (CC)	Total	Motorable	Non-Motorable
1	2	3	4	5	6	7	8	9	10
1.	Arunachal Pradesh	1111	41	15	22	4	1070	915	155
2.	Assam	6076	270	@	270	@	5806	3438	2368
3.	Manipur (d)	417	@	@	@	@	417	417	@
4.	Meghalaya	1081	4	1	2	1	1077	203	874
5.	Mizoram	239	@	@	@	@	239	115	124
6.	Nagaland	725	5	@	5	@	720	720	@
7.	Tripura	1328	11	@	11	@	1317	@	1317
8.	Sub-Total, NER	10977	331	16	310	5	10646	5808	4838
9.	Sikkim (c)	65	1	@	1	@	64	34	30
10.	Total NER	11042	332	16	311	5	10710	5842	4868
11.	India	130346	13916	9471	4109	336	116430	69576	46854

Note: (c)—As on 31st March, 1996; (d)— As on 31st March, 1990; and @ - Not Available.

Source: Basic Road Statistics of India, Ministry of Shipping, Road Transport and Highways, Govt. of India, New Delhi, Oct, 2004.

Appendix 5.5

State-wise Details of Urban Roads by Type of Surface as on 31st March, 2002

(*Length in kms.*)

Sl. No.	Name of the State/NER/India	Total	Surfaced				Un-surfaced		
			Total	Water Bound Macadam (WBM)	Black Top (BT)	Cement Concrete (CC)	Total	Motorable	Non-Motorable
1	2	3	4	5	6	7	8	9	10
1.	Arunachal Pradesh	36	36	0	36	@	0	0	0
2.	Assam	3904	2022	160	1858	4	1882	1238	644
3.	Manipur	135	81	22	59	@	54	54	0
4.	Meghalaya	106	102	0	77	25	4	1	3
5.	Mizoram	10	10	0	10	@	0	0	0
6.	Nagaland	96	94	2	92	@	2	1	1
7.	Tripura	228	187	81	106	@	41	28	13
8.	Sub-Total, NER	4515	2532	265	2238	29	1983	1322	661
9.	Sikkim	36	36	0	36	@	0	0	0
10.	Total NER	4551	2568	265	2274	29	1983	1322	661
11.	India	250122	190102	49260	112907	12923	60020	42220	10359

Note: @ - Not Available.

Source: Basic Road Statistics of India, Ministry of Shipping, Road Transport and Highways, Govt. of India, New Delhi, Oct, 2004.

Appendix 5.6

State-wise Details of Road Length in Relation to Area and Population as on 31st March, 2002

Sl. No.	Name of the State/NER/India	Total Road Length (kms)*	Area (sq. kms)	Population as on 31.03.2002 (lakhs)**	Road Length (kms)	
					Per 100 sq. kms. of Area	Per 1 (one) Lakh of Population
1	2	3	4	5	6	7
1.	Arunachal Pradesh	18365	83743	11	21.93	1669.55
2.	Assam	89486	78438	272	114.09	328.99
3.	Manipur	11434	22327	24	51.21	476.42
4.	Meghalaya	9565	22429	24	42.65	398.54
5.	Mizoram	5075	21081	9	24.07	563.89
6.	Nagaland	21021	16579	20	126.79	1051.05
7.	Tripura	16296	10486	32	155.41	509.25
8.	Sub-Total, NER	171242	255083	392	67.13	436.84
9.	Sikkim	2019	7096	6	28.45	336.50
10.	Total NER	173261	262179	398	66.09	435.33
11.	India	2456647	3287263	10505	74.73	233.86

Note: *Excludes roads reported as constructed under JRY and PMGSY; ** Population figures are from RGI's Office.,

Source: Basic Road Statistics of India, Ministry of Shipping, Road Transport and Highways, Government of India, New Delhi, Oct, 2004.

Appendix 5.7

State-wise Details of Outlay and Expenditure on Roads and Bridges (State Sector)

(Rs. in lakhs)

Sl. No.	Name of the State/ NER/India	Ninth Plan		Tenth Plan Outlay	2002-03 Outlay	2003-04 Outlay
		Outlay	Expenditure			
1	2	3	4	5	6	7
1.	Arunachal Pradesh	87058	58822	78898	10047	10828
2.	Assam	91609	74220	79254	18531	24583
3.	Manipur	39000	24099	22200	2619	3100
4.	Meghalaya	45000	40789	51500	6446	7680
5.	Mizoram	20222	15579	46258	4247	7548
6.	Nagaland	25740	14957	13635	2879	3439
7.	Tripura	34158	16970	24230	3188	6485
8.	Sub-Total, NER	342787	245436	315975	47957	63663
9.	Sikkim	14000	13014	25000	4518	4400
10.	Total NER	356787	258450	340975	52475	68063
11.	India	3046918	3144189	5032082	847251	1095340

Source: Basic Road Statistics of India, Ministry of Shipping, Road Transport and Highways, Government of India, New Delhi, Oct, 2004.

Appendix 5.8

State-wise Details of Motor Vehicles Registered, 2001-02 and 2003-04 (as on 31st March)

(in Number)

Sl. No.	Name of the State/NER/ India	Year/ % increase	Two Wheelers	Auto Rickshaws	Jeeps	Cars	Taxis	Buses (b)	Goods Vehicles	Miscellaneous	Total Vehicles	Average No. of Vehicles per km. of road
1	2	3	4	5	6	7	8	9	10	11	12	13
1.	Arunachal Pradesh*	2001-02	10605	1430	2260	2340	299	665	2878	667	21144	1.15
		2003-04	10605	1430	2260	2340	299	665	2878	667	21144	1.15
		% increase	0	0	0	0	0	0	0	0	0	0
2.	Assam	2001-02	330445	22844	13563	85088	9256	9346	88182	37089	595813	6.66
		2003-04	418780	29806	14266	106063	10368	10286	97506	39744	726819	8.12
		% increase	26.73	30.48	5.18	24.65	12.01	10.06	10.57	7.16	21.99	21.92
3.	Manipur	2001-02**	53695	2263	6185	4870	316	2048	5947	1557	76881	6.72
		2003-04	75333	2521	7872	8030	363	2973	7169	2064	106325	9.30
		% increase	40.30	11.40	27.28	64.89	14.87	45.17	20.55	32.56	38.30	38.39
4.	Meghalaya	2001-02	19395	0	8930	12853	4514	2468	15660	3261	67081	7.01
		2003-04***	21050	2934	9401	14595	5030	2827	14028	3517	73382	7.67
		% increase	8.53	0	5.27	13.55	11.43	14.55	–10.42	7.85	9.39	9.42
5.	Mizoram	2001-02	15146	623	3237	3740	3063	761	4111	3121	33802	6.66
		2003-04	19501	1145	6765	4850	3864	840	4470	710	42145	8.30
		% increase	28.75	83.79	108.99	29.68	26.15	10.38	8.73	–77.25	24.68	24.62

(Contd.)

Appendix-5.8 (*Contd.*)

1	2	3	4	5	6	7	8	9	10	11	12	13
6.	Nagaland	2001-02	42621	10552	35189	34945	2992	4784	40521	5174	176778	8.41
		2003 – 04	36741	8229	21649	23723	13848	3712	50324	13541	171767	8.17
		% increase	–13.80	–22.01	–38.48	–32.11	362.83	–22.41	24.19	161.71	–2.83	–2.85
7.	Tripura	2001-02	32634	7901	1344	4954	1375	1985	5775	1460	57428	3.52
		2003-04	44241	12162	0	8672	257	1596	6916	1703	75547	4.64
		% increase	35.57	53.93	0	75.05	–81.31	–19.60	19.76	16.64	31.55	31.82
8.	Sub Total, NER	2001-02	504541	45613	70708	148790	21815	22057	163074	52329	1028927	6.01
		2003-04	626251	58227	62213	168273	34029	22899	183291	61946	1217129	7.11
		% increase	24.12	27.65	–12.01	13.09	55.99	3.82	12.40	18.38	18.29	18.30
9.	Sikkim	2001-02	4189	0	2267	1042	3417	638	1412	0	12965	6.42
		2003-04	4682	0	2863	1870	4947	893	1972	9	17236	8.54
		% increase	11.77	0	26.29	79.46	44.78	39.97	39.66	0	32.94	33.02
10.	Total NER	2001-02	508730	45613	72975	149832	25232	22695	164486	52329	1041892	6.01
		2003-04	630933	58227	65076	170143	38976	23792	185263	61955	1234365	7.12
		% increase	24.02	27.65	–10.82	13.56	54.47	4.83	12.63	18.40	18.47	18.47
11.	India	2001-02	41478136	1881085	1168868	5717456	684490	668825	3044976	4219191	58863027	23.96
		2003-04	51921973	2167262	1282113	7257624	911289	767593	3748546	4661385	72717785	29.60
		% increase	25.18	15.21	9.69	26.94	33.13	14.77	23.11	10.48	23.54	23.54

Note: * Data relates to 1996-97; ** Data relates to 1997-98; *** Data relates to 2002-03; (0) Data not available; (b) Includes Omni buses.

Source: Statistical Abstract India, 2003, 2005 and 2006, Central Statistical Organization, Govt. of India, New Delhi.

Appendix 5.9

State-wise Details of Railway Network as on 31.03.2004

(Length in kms.)

Sl. No.	Name of the State/NER/India	Broad Gauge (BG)	Metre Gauge (MG)	Narrow Gauge (NG)	Total	Percent of Total Road Length	Length of Railway Line per 100 sq. km. of area
1	2	3	4	5	6	7	8
1.	Arunachal Pradesh	0	1.26	0	1.26	0.007	0.002
2.	Assam	1227.70	1289.53	0	2517.23	2.813	3.209
3.	Manipur	0	1.35	0	1.35	0.012	0.006
4.	Meghalaya	0	0	0	0	0	0
5.	Mizoram	0	1.50	0	1.50	0.030	0.007
6.	Nagaland	11.13	1.72	0	12.85	0.061	0.078
7.	Tripura	0	64.42	0	64.42	0.395	0.614
8.	Sub-Total, NER	1238.83	1359.78	0	2598.61	1.517	1.019
9.	Sikkim	0	0	0	0	0	0
10.	Total NER	1238.83	1359.78	0	2598.61	1.500	0.991
11.	India*	45622	14364	3136	63122	2.569	1.920

* Data relate to 2002-03 (Basic Statistics of India, 2003)

Source: General Manager (Works), N. F. Railway, Maligaon, Guwahati, Assam.

Appendix 5.10

Details of Domestic Traffic of various Airports of North Eastern Region during 2004-05

Sl. No.	*Name of the Airport*	*Average No. of Flights handled per day*	*Average No. of Passengers handled per day*	*Average Cargo handled per day (In Tonnes)*
1	2	3	4	5
1.	Agartala	12	631	9
2.	Aizawl	4	139	1
3.	Bagdogra	9	473	2
4.	Dibrugarh	9	263	3
5.	Dimapur	4	80	1
6.	Guwahati	38	1637	14
7.	Imphal	6	354	5
8.	Jorhat	2	99	0
9.	Kamalpur	0	2	0
10.	Lilabari	1	6	0
11.	Silchar	6	248	1
12.	Tejpur	1	17	0
13.	Teju	1	2	0
14.	Total NER	93	3951	36

Source: India Air Transport Statistics, 2004-05, Statistical Division, Directorate General of Civil Aviation, New Delhi.

Appendix 5.11

Details of Domestic and International Passenger Traffic Handled at various Airports of North Eastern Region during 2004-05

S.I No.	Name of the Airport	Aircraft Movement (No)	Passengers (Number)			Freight (Tonnes)			Mail (Tonnes)		
			Embarked	Disembarked	Total	Loaded	Unloaded	Total	Loaded	Unloaded	Total
1	2	3	4	5	6	7	8	9	10	11	12
1.	Agartala	4503	117218	113115	230333	1106	1763	2869	75	420	495
2.	Aizawl	1368	25494	25279	50773	18	119	137	22	44	66
3.	Bagdogra (Having International Operations)	3148	88161	84459	172620	110	308	418	78	148	226
4.	Dibrugarh	3121	48463	47374	95837	24	478	502	483	37	520
5.	Dimapur	1308	15013	14267	29280	9	148	157	27	29	56
6.	Guwahati (Having International Operations)	13871	299736	297940	597676	1319	2989	4308	292	383	675
7.	Imphal	2236	66871	62232	129103	438	1077	1515	113	238	351
8.	Jorhat	650	17985	18006	35991	23	95	118	14	8	22
9.	Kamalpur	68	357	471	828	0	0	0	0	0	0
10.	Lilabari	218	1136	1195	2331	0	0	0	0	0	0
11.	Silchar	2258	46634	43875	90509	63	186	249	39	50	89
12.	Tejpur	216	2947	3349	6296	2	22	24	5	8	13
13.	Teju	310	611	NA	611	0	0	0	0	0	0
14.	Total NER	33275	730626	711562	1442188	3112	7185	10297	1148	1365	2513

Source: India Air Transport Statistics, 2004-05, Statistical Division, Directorate General of Civil Aviation, New Delhi.

Appendix 5.12

State-wise Investment of NEC Fund through Different Agencies Since Inception to the Year, 2005-06 (Upto February, 2006)

(*Rs. in crores*)

Sl. No.	*Name of the State/NER*	*Schemes implemented by States*	*Road construction by BRO*	*Through Autonomous Institutions*	*Through NEEPCO & PGCI*	*Through AAI/Air connectivity in NER*	*Through CWC, CIWTC, BB, NF Railways etc.*	*Total*	*Percentage of share*
1	2	3	4	5	6	7	8	9	10
1.	Arunachal Pradesh	330.01	254.29	50.03	1362.39	5.00	17.08	2018.80	26.98
2.	Assam	797.85	60.61	95.78	260.25	104.05	196.99	1515.53	20.25
3.	Manipur	184.13	167.88	299.67	11.97	22.19	13.52	699.36	9.35
4.	Meghalaya	264.84	18.72	56.44	126.46	6.35	4.79	477.60	6.38
5.	Mizoram	301.99	197.04	42.53	8.92	7.31	14.58	572.37	7.65
6.	Nagaland	240.38	197.37	3.17	649.72	16.33	7.48	1114.45	14.89
7.	Tripura	421.46	29.07	4.25	8.92	37.41	1.41	502.52	6.72
8.	Sub-Total, NER	2540.66	924.98	551.87	2428.63	198.64	255.85	6900.63	92.22
9.	Sikkim	50.39	–	–	–	–	–	50.39	0.67
10.	Total NER	2591.05	924.98	551.87	2428.63	198.64	255.85	6951.02	92.89
11.	NEC Secretariat and Other Agencies	–	–	–	–	130.00	–	531.98	7.11
12.	Grand Total	2591.05	924.98	551.87	2428.63	328.64	255.85	7483.00	100.00

Note: Though a major portion of Rs. 531.98 crores, indicated under NEC Secretariat and Other Agencies, were invested in the States, the same could not be apportioned as relevant information are not available.

Source: North Eastern Council Secretariat, Shillong.

Appendix 5.13

State-wise Details of Post Offices as on 31.03.2008

Sl. No.	*Name of the State/ NER/India*	*Number of Post Offices*			*Population per Post Office (Based on projected population of respective years)*	*Area served by a Post Office (sq. km.)*
		Total	*Rural*	*Urban*		
1	2	3	4	5	6	7
1.	Arunachal Pradesh	299	282	17	4332	280.08
2.	Assam* (As on 31.03.06)	4006	3706	300	7250	19.58
3.	Manipur	696	685	11	3844	32.08
4.	Meghalaya	486	458	28	5738	46.15
5.	Mizoram	404	347	57	2620	52.19
6.	Nagaland	327	302	25	8280	50.70
7.	Tripura* (As on 31.03.06)	970	895	75	3551	10.82
8.	Sub Total, NER	7188	6675	513	5984	35.49
9.	Sikkim** (As on 31.03.03)	208	195	13	2751	34.12
10.	Total NER	7396	6870	526	5893	35.45
11.	India**As on 31.03.03)	155618	139081	16537	6871	21.12

Sources: (i) Post Master General, North Eastern Circle, Shillong.

(ii) *Statistical Hand Book, Assam, 2006 and Tripura at A Glance, 2006.

(iii) **Department of Post, Ministry of Communication and IT, New Delhi.

Appendix 5.14(a)

State-wise Details of Telecommunication and Cellular Services

Sl. No.	Name of the State /NER/India	No. of Telephone Exchanges	Total capacity of Telephone Exchanges	No. of Telephone connections	No. of Villages provided with Village Public Phone (VPT)	Total No. of PCOs	No. of Internet connections			No. of Cellular Mobile Subscribers (BSNL)
							Broad band	Others	Total	
1	2	3	4	5	6	7	8	9	10	11
1.	Arunachal Pradesh* (As on 31.03.2004)	105	83000	57543	804	1249	AN	NA	1528	1132
2.	Assam** (As on 30.11.2005)	600	682952	551490	22148	NA	1816	16349	18165	229152
3.	Manipur* (As on 31.03.2004)	50	59912	45235	1585	1628	NA	NA	1529	2752
4.	Meghalaya (As on 31.10.2004)	98	92016	69455	2782	1249	NA	NA	1528	1132
5.	Mizoram (As on 31.03.2006)	76	75144	55222	611	782	NA	NA	1529	33955
6.	Nagaland* (As on 31.03.2004)	60	60020	45891	1018	1608	NA	NA	1423	4220
7.	Tripura (As on 31.03.2006)	87	NA	85752	822	2824	NA	NA	4183	38338
8.	Sub-Total, NER	1076	1053044	910588	29770	9340	1816	16349	29885	310681
9.	Sikkim	NA	NA	NA	NA	NA	NA	NA	NA	NA
10.	Total NER	1076	1053044	910588	29770	9340	1816	16349	29885	310681

Sources: (1) *Chief General Manager (BSNL), North East Circle; II,** Chief General Manager (BSNL), Assam, Guwahati.

(2) Statistical Hand Book, at A Glance of the respective State Governments, NA: indicates – Not Available.

Appendix 5.14 (b)

Circle-wise details of Telecommunication and Cellular Services as on March, 2008 and April, 2008

Sl. No.	*Name of the Circle*	*Wireless Total including WLL (F)*										*Total of Wireline Subscriber Base (BSNL only) in 2008*	
		Bharti Airtel in 2008		*Reliance in 2008*		*Aircel in 2008*		*BSNL in 2008*		*Total of all in 2008*			
		March	*April*	*March*	*April*	*March*	*April*	*March*	*April*	*March*	*April*	*March*	*April*
1	2	3	4	5	6	7	8	9	10	11	12	13	14
1.	North East Circle-I (includes the States of Meghalaya, Mizoram and Tripura)	481499	539511	332668	344685	594384	619089	315614	307342	1724165	1810627	212255	211601
2.	Assam Circle	901873	921487	928862	962634	1163684	1201578	918680	1016579	3913099	4102278	430310	426621
3.	North East Circle-II (includes the States of Arunachal Pradesh, Manipur and Nagaland)	–	–	–	–	–	–	394367	380766	394367	380766	130019	127067
4.	Total North East (except Sikkim)	1383372	1460998	1261530	1307319	1758068	1820667	1628661	1704687	6031631	6293671	772584	765289

Source: Website of the Telecom Regulatory Authority of India.

Appendix 5.15

State-wise Details of all India Radio Stations and Doordarshan Kendra's Network as on 01.01.2006

Sl. No.	*Name of the State/NER*	*Type and Number of All India Radio Stations (as on March, 2005)*								*Number of Languages and Dialects Broadcasting*	*Doordarshan Kendra's*	
		Capital Station	*Regional Station*	*North East Service*	*LRS Station*	*Relay Centre*	*CRS*	*CBS (FM)*	*Total*		*No. of Kendra's with Production Centre*	*No. of Relay Kendra's*
1	2	3	4	5	6	7	8	9	10	11	12	13
1.	Arunachal Pradesh	1	3	–	1	–	–	–	5	17	1	49
2.	Assam	1	4	–	4	1	–	1	11	28	3	29
3.	Manipur	1	–	–	–	–	–	–	1	9	1	8
4.	Meghalaya	1	1	1	1	–	2	–	6	8	2	10
5.	Mizoram	1	1	–	–	–	1		3	7	1	8
6.	Nagaland	1	–	–	1	–	2	–	4	18	1	14
7.	Tripura	1	–	–	2	–	–	–	3	5	1	10
8.	Sub-Total, NER	7	9	1	9	1	5	1	33	92*	10	128
9.	Sikkim	1	–	–	–	–	–	–	1	4	1	8
10.	Total NER	8	9	1	9	1	5	1	34	96*	11	136

Note: Total number of Languages broadcast = 6, Total number of Dialects broadcast = 60, *Includes repetation of same Languages/Dialects.

Source: All India Radio and Doordarshan, Guwahati.

Appendix 5.16(a)

State-wise Details of Registered Newspapers and Periodicals as on 2004-05

Sl. No.	Name of the State/NER	Type and Number of Newspapers and Periodicals								Total
		Dailies	Tri-bi-weeklies	Weeklies	Fort- nightlines	Month- lies	Quarter-lies	Annual	Other Periodicals	
1	2	3	4	5	6	7	8	9	10	11
1.	Arunachal Pradesh	4	1	4	–	2	2	–	–	13
2.	Assam	50	11	191	64	108	27	4	21	476
3.	Manipur	55	3	17	12	42	9	4	11	153
4.	Meghalaya	5	4	33	7	17	5	1	4	76
5.	Mizoram	43	14	36	7	24	6	–	4	134
6.	Nagaland	5	–	9	–	1	2	–	–	17
7.	Tripura	24	2	59	9	13	3	–	1	111
8.	Sub-Total, NER	186	35	349	99	207	54	9	41	980
9.	Sikkim	1	2	27	1	1	2	–	3	37
10.	Total NER	187	37	376	100	208	56	9	44	1017

Source: Statistical Abstract India, 2005 and 2006, Central Statistical Organization, Government of India, New Delhi.

Appendix 5.16(b)

State-wise Details of Registered Newspapers and Periodicals by Language as on 2004-05

Sl. No.	*Name of the State/NER*	*Language and Number of Newspapers and Periodicals*							*Total*
		Hindi	*English*	*Assamese*	*Bengali*	*Bi-lingual*	*Multi-lingual*	*Others*	
1	*2*	*3*	*4*	*5*	*6*	*7*	*8*	*9*	*10*
1.	Arunachal Pradesh	1	10	–	–	–	–	2	13
2.	Assam	14	63	239	94	25	6	35	476
3.	Manipur	–	18	–	–	43	13	79	153
4.	Meghalaya	1	21	–	1	13	1	39	76
5.	Mizoram	–	4	–	–	10	5	115	134
6.	Nagaland	–	14	–	–	1	–	2	17
7.	Tripura	–	13	–	84	9	2	3	111
8.	Sub-Total, NER	16	143	239	179	101	27	275	980
9.	Sikkim	1	10	–	–	2	–	24	37
10.	Total NER	17	153	239	179	103	27	299	1017

Source: Statistical Abstract India, 2005 and 2006, Central Statistical Organisation, Government of India, New Delhi.

Appendix 6.1

State-wise Number of Educational Institutions as on 30.09.2004

(*in Numbers*)

Sl. No.	Type of Institution	Name of the North Eastern States/NER										India
		Arunachal Pradesh	Assam	Manipur	Meghalaya	Mizoram	Nagaland	Tripura	Sub-Total, NER	Sikkim	Total, NER	
1	2	3	4	5	6	7	8	9	10	11	12	13
1.	Pre-primary/Pre-Basic Schools	22	199	1	0	0	0	5127	5349	1030	6379	63596
2.	Primary/Jr. Basic Schools	1371	30068	2552	5851	1481	1520	1776	44619	684	45303	767520
3.	Middle/Sr. Basic Schools	495	8143	831	1759	939	480	1001	13648	185	13833	274731
4.	High/Post Basic Schools	136	4629	588	631	445	336	409	7174	111	7285	101777
5.	Pre-Degree Junior College/Higher Secondary Schools	78	745	118	80	67	43	243	1374	50	1424	50272
6.	Technical/Industrial/Arts & Craft Schools	2	27	7	7	1	3	4	51	1	52	5114
7.	Polytechnic Institutes	1	8	1	1	2	3	1	17	2	19	1171
8.	Teachers' Training Schools	0	1	1	7	2	1	2	14	1	15	1465
9.	Others (including Law, Management, MCA/IT, Agriculture etc.)	1	21	1	1	1	18	5	48	1	49	2431
10.	Teachers' Training Colleges	2	40	3	2	2	1	1	51	2	53	1082
11.	Medical Colleges (Allo/Ayur/Homoeo/Unani/Nurs./Pharma. etc.)	1	7	1	0	0	0	1	10	1	11	817

(*Contd.*)

Appendix-6.1 (*Contd.*)

1	2	3	4	5	6	7	8	9	10	11	12	13
12.	Engg., Tech, and Arch. Colleges	1	3	1	0	0	0	1	6	1	7	1302
13.	Arts, Science and Commerce Colleges	10	317	58	54	26	37	14	516	2	518	10377
14.	University	1	5	2	1	1	1	1	12	2	14	298
15.	Grand Total	2121	44213	4165	8394	2967	2443	8586	72889	2073	74962	1281953

Source: Selected Educational Statistics, 2004-2005, Ministry of Human Resource Development, Department of Higher Education, Government of India, New Delhi, 2007.

Appendix 6.2

State-wise Number of Institutions by Management Category as on 30.09.2004

Sl. No.	Type of Institution	Management Category	Number/ Percent	Name of the North Eastern States/NER										India
				Arunachal Pradesh	Assam	Manipur	Megha-laya	Mizoram	Naga-land	Tripura	Sub-Total, NER	Sikkim	Total, NER	
1	2	3	4	5	6	7	8	9	10	11	12	13	14	15
1.	Primary/Jr. Basic Schools (Class I-V)	Govt.	No.	1249	30068	2002	2539	1091	1305	519	38773	504	39277	332565
			Per cent	91.10	100.00	78.45	43.39	73.67	85.86	29.22	86.90	73.68	86.70	43.33
		Local Bodies	No.	0	0	0	0	0	0	1232	1232	0	1232	359772
			Per cent	0	0	0	0	0	0	69.37	2.76	0	2.72	46.87
		Private Aided	No.	4	0	408	2475	104	0	12	3003	0	3003	19593
			Per cent	0.20	0	15.99	42.30	7.02	0	0.68	6.73	0	6.63	2.55
		Private Unaided	No.	118	0	142	837	286	215	13	1611	180	1791	55590
			Per cent	8.61	0	5.56	14.31	19.31	14.14	0.73	3.61	26.32	3.95	7.24
2.	Middle/Sr. Basic Schools (Class VI- VIII)	Govt.	No.	441	6128	307	56	558	270	986	8746	145	8891	118026
			Per cent	89.09	75.25	36.94	3.18	59.42	56.25	98.50	64.08	78.38	64.27	42.96
		Local Bodies	No.	0	0	0	0	0	0	0	0	0	0	80327
			Per cent	0	0	0	0	0	0	0	0	0	0	29.24
		Private Aided	No.	3	0	94	980	95	0	5	1177	0	1177	17616
			Per cent	0.61	0	11.31	55.71	10.12	0	0.50	8.63	0	8.51	6.41
		Private Unaided	No.	51	2015	430	723	286	210	10	3725	40	3765	58762
			Per cent	10.30	24.75	51.74	41.10	30.46	43.75	1.00	27.29	21.62	27.22	21.39

(Contd.)

Appendix-6.2 (*Contd.*)

1	2	3	4	5	6	7	8	9	10	11	12	13	14	15
3.	High/Post Basic Schools (Class IX-X)	Govt.	No.	103	2793	184	21	190	116	386	3793	95	3888	32221
			Per cent	75.74	60.34	31.29	3.33	42.70	34.52	94.38	52.87	85.59	53.37	31.66
		Local Bodies	No.	0	0	0	0	0	0	0	0	0	0	11505
			Per cent	0	0	0	0	0	0	0	0	0	0	11.30
		Private Aided	No.	14	637	102	388	19	220	11	1391	1	1392	29029
			Per cent	10.29	13.76	17.35	61.49	4.27	65.48	2.69	19.39	0.90	19.11	28.52
		Private Unaided	No.	19	1199	302	222	236	0	12	1990	15	2005	29022
			Per cent	13.97	25.90	51.36	35.18	53.03	0	2.93	27.74	13.51	27.52	28.52
4.	Pre-Degree Junior College/Higher Secondary Schools (Class XI - XII)	Govt.	No.	70	646	55	22	20	9	207	1029	44	1073	18137
			Per cent	89.74	86.71	46.61	27.50	29.85	20.93	85.19	74.89	88.00	75.35	36.08
		Local Bodies	No.	0	0	0	0	0	0	0	0	0	0	550
			Per cent	0	0	0	0	0	0	0	0	0	0	1.09
		Private Aided	No.	5	25	0	40	7	34	31	142	3	145	15603
			Per cent	6.41	3.36	0	50.00	10.45	79.07	12.76	10.33	6.00	10.18	31.04
		Private Unaided	No.	3	74	63	18	40	0	5	203	3	206	15982
			Per cent	3.85	9.93	53.39	22.50	59.70	0	2.06	14.78	6.00	14.47	31.79

Source: Selected Educational Statistics, 2004-2005, Ministry of Human Resource Development, Department of Higher Education, Government of India, New Delhi, 2007.

Appendix 6.3

State-wise and Institution-wise Enrolment as on 30.09.2004

(*In Numbers*)

Sl. No.	Type of Institution/Enrolment	Category of students	Name of the North Eastern States/NER										India
			Arunachal Pradesh	Assam	Manipur	Meghalaya	Mizoram	Nagaland	Tripura	Sub-Total, NER	Sikkim	Total, NER	
1	2	3	4	5	6	7	8	9	10	11	12	13	14
1.	Pre-primary/Pre-Basic Schools	Boys	19058	323299	58390	86338	0	55115	121309	663509	13755	677264	2494441
		Girls	14408	316272	54220	91327	0	52516	115920	644663	12176	656839	2267044
		Total	33466	639571	112610	177665	0	107631	237229	1308172	25931	1334103	4761485
2.	Primary/Jr. Basic schools (Class I-V)	Boys	67465	1779825	120434	294425	53980	77519	224809	2618457	56716	2675173	53145577
		Girls	55769	1719330	119073	306120	48827	76735	208685	2534539	54607	2589146	46586332
		Total	123234	3499155	239507	600545	102807	154254	433494	5152996	111323	5264319	99731909
3.	Middle/Sr. Basic Schools (Class VI-VIII)	Boys	50404	617493	91266	57220	28916	52474	68328	966101	13629	979730	30926227
		Girls	40981	579919	81471	57994	27130	47532	62769	897796	15814	913610	25212745
		Total	91385	1197412	172737	115214	56046	100006	131097	1863897	29443	1893340	56138972
4.	High/Post Basic Schools (Class IX - X)	Boys	25433	558613	110956	61431	21503	79381	108891	966208	5182	971390	19238926
		Girls	20739	528168	102070	63663	21658	70143	101745	908186	5322	913508	15364386
		Total	46172	1086781	213026	125094	43161	149524	210636	1874394	10504	1884898	34603312
5.	Pre-Degree Junior College/Higher Secondary Schools (Class XI - XII)	Boys	32874	358319	39154	8266	5279	32435	123840	600167	4028	604195	19048791
		Girls	25663	197716	31126	7540	5004	28949	105870	401868	3448	405316	14322380
		Total	58537	556035	70280	15806	10283	61384	229710	1002035	7476	1009511	33371171
6.	Technical/Industrial/ Arts & Craft Schools	Boys	368	3900	348	890	294	276	316	6392	140	6532	694939
		Girls	0	720	192	52	0	128	100	1192	0	1192	47391
		Total	368	4620	540	942	294	404	416	7584	140	7724	742330

(*Contd.*)

Appendix-6.3 (*Contd.*)

1	2	3	4	5	6	7	8	9	10	11	12	13	14
7.	Polytechnic Institutes	Boys	188	3995	362	417	239	284	341	5826	358	6184	301537
		Girls	89	505	109	127	261	65	179	1335	59	1394	87090
		Total	277	4500	471	544	500	349	520	7161	417	7578	388627
8.	Teachers' Training Schools	Boys	0	80	18	269	125	18	461	971	28	999	59761
		Girls	0	81	45	159	90	69	218	662	49	711	64172
		Total	0	161	63	428	215	87	679	1633	77	1710	123933
9.	Teachers' Training Colleges (B. Ed/B.T)	Boys	41	1216	126	96	54	50	158	1741	119	1860	87143
		Girls	19	1129	180	196	57	42	154	1777	79	1856	68049
		Total	60	2345	306	292	111	92	312	3518	198	3716	155192
10.	Arts, Science & Commerce Colleges (B.A, B.Sc. B.Com)	Boys	3402	108167	7675	10002	3348	6267	11086	149947	2208	152155	3956258
		Girls	2113	77874	5208	9363	2875	4832	8124	110389	1804	112193	2771771
		Total	5515	186041	12883	19365	6223	11099	19210	260336	4012	264348	6728029
11.	University (M.A, M.Sc, M.Com)	Boys	325	6553	645	634	0	248	621	9026	6	9032	439003
		Girls	213	5893	745	905	0	203	606	8565	32	8597	351264
		Total	538	12446	1390	1539	0	451	1227	17591	38	17629	790267
12.	Grand Total	Boys	199558	3761460	429374	519988	113738	304067	660160	5988345	96169	6084514	130392603
		Girls	159994	3427607	394439	537446	105902	281214	604370	5510972	93390	5604362	107142624
		Total	359552	7189067	823813	1057434	219640	585281	1264530	11499317	189559	11688876	237535227

Source: Selected Educational Statistics, 2004-2005, Ministry of Human Resource Development, Department of Higher Education, Government of India, New Delhi, 2007.

Appendix 6.4

State-wise and Institution-wise Number of Teachers as on 30.09.2004

(In Numbers)

Sl. No.	Type of Institution/Number of Teachers	Category of Teachers	Name of the North Eastern States/NER										India
			Arunachal Pradesh	Assam	Manipur	Meghalaya	Mizoram	Nagaland	Tripura	Sub-Total, NER	Sikkim	Total, NER	
1	2	3	4	5	6	7	8	9	10	11	12	13	14
1.	Primary/Jr. Basic Schools (Class I-V)	Male	2518	53811	4939	7300	3015	5159	6145	82887	2559	85446	1318660
		Female	1112	29077	3094	6445	2954	2968	1891	47541	2562	50103	842006
		Total	3630	82888	8033	13745	5969	8127	8036	130428	5121	135549	2160666
2.	Middle/Sr. Basic Schools (Class VI-VIII)	Male	2164	55734	5181	4317	4777	3921	6565	82659	755	83414	992407
		Female	905	17328	3572	3090	2200	2375	2315	31785	417	32202	596873
		Total	3069	73062	8753	7407	6977	6296	8880	114444	1172	115616	1589280
3.	High/Post Basic Schools (Class IX-X)	Male	1250	40077	5475	3056	2586	3904	6195	62543	662	63205	667547
		Female	412	14267	3583	2153	1006	2523	2076	26020	316	26336	415331
		Total	1662	54344	9058	5209	3592	6427	8271	88563	978	89541	1082878
4.	Pre-Degree Junior College/Higher Secondary Schools (Class XI-XII)	Male	1510	16384	1708	456	457	856	6006	27377	267	27644	614269
		Female	384	6525	1367	539	388	901	3193	13297	152	13449	385843
		Total	1894	22909	3075	995	845	1757	9199	40674	419	41093	1000112

(Contd.)

Appendix 6.4 (*Contd.*)

1	*2*	*3*	*4*	*5*	*6*	*7*	*8*	*9*	*10*	*11*	*12*	*13*	*14*
5.	Sub-Total	Male	7442	166006	17303	15129	10835	13840	18925	249480	4243	253723	3592883
		Female	2813	67197	11616	12227	6548	8767	9475	118643	3447	122090	2240053
		Total	10255	233203	28919	27356	17383	22607	28400	368123	7690	375813	5832936
6.	Higher Education Institutions	Total	296	14451	4298	3249	505	1082	929	24810	154	24964	471931
7.	Grand Total	Total	10551	247654	33217	30605	17888	23689	29329	392933	7844	400777	6304867

Source: Selected Educational Statistics, 2004 - 2005, Ministry of Human Resource Development, Department of Higher Education, Government of India, New Delhi, 2007.

Appendix 6.5

State-wise and Institution-wise Student-Teacher Ratio, Number of Female Teachers per 100 Male Teachers and Percentage of Trained Teachers as on 30.09.2004

Sl. No.	Type of Institution	Category	Name of the North Eastern States/NER										India
			Arunachal Pradesh	Assam	Manipur	Megha-laya	Mizoram	Naga-land	Tripura	Sub-Total, NER	Sikkim	Total, NER	
1	2	3	4	5	6	7	8	9	10	11	12	13	14
1.	Primary/Jr. Basic schools (Class I-V)	Student-Teacher Ratio	34	42	30	44	17	19	54	40	22	39	46
		No. of Female Teachers per 100 Male Teachers	44	54	63	88	98	58	31	57	100	59	64
		Percentage of Trained Teachers	22	51	32	45	58	33	25	46	50	46	86
2.	Middle/Sr. Basic Schools (Class VI-VIII)	Student-Teacher Ratio	30	16	20	16	8	16	15	16	24	16	35
		No. of Female Teachers per 100 Male Teachers	42	31	69	72	46	61	35	38	55	39	60
		Percentage of Trained Teachers	29	10	31	36	60	17	23	18	42	19	87
3.	High/Post Basic Schools (Class IX-X)	Student-Teacher Ratio	28	20	24	24	12	23	25	21	11	21	32
		No. of Female Teachers per 100 Male Teachers	33	36	65	70	39	65	34	42	48	42	62
		Percentage of Trained Teachers	49	29	41	36	42	21	26	31	44	31	89

(Contd.)

Appendix 6.5 (*Contd.*)

1	2	3	4	5	6	7	8	9	10	11	12	13	14
4.	Pre-Degree Junior College/Higher Secondary Schools (Class XI-XII)	Student-Teacher Ratio	31	24	23	16	12	35	25	25	18	25	33
		No. of Female Teachers per 100 Male Teachers	25	40	80	118	85	105	53	49	57	49	63
		Percentage of Trained Teachers	66	29	40	36	29	27	39	34	51	34	90
5.	Total (class I-XII)	Student-Teacher Ratio	31	27	24	31	12	21	31	27	21	26	38
		No. of Female Teachers per 100 Male Teachers	38	40	67	81	60	63	50	48	81	48	62
		Percentage of Trained Teachers	37	31	35	41	54	25	34	33	48	33	88
6.	Higher Education Institutions	Student-Teacher Ratio	23	15	9	9	24	13	24	14	43	14	25

Source: Selected Educational Statistics, 2004-2005, Ministry of Human Resource Development, Department of Higher Education, Government of India, New Delhi, 2007.

Appendix 6.6

State-wise and Institution-wise Enrolment of Scheduled Caste (SC) Students as on 30.09.2004

(In Numbers)

Sl. No	Type of Institution/Enrolment	Category of Students	Name of the North Eastern States/NER										India
			Aruna-chal Pradesh	Assam	Manipur	Megha-laya	Mizoram	Naga-land	Tripura	Sub-Total, NER	Sikkim	Total, NER	
1	2	3	4	5	6	7	8	9	10	11	12	13	14
1.	Pre-primary/Pre-Basic Schools	Boys	47	36468	1800	559	0	0	124	38998	0	38998	302842
		Girls	36	34915	1710	457	0	0	99	37217	0	37217	276143
		Total	83	71383	3510	1016	0	0	223	76215	0	76215	578985
2.	Primary/Jr. Basic Schools (Class I - V)	Boys	176	187844	4438	1499	234	0	47239	241430	3104	244534	13762131
		Girls	111	179009	4053	1284	214	0	43834	228505	3110	231615	10994686
		Total	287	366853	8491	2783	448	0	91073	469935	6214	476149	24756817
3.	Middle/Sr. Basic Schools (Class VI-VIII)	Boys	97	87466	2754	1246	94	0	18798	110455	747	111202	5099925
		Girls	59	79617	2603	1084	114	0	16720	100197	832	101029	3597308
		Total	156	167083	5357	2330	208	0	35518	210652	1579	212231	8697233
4.	High/Post Basic Schools (Class IX-X)	Boys	51	46570	1500	477	47	0	11892	60537	287	60824	2181058
		Girls	24	40267	1341	472	37	0	8841	50982	262	51244	1356210
		Total	75	86837	2841	949	84	0	20733	111519	549	112068	3537268

(Contd.)

Appendix 6.6 (*Contd.*)

1	2	3	4	5	6	7	8	9	10	11	12	13	14
5.	Pre-Degree Junior College/Higher Secondary Schools (Class XI - XII)	Boys	37	15942	421	455	12	0	2924	19791	159	19950	1047209
		Girls	16	8473	295	387	13	0	1300	10484	135	10619	633899
		Total	53	24415	716	842	25	0	4224	30275	294	30569	1681108
6.	Total of Primary to Higher Secondary Schools (I - XII)	Boys	361	337822	9113	3677	387	0	80853	432213	4297	436510	22090323
		Girls	210	307366	8292	3227	378	0	70695	390168	4339	394507	16582103
		Total	571	645188	17405	6904	765	0	151548	822381	8636	831017	38672426
7.	Total of Pre-Primary to Higher Secondary Schools (Pre-Primary - XII)	Boys	408	374290	10913	4236	387	0	80977	471211	4297	475508	22393165
		Girls	246	342281	10002	3684	378	0	70794	427385	4339	431724	16858246
		Total	654	716571	20915	7920	765	0	151771	898596	8636	907232	39251411

Source: Selected Educational Statistics, 2004 - 2005, Ministry of Human Resource Development, Department of Higher Education, Government of India, New Delhi, 2007.

Appendix 6.7

State-wise and Institution-wise Enrolment of Scheduled Tribe (ST) Students as on 30.09.2004

(In Numbers)

S.I No.	Type of Institution/ Enrolment	Category of students	Name of the North Eastern States/NER										India
			Arunachal Pradesh	Assam	Manipur	Meghalaya	Mizoram	Nagaland	Tripura	Sub-Total, NER	Sikkim	Total, NER	
1	2	3	4	5	6	7	8	9	10	11	12	13	14
1.	Pre-primary/Pre-Basic Schools	Boys	13147	75614	25720	70797	0	54062	369	239709	0	239709	409453
		Girls	10717	74943	23679	74888	0	48696	254	233177	0	233177	385300
		Total	23864	150557	49399	145685	0	102758	623	472886	0	472886	794753
2.	Primary/Jr. Basic Schools (Class I - V)	Boys	72400	277778	65584	185922	64569	100871	94207	861331	15175	876506	7367246
		Girls	61971	267048	57596	189379	58688	91854	81212	807748	15173	822921	6369350
		Total	134371	544826	123180	375301	123257	192725	175419	1669079	30348	1699427	13736596
3.	Middle/Sr. Basic Schools (Class VI - VIII)	Boys	22373	131875	19415	51996	26207	37893	26284	316043	4396	320439	2395348
		Girls	19430	112394	16460	59008	25099	34851	20788	288030	5309	293339	1775655
		Total	41803	244269	35875	111004	51306	72744	47072	604073	9705	613778	4171003
4.	High/Post Basic Schools (Class IX - X)	Boys	11407	65781	9753	18861	13248	12832	11898	143780	1610	145390	895336
		Girls	8694	47433	8332	18472	13463	12014	8843	117251	1960	119211	576006
		Total	20101	113214	18085	37333	26711	24846	20741	261031	3570	264601	1471342

(Contd.)

Appendix 6.7 (*Contd.*)

1	2	3	4	5	6	7	8	9	10	11	12	13	14
5.	Pre-Degree Junior College/Higher Secondary Schools (Class XI - XII)	Boys	6007	19325	2358	9229	5267	8707	3315	54208	1183	55391	394932
		Girls	3973	11275	1873	8699	4991	7384	2028	40223	1221	41444	219094
		Total	9980	30600	4231	17928	10258	16091	5343	94431	2404	96835	614026
6.	Total of Primary to Higher Secondary Schools (I - XII)	Boys	112187	494759	97110	266008	109291	160303	135704	1375362	22364	1397726	11052862
		Girls	94068	438150	84261	275558	102241	146103	112871	1253252	23663	1276915	8940105
		Total	206255	932909	181371	541566	211532	306406	248575	2628614	46027	2674641	19992967
7.	Total of Pre-Primary to Higher Secondary Schools (Pre-Primary - XII)	Boys	125334	570373	122830	336805	109291	214365	136073	1615071	22364	1637435	11462315
		Girls	104785	513093	107940	350446	102241	194799	113125	1486429	23663	1510092	9325405
		Total	230119	1083466	230770	687251	211532	409164	249198	3101500	46027	3147527	20787720

Source: Selected Educational Statistics, 2004 - 2005, Ministry of Human Resource Development, Department of Higher Education, Government of India, New Delhi, 2007.

Appendix 6.8

State-wise and Class-wise Dropout Rates of all Categories of Students as on 30.09.2004

(*In per cent*)

Sl. No.	Class	Category of students	Name of the North Eastern States								India
			Arunachal Pradesh	Assam	Manipur	Meghalaya	Mizoram	Nagaland	Tripura	Sikkim	
1	2	3	4	5	6	7	8	9	10	11	12
1.	Class I – V	Boys	45.86	51.58	29.71	51.77	50.84	41.79	43.76	52.01	31.81
		Girls	48.01	48.34	32.74	48.15	48.71	43.66	42.58	46.80	25.42
		Total	46.85	50.07	31.18	49.97	49.84	42.69	43.20	49.44	29.00
2.	Class I - VIII	Boys	63.23	72.41	34.47	65.99	68.99	41.09	62.05	72.48	50.49
		Girls	61.90	74.60	30.91	62.43	64.34	43.93	66.42	70.02	51.28
		Total	62.63	73.38	32.80	64.21	66.84	42.49	64.15	71.22	50.84
3.	Class I – X	Boys	69.59	75.18	46.04	79.64	69.52	66.98	73.58	83.34	60.41
		Girls	72.30	74.69	39.58	78.65	64.11	67.63	73.11	81.15	63.88
		Total	70.79	74.96	43.02	79.15	66.95	67.29	73.36	82.30	61.92

Source: Selected Educational Statistics, 2004 - 2005, Ministry of Human Resource Development, Department of Higher Education, Government of India, New Delhi, 2007.

Appendix 6.9

State-wise and Class-wise Dropout Rates of Scheduled Caste (SC) Students as on 30.09.2004

(*In Percentage*)

Sl. No.	Class	Category of Students	Name of the North Eastern States								India
			Arunachal Pradesh	Assam	Manipur	Meghalaya	Mizoram	Nagaland	Tripura	Sikkim	
1	2	3	4	5	6	7	8	9	10	11	12
1.	Class I-V	Boys	17.50	55.85	37.14	52.04		0	35.20	51.82	32.73
		Girls	26.67	49.86	25.68	46.25		0	35.33	45.19	36.14
		Total	20.00	53.15	31.62	49.41	NA	0	35.26	48.55	34.21
2.	Class I-VIII	Boys	34.29	70.15	0.00	63.38		0	62.29	79.83	55.20
		Girls	45.00	70.49	0.00	61.32	NA	0	70.22	70.09	59.95
		Total	38.18	70.30	0.00	62.37		0	66.20	75.49	57.26
3.	Class I-X	Boys	17.86	72.65	1.17	76.08		0	66.77	86.13	69.11
		Girls	15.38	68.98	1.15	74.85	NA	0	73.55	84.11	74.17
		Total	17.07	71.01	1.16	75.48		0	70.02	85.23	71.25

Source: Selected Educational Statistics, 2004–2005, Ministry of Human Resource Development, Department of Higher Education, Government of India, New Delhi, 2007.

Appendix 6.10

State-wise and Class-wise Dropout Rates of Scheduled Tribe (ST) Students as on 30.09.2004

(In Percentage)

Sl. No.	Class	Category of Students	Name of the North Eastern States								India
			Arunachal Pradesh	Assam	Manipur	Meghalaya	Mizoram	Nagaland	Tripura	Sikkim	
1	2	3	4	5	6	7	8	9	10	11	12
1.	Class I-V	Boys	47.91	58.65	46.12	54.17	50.77	39.71	57.27	30.51	42.55
		Girls	47.74	50.15	56.27	47.36	48.68	37.71	60.59	18.27	42.04
		Total	47.83	54.98	51.00	50.80	49.79	38.78	58.84	24.47	42.32
2.	Class I-VIII	Boys	68.03	74.17	57.69	70.68	68.39	44.78	79.83	52.14	64.97
		Girls	66.58	77.41	56.53	68.40	63.85	40.81	83.11	36.05	67.09
		Total	67.37	75.53	57.16	69.55	66.28	42.93	81.40	44.49	65.87
3.	Class I-X	Boys	73.38	78.15	72.27	82.00	69.21	68.66	85.09	73.02	77.75
		Girls	74.89	75.89	72.07	82.87	63.80	68.86	87.06	61.74	80.66
		Total	74.05	77.18	72.18	82.43	66.64	68.75	85.99	67.72	78.97

Source: Selected Educational Statistics, 2004-2005, Ministry of Human Resource Development, Department of Higher Education, Government of India, New Delhi, 2007.

Appendix 6.11

State-wise and Gender-wise Literacy Rates in Rural/Urban Areas as Per 2001 Census

(In Percentage)

Sl. No.	Area Category (Rural/Urban/Total)	Gender Category	Name of the North Eastern States								India
			Arunachal Pradesh	Assam	Manipur	Meghalaya	Mizoram	Nagaland	Tripura	Sikkim	
1	2	3	4	5	6	7	8	9	10	11	12
1.	Rural	Person	47.83	59.73	67.29	56.29	81.27	62.79	69.72	66.82	58.74
		Male	57.65	68.22	77.31	59.24	84.93	67.58	78.40	74.45	70.70
		Female	36.95	50.70	56.95	53.24	77.26	57.52	60.50	58.01	46.13
2.	Urban	Person	78.26	85.34	79.28	86.30	96.13	84.74	89.21	83.91	79.92
		Male	85.19	89.74	88.71	89.05	96.43	87.44	93.21	87.81	86.27
		Female	69.49	80.24	70.01	83.50	95.80	81.42	85.03	79.16	72.86
3.	Total	Person	54.34	63.25	70.53	62.56	88.80	66.59	73.19	68.81	64.84
		Male	63.83	71.28	80.33	65.43	90.72	71.16	81.02	76.04	75.26
		Female	43.53	54.61	60.53	59.61	86.75	61.46	64.91	60.40	53.67

Source: Selected Educational Statistics, 2004-2005, Ministry of Human Resource Development, Department of Higher Education, Government of India, New Delhi, 2007.

Appendix 6.12

State–wise and Gender-wise Literacy Rates of Scheduled Caste (SC) in Rural/Urban Areas as Per 2001 Census

(In Percentage)

Sl. No.	Area Category (Rural/Urban/Total)	Gender Category	Name of the North Eastern States								India
			Arunachal Pradesh	Assam	Manipur	Meghalaya	Mizoram	Nagaland	Tripura	Sikkim	
1	2	3	4	5	6	7	8	9	10	11	12
1.	Rural	Person	65.87	64.92	70.76	51.91	88.89	0	73.59	60.23	51.16
		Male	73.83	74.21	79.79	61.75	88.33	0	80.98	67.56	63.66
		Female	54.37	54.94	61.38	40.55	100.00	0	65.88	52.63	37.84
2.	Urban	Person	69.28	76.86	73.14	63.57	89.30	0	79.51	81.99	68.12
		Male	78.59	84.08	82.86	72.72	88.49	0	85.78	87.92	77.93
		Female	55.57	69.08	63.77	52.99	91.67	0	73.15	76.05	57.49
3.	Total	Person	67.64	66.78	72.32	56.27	89.20	0	74.68	63.04	54.69
		Male	76.31	75.74	81.78	65.86	88.44	0	81.85	70.15	66.64
		Female	54.99	57.14	62.97	45.21	92.16	0	67.24	55.71	41.90

Source: Selected Educational Statistics, 2004-2005, Ministry of Human Resource Development, Department of Higher Education, Government of India. New Delhi, 2007.

Appendix 6.13

State-wise and Gender-wise Literacy Rates of Scheduled Tribe (ST) in Rural/Urban Areas as Per 2001 Census

(*In Percentage*)

Sl. No.	Area Category (Rural/Urban/Total)	Gender Category	Name of the North Eastern States								India
			Arunachal Pradesh	Assam	Manipur	Meghalaya	Mizoram	Nagaland	Tripura	Sikkim	
1	2	3	4	5	6	7	8	9	10	11	12
1.	Rural	Person	45.04	61.29	65.09	56.36	82.00	62.55	55.46	65.37	45.02
		Male	54.33	71.29	72.44	58.72	86.11	67.09	67.19	72.32	57.39
		Female	35.83	51.04	57.58	53.97	77.71	57.72	43.35	58.03	32.44
2.	Urban	Person	77.39	86.75	80.94	86.67	96.77	88.70	91.97	84.89	69.09
		Male	85.92	92.43	87.94	88.95	97.55	91.63	94.45	89.32	77.77
		Female	69.05	80.62	74.28	84.58	96.01	85.60	89.26	80.59	59.87
3.	Total	Person	49.62	62.52	65.85	61.34	89.34	65.95	56.48	67.14	47.10
		Male	58.77	72.34	73.16	63.49	91.71	70.26	67.97	73.81	59.17
		Female	40.56	52.44	58.42	59.20	86.95	61.35	44.60	60.16	34.76

Source: Selected Educational Statistics, 2004-2005, Ministry of Human Resource Development, Department of Higher Education, Government of India, New Delhi, 2007.

Appendix 6.14

State–wise Decadal Changes in Literacy Rate and Male-Female Literacy Gap (1991-2001)

(*In Percentage*)

Sl. No.	Census Year	Category	Name of the North Eastern States								India
			Arunachal Pradesh	Assam	Manipur	Meghalaya	Mizoram	Nagaland	Tripura	Sikkim	
1	2	3	4	5	6	7	8	9	10	11	12
1.	2001 Census	Males	63.83	71.28	80.33	65.43	90.72	71.16	81.02	76.04	75.26
		Females	43.53	54.61	60.53	59.61	86.75	61.46	64.91	60.40	53.67
		Literacy Gap	20.30	16.67	19.80	5.82	3.97	9.70	16.11	15.64	21.59
2.	1991 Census	Males	51.45	61.87	71.63	53.12	85.61	67.62	70.58	65.70	64.13
		Females	29.69	43.03	47.60	44.85	78.60	54.75	49.65	46.76	39.28
		Literacy Gap	21.76	18.84	24.03	8.27	7.01	12.87	20.93	18.94	24.85
3.	Decadal Changes in Literacy Rates	Males	12.38	9.41	8.70	12.31	5.11	3.54	10.44	10.34	11.13
		Females	13.84	11.58	12.93	14.76	8.15	6.71	15.26	13.64	14.39

Source: Selected Educational Statistics, 2004-2005, Ministry of Human Resource Development, Department of Higher Education, Government of India, New Delhi, 2007.

Appendix 6.15

State-wise Budgeted Expenditure (Revenue Account) on Education, 2004-05

Sl. No.	Category of Budget/ Expenditure	Name of the North Eastern States								India
		Arunachal Pradesh	Assam	Manipur	Meghalaya	Mizoram	Nagaland	Tripura	Sikkim	
1	2	3	4	5	6	7	8	9	10	11
1.	Total Budget (Centre/States, Rev. Account) (RE) (In crore)	1536.70	15596.87	1674.10	1617.13	1484.07	1822.65	2203.52	1789.38	819231.91
2.	Expenditure (Rev. Acct) on Edu. & Trg. by Edu. and other Deptts. (RE) (In crore)	175.66	3091.58	326.07	299.63	237.33	265.18	564.76	164.25	104566.00
3.	Projected population as on 01.03.2004 (In crore)	0.11	2.79	0.23	0.24	0.09	0.21	0.33	0.06	107.91
4.	Per Capita Expenditure (In Rupees)	1539.53	1108.97	1448.56	1243.28	2568.51	1282.30	1698.53	2927.81	969.00
5.	Percentage of Expenditure (RE) on Edn. & Trg, by Edu. and other Deptts to total Budget	11.43	19.82	19.48	18.53	15.99	14.55	25.63	9.18	12.76

Source: Selected Educational Statistics, 2004-2005, Ministry of Human Resource Development, Department of Higher Education, Government of India, New Delhi, 2007.

Appendix 7.1

State-wise Number of Health Institutions and other Health Infrastructure as on 31.03.2007

Sl. No.	Name of the State/NER/India	Number of Health Institutions/Health Centers						Other Health Institutions					
		Medical College (s)	District Hospitals	Sub–Centers	PHCs	CHCs	Total	Ayurvedic Hospitals	Ayurvedic Dispensaries	Unani Dispensaries	Homoeopathic Hospitals	Homoeopathic Dispensaries	Total
1	2	3	4	5	6	7	8	9	10	11	12	13	14
1.	Arunachal Pradesh	–	14	379	85	31	509	1	2	–	1	44	48
2.	Assam	3	20	5109	610	100	5842	1	393	1	3	75	473
3.	Manipur	1	13	420	72	16	522	–	–	–	–	–	–
4.	Meghalaya	–	3	398	103	26	530	1	7	–	–	4	12
5.	Mizoram	–	8	366	57	9	440	–	–	–	6	1	7
6.	Nagaland	–	11	397	84	21	513	–	–	–	–	–	–
7.	Tripura	2	2	579	75	10	668	1	40	–	9	66	116
8.	Sub-Total, NER	6	71	7648	1086	213	9024	4	442	1	19	190	656
9.	Sikkim	1	4	147	24	4	180	1	1	–	7	1	10
10.	Total NER	7	75	7795	1110	217	9204	5	443	1	26	191	666
11.	India	NA	NA	145272	22370	4045	171687	NA	NA	NA	NA	NA	NA

Source: Website of the Ministry of Health and Family Welfare, Government of India, New Delhi.

Appendix 7.2

State-wise Establishment of Health Infrastructure During Five Year Plans

(In Numbers)

Sl. No.	Name of the State/NER/India	Sub-Centres Functioning at the End of				PHCs Functioning at the End of				CHCs Functioning at the End of			
		Seventh Plan (1985-90)	Eighth Plan (1992-97)	Nineth Plan (1997-02)	Tenth Plan (2002-07)	Seventh Plan (1985-90)	Eighth Plan (1992-97)	Nineth Plan (1997-02)	Tenth Plan (2002-07)	Seventh Plan (1985-90)	Eigth Plan (1992-97)	Nineth Plan (1997-02)	Tenth Plan (2002-07)
1	2	3	4	5	6	7	8	9	10	11	12	13	14
1.	Arunachal Pradesh	155	223	273	379	24	45	65	85	6	9	20	31
2.	Assam	5109	5109	5109	5109	449	610	610	610	60	100	100	100
3.	Manipur	420	420	420	420	64	69	69	72	10	16	16	16
4.	Meghalaya	272	377	413	398	56	81	85	103	3	10	13	26
5.	Mizoram	220	324	346	366	35	55	58	57	4	6	9	9
6.	Nagaland	244	244	302	397	33	33	46	84	4	5	9	21
7.	Tripura	506	537	539	579	49	55	58	75	8	11	11	10
8.	Sub Total, NER	6926	7234	7402	7648	710	948	991	1086	95	157	178	213
9.	Sikkim	132	147	147	147	20	24	24	24	2	2	2	4
10.	Total NER	7058	7381	7549	7795	730	972	1015	1110	97	159	180	217
11.	India	130165	136258	137311	145272	18671	22149	22875	22370	1910	2633	3054	4045

Source: Website of the Ministry of Health and Family Welfare, Govt. of India, New Delhi.

Appendix 7.3

State-wise Position of Health Infrastructure as Per 2001 Population Census (As on March, 2007)

(*In Numbers*)

Sl. No.	Name of the State/NER/India	Total Population in Rural Areas	Tribal Population in Rural Areas	Position of Sub-Centres			Position of PHCs			Position of CHCs		
				Required	In Position	Shortfall	Required	In Position	Shortfall	Required	In position	Shortfall
1	2	3	4	5	6	7	8	9	10	11	12	13
1.	Arunachal Pradesh	prescribed	6J6278	254	379	*	39	85	*	9	31	*
2.	Assam	23216288	3154546	5063	5109	*	826	610	216	206	100	106
3.	Manipur	1590820	705912	412	420	*	64	72	*	16	16	0
4.	Meghalaya	1864711	1682670	597	398	199	90	103	*	22	26	*
5.	Mizoram	447567	430883	146	366	*	22	57	*	5	9	*
6.	Nagaland	1647249	1544022	535	397	138	80	84	*	20	21	*
7.	Tripura	2653453	967997	659	579	80	104	75	29	26	10	16
8.	Sub-Total, NER	31420088	9092308	7666	7648	417	1225	1086	245	304	213	122
9.	Sikkim	480981	101909	109	147	*	17	24	*	4	4	0
10.	Total NER	31901069	9194217	7775	7795	417	1242	1110	245	308	217	122
11.	India	742490639	77338597	158792	145272	20855	26022	22370	4833	6491	4045	2525

Note: (i) The requirement is calculated on the basis of total and tribal population of Census 2001 in rural areas using the prescribed norms.
(ii) All India shortfall is derived by adding state-wise figures of shortfall ignoring the existing surplus in some of the states.
(iii) *indicates surplus.

Source: Website of the Ministry of Health and Family Welfare, Govt. of India, New Delhi.

Appendix 7.4

State-wise Position of Doctors, Specialists and other Health Workers in Different Health Institutions as on March, 2007

(In Numbers)

Sl. No.	Name of the State/NER/India	Position at Sub-Centres and PHCs			Position at Sub-Centres			Position at PHCs					
		Multipurpose Workers (Female/ANM)			Health Workers (Male)/MPW (M)			Health Assistants (Female)/LHV			Health Assistants (Male)		
		Required	In Position	Shortfall	Required	In Position	Shortfall	Required	In Position	Shortfall	Required	In Position	Shortfall
1	2	3	4	5	6	7	8	9	10	11	12	13	14
1.	Arunachal Pradesh	464	454	10	379	23	356	85	16	69	85	26	59
2.	Assam	5719	NA	NA	5109	NA	NA	610	NA	NA	610	NA	NA
3.	Manipur	492	487	5	420	420	0	72	55	17	72	52	20
4.	Meghalaya	501	608	*	398	273	125	103	75	28	103	87	16
5.	Mizoram	423	421	2	366	303	63	57	57	0	57	57	0
6.	Nagaland	481	342	139	397	300	97	84	15	69	84	15	69
7.	Tripura	654	642	12	579	268	311	75	62	13	75	93	*
8.	Sub-Total, NER	8734	2954	168	7648	1587	952	1086	280	196	1086	330	164
9.	Sikkim	171	267	*	147	147	0	24	18	6	24	8	16
10.	Total NER	8905	3221	168	7795	1734	952	1110	298	202	1110	338	180
11.	India	167642	147439	21157	145272	62881	77615	22370	15546	7142	22370	20234	6261

Note: Same as Appendix-7.3; NA—indicates Not Available.
Source: Website of the Ministry of Health and Family Welfare, Govt. of India, New Delhi.

Appendix 7.4 (Contd.)

State-wise Position of Doctors, Specialists and other Health Workers in Different Health Institutions as on March, 2007

(*In Numbers*)

Sl. No.	Name of the State/NER/India	Position at PHCs			Position at CHCs								
		Doctors			Surgeons			Obstetricians and Gynaecologists			Physicians		
		Required	In Position	Shortfall	Required	In Position	Shortfall	Required	In Position	Shortfall	Required	In Position	Shortfall
1	2	15	16	17	18	19	20	21	22	23	24	25	26
1.	Arunachal Pradesh	85	78	7	31	0	31	31	0	31	31	0	31
2.	Assam	610	NA	NA	100	NA	NA	100	NA	NA	100	NA	NA
3.	Manipur	72	103	*	16	1	15	16	0	16	16	0	16
4.	Meghalaya	103	106	*	26	0	26	26	0	26	26	1	25
5.	Mizoram	57	39	18	9	0	9	9	0	9	9	0	9
6.	Nagaland	84	53	31	21	0	21	21	0	21	21	0	21
7.	Tripura	75	150	*	10	0	10	10	0	10	10	2	8
8.	Sub-Total, NER	1086	529	56	213	1	112	213	0	113	213	3	110
9.	Sikkim	24	38	*	4	1	3	4	1	3	4	1	3
10.	Total NER	1110	567	56	217	2	115	217	1	116	217	4	113
11.	India	22370	22608	1410	4045	1054	2353	4045	1357	2050	4045	1083	2341

Note: Same as Appendix - 7.3; NA—indicates Not Available.

Source: Website of the Ministry of Health and Family Welfare, Govt. of India, New Delhi.

Appendix 7.4 **(Contd.)**

State-wise Position of Doctors, Specialists and Other Health Workers in Different Health Institutions as on March, 2007

(In Numbers)

Sl. No.	Name of the State/NER/India	Position at CHCs								
		Paediatricians			Total Specialists (Respective Totals from Columns 18 to 29)			Radiographers		
		Required	In Position	Shortfall	Required	In Position	Shortfall	Required	In Position	Shortfall
1	2	27	28	29	30	31	32	33	34	35
1.	Arunachal Pradesh	31	0	31	124	0	124	31	22	9
2.	Assam	100	NA	NA	400	NA	NA	100	NA	NA
3.	Manipur	16	0	16	64	1	63	16	7	9
4.	Meghalaya	26	0	26	104	1	103	26	25	1
5.	Mizoram	9	0	9	36	0	36	9	9	0
6.	Nagaland	21	0	21	84	0	84	21	11	10
7.	Tripura	10	0	10	40	2	38	10	4	6
8.	Sub-Total, NER	213	0	113	852	4	448	213	78	35
9.	Sikkim	4	2	2	16	5	11	4	9	*
10.	Total NER	217	2	115	868	9	459	217	87	35
11.	India	4045	898	2509	16180	5117	9455	4045	1740	1398

Note: Same as Appendix-7.3; NA—indicates Not Available.
Source: Website of the Ministry of Health and Family Welfare, Govt. of India, New Delhi.

Appendix 7.4 (Contd.)

State-wise Position of Doctors, Specialists and other Health Workers in Different Health Institutions as on March, 2007

(In Numbers)

Sl. No.	Name of the State/NER/India	Position at PHCs and CHCs								
		Pharmacists			Laboratory Technicians			Nurses and Midwives		
		Required	In Position	Shortfall	Required	In Position	Shortfall	Required	In Position	Shortfall
1	2	36	37	38	39	40	41	42	43	44
1.	Arunachal Pradesh	116	31	85	116	18	98	302	105	197
2.	Assam	710	NA	NA	710	NA	NA	1310	NA	NA
3.	Manipur	88	26	62	88	41	47	184	169	15
4.	Meghalaya	129	113	16	129	130	*	285	174	111
5.	Mizoram	66	35	31	66	31	35	120	243	*
6.	Nagaland	105	85	20	105	45	60	231	520	*
7.	Tripura	85	56	29	85	42	43	145	268	*
8.	Sub-Total, NER	1299	346	243	1299	307	283	2577	1479	323
9.	Sikkim	28	0	28	28	32	*	52	90	*
10.	Total NER	1327	346	271	1327	339	283	2629	1569	323
11.	India	26415	17919	4910	26415	12101	9795	50685	29776	17262

Note: Same as Appendix-7.3, NA—indicates Not Available

Source: Website of the Ministry of Health and Family Welfare, Govt. of India, New Delhi.

Appendix 7.5

State-wise Number of Sub-Centers without ANMs or/and Health Workers (M) as on March, 2007

(In Numbers)

Sl. No.	*Name of the State/NER/India*	*Position of Sub-Centers*			
		Sub-Centers Functioning	*Without HW (F)/ANMs*	*Without HW (M)*	*Without Both*
1	2	3	4	5	6
1.	Arunachal Pradesh	379	100	275	100
2.	Assam	5109	80	4997	80
3.	Manipur	420	0	99	0
4.	Meghalaya	398	0	123	0
5.	Mizoram	366	20	50	5
6.	Nagaland	397	59	59	59
7.	Tripura	579	137	237	102
8.	Sub Total, NER	7648	396	5840	346
9.	Sikkim	147	0	0	0
10.	Total NER	7795	396	5840	346
11.	India	145272	6937	52634	4711

Source: Website of the Ministry of Health and Family Welfare, Govt. of India, New Delhi.

Appendix 7.6

State-wise Number of Primary Health Centers (PHCs) with Doctor and without Doctor/Lab Technician/Pharmacist (as on March, 2007)

(In Numbers)

Sl. No.	Name of the State/NER/India	Total PHCs Functioning	Position of PHCs							
			With 4+ Doctors	With 3 Doctors	With 2 Doctors	With 1 Doctor	Without Doctor	Without Lab Tech.	Without Pharmacist	With Lady Doctor
1	2	3	4	5	6	7	8	9	10	11
1.	Arunachal Pradesh	85	NA	NA	NA	NA	NA	78	78	0
2.	Assam	610	26	80	314	190	0	185	0	NA
3.	Manipur	72	0	0	32	39	1	44	23	21
4.	Meghalaya	103	2	0	15	86	0	5	26	48
5.	Mizoram	57	0	0	1	38	18	20	22	13
6.	Nagaland	84	NA	NA	NA	NA	NA	83	23	0
7.	Tripura	75	9	18	24	18	6	40	20	11
8.	Sub-Total, NER	1086	37	98	386	371	25	455	192	93
9.	Sikkim	24	0	1	12	11	0	0	24	19
10.	Total NER	1110	37	99	398	382	25	455	216	112
11.	India	22370	259	720	3776	9595	807	7558	3073	3109

Note: NA—indicates Not Available.

Source: Website of the Ministry of Health and Family Welfare, Govt. of India, New Delhi.

Appendix 7.7

State–wise Number of Training Schools and Health and Family Welfare Training Centres (as on March, 2006)

(In Numbers)

Sl. No.	*Name of the State/NER/India*	*ANM/HW (F) Schools Funded by Govt. of India*	*LHV/HA (F) Promotional Schools Established by Govt. of India*	*Health and Family Welfare Training Centers*	*MPW (M) Training Centers*
1	2	3	4	5	6
1.	Arunachal Pradesh	1	0	0	0
2.	Assam	22	1	1	0
3.	Manipur	1	1	1	1
4.	Meghalaya	2	0	1	0
5.	Mizoram	1	0	0	1
6.	Nagaland	2	0	0	0
7.	Tripura	3	1	0	1
8.	Sub-Total, NER	32	3	3	3
9.	Sikkim	1	1	0	0
10.	Total NER	33	4	3	3
11.	India	*336*	42	47	56

Source: Website of the Ministry of Health and Family Welfare, Govt. of India, New Delhi.

Appendix 7.8

State-wise Details of Rural Healthcare Infrastructure, Average Number of Villages and Rural Population (2001 Census) Covered (as on March, 2007)

(In Numbers)

Sl. No.	Name of the State/NER/India	Average Number of Villages Covered by a			Number of Sub-Centres per PHC	Number of PHCs per CHC	Average Rural Population (2001 Census) Covered by a		
		Sub-Centre	PHC	CHC			Sub-Centre	PHC	CHC
1	2	3	4	5	6	7	8	9	10
1.	Arunachal Pradesh	11	48	131	4	3	2296	10236	28067
2.	Assam	5	43	263	8	6	4544	38059	232163
3.	Manipur	6	33	149	6	5	3788	22095	99426
4.	Meghalaya	15	59	232	4	4	4685	18104	71720
5.	Mizoram	2	14	91	6	6	1223	7852	49730
6.	Nagaland	3	16	63	5	4	4149	19610	78440
7.	Tripura	2	12	87	8	8	4583	35379	265345
8.	Sub-Total, NER	5	38	196	7	5	4222	29733	151597
9.	Sikkim	3	19	113	6	6	3272	20041	120245
10.	Total NER	5	38	195	7	5	4204	29524	151019
11.	India	4	29	158	6	6	5111	33191	183558

Source: Website of the Ministry of Health and Family Welfare, Govt. of India, New Delhi.

Appendix 7.9

State-wise Number of Medical Institutions, Medical Staff, Hospital Beds and Different Rates

Sl. No.	Name of the State /NER/India	Total Number of Medical Institutions (Hospitals, PHCs, CHCs, Sub–Centres and Dispensaries)	Total Number of Doctors	Total Number of Health Workers (Nurses, Midwives, Health Workers (Male) etc.)	Total Number of Beds	Total Number of Patients Treated (In '00)	Average Number of the following per Thousand Population (As per Projected Population of the Respective Years)				Average Number of Patients (in '00) Treated/Attended by a	
							Medical Institution	Doctor	Health Worker	Bed	Doctor	Health Worker
1	2	3	4	5	6	7	8	9	10	11	12	13
1.	Arunachal Pradesh (During 2005-06)	635	527	517	2218	NA	0.51	0.43	0.42	1.80	NA	NA
2.	Assam (During 2004-05)	5987	691	1671	7083	NA	0.21	0.02	0.06	0.25	NA	NA
3.	Manipur (During 2002-03)	541	945	1148	2395	11568	0.23	0.39	0.48	1.00	12.24	10.08
4.	Meghalaya (During 2005-06)	583	568	2086	3166	20810	0.22	0.21	0.79	1.20	36.64	9.98
5.	Mizoram (During 2005-06)	427	155	1175	2180	NA	0.42	0.15	1.17	2.16	NA	NA
6.	Nagaland (During 2001-02)	513	367	672	2183	NA	0.25	0.18	0.32	1.05	NA	NA
7.	Tripura (During 2005-06)	759	883	1323	2653	26884	0.22	0.26	0.38	0.77	30.45	20.32

(Contd.)

Appendix-7.9 (*Contd.*)

1	2	3	4	5	6	7	8	9	10	11	12	13
8.	Sub-Total, NER	9445	4133	8592	21878	NA	0.23	0.10	0.21	0.53	NA	NA
9.	Sikkim (During 2001-02)	181	182	1028	920	5056	0.32	0.33	1.85	1.65	27.78	4.92
10.	Total, NER	9626	4313	9620	22798	NA	0.23	0.10	0.23	0.54	NA	NA
11.	India (In 2005)	199373	656111	865135	914543	NA	0.18	0.59	0.78	0.82	NA	NA

Note: NA indicates-Not Available

Source: (i) Statistical Hand Book/Statistical Abstract/Other Publications of the respective State Governments

(ii) Economic Survey, 2006-07, Ministry of Finance, Govt. of India, New Delhi.

Appendix 7.10

State-wise Achievement of Family Welfare Programme

Sl. No.	Name of the State/NER/India	Number of Sterilisations during 2002-03	Cumulative number of Sterilisations up to 2002-03		Number of Sterilisations during 2004-05	Number of IUD Insertions during 2002-03	Cumulative Number of IUD Insertions up to 2002-03		Number of IUD Insertions during 2004-05	Number of Conventional Contraceptive Users during 2002-03		Number of Conventional Contraceptive Users during 2004-05	
			Number	Rate*			Number	Rate*		Number	Rate*	Number	Rate*
1	2	3	4	5	6	7	8	9	10	11	12	13	14
1.	Arunachal Pradesh	1111	30423	27.9	2101	2433	48613	44.6	2766	2798	2.6	2424	2.2
2.	Assam	34104	1829713	68.7	39555	41023	829382	31.1	39966	65420	2.5	70866	2.7
3.	Manipur	1671	93249	39.0	518	6805	166904	69.9	6693	4963	2.1	6959	3.0
4.	Meghalaya	2483	34719	15.1	2205	2590	43317	18.8	2606	5305	2.3	6139	2.6
5.	Mizoram	4057	78330	87.9	2140	2332	46494	52.2	2430	4600	5.2	7665	8.6
6.	Nagaland	900	24094	12.1	754	5109	31169	15.7	1749	4230	2.1	1083	0.5
7.	Tripura	3353	208006	65.2	2274	3279	63744	20.0	3013	39590	12.4	32560	10.2
8.	Sub-Total, NER	47679	2298534	60.0	49547	63571	1229623	32.1	59223	126906	3.3	127696	3.3
9.	Sikkim	569	21432	39.7	1173	905	27210	50.4	1252	5378	10.0	8073	14.9
10.	Total NER	48248	2319966	59.7	50720	64476	1256833	32.3	60475	132284	3.4	135769	3.5
11.	India	4731438	129817807	124.0	4920144	6108035	113305761	108.2	6169003	25923540	24.8	33482977	32.5

Note: * Rate relates to per thousand population of 2001 Census.

Source: Statistical Abstract, India, 2003, 2005 & 2006, Central Statistical Organization, New Delhi.

Appendix 7.11

State-wise Details of Sterilisation

Sl. No.	Name of the State/NER/India	Total Number of Eligible Couples as on 31.03.08 (in '000)		Achievement during April to June			Sterilisation per 10,000 Unsterilised Couples	Estimated Unsterilised Couples Exposed to Higher Order of Birth 3 & 3+ (in '000)	Sterilisation per 10,000 Unsterilised Couples Exposed to Higher Order of Birth 3 & 3+
		Total No.	Unsterilised	2008-09	2007-08	% Change			
1	2	3	4	5	6	7	8	9	10
1.	Arunachal Pradesh	182	141	1055	410	157.4	74.7	73	145
2.	Assam	4396	3816	9779	2049	377.3	25.6	1561	63
3.	Manipur	307	280	55	46	18.9	2.0	111	5
4.	Meghalaya	358	324	567	540	5.0	17.5	184	31
5.	Mizoram	125	71	408	539	–24.3	57.2	30	136
6.	Nagaland	250	225	372	331	12.4	16.5	128	29
7.	Tripura	539	530	1891	789	139.7	35.6	128	148
8.	Sub-Total, NER	6157	5387	14127	4704	200.3	26.2	2215	68
9.	Sikkim	84	52	112	279	-59.9	18.0	21	53
10.	Total NER	6241	5449	14239	4983	185.7	26.1	2236	68
11.	India	193460	119365	686641	656981	4.5	57.5	49059	140

Source: Website of the Ministry of Health and Family Welfare, Government of India, New Delhi.

Appendix 7.12

State-wise Estimated Birth Rate, Death Rate, Natural Growth Rate and Infant Mortality Rate, 2006 (as per SRS Bulletin, October, 2007)

Sl. No.	Name of the State/NER/India	Birth Rate			Death Rate			Natural Growth Rate			Infant Mortality Rate		
		Total	Rural	Urban	Total	Rural	Urban	Total	Rural	Urban	Total	Rural	Urban
1	2	3	4	5	6	7	8	9	10	11	12	13	14
1.	Arunachal Pradesh	18.9	19.8	16.5	7.3	7.9	5.8	11.6	11.9	10.7	56	62	38
2.	Assam	24.6	26.1	15.4	8.7	9.2	5.8	15.9	17.0	9.6	67	70	42
3.	Manipur	13.4	13.5	13.1	4.5	4.4	4.6	9.0	9.1	8.6	11	11	11
4.	Meghalaya	24.7	26.4	17.1	8.0	8.5	5.8	16.7	17.8	11.3	53	54	43
5.	Mizoram	17.8	21.6	14.0	5.5	6.2	4.8	12.3	15.4	9.2	25	32	13
6.	Nagaland	17.3	16.8	19.2	4.8	4.9	4.1	12.5	11.9	15.0	20	18	27
7.	Tripura	16.6	17.3	13.4	6.3	6.2	6.8	10.3	11.1	6.7	36	37	30
8.	Sikkim	19.2	19.5	17.7	5.6	5.7	4.7	13.7	13.8	13.0	33	35	16
9.	India	23.5	25.2	18.8	7.5	8.1	6.0	16.0	17.2	12.8	57	62	39

Source: SRS Bulletin, October, 2007, Registrar General of India, New Delhi.

Appendix 7.13

State–wise Percentage Distribution of Households Living in Various Types of Houses

Sl. No.	Name of the State/NER/India	Total/Rural/Urban	As per 1991 Census			As per 2001 Census		
			Pucca	Semi–Pucca	Kutcha	Pucca/ Permanent	Semi– Pucca/ Permanent	Kutcha/ Unclassified
1	2	3	4	5	6	7	8	9
1.	Arunachal Pradesh	T	14.94	11.72	73.34	20.68	18.16	61.16
		R	5.75	9.78	84.48	13.43	15.18	71.39
		U	28.03	33.62	38.35	44.20	27.14	28.66
2.	Assam	T	14.62	15.16	70.22	19.47	31.23	49.12
		R	–	–	–	14.21	30.31	55.49
		U	–	–	–	52.01	36.99	10.99
3.	Manipur	T	5.40	40.65	53.95	8.39	55.13	36.47
		R	1.20	13.94	84.87	4.79	52.26	42.95
		U	9.38	33.21	56.96	19.05	63.85	17.10
4.	Meghalaya	T	13.30	33.72	52.98	22.14	37.49	40.37
		R	7.03	20.86	72.12	14.56	36.74	48.70
		U	30.67	54.19	15.14	50.12	39.74	10.14

(Contd.)

Appendix 6.5 (*Contd.*)

1	2	3	4	5	6	7	8	9
5.	Mizoram	T	19.10	42.52	38.38	52.84	25.69	21.47
		R	1.61	13.77	84.63	32.42	29.71	37.86
		U	24.28	49.48	26.24	72.98	21.56	5.46
6.	Nagaland	T	12.62	36.47	50.91	16.19	50.50	33.30
		R	4.83	19.30	75.88	9.43	52.05	38.53
		U	38.32	35.70	25.98	43.58	43.94	12.48
7.	Tripura	T	5.50	20.71	73.79	9.81	45.99	44.19
		R	1.43	6.41	92.16	3.99	44.53	51.48
		U	20.70	24.12	55.17	36.13	51.66	12.21
8.	Sikkim	T	26.95	39.11	33.94	37.87	46.26	16.07
		R	–	–	–	31.79	50.21	18.00
		U	–	–	–	79.38	18.18	2.44
9.	India	T	41.61	30.95	27.44	51.62	30.13	18.24
		R	–	–	–	41.10	35.73	23.17
		U	–	–	–	79.34	15.39	5.27

Source: Statistical Abstract, India, 2005 and 2006, Central Statistical Organization, New Delhi.

Appendix 7.14

State-wise Distribution of Households/Habitations having Safe Drinking Water Facilities

Sl. No.	Name of the State/NER/India	Percentage of Households having Safe Drinking Water Facilities (As per 2001 Census)			Coverage of Habitations under Rural Water Supply (As on April 1, 2006)							
					Status of Habitations				Status of Habitations (in %)			
		Total	Rural	Urban	Not Covered	Partially Covered	Fully Covered	Total	Not Covered	Partially Covered	Fully Covered	Total
1	2	3	4	5	6	7	8	9	10	11	12	13
1.	Arunachal Pradesh	77.5	73.7	90.7	34	309	3955	4298	0.8	7.2	92.0	100.0
2.	Assam	58.8	56.8	70.4	144	4803	65608	70555	0.2	6.8	93.0	100.0
3.	Manipur	37.0	29.3	59.4	0	0	2791	2791	0	0	100.0	100.0
4.	Meghalaya	39.0	29.5	73.5	7	127	8502	8636	0.1	1.5	98.4	100.0
5.	Mizoram	36.0	23.8	47.8	0	26	781	807	0	3.2	96.8	100.0
6.	Nagaland	46.5	47.5	42.3	16	609	900	1525	1.1	39.9	59.0	100.0
7.	Tripura	52.5	45.0	85.8	0	0	7412	74120	0	0	100.0	100.0
8.	Sikkim	70.7	67.0	97.1	0	0	1679	1679	0	0	100.0	100.0
9.	India	77.9	73.2	90.0	3052	38894	1380337	1422283	0.2	2.7	97.1	100.0

Sources: (i) Statistical Abstract, India, 2005 and 2006, Central Statistical Organization, New Delhi.

(ii) Economic Survey, 2006-2007, Ministry of Finance, New Delhi.

Appendix 7.15

State-wise Distribution of Households having Toilet Facilities

Sl. No.	*Name of the State/NER/India*	*Percentage of Households having Toilet Facilities*				
		As per 2001 Census			*As per NSS 58th Round (July, 02 to Dec, 02)*	
		Total	*Rural*	*Urban*	*Rural*	*Urban*
1	2	3	4	5	6	7
1.	Arunachal Pradesh	56.30	47.34	86.95	NR	99.40
2.	Assam	64.64	59.57	94.60	86.20	98.20
3.	Manipur	82.03	77.50	95.31	93.70	100.00
4.	Meghalaya	51.19	40.10	91.58	67.80	99.10
5.	Mizoram	89.02	79.74	98.03	96.40	100.00
6.	Nagaland	70.57	64.64	94.12	96.20	100.00
7.	Tripura	81.45	77.93	96.96	94.20	99.20
8.	Sikkim	63.38	59.35	91.79	89.30	99.30
9.	India	36.41	21.92	73.72	23.70	82.90

Note: NR—indicates Not Reported.

Source: Statistical Abstract, India, 2005 and 2006, Central Statistical Organization, New Delhi.

Appendix 7.16

State-wise Distribution of Households by Type of Latrine

Sl. No.	Name of the State/NER/India	Percentage Distribution of Households by Type of Latrine as per NSS 58th round (July, 02 to Dec, 02)											
		In Rural Areas						In Urban Areas					
		No Latrine	Service Latrine	Septic Tank/ Flush	Others	Not Reported	Total	No Latrine	Service Latrine	Septic Tank/ Flush	Others	Not Reported	Total
1	2	3	4	5	6	7	8	9	10	11	12	13	14
1.	Arunachal Pradesh	28.7	16.2	12.1	42.8	0.2	100.0	0.6	51.6	20.3	27.3	0.2	100.0
2.	Assam	13.8	1.6	10.4	74.2	0.0	100.0	1.8	1.5	76.2	20.5	0.0	100.0
3.	Manipur	6.3	14.1	17.1	62.4	0.1	100.0	0.0	26.5	45.6	27.9	0.0	100.0
4.	Meghalaya	32.2	2.2	3.7	61.9	0.0	100.0	0.9	2.1	77.7	19.3	0.0	100.0
5.	Mizoram	3.6	6.6	15.7	74.1	0.0	100.0	0.0	7.2	55.8	37.0	0.0	100.0
6.	Nagaland	3.8	8.8	36.1	51.3	0.0	100.0	0.0	4.2	72.0	23.8	0.0	100.0
7.	Tripura	5.8	4.2	3.0	87.0	0.0	100.0	0.8	9.8	43.2	46.2	0.0	100.0
8.	Sikkim	10.7	0.3	47.1	41.9	0.0	100.0	0.7	0.0	92.3	7.0	0.0	100.0
9.	India	76.3	1.9	11.8	10.0	0.0	100.0	17.9	4.1	70.7	7.3	0.0	100.0

Source: Statistical Abstract, India, 2005 and 2006, Central Statistical Organization, New Delhi.

Appendix 8.1

State-wise Identified Power Potentiality and its Demand and Supply

Sl. No.	Name of the State/NER/India	Hydel Power Potential Identified and its Development (In MW)				Power Requirement and its Availability (In MU) as on March, 2005			
		Identified Capacity	Capacity Developed	Capacity under Development	Capacity to be Developed {3– (4+5)}	Require-ment	Availability	Surplus / Deficit (+) or (–)	Surplus / Deficit in %
1	2	3	4	5	6	7	8	9	10
1.	Arunachal Pradesh	50328	416	2600	47312	14	14	0	0.0
2.	Assam	680	275	100	305	313	293	–20	–6.4
3.	Manipur	1784	105	90	1589	35	34	–1	–2.9
4.	Meghalaya	2394	185	84	2125	117	98	–19	–16.2
5.	Mizoram	2196	–	60	2136	20	19	–1	–5.0
6.	Nagaland	1574	99	–	1475	29	29	0	0.0
7.	Tripura	15	15	–	–	57	51	–6	–10.5
8.	Sub-Total, NER	58971	1095	2934	54942	585	538	–47	–8.0
9.	Sikkim	4286	84	510	3692	NA	NA	NA	NA
10.	Grand Total, NER	63257	1179	3444	58634	585	538	–47	–8.0
11.	India	NA	NA	NA	NA	53192	49259	–3933	–7.4

Source: North Eastern Region-VISION-2020, Ministry of Development of North Eastern Region, North Eastern Council, Vol. III, pp. 104, 250.

Appendix 8.2

State-wise Electricity-Installed Capacity, Generation and Consumption during 2004-05 and 2005-06

Sl. No.	Name of the State/NER/ India	Installed Capacity (In '000 Kw)					Electricity Generated (In Gwh)					Consumption in Power Station Auxiliaries (Gwh)	Net Total Electricity Generated (Gwh) (Col. 12-13)	Total Consumption (Gwh)	Per Capita Consumption (2004–05) (kWh)	Per capita consumption (2005–06)@ (kWh)
		Hydro	Steam	Diesel & Wind	Gas	Total	Hydro	Steam	Diesel & Wind	Gas	Gross Total					
1	2	3	4	5	6	7	8	9	10	11	12	13	14	15	16	17
1.	Arunachal Pradesh	19	–	16	–	35	2	–	–	–	2	–	2	166.5	144.8	297.7
2.	Assam	2	330	21	269	622	–	–	–	903	903	44	859	1838.0	85.3	170.7
3.	Manipur	2	–	45	–	47	–	–	1	–	1	–	1	177.6	70.5	215.2
4.	Meghalaya	186	–	2	–	188	638	–	–	–	638	2	636	855.9	352.2	517.5
5.	Mizoram	4	–	52	–	56	5	–	1	–	6	–	6	125.7	133.7	250.2
6.	Nagaland	26	–	2	–	28	3	–	–	–	3	–	3	183.2	87.2	179.3
7.	Tripura	16	–	5	107	128	68	–	–	487	555	8	547	380.0	113.1	190.6
8.	Sub–Total, NER	255	330	143	376	1104	716	–	2	1390	2108	54	2054	3726.9	96.9*	201.8*
9.	Sikkim	32	–	5	–	37	59	–	–	–	59	–	59	266.7	397.7	429.8
10.	Grand Total, NER	287	330	148	376	1141	775	–	2	1390	2167	54	2113	3993.6	102.4*	204.9*
11.	India	30942	67791	4181	11910	114824	84610	424244	6855	61525	577234	41590	535644	386133.7	411.1	631.4

Source: Statistical Abstract, India, 2005 and 2006; Central Statistical Organisation, New Delhi.

@ – data collected from the website of the Ministry of Power, New Delhi. * indicates estimated figure.

Appendix 8.3

State-wise Quantity of Electricity Sold to Ultimate Consumers during 2004-05

In Gwh)

Sl. No.	Name of the State/NER/India	Domestic	Commercial	Industrial Power at Low & Medium Voltage	Industrial Power at High Voltage	Public Lighting	Traction	Agriculture	Public Water Works & Sewage Pumping	Miscellaneous	Total Sold to Ultimate Consumers
1	2	3	4	5	6	7	8	9	10	11	12
1.	Arunachal Pradesh	65.00	13.50	4.50	A	8.75	–	–	7.75	67.00	166.50
2.	Assam	722.02	227.54	85.52	505.49	5.90	–	14.31	30.23	246.94	1837.95
3.	Manipur	113.42	12.30	7.11	0.93	3.17	–	0.22	8.58	31.86	177.59
4.	Meghalaya	171.58	38.53	5.28	485.54	1.48	–	0.93	24.63	127.90	855.87
5.	Mizoram	84.72	6.53	1.93	–	5.81	–	–	18.03	8.65	125.67
6.	Nagaland	120.02	18.29	3.65	A	0.69	–	–	0.19	40.34	183.18
7.	Tripura	148.47	32.74	50.17	A	7.32	–	70.98	55.52	14.81	380.01
8.	Sub-Total, NER	1425.23	349.43	158.16	991.96	33.12	–	86.44	144.93	537.50	3726.77
9.	Sikkim	98.50	56.00	27.00	–	45.20	–	–	–	–	226.70
10.	Grand Total, NER	1523.73	405.43	185.16	991.96	78.32	–	86.44	144.93	537.50	3953.47
11.	India	95659.47	31381.23	32334.67	104354.58	4967.58	9495.33	88555.35	9618.49	8866.96	385233.66

Source: Statistical Abstract, India, 2005 and 2006, Central Statistical Organization, New Delhi.

Note: A—indicates, the amount included in Industrial power at low and medium voltage.

Appendix 8.3 (Contd.)

State-wise Quantity of Electricity Sold to Ultimate Consumers During 2004-05

(In Percentage)

Sl. No.	Name of the State/NER/India	Domestic	Commercial	Industrial Power at Low & Medium Voltage	Industrial Power at High Voltage	Public Lighting	Traction	Agriculture	Public Water Works & Sewage Pumping	Miscellaneous	Total Sold to Ultimate Consumers
1	2	13	14	15	16	17	18	19	20	21	22
1.	Arunachal Pradesh	39.04	8.11	2.70	–	5.26	–	–	4.65	40.24	100.00
2.	Assam	39.28	12.38	4.65	27.50	0.32	–	0.78	1.65	13.44	100.00
3.	Manipur	63.87	6.93	4.00	0.52	1.79	–	0.12	4.83	17.94	100.00
4.	Meghalaya	20.05	4.50	0.62	56.73	0.17	–	0.11	2.88	14.94	100.00
5.	Mizoram	67.41	5.20	1.54	–	4.62	–	–	14.35	6.88	100.00
6.	Nagaland	65.52	9.99	1.99	–	0.38	–	–	0.10	22.02	100.00
7.	Tripura	39.07	8.61	13.20	–	1.93	–	18.68	14.61	3.90	100.00
8.	Sub-Total, NER	38.27	9.37	4.24	26.61	0.88	–	2.32	3.89	14.42	100.00
9.	Sikkim	43.45	24.70	11.91	–	19.94	–	–	–	–	100.00
10.	Grand Total, NER	38.54	10.26	4.68	25.09	1.98	–	2.19	3.67	13.59	100.00
11.	India	24.83	8.15	8.39	27.09	1.29	2.46	22.99	2.50	2.30	100.00

Source: Statistical Abstract, India, 2005 and 2006, Central Statistical Organisation, New Delhi.

Appendix 8.4

State-wise Electricity Installed Capacity and Generation in Different Years

Sl. No	Name of the State/ NER /India	Installed Capacity in (Mw) during					Generation in (Gwh) during				
		1996-97	1999-00	2003-04	2005-06	% Increase in 2005-06 over 1996-97 i.e. withih a Gap of 9 Years	1996-97	1999-00	2003-04	2004-05	% Increase in 2004-05 over 1996-97 i.e. within a Gap of 8 Years
1	2	3	4	5	6	7	8	9	10	11	12
1.	Arunachal Pradesh	40(60.0)	45(64.4)	34(52.9)	60(55.0)	50.0	6.1	55.0	29.0	2.0	–
2.	Assam	597(0.3)	622(0.3)	622(0.3)	1131(47.4)	89.4	129.6	945.0	827.0	859.0	562.8
3.	Manipur	12(25.0)	12(25.0)	47(4.3)	158(52.5)	1216.7	0.3	1.0	0.0	1.0	233.3
4.	Meghalaya	189(98.9)	189(98.9)	188(98.9)	288(89.7)	52.4	54.1	674	595.0	636.0	1075.6
5.	Mizoram	26(19.2)	37(21.6)	33(12.1)	117(32.5)	350.0	1.4	14.0	11.0	6.0	328.6
6.	Nagaland	6(66.7)	6(66.7)	27(92.6)	103(76.5)	1616.7	0.3	3.0	24.0	3.0	900.0
7.	Tripura	77(20.8)	86(18.6)	127(12.6)	245(31.9)	218.2	19.1	308.0	492.0	547.0	2763.9
8.	Sub-Total, NER	947(26.5)	997(23.6)	1078(24.7)	2102(45.8)	122.0	210.9	2000.0	1978.0	2054.0	873.9
9.	Sikkim	36(91.7)	38(88.8)	37(86.9)	116((34.5)	222.2	6.1	52.0	36.0	59.0	867.2
10.	Grand Total, NER	983(27.9)	1035(24.0)	1115(25.7)	2218(46.3)	125.6	217.0	2052.0	2014.0	2113.0	873.7
11.	India	87595(24.7)	97884(29.0)	112684(26.2)	126994(26.1)	45.0	36708.3	448166.0	525301.0	552655.0	1405.5

Source: Statistical Abstract, India, 2005 and 2006, Central Statistical Organisation, New Delhi and NER – VISION-2020,. Ministry of DONER, NEC, Vol. III.

Note: Figure within bracket indicates the percentage of Hydel Power in Cols. 3 to 6.

Appendix 8.5

State-wise Electricity Consumption by End Consumers from 1996 to 2005

(In Gwh)

Sl. No	Name of the State/NER /India	Electricity Consumed by End Consumers During								
		1997-98	1998-99	1999-00	2000-01	2001-02	2002-03	2003-04	2004-05	% Increase in 2004-05 over 1997-98 i.e. within a Gap of 7 Years
1	2	3	4	5	6	7	8	9	10	11
1.	Arunachal Pradesh	111.3	99.6	81.0	102.4	75.2	79.2	125.0	166.5	49.6
2.	Assam	1871.6	1752.9	1809.0	1911.2	1818.0	1960.8	1920.4	1838.0	–1.8
3.	Manipur	322.2	179.9	173.1	176.9	168.7	178.6	175.4	177.6	–44.9
4.	Meghalaya	321.4	348.5	386.4	417.2	550.7	713.0	797.0	855.9	166.3
5.	Mizoram	83.7	103.4	113.8	136.8	132.4	147.7	123.0	125.7	50.2
6.	Nagaland	131.9	128.4	138.2	165.5	117.2	126.5	136.2	183.2	38.9
7.	Tripura	314.6	396.9	356.1	303.0	348.0	363.0	414.3	380.0	20.8
8.	Sub-Total, NER	3156.7	3009.6	3057.6	3213.0	3210.2	3568.8	3691.3	3726.9	18.1
9.	Sikkim	92.5	98.0	105.8	103.2	123.3	73.3	182.2	226.7	145.1
10.	Grand Total, NER	3249.2	3107.6	3163.4	3316.2	3333.5	3642.1	3873.5	3953.6	21.7
11.	India	296748.9	309734.1	312841.1	316599.6	322459.3	339598.3	360937.2	386133.7	30.1

Source: Statistical Abstract, India, 2005 and 2006, Central Statistical Organisation, New Delhi and NER – VISION – 2020,. Ministry of DONER, NEC, Vol. III.

Appendix 8.6

State–wise Number of Towns and Villages Electrified

Sl. No.	Name of the State/NER/India	Towns			Villages		
		Total Number (2001 Census)	Number Electrified as on 31.3.2005	Percentage Electrified	Total Number (2001 Census)	Number Electrified as on 31.3.2005	Percentage Electrified
1	2	3	4	5	6	7	8
1.	Arunachal Pradesh	17	17	100	3863	1867	48.3
2.	Assam	125	125	100	39015*	20006*	51.3
3.	Manipur	33	33	100	2315	1903	82.2
4.	Meghalaya	16	16	100	5782	3328	57.6
5.	Mizoram	22	22	100	707	570	80.6
6.	Nagaland	9	9	100	1278	855	66.9
7.	Tripura	23	23	100	858	491	57.2
8.	Sub-Total, NER	245	245	100	14803	9014	53.9
9.	Sikkim	9	9	100	450	425	94.4
10.	Grand Total, NER	254	254	100	15253	9439	54.3
11.	India	5161	5161	100	593732	439800	74.1

Source: Statistical Abstract, India, 2005 and 2006, Central Statistical Organisation, New Delhi.

Note: * – Indicates, Data are Tentative.

Appendix 8.7

State-wise Distribution of Households having Electricity

Sl. No.	Name of the State / NER / India	Percentage of Households having Electricity						
		As per 2001 Census			As per NSS 59th round (Jan, 03 to Dec, 03)		As per NSS 60th Round (Jan, 04 to June, 04)	
		Total	Rural	Urban	Rural	Urban	Rural	Urban
1	2	3	4	5	6	7	8	9
1.	Arunachal Pradesh	54.69	44.53	89.42	NR	NR	50.8	NR
2.	Assam	24.90	16.54	74.29	25.4	82.8	25.8	95.9
3.	Manipur	60.04	52.53	81.99	68.5	NR	80.9	95.7
4.	Meghalaya	42.74	30.26	88.14	66.4	NR	NR	NR
5.	Mizoram	69.63	44.14	94.42	NR	NR	NR	99.7
6.	Nagaland	63.60	56.88	90.33	NR	NR	NR	NR
7.	Tripura	41.84	31.75	86.36	57.4	NR	63.2	NR
8.	Sikkim	77.76	75.02	97.09	NR	NR	NR	NR
9.	India	55.85	43.53	87.58	51.6	90.8	53.5	92.2

Note: NR—indicates Not Reported.

Source: Statistical Abstract, India, 2005 and 2006, Central Statistical Organization, New Delhi.

Appendix 9.1

State-wise Position of Large and Medium Industries and Growth of Small Scale Industries (SSI) in North Eastern Region

Sl. No.	*Name of the State / NER / India*	*Large and Medium Industries As on March,2003*		*Number and Percentage Increase of SSI during 1997-98 to 2002-03*						
		Number of Units	*% to NER*	*Number (N) / % Increase over Previous Year (P)*	*1997-1998*	*1998-1999*	*1999-2000*	*2000-2001*	*2001-2002*	*2002-2003*
1	2	3	4	5	6	7	8	9	10	11
1.	Arunachal Pradesh	15	7.04	N	4456	4546	4694	4750	4797	5022
				P	7.00	2.01	3.26	1.19	1.00	4.70
2.	Assam	120	56.34	N	34258	36482	38303	40419	42947	45193
				P	6.84	6.49	4.99	5.52	6.25	5.23
3.	Manipur	12	5.63	N	5322	5447	5587	5778	5868	5974
				P	3.08	2.35	2.57	3.42	1.54	1.81
4.	Meghalaya	49	23.00	N	2982	3247	3505	3778	4044	4213
				P	8.87	8.87	7.94	7.79	7.04	4.18
5.	Mizoram	1	0.47	N	3907	4313	4490	4610	4970	5293
				P	6.40	10.39	4.10	2.67	7.94	6.49

(Contd.)

Appendix 9.1 (*Contd.*)

1	2	3	4	5	6	7	8	9	10	11
6.	Nagaland	5	2.35	N	712	982	1276	1600	1969	2513
				P	15.78	37.92	29.93	25.39	23.06	27.63
7.	Tripura	8	3.76	N	1798	1867	1931	1967	2000	2020
				P	3.90	3.83	3.31	1.86	1.67	1.00
8.	Sikkim	3	1.41	N	294	306	322	333	341	351
				P	4.60	4.06	5.53	3.08	2.39	2.92
9.	Total NER	213	100.00	N	53729	57190	60108	63235	66936	70579
				P	6.25	6.44	5.10	5.20	5.85	5.44

Source: Indian Institute of Entrepreneurship (IIE), Guwahati

Appendix 9.2

State-wise Details of Working/Closed SIS Units and their Percentage Distribution According to Principal Characteristics

Sl. No.	Name of the State / NER / India	Status of Registered SSI Units as on 2001 -02				Percentage Distribution of Principal Characteristics of Registered SSI Units				
		Number of Working Units	Number of Closed Units	% of Closed Units to NER	% of Closed Units to All India	Number of Working Units	Market Value of Fixed Assets	Original Value of Plant & Machine rise (P&M)	Employment	Gross Output
1	2	3	4	5	6	7	8	9	10	11
1.	Arunachal Pradesh	255	248	1.51	0.03	0.02	0.02	0.01	0.02	0.02
2.	Assam	14453	10338	63.05	1.16	1.05	0.52	0.73	1.05	0.57
3.	Manipur	4599	1226	7.48	0.14	0.33	0.09	0.07	0.32	0.05
4.	Meghalaya	1939	1908	11.64	0.22	0.14	0.04	0.07	0.17	0.05
5.	Mizoram	2733	1313	8.01	0.15	0.20	0.07	0.09	0.15	0.03
6.	Nagaland	568	129	0.79	0.01	0.04	0.06	0.07	0.08	0.05
7.	Tripura	959	1077	6.57	0.12	0.07	0.26	0.08	0.19	0.08
8.	Sikkim	174	155	0.95	0.02	0.01	0.01	0.01	0.02	0.01
9.	Total NER	25680	16394	100.00	1.85	NA	NA	NA	NA	NA
10.	India	1374974	887427	–	100.00	100.00	100.00	100.00	100.00	100.00

Source: Indian Institute of Entrepreneurship (IIP), Guwahati.

Note: NA—Indicate Not Available

Appendix 9.3

State-wise Percentage Distribution of Sick SSI Units and Entrepreneurs Trained by IIE and Units Set-up for NEC, IDBI and SIDBI Sponsored Programmes (April,1994 to March, 2004)

Sl. No.	Name of the State / NER / India	Percentage Distribution of Sick Units (as per census of SSI, 2001-02)				Details of Entrepreneurs Trained by IIE and Units set-up (During April,1994—March, 2004)							
		Sick Units (Erosion of Net worth or Delay in Repayment)	Incipient Sick Units (Continuous Decline in Gross Output)	Sick / Incipient Sick Units	Sick Units as per RBI Criteria	No. of Entrepre -neurs Trained	Applied for Bank Finance		Units set-up		Units set-up with Bank Finance		
							Num-ber	% of (8) to (7)	Num-ber	% of (10) to (7)	% of (10) to (8)	Num-ber	% of (13) to (8)
1	2	3	4	5	6	7	8	9	10	11	12	13	14
1.	Arunachal Pradesh	0.02	0.01	0.01	0.02	172	91	52.90	82	47.67	90.11	41	45.05
2.	Assam	1.23	1.01	1.02	0.98	623	297	47.67	213	34.19	71.72	76	25.59
3.	Manipur	0.12	0.53	0.50	0.12	354	153	43.22	125	35.31	81.70	46	30.07
4.	Meghalaya	0.22	0.06	0.08	0.26	323	161	49.85	100	30.96	62.11	38	23.60
5.	Mizoram	0.02	0.01	0.01	0.01	100	65	65.00	24	24.00	36.92	14	21.50
6.	Nagaland	0.01	0.00	0.00	0.01	158	95	60.13	57	36.08	60.00	31	32.63
7.	Tripura	0.45	0.21	0.20	0.54	235	120	51.06	55	23.40	45.83	27	22.50
8.	Sikkim	0.02	0.01	0.01	0.01	34	15	44.12	5	14.71	33.33	2	13.33
9.	Total NER	NA	NA	NA	NA	1999	997	49.87	661	33.07	66.29	275	27.58
10.	India	100.00	100.00	100.00	100.00	NA	NA	NA	NA	NA	NA	NA	NA

Source: Indian Institute of Entrepreneurship (IIP), Guwahati.

Note: NA—Not Available.

Appendix 9.4

State-wise Rural-Urban Distribution of Small-Scale Industries (SSI) According to Activities and their Gross Output and Employment, 2001-02

Sl. No.	Name of the State / NER / India	Distribution of SSI Units in per cent							Gross Output and Employment in SSI			
		Manufacturing		Repairing and Maintenance		Services		Total	Output (Rs. in Lakhs)	Per cent of Total Output	Employment (In No.)	Per cent of Total Employment
		Rural	Urban	Rural	Urban	Rural	Urban					
1	2	3	4	5	6	7	8	9	10	11	12	13
1.	Arunachal Pradesh	12.38	22.20	2.24	29.47	3.67	30.03	100.00	5645.4	0.02	3687	0.01
2.	Assam	32.70	8.99	18.89	8.14	22.30	8.98	100.00	330255.9	1.17	429003	1.72
3.	Manipur	52.44	13.30	6.90	7.24	12.48	7.64	100.00	47985.9	0.17	136811	0.55
4.	Meghalaya	47.32	12.61	0.79	16.59	2.55	20.14	100.00	33872.4	0.12	65586	0.26
5.	Mizoram	17.04	32.53	0.03	2.69	31.64	16.08	100.00	14113.5	0.05	24850	0.10
6.	Nagaland	62.77	11.75	9.88	1.22	9.44	4.95	100.00	36695.1	0.13	56795	0.23
7.	Tripura	10.06	15.14	5.83	12.00	22.56	34.40	100.00	31049.7	0.11	56962	0.23
8.	Sikkim	32.07	31.79	0.00	2.99	1.09	32.07	100.00	2822.7	0.01	1322	0.01
9.	Total NER	NA	NA	NA	NA	NA	NA	NA	502440.6	1.78	775016	3.11
10.	India	25.31	14.38	8.37	7.99	21.53	22.42	100.00	28226998.0	100.00	24932763	100.00

Source: Third Census Report, Small-Scale Industry, 2001-02.

Appendix 9.5

State-wise Details of Handlooms and Handicrafts, 1995-96

Sl. No.	Name of the State/NER/India	Type of Handlooms in Number			Details of Handicrafts					
		Working Looms	Idle Looms	Total Looms	Units		Artisans		Production	
					Number	Percentage to Total	Number	Percentage to Total	Rs. in Crores	Percentage to Total
1	2	3	4	5	6	7	8	9	10	11
1.	Arunachal Pradesh	45060	456	45516	4044	0.31	15735	0.38	855.56	3.25
2.	Assam	1298731	110437	1409168	30360	2.39	100482	2.45	7820.94	29.72
3.	Manipur	266915	3346	270261	98051	7.74	379988	9.29	147.60	0.56
4.	Meghalaya	7783	418	8201	11512	0.90	53564	1.31	2580.67	9.80
5.	Mizoram	14388	9406	23794	2213	0.17	5260	0.12	5.93	0.02
6.	Nagaland	71636	5867	77503	17603	1.39	79878	1.95	9463.99	35.98
7.	Tripura	116659	2413	119072	77375	6.11	244495	5.98	60.80	0.23
8.	Sub-Total, NER	1821172	132343	1953515	241158	19.05	879402	21.43	20935.49	79.56
9.	Sikkim	NA	NA	NA	2198	0.17	9768	0.23	5.59	0.02
10.	Grand Total, NER	1821172	132343	1953515	243356	19.22	889170	21.71	20941.08	79.58
11.	India	NA	NA	NA	1266009	100.00	4103293	100.00	26312.13	100.00

Source: NER Data Bank, based on Handloom and Handicraft Census of India, 1995-96.

Appendix 9.6

State-wise Details of Physical Performance of Khadi and Village Industries During 2002-03

Sl. No.	Name of the State / NER / India	Production (Rs. In lakh)				Sales (Rs. In lakh)				Employment (In lakh Persons)				Earnings (Rs. In lakh)			
		Khadi	Poly-ester	V.I.	Total	Khadi	Poly-ester	V.I.	Total	Khadi	Poly-ester	V.I.	Total	Khadi	Poly-ester	V.I.	Total
1	2	3	4	5	6	7	8	9	10	11	12	13	14	15	16	17	18
1.	Arunachal Pradesh	3.57	–	314.31	317.88	9.21	0.06	437.64	446.91	*	–	0.01	0.01	1.87	–	148.99	150.86
2.	Assam	446.69	9.34	5628.05	6084.08	355.27	9.53	5366.29	5731.09	0.10	*	1.12	1.12	168.02	2.50	2248.16	2418.68
3.	Manipur	47.57	3.33	5949.95	6000.85	58.67	5.18	5598.07	5661.92	0.10	*	0.61	0.61	21.45	0.57	2610.66	2632.68
4.	Meghalaya	4.42	1.15	3096.04	3101.61	6.23	0.34	3836.07	3842.64	*	*	0.25	0.25	2.01	0.36	1947.87	1950.24
5.	Mizoram	2.70	–	3766.74	3769.44	2.91	–	5060.91	5063.82	*	*	0.23	0.23	3.44	–	1489.23	1492.67
6.	Nagaland	56.01	–	4527.93	4583.94	55.68	1.40	5452.34	5509.06	0.01	*	0.29	0.30	13.17	–	2998.54	3011.71
7.	Tripura	3.30	–	2231.99	2235.29	9.50	–	2370.35	2379.85	*	*	0.28	0.28	2.20	–	645.16	647.36
8.	Sub–Total, NER	564.26	13.82	25515.01	26093.09	497.47	16.51	28121.67	28635.29	0.21	NA	2.79	2.80	212.16	3.43	12088.61	12304.20
9.	Sikkim	4.34	–	369.17	373.51	11.56	–	211.34	222.90	*	*	0.06	0.06	1.31	–	103.65	104.96
10.	Grand Total, NER	568.60	13.82	25884.18	26466.60	509.03	16.51	28333.01	28858.19	0.21	NA	2.85	2.86	213.47	3.43	12192.26	12409.16

Source: Commissioner for Khadi and Village Industries, Guwahati.

Note: *means Less than 500; NA—Not available.

Appendix 9.6 (Contd.)

State-wise Details of Physical Performance of Khadi and Village Industries during 2003-04

Sl. No.	Name of the State/NER /India	Production (Rs. In lakh)				Sales (Rs. In lakh)				Employment (In lakh Persons)				Earnings (Rs. In lakh)			
		Khadi	Poly-ester	V.I.	Total	Khadi	Poly-ester	V.I.	Total	Kha-di	Poly-ester	V.I.	Total	Khadi	Poly-ester	V.I.	Total
1	2	3	4	5	6	7	8	9	10	11	12	13	14	15	16	17	18
1.	Arunachal Pradesh	5.52	0.11	462.91	468.54	12.14	0.25	570.82	583.21	*	–	0.01	0.01	2.06	0.02	183.34	185.42
2.	Assam	395.38	10.35	7612.20	8017.93	297.86	10.52	9673.13	9981.51	0.10	*	1.12	1.22	139.21	2.97	3304.32	3446.50
3.	Manipur	58.74	–	5970.50	6029.24	63.39	–	6006.49	6069.88	0.10	*	0.61	0.71	9.75	–	2680.39	2690.14
4.	Meghalaya	5.41	1.00	3196.03	3202.44	6.10	1.20	3289.91	3297.21	*	*	0.25	0.25	–	–	1998.65	1998.65
5.	Mizoram	49.02	–	4008.78	4057.80	41.79	–	4176.23	4218.02	*	*	0.26	0.26	2.74	–	1658.34	1661.08
6.	Nagaland	40.95	–	4732.75	4773.70	47.78	1.31	5151.19	5200.28	0.01	*	0.29	0.30	17.49	–	3137.86	3155.35
7.	Tripura	2.08	–	3601.81	3603.89	1.32	–	4253.87	4255.19	*	*	0.30	0.30	–	–	1252.43	1252.43
8.	Sub–Total, NER	557.10	11.46	29584.98	30153.54	470.38	13.28	33121.64	33605.30	0.21	*	2.84	3.05	171.25	2.99	14215.33	14389.57
9.	Sikkim	7.27	–	433.91	441.18	8.98	0.02	523.45	532.45	*	*	0.06	0.06	–	–	134.85	134.85
10.	Grand Total, NER	564.37	11.46	30018.89	30594.72	479.36	13.30	33645.09	34137.75	0.21	*	2.90	3.11	171.25	2.99	14350.18	14524.42

Source: Commissioner for Khadi and Village Industries, Guwahati.

Note: *means Less than 500.

Appendix 9.7

State-wise Details of Sericulture Activities from 1999-2004

Sl. No.	Name of the State/NER/India	Area covered under Mulberry Cultivation (In hectares)				Production of Mulberry Reeling Cocoons (MT)				Production of Oak Tasar Reeling Cocoons (lakh nos.)			
		1999-2000	2000-2001	2002-2003	2003-2004	1999-2000	2000-2001	2002-2003	2003-2004	1999-2000	2000-2001	2002-2003	2003-2004
1	2	3	4	5	6	7	8	9	10	11	12	13	14
1.	Arunachal Pradesh	219.00	526.00	230.20	237.40	3.00	8.10	18.00	0.70	0.44	0.50	1.08	0.60
2.	Assam	3200.00	3442.00	4151.70	4477.42	194.00	219.89	158.16	80.00	–	–	0.38	0.38
3.	Manipur	5403.00	6186.00	7413.00	NA	560.00	320.00	221.20	NA	11.20	2.52	8.40	NA
4.	Meghalaya	160.00	270.00	67.20	917.72	16.00	22.56	18.05	21.43	–	–	NA	NA
5.	Mizoram	1200.00	2000.00	1557.60	2209.60	18.00	399.00	15.00	45.00	–	2.66	3.09	2.70
6.	Nagaland	688.00	688.00	305.20	305.20	2.68	4.10	3.29	2.99	6.30	–	1.32	2.55
7.	Tripura	675.00	906.00	675.00	–	35.00	38.00	39.50	39.50	NIL	NIL	–	–
8.	Sub–Total, NER	11545.00	14022.00	14399.90	8147.34	828.68	1011.65	473.20	189.62	17.94	5.68	14.27	6.23
9.	Sikkim	NA	NA	NA	NA	NA	NA	NA	NA	NA	NA	NA	NA
10.	Grand Total, NER	11545.00	14022.00	14399.90	8147.34	828.68	1011.65	473.20	189.62	17.94	5.68	14.27	6.23

Source: Office of the Director (NE), Central Silk Board, Guwahati.

Note: NA—Not available.

Appendix 9.7 (Contd.)

State-wise Details of Sericulture Activities from 1999-2004

Sl. No.	Name of the State/NER/India	Production of Eri Cut Cocoons (MT) in					Production of Muga Reeling Cocoons (Lakh Nos.)				
		1998-1999	1999-2000	2000-2001	2002-2003	2003-2004	1998-1999	1999-2000	2000-2001	2002-2003	2003--2004
1	2	15	16	17	18	19	20	21	22	23	24
1.	Arunachal Pradesh	16.50	6.40	13.40	15.00	4.00	10.05	1.65	6.37	12.93	7.50
2.	Assam	640.00	629.00	595.84	634.77	652.61	3430.00	4126.00	5106.00	4781.48	4549.55
3.	Manipur	485.00	482.00	419.00	256.00	NA	3.36	4.20	4.45	1.20	NA
4.	Meghalaya	213.27	267.80	315.65	360.74	422.53	76.12	121.10	127.70	216.96	289.91
5.	Mizoram	4.92	5.00	14.00	0.93	3.80	–	–	2.75	1.75	4.00
6.	Nagaland	35.86	37.22	40.00	101.24	119.70	1.17	0.96	3.25	1.70	2.65
7.	Tripura	NA	NA	NA	–	–	NA	NA	NA	–	–
8.	Sub-Total, NER	1395.55	1427.42	1397.89	1368.68	1202.64	3520.70	4253.91	5250.52	5016.02	4853.61
9.	Sikkim	NA	NA	NA	NA	NA	NA	NA	NA	NA	NA
10.	Grand Total, NER	1395.55	1427.42	1397.89	1368.68	1202.64	3520.70	4253.91	5250.52	5016.02	4853.61

Source: Office of the Director (NE), Central Silk Board, Guwahati.

Note: NA—Not available.

Appendix 9.8

State-wise Details of Factories, Input, Output, Workers, Emoluments, Net Value Added at Industry in 2003-04 and 2004-05

(Value in Rs. Ten Million, Others in Number)

Sl. No.	Name of the State/NER/India	Year / % increase	Item-wise Details								
			Number of Factories	Fixed Capital	Working Capital	Productive Capital	Invested Capital	Number of Workers	Total Persons Engaged	Wages to Workers	Total Emoluments
1	2	3	4	5	6	7	8	9	10	11	12
1.	Assam	2003-04	1570	6696	1946	8642	9321	95936	113993	306	518
		2004-05	1710	7030	2043	9073	10226	101265	119548	336	561
		% increase (+) or decrease (–)	8.92	4.99	4.98	4.99	9.71	5.55	4.87	9.80	8.30
2.	Manipur	2003-04	45	6	2	440	8	1090	1231	2	2
		2004-05	55	9	6	14	13	1607	1835	3	4
		% increase (+) or decrease (–)	22.22	8.33	200.00	–96.82	62.50	47.43	49.07	50.00	100.00
3.	Meghalaya	2003-04	47	107	76	*	157	1773	2228	5	9
		2004-05	58	147	161	308	217	2405	3037	13	23
		% increase (+) or decrease (–)	23.40	37.38	111.84	*	38.22	35.65	36.31	160.00	155.55

(Contd.)

Appendix 9.8 (*Contd.*)

1	2	3	4	5	6	7	8	9	10	11	12
4.	Nagaland	2003-04	120	28	28	*	64	2356	2802	4	6
		2004-05	113	27	36	63	65	2332	2821	5	7
		% increase (+) or decrease (–)	–5.83	–3.57	28.57	*	1.56	–1.02	0.68	25.00	16.67
5.	Tripura	2003-04	269	50	63	*	118	13105	14508	20	27
		2004-05	275	61	101	161	149	13818	15392	21	29
		% increase (+) or decrease (–)	2.23	22	60.32	*	26.27	5.44	6.09	5	7.41
6.	Total NER	2003-04	2051	6887	2115	9082	9668	114260	134762	337	562
		2004-05	2211	7274	2347	9619	10670	121427	143869	378	624
		% increase (+) or decrease (–)	7.80	5.62	10.97	5.91	10.36	6.27	6.76	12.17	11.03
7.	India	2003-04	129074	473331	119231	592562	679598	6086908	7870081	30478	58337
		2004-05	136353	512346	160054	672399	758694	6599298	8453624	33635	64408
		% increase (+) or decrease (–)	5.64	8.24	34.24	13.47	11.64	8.42	7.41	10.36	10.41

Note: *means the amount is very less.

Source: Annual Survey of Industries, 2006-07, Central Statistical Organization, Govt. of India, Kolkata.

Appendix 9.8 (*Contd.*)

State-wise Details of Factories, Input, Output, Workers, Emoluments, Net Value Added at Industry in 2003-04 and 2004-05

(Value in Rs. Ten Million, Others in Number)

Sl. No.	Name of the State / NER / India	Year /% increase	Item-wise Details						
			Fuels Consumed	Materials Consumed	Total Input	Products and By-Products	Total Output	Depreciation	Net Value Added
1	2	3	13	14	15	16	17	18	19
1.	Assam	2003-04	697	9887	12093	15065	16306	473	3741
		2004-05	832	12997	17820	19915	22050	509	3721
		% increase (+) or decrease (–)	19.37	31.45	47.36	32.19	35.23	7.61	–0.53
2.	Manipur	2003-04	3	10	14	17	18	1	3
		2004-05	4	21	28	33	35	1	6
		% increase (+) or decrease (–)	33.33	110.00	100.00	94.12	94.44	0.00	100.00
3.	Meghalaya	2003-04	48	217	312	359	377	13	52
		2004-05	58	340	460	538	568	16	92
		% increase (+) or decrease (–)	20.83	56.68	47.43	49.86	50.66	23.08	76.92
4.	Nagaland	2003-04	4	71	84	97	104	2	18
		2004-05	5	74	88	104	110	2	20
		% increase (+) or decrease (–)	25.00	4.22	4.76	7.22	5.77	0.00	11.11

(*Contd.*)

Appendix 9.8 (Contd.)

1	2	3	13	14	15	16	17	18	19
5.	Tripura	2003-04	19	189	284	286	358	6	68
		2004-05	22	276	378	494	616	7	231
		% increase (+) or cecrease (–)	15.79	46.03	33.10	72.73	72.07	16.67	239.71
6.	Total NER	2003-04	771	10374	12787	15824	17163	495	3882
		2004-05	921	13708	18774	21084	23379	535	4070
		% increase (+) or decrease (–)	19.45	32.14	46.82	33.24	36.22	8.08	4.84
7.	India	2003-04	73713	793285	1039624	1135722	1287380	44823	202933
		2004-05	85854	1024347	1362942	1445203	1672561	49713	259907
		% increase (+) or decrease (–)	16.47	29.13	31.1	27.25	29.92	10.91	28.07

Source: Annual Survey of Industries, 2006 - 07, Central Statistical Organization, Govt. of India, Kolkata.

Note: * means the amount is very less.

Appendix 9.8 (Contd.)

State-wise Details of Factories, Input, Output, Workers, Emoluments, Net Value Added at Industry in 2003-04 and 2004-05

(Value in Rs. Ten Million, Others in Number)

Sl. No.	Name of the State/NER/India	Year/% Increase	Item-wise Details			Value of Addition in Stock			
			Rent Paid for Fixed Assets	Interest Paid	Gross Fixed Capital Formation	Total	Materials, Fuels etc.	Semi Finished Goods	Finished Goods
1	2	3	20	21	22	23	24	25	26
1.	Assam	2003-04	29	272	1091	653	233	76	344
		2004-05	24	222	692	511	276	92	143
		% increase (+) or decrease (–)	–17.24	–18.38	–36.57	–21.75	18.45	21.05	–58.43
2.	Manipur	2003-04	–	–	1	0	–	–	–
		2004-05	0	1	0	2	2	0	0
		% increase (+) or decrease (–)	–	–	–	–	–	–	–
3.	Meghalaya	2003-04	2	5	15	11	7	2	3
		2004-05	2	6	12	3	1	3	5
		% increase (+) or decrease (–)	0.00	20.00	–20.00	–72.73	–85.71	50.00	66.67
4.	Nagaland	2003-04	–	3	2	5	7	–	–1
		2004-05	0	3	3	0	1	0	–1
		% increase (+) or decrease (–)	–	0.00	50.00	–	–85.71	–	0.00

(Contd.)

Appendix 9.8 (*Contd.*)

1	2	3	20	21	22	23	24	25	26
5.	Tripura	2003-04	1	4	5	18	16	–	2
		2004-05	2	5	12	19	–3	18	4
		% increase (+) or decrease (–)	100.00	25.00	140.00	5.55	–118.75	–	100.00
6.	Total NER	2003-04	32	284	1114	687	263	78	377
		2004-05	28	237	719	535	277	113	151
		% increase (+) or decrease (–)	–12.50	–16.55	–35.46	–22.13	5.32	44.87	–59.95
7.	India	2003-04	4161	33972	57534	16653	13188	1308	2156
		2004-05	4538	32454	74590	34822	23775	6420	4627
		% increase (+) or decrease (–)	9.06	–4.47	29.65	109.10	80.28	390.82	114.61

Source: Annual Survey of Industries, 2006-07, Central Statistical Organization, Govt. of India, Kolkata.

Note: * means the amount is very less.

Appendix 10.1

Domestic and Foreign Tourists Visited India from 1991 to 2007

Sl. No.	Year	Type and Number of Tourists Visited		Total	Annual Growth Rate (in per cent)		
		Domestic	Foreign		Domestic	Foreign	Total
1	2	3	4	5	6	7	8
1.	1991	66670303	3146652	69816955	–	–	–
2.	1992	81455861	3095160	84551021	22.2	–1.6	21.1
3.	1993	105811696	3541727	109353423	29.9	14.4	29.3
4.	1994	127118655	4030216	131148871	20.1	13.8	19.9
5.	1995	136643600	4641279	141284879	7.5	15.2	7.7
6.	1996	140119672	5030342	145150014	2.5	8.4	2.7
7.	1997	159877208	5500419	165377627	14.1	9.3	13.9
8.	1998	168196000	5539704	173735704	5.2	0.7	5.1
9.	1999	190671034	5832015	196503049	13.4	5.3	13.1
10.	2000	220106911	5893542	226000453	15.4	1.1	15.0
11.	2001	236469599	5436261	241905860	7.4	–7.8	7.0
12.	2002	269598028	5157518	274755546	14.0	–5.1	13.6
13.	2003	309038335	6708479	315746814	14.6	30.1	14.9
14.	2004	366267522	8360278	374627800	18.5	24.6	18.6
15.	2005	391948589	9949676	401898265	7.0	19.0	7.3
16.	2006	462310177	11747914	474058091	18.0	18.1	18.0
17.	2007	526564364	13230839	539795203	13.9	12.6	13.9

Source: Govt. of India, Ministry of Tourism (Market Research Division), New Delhi.

Appendix 10.2

State-wise Domestic and Foreign Tourists Visited North Eastern States from 2001 to 2007

Sl. No.	Name of the State/NER/India	During 2001			During 2002			During 2003		
		Domestic	Foreign	Total	Domestic	Foreign	Total	Domestic	Foreign	Total
1	2	3	4	5	6	7	8	9	10	11
1.	Arunachal Pradesh	6349	323	6672	4372	187	4559	2195	123	2318
2.	Assam	1010651	6171	1016822	1953915	6409	1960324	2156675	6610	2163285
3.	Manipur	76527	183	76710	89633	221	89854	92923	257	93180
4.	Meghalaya	178697	2390	181087	268609	3146	271755	371953	6304	378257
5.	Mizoram	28771	152	28923	29417	259	29676	35129	279	35408
6.	Nagaland	9948	926	10874	14263	657	14920	5605	743	6348
7.	Tripura	254912	1512	256424	260586	2602	263188	257331	3196	260527
8.	Sub-total, NER	1565855	11657	1577512	2620795	13481	2634276	2921811	17512	2939323
9.	Sikkim	203306	31028	234334	159342	8566	167908	179661	11966	191627
10.	Total NER	1769161	42685	1811846	2780137	22047	2802184	3101472	29478	3130950
11.	India	236469599	5436261	241905860	269598028	5157518	274755546	309038335	6708479	315746814

Source: Government of India, Ministry of Tourism (Market Research Division), New Delhi.

Appendix 10.2 (Contd.)

State-wise Domestic and Foreign Tourists Visited North Eastern States from 2001 to 2007

(In Numbers)

Sl. No.	Name of the State/NER/ India	During 2004			During 2005			During 2006			During 2007		
		Domestic	Foreign	Total	Domestic	Foreign	Total	Domestic	Foreign	Total	Domestic	Foreign	Total
1	2	12	13	14	15	16	17	18	19	20	21	22	23
1.	Arunachal Pradesh	4740	269	5009	50560	313	50873	80137	706	80843	91100	2212	93312
2.	Assam	2288093	7285	2295378	2467652	10782	2478434	3268657	11151	3279808	3436833	12899	3449732
3.	Manipur	93476	249	93725	94299	316	94615	116984	295	117279	101484	396	101880
4.	Meghalaya	433495	12407	445902	375901	5099	381000	401529	4287	405816	457685	5267	462952
5.	Mizoram	38598	326	38924	44715	273	44988	50987	436	51423	43161	669	43830
6.	Nagaland	10056	1084	11140	17470	883	18353	15850	426	16276	22085	936	23021
7.	Tripura	260907	3171	264078	216330	2677	219007	230645	3245	233890	244795	3181	247976
8.	Sub-total, NER	3129365	24791	3154156	3266927	20343	3287270	4164789	20546	4185335	4397143	25560	4422703
9.	Sikkim	230719	14646	245365	251744	16523	268267	292486	18026	310512	329075	17498	346573
10.	Total NER	3360084	39437	3399521	3518671	36866	3555537	4457275	38572	4495847	4726218	43058	4769276
11.	India	366267522	8360278	374627800	391948589	9949676	401898265	462310177	11747914	474058091	526564364	13230839	539795203

Source: Government of India, Ministry of Tourism (Market Research Division), New Delhi.

Appendix 10.3

State-wise Growth of Domestic and Foreign Tourists from 2001-2002 to 2006-2007

Sl. No.	Name of the State/ NER/India	Growth during 2001-2002			Growth during 2002-2003			Growth during 2003-2004		
		Domestic	Foreign	Total	Domestic	Foreign	Total	Domestic	Foreign	Total
1	2	3	4	5	6	7	8	9	10	11
1.	Arunachal Pradesh	–31.14	–42.10	–31.67	–49.79	–34.22	–49.16	115.95	118.70	116.09
2.	Assam	93.33	3.86	92.79	10.38	3.14	10.35	6.09	10.21	6.11
3.	Manipur	17.13	20.76	17.13	3.67	16.29	3.70	0.60	–3.11	0.58
4.	Meghalaya	50.32	31.63	50.07	38.47	100.38	39.19	16.55	96.81	17.88
5.	Mizoram	2.25	70.39	2.60	19.42	7.72	19.32	9.87	16.85	9.93
6.	Nagaland	43.38	–29.05	37.21	–60.70	13.09	–57.45	79.41	45.90	75.49
7.	Tripura	2.23	72.09	2.64	–1.25	–22.83	–1.01	1.39	–0.78	1.36
8.	Sub-total NER	67.32	15.65	66.99	11.49	29.90	11.58	7.10	41.57	7.31
9.	Sikkim	–21.62	–72.39	–28.35	12.75	39.69	14.13	28.42	22.40	28.04
10.	Total NER	57.14	–48.35	54.66	11.56	33.70	11.73	8.34	33.78	8.58
11.	India	14.01	–5.13	13.58	14.63	30.07	14.92	18.52	24.62	18.65

Source: Government of India, Ministry of Tourism (Market Research Division), New Delhi.

Appendix 10.3 (*Contd.*)

State-wise Growth of Domestic and Foreign Tourists from 2001-2002 to 2006-2007

(*In Percentage*)

Sl. No.	Name of the State/NER/India	Growth during 2004-2005			Growth during 2005-2006			Growth during 2006-2007			Growth during 2001-2007 (i.e. in a gap of 6 years)		
		Domestic	Foreign	Total	Domestic	Foreign	Total	Domestic	Foreign	Total	Domestic	Foreign	Total
1	2	12	13	14	15	16	17	18	19	20	21	22	23
1.	Arunachal Pradesh	966.67	16.36	915.63	58.50	125.56	58.91	13.68	213.31	15.42	1334.87	584.83	1298.56
2.	Assam	7.85	48.00	7.97	32.46	3.42	32.33	5.15	15.68	5.18	240.06	109.03	239.27
3.	Manipur	0.88	26.91	0.95	24.06	–6.65	23.95	–13.25	34.24	–13.13	32.16	116.39	32.81
4.	Meghalaya	–13.29	–58.90	–14.56	6.82	–15.92	6.51	13.99	22.86	14.08	156.12	120.38	155.65
5.	Mizoram	15.85	–16.26	15.58	14.03	59.71	14.30	–15.35	53.44	–14.77	50.02	340.13	51.54
6.	Nagaland	73.73	–18.54	64.75	–9.27	–51.76	–11.32	39.34	119.72	41.44	122.00	1.08	111.71
7.	Tripura	–17.08	–15.58	–17.07	6.62	21.22	6.80	6.13	–1.97	6.02	–3.97	110.38	–3.29
8.	Sub-total, NER	4.40	–17.94	4.22	27.48	1.00	27.32	5.58	24.40	5.67	180.81	119.27	180.36
9.	Sikkim	9.11	12.82	9.33	16.18	9.10	15.75	12.51	–2.93	11.61	61.86	–43.61	47.90
10.	Total NER	4.72	–6.52	4.59	26.67	4.63	26.45	6.03	11.63	6.08	167.14	0.87	163.23
11.	India	7.01	19.01	7.28	17.95	18.07	17.95	13.90	12.62	13.87	122.68	143.38	123.14

Source: Government of India, Ministry of Tourism (Market Research Division), New Delhi.

Appendix 11.1

Position of Employment and Unemployment in India in Different Years (By Usual Principal Status)

Sl. No.	Status	Position in million in				Growth in per cent per annum		
		1983	1993-1994	1999-2000	2004-2005	1983 to 1993-94	1993-94 to 1999-2000	1999-2000 to 2004-05
1	2	3	4	5	6	7	8	9
1.	Labour Force	277.34	343.56	377.88	428.37	2.06	1.60	2.54
2.	Workforce	269.36	334.54	367.37	415.27	2.09	1.57	2.48
3.	Number of unemployed	7.98	9.02	10.51	13.10	1.30	2.75	2.93
4.	Unemployment rate (As a proportion of labour force in per cent)	2.88	2.62	2.78	3.06			

Source: Economic Survey, 2006-07; Ministry of Finance, Government of India, New Delhi.

Appendix 11.2

Details of Unemployment Rates in India for Different Rounds of the NSS

Sl. No.	Category/Round of NSS	Rural					
		Males			Females		
		Usual	CWS	CDS	Usual	CWS	CDS
1	2	3	4	5	6	7	8
1.	55th round (1999-2000)	2.1	3.9	7.2	1.5	3.7	7.0
2.	61st round (July, 2004-June, 2005)	2.1	3.8	8.0	3.1	4.2	8.7

Sl.No.	Category / Round of NSS	Urban					
		Males			Females		
		Usual	CWS	CDS	Usual	CWS	CDS
1.	55th round (1999-2000)	4.8	5.6	7.3	7.1	7.3	9.4
2.	61st round (July,2004-June, 2005)	4.4	5.2	7.5	9.1	9.0	11.6

Note: Usual: Usual Principal Status; CWS: Current Weekly Status; CDS: Current Daily Status

Source: Economic Survey, 2006-2007, Ministry of Finance, Government of India, New Delhi.

Appendix 11.3

State-wise Employment Exchange Statistics (All Categories) for the Years, 2000 and 2005

Sl. No.	Name of the State/NER/ India	Reference Year	No of Employment Exchanges/ UEIGBs *	No in Thousands					% of Live Register to Total Live Register (NER/India)	% of Placement to Submission
				Registration	Vacancies Notified	Submissions	Placements	Live Register *		
1	2	3	4	5	6	7	8	9	10	11
1.	Arunachal Pradesh	2000	8	7.4	0.4	1.6	@	21.0	0.9	@
		2005	10	4.9	@	3.6	@	25.1	0.9	0.0
2.	Assam	2000	53	137.2	3.5	49.8	1.3	1442.3	62.2	2.6
		2005	52	218.4	3.9	73.2	0.4	1760.8	62.1	0.5
3.	Manipur	2000	11	10.5	0.7	11.9	@	391.9	16.9	0.0
		2005	11	76.1	24.0	94.6	0.3	532.3	18.8	0.3
4.	Meghalaya	2000	10	11.8	0.4	3.4	0.2	35.4	1.5	5.9
		2005	11	9.0	0.9	2.8	@	38.0	1.3	0.0
5.	Mizoram	2000	3	15.2	0.8	10.0	0.3	88.7	3.8	3.0
		2005	3	2.8	0.8	2.3	NA	34.4	1.2	0.0
6.	Nagaland	2000	7	9.4	0.2	1.5	0.1	37.2	1.6	6.7
		2005	7	7.8	@	0.3	@	44.3	1.6	0.0
7.	Tripura	2000	5	23.8	0.3	3.6	0.9	303.9	13.1	25.0
		2005	5	24.9	0.2	1.7	0.2	399.7	14.1	11.8

(Contd.)

Appendix 11.3 (*Contd.*)

1	2	3	4	5	6	7	8	9	10	11
8.	Sub-Total, NER	2000	97	215.3	6.3	81.8	2.8	2320.4	100.0	3.4
		2005	99	343.9	29.8	178.5	0.9	2834.6	100.0	0.5
9.	Sikkim	2000			N			A		
		2005			N			A		
10.	Total NER	2000	97	215.3	6.3	81.8	2.8	2320.4	5.6	3.4
		2005	99	343.9	29.8	178.5	0.9	2834.6	7.2	0.5
11.	India	2000	958	6041.9	284.5	2322.8	177.7	41343.6	100.0	7.7
		2005	947	5437.1	349.2	2402.0	173.2	39347.8	100.0	7.2

Source: Employment Exchange Statistics, Government of India, Ministry of Labour and Employment, Directorate General of Employment and Training, Shram Shakti Bhawan, New Delhi-110 001.

Note: * – At the end of the Year; @-Figure less than 50

Appendix 11.4

State-wise Number of Job-Seekers on the Live Register According to Age Group for the Years, 1999 and 2004

(No. in Thousands)

Sl. No.	Name of the State / NER / India	Reference Year	Age Group in Years						Total
			Up to 19	20 – 29	30 – 39	40 – 49	50 – 59	Above 60	
1	2	3	4	5	6	7	8	9	10
1.	Arunachal Pradesh	1999	2.7	11.9	1.1	0.2	@	0.0	15.9
		2004	5.0	11.5	4.5	1.3	0.3	0.0	22.6
2.	Assam	1999	293.5	771.6	302.8	85.8	28.5	8.1	1490.3
		2004	368.4	873.2	318.7	66.8	4.5	0.4	1632.0
3.	Manipur	1999	88.6	210.2	72.0	12.1	2.8	@	385.7
		2004	100.7	239.4	94.3	19.2	4.0	0.1	457.7
4.	Meghalaya	1999	13.2	13.9	6.3	2.2	0.5	0.0	36.1
		2004	8.2	19.4	8.0	1.4	0.3	0.0	37.3
5.	Mizoram	1999	8.8	72.2	12.5	0.0	0.0	0.0	93.5
		2004	2.9	29.4	2.6	0.0	0.0	0.0	34.9

(Contd.)

Appendix 11.4 (*Contd.*)

1	2	3	4	5	6	7	8	9	10
6.	Nagaland	1999	7.5	25.5	3.3	0.2	@	0.0	36.5
		2004	20.8	17.2	5.5	0.3	0.1	0.0	43.9
7.	Tripura	1999	102.4	114.4	50.1	14.6	4.3	0.0	285.8
		2004	136.6	157.7	69.9	11.6	2.1	0.0	377.9
8.	Sub-Total, NER	1999	516.7	1219.7	448.1	115.1	36.1	8.1	2343.8
		2004	642.6	1347.8	503.5	100.6	11.3	0.5	2606.3
9.	Sikkim	1999		N			A		
		2004		N			A		
10.	Total NER	1999	516.7	1219.7	448.1	115.1	36.1	8.1	2343.8
		2004	642.6	1347.8	503.5	100.6	11.3	0.5	2606.3
11.	India	1999	8282.3	20782.1	9394.8	1600.5	267.6	44.1	40371.4
		2004	8814.2	19948.4	9443.9	1954.3	264.6	32.3	40457.7

Source: Employment Exchange Statistics, Government of India, Ministry of Labour and Employment, Directorate General of Employment and Training, Shram Shakti Bhawan, New Delhi-110 001.

Note: @–Figure less than 50.

Appendix 11.5

State-wise Employment Exchange Statistics on Women Job-Seekers for the Years, 2000 and 2005

Sl. No.	*Name of the State/ NER/India*	*Reference Year*	*No. of Employment Exchanges/UEIGBs **	*No in Thousands*			*% of Placement to Registration*
				Registration	*Placements*	*Live Register**	
1	2	3	4	5	6	7	8
1.	Arunachal Pradesh	2000	8	2.9	–	7.0	–
		2005	10	1.6	0.1	7.8	6.3
2.	Assam	2000	53	29.1	0.3	307.5	1.0
		2005	52	78.9	0.1	395.9	0.1
3.	Manipur	2000	11	2.0	@	105.1	NA
		2005	11	22.1	NA	138.9	NA
4.	Meghalaya	2000	10	4.9	@	14.6	NA
		2005	11	3.8	@	15.3	NA
5.	Mizoram	2000	3	3.0	0.1	26.1	3.3
		2005	3	1.3	NA	12.4	NA
6.	Nagaland	2000	7	2.5	@	9.1	NA
		2005	7	1.8	@	12.7	NA

(Contd.)

Appendix 11.5 (*Contd.*)

1	2	3	4	5	6	7	8
7.	Tripura	2000	5	7.1	0.3	114.6	4.2
		2005	5	8.9	0.1	146.3	1.1
8.	Sub-Total, NER	2000	97	51.5	0.7	584.0	1.4
		2005	99	118.4	0.3	729.3	0.3
9.	Sikkim	2000			N	A	
		2005			N	A	
10.	Total NER	2000	97	51.5	0.7	584.0	1.4
		2005	99	118.4	0.3	729.3	0.3
11.	India	2000	958	1646.3	35.7	10457.3	2.2
		2005	947	1606.9	32.4	10605.6	2.0

Source: Employment Exchange Statistics, Government of India, Ministry of Labour and Employment, Directorate General of Employment and Training, Shram Shakti Bhawan, New Delhi–110 001.

Note: * – At the end of the Year; @–Figure less than 50.

Appendix 11.6

State-wise Employment Exchange Statistics on SC, ST and OBC Job-Seekers for the Years, 1999 and 2004

(*No. in Thousands*)

Sl. No.	Name of the State/ NER/India	Reference Year	Scheduled Caste (SC)				Scheduled Tribe (ST)				Other Backward Class (OBC)			
			Registration	Placements	Live Register*	% of placement to Registration	Registration	Placements	Live Register *	% of placement to Registration	Registration	Placements	Live Register *	% of placement to Registration
1	2	3	4	5	6	7	8	9	10	11	12	13	14	15
1.	Arunachal Pradesh	1999	@	@	0.3	NA	1.6	NA	6.4	NA	0.1	@	0.2	NA
		2004	0.1	NA	0.9	NA	0.9	NA	12.1	NA	@	NA	0.2	NA
2.	Assam	1999	9.8	0.1	92.5	1.0	19.4	0.1	162.0	0.5	18.0	0.2	174.8	1.1
		2004	10.9	@	102.8	NA	20.1	@	192.5	NA	27.1	@	227.6	NA
3.	Manipur	1999	1.1	NA	5.9	NA	7.8	@	113.5	NA	0.1	NA	0.2	NA
		2004	0.2	NA	6.6	NA	4.7	NA	134.9	NA	@	NA	0.4	NA
4.	Meghalaya	1999	@	@	0.2	NA	9.1	@	28.7	NA	@	@	0.2	NA
		2004	@	NA	0.1	NA	7.2	@	28.6	NA	@	@	0.2	NA
5.	Mizoram	1999	NA	NA	NA	NA	21.8	0.3	76.9	1.4	NA	NA	NA	NA
		2004	NA	NA	NA	NA	0.7	NA	41.5	NA	NA	NA	NA	NA

(*Contd.*)

Appendix 11.6 (*Contd.*)

1	2	3	4	5	6	7	8	9	10	11	12	13	14	15
6.	Nagaland	1999	@	NA	0.2	NA	16.1	0.3	34.9	1.9	NA	NA	@	NA
		2004	@	NA	0.2	NA	11.0	@	43.3	NA	NA	NA	NA	NA
7.	Tripura	1999	1.3	@	43.4	NA	2.0	@	38.2	NA	0.2	NA	1.9	NA
		2004	2.4	0.1	64.7	4.2	3.4	0.2	65.4	5.9	1.4	@	11.9	NA
8.	Sub-Total, NER	1999	12.2	0.1	142.5	0.8	77.8	0.7	460.6	0.9	18.4	0.2	177.3	1.1
		2004	13.6	0.1	175.3	0.7	48.0	0.2	518.3	0.4	28.5	NA	240.3	NA
9.	Sikkim	1999			N				A					
		2004			N				A					
10.	Total NER	1999	12.2	0.1	142.5	0.8	77.8	0.7	460.6	0.9	18.4	0.2	177.3	1.1
		2004	13.6	0.1	175.3	0.7	48.0	0.2	518.3	0.4	28.5	NA	240.3	NA
11.	India	1999	760.2	28.6	5948.0	3.8	273.8	17.6	1762.4	6.4	936.9	24.2	6838.4	2.6
		2004	718.5	15.7	6470.0	2.2	277.7	8.3	2218.4	3.0	952.0	13.7	8205.3	1.4

Source: Employment Exchange Statistics, Government of India, Ministry of Labour and Employment, Directorate General of Employment and Training, Shram Shakti Bhawan, New Delhi-110 001.

Note: * – At the end of the Year; @ – Figure less than 50; NA — Not available

Appendix 11.7

State-wise Distribution of Workers, Non-workers and their Percentages as per 2001 census

Sl. No	Name of the State/ NER/India	Rural/ Urban/ Total	Total Workers			Total non-workers			Percentage of total workers to total population			Percentage of total non-workers to total population		
			Male	Female	Total	Male	Female	Total	Male	Female	Total	Male	Female	Total
1	2	3	4	5	6	7	8	9	10	11	12	13	14	15
1.	Arunachal Pradesh	R	230320	171690	402010	224360	243717	468077	50.66	41.33	46.20	49.34	58.67	53.80
		U	63292	17600	80892	61969	85020	146989	50.53	17.15	35.50	49.47	82.85	64.50
		T	293612	189290	482902	286329	328737	615066	50.63	36.54	43.98	49.37	63.46	56.02
2.	Assam	R	5899204	2497565	8396769	6040741	8778778	14819519	49.41	22.15	36.17	50.59	77.85	63.83
		U	971756	170066	1141822	865336	1432082	2297418	52.90	10.61	33.20	47.10	89.39	66.80
		T	6870960	2667631	9538591	6906077	10210860	17116937	49.88	20.17	35.78	50.12	79.29	64.22
3.	Manipur	R	398374	324713	723087	410579	457154	867733	49.25	41.53	45.45	50.75	58.47	54.55
		U	128842	93284	222126	157839	196003	353842	44.94	32.25	38.57	55.06	67.75	61.43
		T	527216	417997	945213	568418	653157	1221575	48.12	39.02	43.62	51.88	60.98	56.38
4.	Meghalaya	R	468095	354436	822531	478904	563276	1042180	49.43	38.62	44.11	50.57	61.38	55.89
		U	100396	47219	147615	128692	177804	306496	43.82	20.98	32.51	56.18	79.02	67.49
		T	568491	401655	970146	607596	741080	1348676	48.34	35.15	41.84	51.66	64.85	58.16
5.	Mizoram	R	138855	117189	256044	93871	97652	191523	59.66	54.55	57.21	40.33	45.45	42.79
		U	124153	86962	211115	102230	127661	229891	54.84	40.52	47.87	45.16	59.48	52.13
		T	263008	204151	467159	196101	225313	421414	57.29	47.54	52.57	42.71	52.46	47.43

(Contd.)

Appendix 11.7 (*Contd.*)

1	2	3	4	5	6	7	8	9	10	11	12	13	14	15
6.	Nagaland	R	406859	334580	741439	452857	452953	905810	47.32	42.48	45.01	52.68	57.52	54.99
		U	82109	24248	106357	105316	131114	236430	43.81	15.61	31.03	56.19	84.39	68.97
		T	488968	358828	847796	558173	584067	1142240	46.70	38.06	42.60	53.30	61.94	57.40
7.	Tripura	R	687482	294965	982447	676156	994850	1671006	50.42	22.87	37.03	49.58	77.13	62.97
		U	143864	33250	177114	134723	233913	368636	51.64	12.45	32.45	48.36	87.55	67.55
		T	831346	328215	1159561	810879	1228763	2039642	50.62	21.08	36.25	49.38	78.92	63.75
8.	Sub–Total, NER	R	8229189	4095138	12324327	8377468	11588380	19965848	49.53	26.11	38.17	50.45	73.89	61.83
		U	1614412	472629	2087041	1556105	2383597	3939702	50.92	16.55	34.63	49.08	83.45	65.37
		T	9843601	4567767	14411368	9933573	13971977	23905550	49.77	24.64	37.61	50.23	75.36	62.39
9.	Sikkim	R	147560	91442	239002	108214	133765	241979	57.69	40.60	49.69	42.31	59.40	50.31
		U	18156	5885	24041	14554	21275	35829	55.51	21.67	40.16	44.49	78.33	59.84
		T	165716	97327	263043	122768	155040	277808	57.44	38.57	48.64	42.56	61.43	51.36
10.	Total, NER	R	8376749	4186580	12563329	8485682	11722145	20207827	49.68	26.32	38.34	50.32	73.68	61.66
		U	1632568	478514	2111082	1570659	2404872	3975531	50.97	16.60	34.68	49.03	83.40	65.32
		T	10009317	4665094	14674411	10056341	14127017	24183358	49.88	24.82	37.76	50.12	75.18	62.24
11.	India	R	198839153	111116917	309956070	182763521	249771048	432534569	52.11	30.79	41.75	47.89	69.21	58.25
		U	76175323	16103331	92278654	74378775	119462260	193841035	50.60	11.88	32.25	49.40	88.12	67.75
		T	275014476	127220248	402234724	257142296	369233308	626375604	51.68	25.63	39.10	48.32	74.37	60.90

Source: Registrar General of India, New Delhi.

Appendix 11.8

State-wise Total Number of Population and Population in the Age Group 15-29 Years as per 2001 census and their Percentages

Sl. No.	*Name of the State / NER / India*	*Age group-wise population in thousands*				*Age group-wise percentage to total population*		
		All ages (i.e. Total population)	*Age Group, Years*			*Age Group, Years*		
			15-19	*20-29*	*15 -29*	*15-19*	*20-29*	*15-29*
1	2	3	4	5	6	7	8	9
1.	Arunachal Pradesh	1097.97	110.56	178.94	289.50	10.07	16.30	26.37
2.	Assam	26655.53	2610.79	4631.07	7241.86	9.97	17.37	27.17
3.	Manipur	2166.79	222.48	431.86	654.34	10.27	19.93	30.20
4.	Meghalaya	2318.82	249.78	379.32	629.10	10.77	16.36	27.13
5.	Mizoram	888.57	98.63	172.95	271.58	11.10	19.46	30.56
6.	Nagaland	1990.04	266.10	373.37	639.47	13.37	18.76	32.13
7.	Tripura	3199.20	339.44	553.07	892.51	10.61	17.29	27.90
8.	Sub-Total, NER	33316.92	3897.78	6720.58	10618.36	10.17	17.54	27.71
9.	Sikkim	540.85	63.44	102.72	166.16	11.73	18.99	30.72
10.	Total NER	33857.77	3961.22	6823.30	10784.52	10.19	17.56	27.75
11.	India	1028610.33	100215.89	173186.53	273402.42	9.74	16.84	26.58

Source: Registrar General of India, New Delhi.

Appendix 11.9

State-wise Percentage Distribution of Workers as Cultivators, Agricultural Labourers and other Workers in Different Census Years

(In Percentage to Total Workers)

Sl. No.	Name of the State / NER / India	Cultivators			Agricultural Labourers			Other workers		
		Census years			Census years			Census years		
		1981	1991	2001	1981	1991	2001	1981	1991	2001
1	2	3	4	5	6	7	8	9	10	11
1.	Arunachal Pradesh	71.3	60.8	57.8	2.5	5.4	3.9	26.3	33.7	37.0
2.	Assam	NA	54.8	39.1	NA	12.6	13.3	NA	31.7	44.0
3.	Manipur	63.6	59.9	40.2	5.0	10.3	12.0	31.4	23.8	37.6
4.	Meghalaya	62.6	56.3	48.1	10.0	13.0	17.7	27.5	30.4	32.0
5.	Mizoram	70.6	62.3	54.9	2.5	5.4	5.7	26.9	31.2	37.9
6.	Nagaland	72.3	72.7	64.7	0.8	1.6	3.7	26.9	25.3	29.0
7.	Tripura	43.3	38.7	27.0	24.0	24.2	23.8	32.7	35.2	46.1
8.	Sikkim	60.1	58.0	49.9	3.3	8.2	6.5	36.6	33.1	42.0
9.	India	41.5	39.7	31.6	25.1	27.4	26.7	33.4	30.5	37.5

Note: NA – indicates Not Available.

Source:– Registrar General of India, New Delhi.

Appendix 11.10

State-wise Changes in the Percentage Distribution of Workers as Cultivators, Agricultural Labourers and other Workers During Inter-Census Periods

(In Percentage)

Sl. No.	Name of the State / India	Cultivators			Agricultural Labourers			Other workers		
		Changes in (+ or –)			Changes in (+ or –)			Changes in (+ or –)		
		1981-1991	1991-2001	1981-2001	1981-1991	1991-2001	1981 2001	1981-1991	1991-2001	1981-2001
1	2	3	4	5	6	7	8	9	10	11
1.	Arunachal Pradesh	–10.5	–3.0	–13.5	2.9	–1.5	1.4	7.4	3.3	10.7
2.	Assam	NA	–15.7	NA	NA	0.7	NA	NA	12.3	NA
3.	Manipur	–3.7	–19.7	–23.4	5.3	1.7	7.0	–7.6	13.8	6.2
4.	Meghalaya	–6.3	–8.2	–14.5	3.0	4.7	7.7	2.9	1.6	4.5
5.	Mizoram	–8.3	–7.4	–15.7	2.9	0.3	3.2	4.3	6.7	11.0
6.	Nagaland	0.4	–8.0	–7.6	0.8	2.1	2.9	–1.6	3.7	2.1
7.	Tripura	–4.6	–11.7	–16.3	0.2	–0.4	–0.2	2.5	10.9	13.4
8.	Sikkim	–2.1	–8.1	–10.2	4.9	–1.7	3.2	–3.5	8.9	5.4
9.	India	–1.8	–8.1	–9.9	2.3	–0.7	1.6	–2.9	7.0	4.1

Note: NA – indicates Not Available.

Source: Registrar General of India, New Delhi.

Appendix 11.11(a)

State-wise Percentage Distribution of Usually Employed by Category of Employment in Different Years (Rural)

(*In Percentage*)

Sl. No.	Name of the State/ NER/India	In 1993-94			In 1999-2000			In 2004-05		
		Principal and Subsidiary Status			Principal and Subsidiary Status			Principal and Subsidiary Status		
		Self-employed	Regularly employed	Casual labour	Self-employed	Regularly employed	Casual labour	Self-employed	Regularly employed	Casual labour
1	2	3	4	5	6	7	8	9	10	11
1.	Arunachal Pradesh	85.4	12.3	2.3	79.3	12.6	8.1	83.3	10.8	5.9
2.	Assam	57.8	14.4	27.8	58.2	16.6	25.2	71.0	9.1	19.9
3.	Manipur	83.0	12.1	4.9	80.0	10.0	10.0	85.1	9.5	5.4
4.	Meghalaya	79.7	6.3	14.0	79.6	4.4	16.0	81.0	5.0	14.1
5.	Mizoram	91.1	7.3	1.4	89.0	8.4	2.6	91.4	6.7	1.8
6.	Nagaland	78.1	19.2	2.7	82.1	16.6	1.3	88.3	11.0	0.7
7.	Tripura	56.9	12.8	30.3	47.2	11.1	41.7	52.8	10.2	37.0
8.	Sikkim	57.0	27.0	16.0	62.0	26.1	11.9	67.8	25.2	7.0
9.	India	58.1	6.6	35.3	55.8	6.8	37.4	60.2	7.1	32.8

Source: NSS Reports on Employment and Un-employment, No. 409, 458, 515, Central Statistical Organisation, New Delhi.

Appendix 11.11(b)

State-wise Percentage Distribution of Usually Employed by Category of Employment in Different Years (Urban)

(In Percentage)

Sl. No.	Name of the State/ NER/India	In 1993-94			In 1999-2000			In 2004-05		
		Principal and Subsidiary Status			Principal and Subsidiary Status			Principal and Subsidiary Status		
		Self-employed	Regularly employed	Casual labour	Self-employed	Regularly employed	Casual labour	Self-employed	Regularly employed	Casual labour
1	2	3	4	5	6	7	8	9	10	11
1.	Arunachal Pradesh	22.0	69.5	8.5	24.1	59.0	16.9	42.7	48.8	8.2
2.	Assam	45.3	43.1	11.6	44.7	42.9	12.4	42.3	45.1	12.6
3.	Manipur	63.9	33.3	2.8	60.3	30.6	9.1	65.4	29.9	4.6
4.	Meghalaya	34.1	55.8	10.1	26.3	56.4	17.3	20.1	70.8	9.1
5.	Mizoram	61.0	33.1	5.9	49.5	33.8	16.7	59.0	34.1	6.9
6.	Nagaland	39.1	54.4	6.5	24.2	71.7	4.1	62.2	33.8	4.1
7.	Tripura	38.8	48.3	12.9	31.3	53.0	15.7	40.7	46.0	13.3
8.	Sikkim	45.3	48.2	6.5	32.7	56.5	10.8	40.4	57.2	2.4
9.	India	42.4	39.5	18.1	42.2	40.0	17.8	45.4	39.5	15.0

Source: NSS Reports on Employment and Un-Employment, No. 409, 458, 515, Central Statistical Organization, New Delhi.

Appendix 11.12

State-wise and Sector-wise Distribution of Public and Private Employment in the Organised Sector During 1981-2002

(*In Lakhs*)

Sl. No.	Name of the State/ NER/India	Public Sector in								Private Sector in							
		1981	1991	1997	1998	1999	2000	2001	2002	1981	1991	1997	1998	1999	2000	2001	2002
1	2	3	4	5	6	7	8	9	10	11	12	13	14	15	16	17	18
1.	Assam	3.58	5.01	5.49	5.35	5.32	5.36	5.37	5.26	4.99	5.49	5.67	5.57	5.50	5.49	5.79	5.38
2.	Manipur	0.36	0.55	0.78	0.78	0.80	0.64	0.80	0.80	0.01	0.01	0.02	0.02	0.02	0.02	0.03	0.03
3.	Meghalaya	0.44	0.64	0.69	0.70	0.71	0.73	0.73	0.73	0.04	0.05	0.08	0.08	0.09	0.09	0.09	0.09
4.	Mizoram	0.15	0.33	0.40	0.40	0.40	0.35	0.40	0.40	0.01	0.01	0.02	0.01	0.01	0.02	0.01	0.01
5.	Nagaland	0.39	0.64	0.69	0.73	0.74	0.74	0.74	0.74	0.01	0.02	0.03	0.03	0.03	0.03	0.03	0.03
6.	Tripura	0.62	0.88	1.00	1.00	1.00	1.10	1.10	1.10	0.06	0.10	0.11	0.11	0.10	0.13	0.13	0.13
7.	Total NER	5.54	8.05	9.05	8.96	8.97	8.92	9.14	9.03	5.12	5.68	5.93	5.82	5.75	5.78	6.08	5.67
8.	India	155.00	191.00	196.00	194.00	194.20	193.00	191.40	187.70	73.95	76.76	86.90	87.50	86.98	86.46	86.52	84.32

Source: North Eastern Region–VISION-2020, Ministry of Development of North Eastern Region, North Eastern Council—Vol. III, May, 2008.

Appendix 11.13

State-wise Percentage Distribution of Unemployment in the North Eastern Region in Different Years

(In per cent of Labour Force)

Sl. No.	Name of the State / NER / India	In 1983			In 1993-94			In 1999-2000		
		Male	Female	Total	Male	Female	Total	Male	Female	Total
1	2	3	4	5	6	7	8	9	10	11
1.	Arunachal Pradesh	NA	NA	NA	1.3	0.5	1.0	1.0	0.9	0.9
2.	Assam	2.2	2.4	2.2	4.6	9.5	5.6	3.7	8.0	4.6
3.	Manipur	0.6	0.0	0.4	2.2	1.0	1.8	3.7	3.1	3.5
4.	Meghalaya	1.8	0.9	1.5	0.5	0.3	0.5	0.9	0.9	0.9
5.	Mizoram	0.3	1.0	0.4	0.9	0.5	0.8	2.5	1.3	2.0
6.	Nagaland	0.4	0.0	0.3	3.2	0.6	2.4	4.0	2.9	3.5
7.	Tripura	2.1	7.7	3.9	2.2	8.4	3.4	1.6	4.5	1.9
8.	Sikkim	2.6	1.3	2.2	0.7	1.9	1.0	3.6	2.7	3.4
9.	India	2.3	1.3	2.0	2.1	1.7	2.0	2.5	1.8	2.3

Source: North Eastern Region—VISION-2020, Ministry of Development of North Eastern Region, North Eastern Council-Vol. III, May, 2008.

Note: NA = Not available

Appendix 11.14

State-wise Percentage Distribution of Unemployment Among the Youth of the Age Group 15-29 Years (Usual Principal Status) (Rural)

(*In Percentage*)

Sl. No.	Name of the State / NER / India	Unemployment rate in 1999-2000											
		Male (in the age group)				Female (in the age group)				Total (in the age group)			
		15-19	20-24	25-29	15-29	15-19	20-24	25-29	15-29	15-19	20-24	25-29	15-29
1	2	3	4	5	6	7	8	9	10	11	12	13	14
1.	Arunachal Pradesh	4.1	4.3	1.1	2.5	0.9	1.1	0.0	0.4	1.8	2.6	0.7	1.5
2.	Assam	10.3	13.8	7.2	10.2	20.3	32.9	19.4	24.5	11.4	17.1	9.3	12.5
3.	Manipur	6.4	5.6	4.4	5.2	0.0	10.7	6.2	7.2	4.7	7.2	4.9	5.8
4.	Meghalaya	2.2	1.5	0.0	1.1	0.0	1.6	0.4	0.7	1.2	1.6	0.2	1.0
5.	Mizoram	0.2	2.6	10.3	4.9	0.0	0.0	4.1	1.4	0.0	1.6	8.0	3.4
6.	Nagaland	2.9	15.3	8.3	9.9	9.2	14.5	5.3	10.0	5.3	15.0	7.6	10.0
7.	Tripura	3.7	2.2	1.8	2.8	12.7	5.7	18.2	12.8	6.1	2.5	3.9	3.9
8.	Sikkim	7.4	8.4	13.1	10.2	0.0	10.3	2.5	5.0	4.9	8.9	9.5	8.4
9.	India	6.5	6.2	3.2	5.1	4.1	4.9	2.4	3.7	5.7	5.8	2.8	4.6

Source: North Eastern Region–VISION-2020, Ministry of Development of North Eastern Region, North Eastern Council–Vol. III, May, 2008.

Appendix 11.14 (Contd.)

State-wise Percentage Distribution of Unemployment Among the Youth of the Age Group 15-29 Years (Usual Principal Status) (Rural)

(In Percentage)

Sl. No.	Name of the State/ NER/India	Unemployment rate in 2004-2005											
		Male (in the age group)				Female (in the age group)				Total (in the age group)			
		15-19	20-24	25-29	15-29	15-19	20-24	25-29	15-29	15-19	20-24	25-29	15-29
1	2	15	16	17	18	19	20	21	22	23	24	25	26
1.	Arunachal Pradesh	2.1	3.6	3.2	3.0	0.9	1.3	2.5	1.7	1.3	2.6	2.9	2.5
2.	Assam	10.3	11.1	5.1	8.5	19.1	17.2	10.0	15.3	12.1	12.3	5.8	9.7
3.	Manipur	8.2	3.0	5.6	5.1	0.0	2.9	2.5	2.3	4.8	3.0	4.4	3.9
4.	Meghalaya	0.0	0.6	0.1	0.2	0.0	2.6	1.1	1.6	0.0	1.6	0.6	0.8
5.	Mizoram	0.7	2.4	2.2	2.0	0.0	0.4	0.0	0.3	0.5	1.5	1.4	1.3
6.	Nagaland	8.2	26.9	19.2	20.8	8.1	15.0	4.1	9.5	7.8	20.1	12.4	14.9
7.	Tripura	33.6	31.2	13.1	25.7	65.7	67.1	45.2	60.8	40.9	39.1	18.5	33.0
8.	Sikkim	10.3	13.0	3.5	8.6	0.0	6.4	3.7	4.0	7.1	10.7	3.6	7.0
9.	India	7.9	6.2	2.3	5.2	6.7	9.3	5.2	7.0	7.5	7.0	3.3	5.7

Source: North Eastern Region–VISION-2020, Ministry of Development of North Eastern Region, North Eastern Council–Vol.III, May, 2008.

Appendix 11.15

State-wise Percentage Distribution of Unemployment Among the Youth of the Age Group 15-29 Years (Usual Principal Status) (Urban)

(In Percentage)

Sl. No.	Name of the State/ NER/India	Unemployment Rate in 1999 – 2000											
		Male (in the Age Group)				Female (in the Age Group)				Total (in the Age Group)			
		15 –19	20 –24	25 –29	15 –29	15 –19	20–24	25 –29	15 –29	15 –19	20 –24	25 –29	15 –29
1	2	3	4	5	6	7	8	9	10	11	12	13	14
1.	Arunachal Pradesh	0.0	14.2	8.9	9.1	54.1	31.6	2.6	18.5	11.8	21.6	7.1	11.9
2.	Assam	20.5	34.4	15.5	22.2	0.8	70.5	55.7	45.0	12.7	39.0	22.8	26.6
3.	Manipur	8.6	21.4	23.9	22.6	61.1	6.9	29.1	24.2	30.8	17.3	25.4	23.1
4.	Meghalaya	6.1	14.9	10.2	11.9	19.5	13.1	21.2	17.7	10.4	14.4	15.4	14.3
5.	Mizoram	4.9	11.3	14.8	12.7	17.1	6.1	3.8	6.0	6.3	9.1	11.1	10.3
6.	Nagaland	0.0	34.0	30.8	31.1	0.0	55.5	10.6	23.3	0.0	41.0	24.6	28.3
7.	Tripura	1.1	35.2	23.4	22.1	0.0	35.3	6.9	17.3	0.9	35.1	21.2	21.4
8.	Sikkim	22.1	13.2	15.4	15.6	0.0	49.5	16.7	29.9	16.7	23.4	15.6	19.0
9.	India	15.4	13.9	7.5	11.5	15.5	22.6	11.5	16.6	15.4	15.4	8.2	12.4

Source: North Eastern Region – VISION – 2020, Ministry of Development of North Eastern Region, North Eastern Council – Vol. III, May, 2008.

Appendix 11.15 (Contd.)

State-wise Percentage Distribution of Unemployment Among the Youth of the Age Group 15-29 Years (Usual Principal Status) (Urban)

(In Percentage)

Sl. No.	Name of the State / NER / India	Unemployment Rate in 2004-2005											
		Male (in the Age Group)				Female (in the Age Group)				Total (in the Age Group)			
		15-19	20-24	25-29	15-29	15-19	20-24	25-29	15-29	15-19	20-24	25-29	15-29
1	2	15	16	17	18	19	20	21	22	23	24	25	26
1.	Arunachal Pradesh	12.9	10.7	2.3	5.6	7.1	11.3	3.7	7.4	9.5	10.9	2.7	4.9
2.	Assam	12.6	26.9	19.8	20.9	19.7	50.0	19.4	33.4	14.1	32.8	19.5	23.3
3.	Manipur	5.5	22.6	19.3	19.7	1.2	11.4	28.7	18.5	2.9	19.0	22.4	19.3
4.	Meghalaya	29.4	3.0	12.8	12.9	3.0	14.8	15.3	12.0	14.6	8.7	14.0	12.5
5.	Mizoram	2.8	7.4	2.1	4.4	0.0	5.9	7.6	6.2	1.8	6.7	4.5	4.9
6.	Nagaland	0.0	33.2	19.7	22.1	0.0	55.2	23.7	35.5	0.0	43.4	21.4	27.7
7.	Tripura	55.4	54.0	34.0	45.4	69.1	94.8	77.6	83.7	60.7	70.3	52.6	61.4
8.	Sikkim	21.7	7.9	0.0	6.7	0.0	24.6	0.0	6.3	16.9	10.5	0.0	8.0
9.	India	14.0	12.5	5.8	10.0	15.6	25.8	15.8	19.9	14.5	15.2	7.6	11.9

Source: North Eastern Region – VISION – 2020, Ministry of Development of North Eastern Region, North Eastern Council, Vol. III, May, 2008.

Appendix 12.1

State-wise Composition of Gross State Domestic Product (GSDP) Based on the Averages for the Period from 2000–01 to 2004–05

(In Percentage)

Sl. No.	Name of the State/NER/India	Primary Sector					Secondary Sector					
		Agriculture	Forestry & Logging	Fishing	Mining & Quarrying	Sub–Total of Primary Sector	Manufacturing: Registered	Manufacturing: Unregistered	Manufacturing Total	Construction	Electricity	Sub–total of Secondary Sector
1	2	3	4	5	6	7	8	9	10	11	12	13
1.	Arunachal Pradesh	25.2	3.5	1.1	1.5	31.3	0.0	3.6	3.6	16.0	3.6	23.2
2.	Assam	28.3	1.8	2.2	6.2	38.5	7.2	2.2	9.4	4.5	1.1	15.0
3.	Manipur	22.3	1.8	3.0	0.0	27.1	0.1	8.6	8.7	12.5	2.3	23.5
4.	Meghalaya	21.3	1.0	0.8	8.7	31.8	0.7	1.5	2.2	9.5	3.5	15.2
5.	Mizoram	20.4	0.9	1.1	0.1	22.5	0.3	0.9	1.2	11.5	1.7	14.4
6.	Nagaland	33.1	2.5	0.6	0.1	36.3	0.4	0.4	0.8	10.9	0.4	12.1
7.	Tripura	19.6	1.4	1.9	0.8	23.7	1.5	1.3	2.8	19.3	2.5	24.6
8.	Sikkim	16.9	1.9	0.1	0.1	19.0	2.9	0.0	2.9	17.9	4.7	25.5
9.	Total, NER	26.2	1.8	1.8	4.4	34.2	4.4	2.3	6.7	8.5	1.6	16.8
10.	India	20.2	0.9	1.0	2.2	24.3	10.2	5.0	15.2	6.0	2.3	23.5

Source: North Eastern Region – VISION-2020, Ministry of Development of North Eastern Region, North Eastern Council, Vol.-III.

Appendix 12.1 (Contd.)

State-wise Composition of Gross State Domestic Product (GSDP) Based on the Averages for the Period from 2000-01 to 2004-05

(In Percentage)

Sl. No.	Name of the State/NER/India	Tertiary Sector											Gross State Domestic Product (GSDP)
		Rail-ways	Trans-port by other Means	Storage	Commu-nication	Total of Transport, Storage & communi-cation	Trade, Hotels and Restau-rants	Ban-king and Insu-rance	Real Estate, Ownership of Dwellings and Business Services	Public Adminis-tration	Other Services	Sub-Total of Tertiary Sector	
1	2	14	15	16	17	18	19	20	21	22	23	24	25
1.	Arunachal Pradesh	0.0	4.8	0.0	2.2	7.0	4.3	2.7	2.5	17.3	11.7	45.5	100.0
2.	Assam	1.1	2.0	0.0	2.4	5.5	15.4	4.9	3.7	7.0	10.0	46.5	100.0
3.	Manipur	0.0	4.3	0.0	1.5	5.8	9.7	1.6	3.8	16.9	11.6	49.4	100.0
4.	Meghalaya	0.0	4.3	0.0	0.9	5.2	14.7	2.5	9.0	13.6	8.0	53.0	100.0
5.	Mizoram	0.0	2.3	0.0	1.0	3.3	9.1	2.6	14.0	21.0	13.1	63.1	100.0
6.	Nagaland	0.0	17.0	0.0	0.4	17.4	5.3	1.3	8.7	12.1	6.8	51.6	100.0
7.	Tripura	0.0	3.0	0.1	3.3	6.4	12.3	2.2	2.6	15.1	13.1	51.7	100.0
8.	Sikkim	0.0	1.9	0.0	0.0	1.9	7.1	2.6	5.8	17.5	20.6	55.5	100.0
9.	Total, NER	0.6	3.8	0.0	2.0	6.4	13.0	3.7	4.8	10.6	10.5	49.0	100.0
10.	India	1.2	5.0	0.1	2.7	9.0	15.2	5.8	7.6	6.3	8.3	52.2	100.0

Source: North Eastern Region–VISION-2020, Ministry of Development of North Eastern Region, North Eastern Council, Vol.-III.

Appendix 12.2

State-wise Sectoral Composition of Gross State Domestic Product (GSDP) for 1995-96, 2000-01 and 2004-05

Sl. No.	Name of the State/NER/India	Sector	Composition			Coefficient of Variation		
			1995-96	2000-01	2004-05	1995-96 to 1999-00	2000-01 to 2004-05	1995-96 to 2004-05
1	2	3	4	5	6	7	8	9
1.	Arunachal Pradesh	Primary	38.00	37.33	31.49	7.26	6.60	8.00
		Secondary	31.58	19.01	22.14	15.88	8.25	15.85
		Tertiary	30.41	43.67	46.37	13.96	2.69	12.70
2.	Assam	Primary	46.28	42.06	41.57	3.00	0.83	4.76
		Secondary	15.15	15.89	15.35	6.01	5.42	6.16
		Tertiary	38.57	42.05	43.08	3.07	2.08	6.10
3.	Manipur	Primary	33.62	31.94	26.42	5.66	7.57	10.00
		Secondary	19.62	19.29	21.01	5.04	3.38	4.08
		Tertiary	46.76	48.77	52.57	1.94	2.91	5.31
4.	Meghalaya	Primary	32.04	31.22	29.85	1.40	1.82	2.79
		Secondary	14.14	15.46	14.74	3.13	3.05	3.16
		Tertiary	53.82	53.32	55.41	0.78	1.60	1.56
5.	Mizoram	Primary	28.79	27.48	21.78	9.35	9.67	11.12
		Secondary	15.42	9.56	14.74	7.65	17.76	13.35
		Tertiary	55.79	62.96	63.48	4.46	1.26	4.91

(Contd.)

Appendix 12.2 (*Contd.*)

6.	Nagaland	Primary	22.62	29.31	34.47	9.63	6.11	13.83
		Secondary	19.27	16.33	12.23	17.12	14.09	23.12
		Tertiary	58.11	54.36	53.30	3.83	2.07	3.20
7.	Tripura	Primary	34.31	27.91	27.84	2.12	3.15	8.78
		Secondary	12.94	20.14	21.90	5.62	5.98	20.63
		Tertiary	52.76	51.95	50.26	1.07	1.31	1.78
8.	Sikkim	Primary	35.74	26.33	18.59	19.04	13.61	24.46
		Secondary	20.30	23.30	36.24	6.80	15.99	26.05
		Tertiary	43.96	50.37	45.17	11.54	4.41	8.63
9.	NER	Primary	41.21	37.39	35.96	1.78	1.45	5.17
		Secondary	16.15	16.54	16.82	4.65	3.90	4.08
		Tertiary	42.63	46.06	47.22	1.79	1.47	4.65

Source: North Eastern Region – VISION-2020. Ministry of Development of North Eastern Region, North Eastern Council, Vol.-III.

Appendix 12.3

State-wise and Year-wise Net State Domestic Product (NSDP) at Current Price and its Growth from 1999-2000 to 2005-06

Sl. No.	Name of the State/ NER/India	Years–wise NSDP (Rs. in crores)							Growth of NSDP (In percentage)					
		1999-2000	2000-2001	2001-2002	2002-2003	2003-2004	2004-2005	2005-2006	2000-2001	2001-2002	2002-2003	2003-2004	2004-2005	2005-2006
1	2	3	4	5	6	7	8	9	10	11	12	13	14	15
1.	Arunachal Pradesh	1504	1686	1986	1954	2237	2590	2767	12.1	17.8	–1.6	14.5	15.8	6.8
2.	Assam	31978	33743	35069	39397	42914	46727	52500	5.5	3.9	12.3	8.9	8.9	12.4
3.	Manipur	2954	2814	2975	3142	3564	4541	5120	–4.7	5.7	5.6	13.4	27.4	12.8
4.	Meghalaya	3269	3695	4220	4440	4969	5319	5757	13.0	14.2	5.2	11.9	7.0	8.2
5.	Mizoram	1410	1567	1752	1933	2083	2181	NA	11.1	11.8	10.3	7.8	4.7	NA
6.	Nagaland	2556	3286	3874	4382	4699	4980	NA	28.6	17.9	13.1	7.2	6.0	NA
7.	Tripura	4496	5114	5889	6223	6990	7648	8375	13.7	15.2	5.7	12.3	9.4	9.5
8.	Sikkim	765	855	956	1078	1209	1356	1527	11.8	11.8	12.8	12.2	12.2	12.6
9.	India	1600932	1719120	1867735	2010536	2264715	2523442	2871731	7.4	8.6	7.6	12.6	11.4	13.8

Source: Economic Survey, 2007-08, Ministry of Finance, Government of India, New Delhi.

Appendix 12.4

State-wise and Year-wise Per Capita Net State Domestic Product (NSDP) at Current Price and its Growth from 1999-2000 to 2005-06

Sl. No.	Name of the State/NER/India	Year–wise Per Capita NSDP (In rupees)							Growth of Per Capita NSDP (In Percentage)					
		1999–2000	2000–2001	2001–2002	2002–2003	2003–2004	2004–2005	2005–2006	2000–2001	2001–2002	2002–2003	2003–2004	2004–2005	2005–2006
1	2	3	4	5	6	7	8	9	10	11	12	13	14	15
1.	Arunachal Pradesh	14054	15452	17893	17434	19707	22542	23788	9.9	15.8	–2.6	13.0	14.4	5.5
2.	Assam	12269	12797	13153	14600	15687	16825	18598	4.3	2.8	11.0	7.4	7.3	10.5
3.	Manipur	13260	12369	12801	13250	14728	18386	20326	–6.7	3.5	3.5	11.2	24.8	10.6
4.	Meghalaya	14611	16100	17936	18756	20729	21915	23420	10.2	11.4	4.6	10.5	5.7	6.9
5.	Mizoram	16443	17826	19430	20896	21963	22417	NA	8.4	9.0	7.5	5.1	2.1	NA
6.	Nagaland	13819	16903	18961	20407	20821	20998	NA	22.3	12.2	7.6	2.0	0.9	NA
7.	Tripura	14119	15983	18368	19059	21138	22836	24706	13.2	14.9	3.8	10.9	8.0	8.2
8.	Sikkim	14890	16077	17324	19428	21476	23791	26412	8.0	7.8	12.1	10.5	10.8	11.0
9.	India	15839	16648	17800	18899	20936	22946	25716	5.1	6.9	6.2	10.8	9.6	12.1

Source: Economic Survey, 2007-08, Ministry of Finance, Government of India, New Delhi.

Note: NA–indicates not available.

Appendix 12.5

State-wise and Year-wise Net State Domestic Product (NSDP) at 1993-94 Price and its Growth from 1993-94 to 2002-03 (Position as on 30.06.2003)

Sl. No.	Name of the State/NER/India	Year–wise NSDP (Rs. In crores)									
		1993-1994	1994-1995	1995-1996	1996-1997	1997-1998	1998-1999	1999-2000	2000-2001	2001-2002	2002-2003
1	2	3	4	5	6	7	8	9	10	11	12
1.	Arunachal Pradesh	796	796	915	860	884	910	908	1039	1037	NA
2.	Assam	13477	13796	14125	14467	14704	14574	15078	15671	16155	16785
3.	Manipur	1141	1110	1147	1258	1373	1396	1581	1552	1629	1708
4.	Meghalaya	1309	1353	1508	1562	1663	1844	2000	2150	2228	2338
5.	Mizoram	NA	NA	NA	NA	NA	NA	NA	NA	NA	NA
6.	Nagaland	1251	1348	1445	1547	1684	1605	1614	2230	NA	NA
7.	Tripura	1619	1601	1733	1923	2132	2333	2532	2999	3325	NA
8.	Sikkim	337	329	365	409	470	516	527	NA	NA	NA
9.	India	697992	747573	800411	862808	901734	960555	1019298	1062492	1125286	1168224

Source: Central Statistical Organisation, Government of India, New Delhi;

Note: NA–means not available.

Appendix 12.5 (Contd.)

State-wise and Year-wise Net State Domestic Product (NSDP) at 1993-94 Price and its Growth from 1993-94 to 2002-03

(Position as on 30.06.2003)

Sl. No.	Name of the State/NER/India	Growth of NSDP (In Percentage)								
		1994-1995	1995-1996	1996-1997	1997-1998	1998-1999	1999-2000	2000-2001	2001-2002	2002-2003
1	2	13	14	15	16	17	18	19	20	21
1.	Arunachal Pradesh	0.00	14.95	–6.01	2.79	2.94	–0.22	14.43	–0.19	NA
2.	Assam	2.37	2.38	7.25	1.64	–0.88	3.46	3.93	3.09	3.90
3.	Manipur	–2.72	3.33	9.68	9.14	1.67	13.25	–1.83	4.96	4.85
4.	Meghalaya	3.36	11.45	3.58	6.47	10.88	8.46	7.50	3.63	4.94
5.	Mizoram	NA	NA	NA	NA	NA	NA	NA	NA	NA
6.	Nagaland	7.75	7.19	7.06	8.85	–4.69	0.56	36.17	NA	NA
7.	Tripura	–1.11	8.24	10.96	10.87	9.43	8.53	18.44	10.87	NA
8.	Sikkim	–2.37	10.94	12.05	14.91	9.79	2.13	NA	NA	NA
9.	India	7.10	7.07	7.79	4.51	6.52	6.11	4.24	5.91	3.82

Source: Central Statistical Organization, Government of India, New Delhi.

Note: NA–means not available.

Appendix 12.6

State-wise and Year-wise Per-Capita Net State Domestic Product (NSDP) at 1993-94 Price and its Growth from 1993-94 to 2002-03

(*Position as on 30. 06. 2003*)

Sl. No.	*Name of the State/NER/India*	*Year–wise Per Capita NSDP (In rupees)*									
		1993 - 1994	*1994 - 1995*	*1995- 1996*	*1996- 1997*	*1997- 1998*	*1998- 1999*	*1999- 2000*	*2000- 2001*	*2001- 2002*	*2002- 2003*
1	*2*	*3*	*4*	*5*	*6*	*7*	*8*	*9*	*10*	*11*	*12*
1.	Arunachal Pradesh	8559	8342	9352	8590	8634	8712	8521	9575	9413	NA
2.	Assam	5715	5737	5760	5793	5796	5664	5785	5943	6059	6220
3.	Manipur	5811	5507	5543	5920	6295	6234	6873	6573	6715	6858
4.	Meghalaya	6893	6941	7537	7605	7883	8517	9003	9427	9514	9727
5.	Mizoram	NA	NA	NA	NA	NA	NA	NA	NA	NA	NA
6.	Nagaland	9129	9410	9646	9880	10287	9118	8726	11473	NA	NA
7.	Tripura	5534	5364	5707	6239	6828	7396	7967	9397	10255	NA
8.	Sikkim	7550	7113	7633	8236	9125	9666	10250	NA	NA	NA
9.	India	7690	8070	8489	9007	9244	9650	10071	10313	10774	10964

Source: Central Statistical Organization, Government of India, New Delhi.

Note: NA–means not available.

Appendix 12.6 (Contd.)

State-wise and Year-wise Per-Capita Net State Domestic Product (NSDP) at 1993-94 Price and its Growth from 1993-94 to 2002-03

(Position as on 30.06.2003)

Sl. No.	Name of the State/NER/India	Growth of Per Capita NSDP (In percentage)								
		1994-1995	1995-1996	1996-1997	1997-1998	1998-1999	1999-2000	2000-2001	2001-2002	2002-2003
1	2	13	14	15	16	17	18	19	20	21
1.	Arunachal Pradesh	–2.53	12.11	–8.15	0.51	0.90	–2.19	12.37	–1.69	NA
2.	Assam	0.38	0.40	0.57	0.05	–2.28	2.14	2.73	1.95	2.66
3.	Manipur	–5.23	0.65	6.80	6.33	–0.97	10.25	–4.36	2.16	2.10
4.	Meghalaya	0.68	8.59	0.90	3.65	8.04	5.71	4.71	0.92	2.24
5.	Mizoram	NA	NA	NA	NA	NA	NA	NA	NA	NA
6.	Nagaland	3.08	2.51	2.43	4.12	–11.36	–4.30	31.48	NA	NA
7.	Tripura	–3.07	6.39	9.32	9.44	8.32	7.75	17.95	9.13	NA
8.	Sikkim	–5.79	7.31	7.90	10.79	5.93	6.04	NA	NA	NA
9.	India	4.94	5.19	6.10	2.63	4.39	4.36	2.40	4.47	1.76

Source: Central Statistical Organization, Government of India, New Delhi.
Note: NA–means not available.

Appendix 13.1

State–wise Poverty Ratio

(In Percentage)

Sl. No.	Name of the State / NER / India	Rural			Urban			Combined		
		In the Year			In the Year			In the Year		
		1973-74	*1993-94*	*1999-2000*	*1973-74*	*1993-94*	*1999-2000*	*1973-74*	*1993-94*	*1999-2000*
1	2	3	4	5	6	7	8	9	10	11
1.	Arunachal Pradesh	52.67	45.01	40.04	36.92	7.73	7.47	51.93	39.35	33.47
2.	Assam	52.67	45.01	40.04	36.92	7.73	7.47	51.21	40.86	36.09
3.	Manipur	52.67	45.01	40.04	36.92	7.73	7.47	49.96	33.78	28.54
4.	Meghalaya	52.67	45.01	40.04	36.92	7.73	7.47	50.32	25.66	19.47
5.	Mizoram	52.67	45.01	40.04	36.92	7.73	7.47	50.32	25.66	19.47
6.	Nagaland	52.67	45.01	40.04	36.92	7.73	7.47	50.81	37.92	32.67
7.	Tripura	52.67	45.01	40.04	36.92	7.73	7.47	51.00	39.01	34.44
8.	Total NER	–	–	–	–	–	–	50.79	34.60	29.16
9.	India	56.44	37.27	27.09	49.01	32.36	23.62	54.88	35.97	26.1

Source: Economic Survey, India, 2001–2002.

Appendix 14.1

State–wise Human Development Indices

Sl. No.	Name of the State/NER/India	Females per 100 Males (2001 Census)	Percentage of Literacy (2001 Census)		Literacy Gap	Enrollment Ratio as on 30.09.2004		Male–Female Teachers Ratio as on 30.09.2004		Workers Ratio
			Male	Female		Girls per 100 Boys in		Female Teachers per 100 Male Teachers		No. of Female Workers per 100 Male Workers (2001 Census)
						High/Post Basic Schools (Class IX-X)	Pre-Degree Junior College/HSS (Class XI-XII)	High/Post Basic Schools (Class IX-X)	Pre-Degree Junior College/HSS (Class XI-XII)	
1	2	3	4	5	6	7	8	9	10	11
1.	Arunachal Pradesh	89	63.83	43.53	20.30	82	78	33	25	64
2.	Assam	93	71.28	54.61	16.67	94	55	36	40	39
3.	Manipur	98	80.33	60.53	19.80	92	79	65	80	79
4.	Meghalaya	97	65.34	59.61	5.73	104	91	70	118	71
5.	Mizoram	94	90.72	86.75	3.97	101	95	39	85	78
6.	Nagaland	90	71.16	61.46	9.70	88	89	65	105	73
7.	Tripura	95	81.02	64.91	16.11	93	85	34	53	39
8.	Sub Total, NER	94	72.53	56.96	15.57	94	67	42	49	46
9.	Sikkim	87	76.04	60.40	15.64	103	86	48	57	59
10.	Total NER	94	72.58	57.01	15.57	94	67	42	49	47
11.	India	93	75.26	53.67	21.59	80	75	62	63	46

Source: Different Reports of State Directorates, RGI, CSO and other Ministries.

Appendix 14.1 (Contd.)

State–wise Human Development Indices

Sl. No.	Name of the State / NER / India	Percentage of Households (as per 2001 Census)				Per Capita Consumption of Electricity (Kwh), 2004-05	Tele Density, i.e. No. of Telephone (s) per 100 Population as on Dec.,04	Birth Rate, 2006	Death Rate, 2006	Infant Mortality Rate, 2005-06 (NFHS, 1, 2 & 3)	Average Number of Doctor(s) per 1000 Population	Average Number of Bed(s) per 1000 Population	Per capita Net State Domestic Product at Current Price in Rs. (2005-06)
		Living in Pucca/ Permanent Houses	Having Safe Drinking Water Facility	Having Toilet Facility	Having Electricity								
1	2	12	13	14	15	16	17	18	19	20	21	22	23
1.	Arunachal Pradesh	20.68	77.5	56.30	54.69	144.8	6.22	18.9	7.3	61	0.43	1.80	23788
2.	Assam	19.47	58.8	64.64	24.90	85.3	2.44	24.6	8.7	66	0.02	0.25	18598
3.	Manipur	8.39	37.0	82.03	60.04	70.5	2.41	13.4	4.5	30	0.39	1.00	20326
4.	Meghalaya	22.14	39.0	51.19	42.74	352.2	3.73	24.7	8.0	45	0.21	1.20	23420
5.	Mizoram	52.84	36.0	89.02	69.63	133.7	7.13	17.8	5.5	34	0.15	2.16	22417
6.	Nagaland	16.19	46.5	70.57	63.60	87.2	2.98	17.3	4.8	38	0.18	1.05	20998
7.	Tripura	9.81	52.5	81.45	41.84	113.1	2.95	16.6	6.3	52	0.26	0.77	24706

(Contd.)

Appendix 14.1 (*Contd.*)

1	2	12	13	14	15	16	17	18	19	20	21	22	23
8.	Sub Total, NER	NA	NA	NA	NA	NA	NA	NA	NA	NA	0.10	0.53	NA
9.	Sikkim	37.87	70.7	63.38	77.76	397.7	2.80	19.2	5.6	34	0.33	1.65	26412
10.	Total NER	NA	NA	NA	NA	NA	NA	NA	NA	NA	0.10	0.54	NA
11.	India	51.62	77.9	36.41	55.85	411.1	7.02	23.5	7.5	57	0.59	0.82	25716

Source: Different Reports of State Directorates, RGI, CSO and other Ministries.

Bibliography

A paper on "Social Context of Education in Manipur" by Ms. Salam Jeebanlata, Centre for Educational Studies, SSS, J.N.U., New Delhi.

A Resource Atlas of Arunachal Pradesh, 1999, by Surendra Singh, North Eastern Hill University, Shillong.

An Introduction to the Economy of Meghalaya by D.D. Mali, Ratna's Mascot, G.S. Road, Shillong.

Arunachal Pradesh at a Glance, 2004, Directorate of Economics and Statistics, Govt. of Arunachal Pradesh, Itanagar.

Arunachal through the ages by J.N. Chowdhury, published by Smti Jaya Chowdhury, Shillong, 1982.

Basic Road Statistics of India, Ministry of Shipping, Road Transport and Highways, Govt. of India, New Delhi, Oct., 2004.

British Policy in the North East Frontier Agency by M.L. Bose, Concept Publishing Company, New Delhi, 1979.

Census Publications of the Registrar General of India, New Delhi.

Economic Problems and Planning in North East India by A.K. Agarwal, Sterling Publisher Private Limited, New Delhi, 1987.

Economic Review of Tripura, 2003-04, Directorate of Economics and Statistics, Planning (Statistics) Department, Govt. of Tripura. Agartala.

Economic Survey, 2006-2007, Government of India, Ministry of Finance, New Delhi.

Economic Survey, 2007-2008, Government of India, Ministry of Finance, New Delhi.

Economic Survey, Assam, 2005-06, Directorate of Economics and Statistics, Govt. of Assam, Guwahati.

Economic Survey, Manipur, 2002-03, Directorate of Economics and Statistics, Government of Manipur, Imphal.

Employment Exchange Statistics, Govt. of India, Ministry of Labour and Employment, Directorate General of Employment and Training, Shram Shakti Bhawan, New Delhi.

Fertiliser Statistics, 2005-06, the Fertiliser Association of India, New Delhi.

Glimpses of the Early History of Arunachal Pradesh by L.N. Chakavarty, published by the Director of Research, Govt. of Arunachal Pradesh, 1973.

Human Development Report 2004, Cultural Liberty in Today's Diverse World, United Nations Development Programme (UNDP), Oxford University Press.

Human Development Report, 1990, United Nations Development Programme (UNDP), Oxford University Press.

Human Development Report, 1992, United Nations Development Programme (UNDP), Oxford University Press.

Human Development Report, 1994, United Nations Development Programme (UNDP), Oxford University Press.

India Air Transport Statistics, 2004-05, Statistical Division, Directorate General of Civil Aviation, New Delhi.

Manorama Year Book, 1984, Manorama Publishing House, Kottayam.

Minutes of the Fifth Sectoral Summit of the North Eastern Council, Shillong, held at Aizawl on 18th and 11th May, 2007.

Minutes of the Seventh Special Sectoral Summit of the North Eastern Council, Shillong, held at Kohima on 31st July and 1st August, 2007.

Minutes of the Third Sectoral Summit of the North Eastern Council, Shillong, held in Guwahati from 9th to 11th March, 2007.

Mizoram (Historical, Geographical, Social, Economic, Political and Administrative) by S.N. Singh, Mittal Publications.

North Eastern Region – VISION – 2020, Ministry of Development of North Eastern Region, North Eastern Council, Shillong – Vol.-II and III.

NSS Reports of the Central Statistical Organisation, New Delhi.

Peace and Development in Northeast by P.L. Sanjeev Reddy and P.C. Shekar Reddy, Mittal Publications, New Delhi.

Report of Working Group on Transport Sector for preparation of perspective plan in the North Eastern Region up to 2000 AD, NEC Secretariat, August, 1987.

Report on Annual Survey of Industries, 2002-03, Central Statistical Organisation (Industrial Statistics Wing), Kolkata.

Report on Tourism, Govt. of India, Ministry of Tourism (Market Research Division), New Delhi.

Reports of Indian Institute of Entrepreneurship (IIE), Guwahati.

Reports on Khadi and Village Industries by Commissioner for Khadi and Village Industries, Guwahati.

Sceptical Essays by Bertrand Russell, Unwin Hyman Limited, 15-17 Broadwick Street, London.

School Organisation and Administration by J.C. Aggarwal, Doaba House, Booksellers & Publishers, Delhi.

Selected Educational Statistics, 2004-05, Ministry of Human Resource Development, Department of Higher Education, Govt. of India, New Delhi, 2007.

Sikkim-Land and People by B. Bhattacharya, Omsons Publications, New Delhi.

Social History of Assam by M.L. Bose, Concept Publishing Company, New Delhi.

Socio-Economic Review, 2003, Directorate of Economics and Statistics, Govt. of Meghalaya, Shillong.

SRS Bulletins of the Registrar General of India, New Delhi.

State Level Reports of the NEDFI, Guwahati

State of Forest Report, 2003, Forest Survey of India, Ministry of Environment and Forest, Dehradun.

Statistical Abstract India, 2003, 2005, 2006, Central Statistical Organisation, Govt. of India, New Delhi.

Statistical Abstract of the North Eastern Region, North Eastern Council, Shillong.

Statistical Hand Book, Economic Review, Report on Manpower Development, Report on State Domestic Product etc. published by the Directorate of Economics and Statistics of the North Eastern States.

The Assam Tribune, 7th January, 2006.

The Beautiful India—Nagaland by S.A. Rahman (Chief Editor), published by Reference Press, New Delhi.

The Indian Express (Best of India), dated 10-14 March, 2010.

The Shillong Times, 18th June, 2008.

The Shillong Times, Shillong, dated 6th September, 2008.

The Times of India, 1st June, 2008.

The Times of India, 31st May, 2008.

The Times of India, Guwahati, dated 3rd June, 2008.

Third Census Report, Small Scale Industry, 2001-02.

Tripura: Its History and Culture by Omesh Saigal, published by Concept Publishing Company, New Delhi, 1978.

Website of the Ministry of Health and Family Welfare, Government of India, New Delhi.

Website of the Ministry of Human Resource Development, Government of India, New Delhi.

Website of the NEDFI, Guwahati.

Website of the Telecom Regulatory Authority of India.

Index